Mending the Broken Pieces

Religion in Contemporary Africa Series

The Religion in Contemporary Africa Series (RCAS) aims at publishing innovative research relevant to the diverse and changing religious scene in contemporary Africa. One of the principal objectives of the Series is to facilitate the dissemination of research by young African scholars. The Series includes books from a range of disciplines: the academic study of religions, anthropology, sociology and related disciplines in the human and social sciences.

Series editors are James L. Cox, Professor of Religious Studies in the University of Edinburgh, and Gerrie ter Haar, Professor of Religion and Development in the Institute of Social Studies, The Hague, Netherlands. They can be contacted at: <j.cox@ed.ac.uk> or <terhaar@iss.nl>.

Previous Publications in the Religion in Contemporary Africa Series

1. Abel Ugba. *Shades of Belonging: African Pentecostals in Twenty-first Century Ireland.*

2. James L. Cox and Gerrie ter Haar (eds.). *Uniquely African? African Christian Identity from Cultural and Historical Perspectives.*

3. Matthews A. Ojo. *The End-Time Army. Charismatic Movements in Modern Nigeria.*

4. Leslie S. Nthoi. *Contesting Sacred Space. A Pilgrimage Study of the Mwali Cult of Southern Africa.*

5. Gerrie ter Haar (ed.). *Imagining Evil. Witchcraft Beliefs and Accusations in Contemporary Africa.*

6. Asonzeh Ukah (ed.). *A New Paradigm of Pentecostal Power. A Study of the Redeemed Christian Church of God in Nigeria.*

7. Afe Adogame (ed.). *Who is Afraid of the Holy Ghost? Pentecostalism and Globalization in Africa and Beyond.*

8. Frieder Ludwig and J. Kwabena Asamoah-Gyadu (ed.). *African Christian Presence in the West: New Immigrant Congregations and Transnational Networks in North America and Europe.*

MENDING
THE BROKEN PIECES

*Indigenous Religion
and Sustainable
Rural Development
in Northern Ghana*

Rose Mary Amenga-Etego

AFRICA WORLD PRESS

TRENTON | LONDON | CAPE TOWN | NAIROBI | ADDIS ABABA | ASMARA | IBADAN | NEW DELHI

AFRICA WORLD PRESS
541 West Ingham Avenue | Suite B
Trenton, New Jersey 08638

Book and cover design: Saverance Publishing Services

Library of Congress Cataloging-in-Publication Data

Amenga-Etego, Rose Mary.
  Mending the broken pieces : indigenous religion and sustainable rural development in northern Ghana / Rose Mary Amenga-Etego.
     p. cm.
  Based on the author's dissertation (Ph. D.).
  Includes bibliographical references and index.
  ISBN 1-59221-813-X (hard cover) -- ISBN 1-59221-814-8 (pbk.) 1. Ghana--Religion. 2. Frafra (African people)--Religion. 3. Sustainable development--Religious aspects. 4. Economics--Religious aspects. 5. Religion--Economic aspects. I. Title.
  BL2470.G6A44 2011
  306.6'996835--dc22

                              2010054157

To my husband

Amenga-Mmi Akinaam N. Amenga-Etego

and sons

Winenbinge B. and Kangu P. Amenga-Etego

Table of Contents

Preface

This study examines the debate between African Traditional Religion (ATR) and sustainable rural development among the Nankani of Northern Ghana. The question as to whether or not ATR has an impact on the continent's development has risen to the fore as economic crisis deepens in relation to the global context. The study interrogates the concept 'sustainable rural development', and the current emphasis on gender as a fundamental part of development, from the religio-cultural perspective of the Nankani. With indigenous epistemological underpinnings, the study examines the subject from the perspective of a 'native researcher', within the much polarized "insider/outsider" debate of contemporary discourses on theory and method.

Emerging from my PhD dissertation, I argue that even though ATR as a religion and a subject of study has gained positive grounds and understanding in recent times, its role in development and gender discourses is yet to receive such a status. At the moment, most of the studies in these areas are centred on the limitative aspects of traditional worldviews and the negative effects of their practices. This study moves beyond that stand to engage the discourses at different levels, opening up the issues for further discussions. The study interrogates the underlying influences of ATR in development through an in-depth examination of the intricate dynamics of the internal processes of the Nankani religio-cultural system. Through this, it provides a new ground for knowing, understanding and dialoguing with the Nankani as an identifiable group and, possibly, other rural African communities.

Discussed in seven chapters, the study has two main parts with two additional chapters serving as the general introduction and conclusion. The two additional chapters are identified as chapters one and seven respectively. In chapter one, I have sought to establish the fundamental role of the African indigenous religio-cultural system to the understanding of the African and his/her ways of thought and action. The chapter outlines the underlying problem through an active engagement with the opposing views in the development arena from the onset, using the indigenous knowledge systems of the Nankani. The latter was obtained from oral sources, derived from an extensive field study.

Part one of the book is made up of three chapters, consisting of chapters two, three and four. Chapter two identifies the Nankani and their religio-cultural experiences and practices. Ethnographically inclined, the chapter takes the historical development of the people into consideration as they reconstruct their religio-cultural identity in the face of socio-political change and religious pluralism. This is followed up with chapter three where the concept of sustainable development is interrogated and contextualized within the Nankani traditional milieu. With a historical approach, the chapter engages the practical issues of modern development as encountered by the people through the NGO community and development workers in their midst. From the ensuing discussion, the fourth chapter engages both the community's perspective and understanding of gender as a developmental and analytical tool in contemporary discourses. Drawing examples from the development initiatives in the community, the study investigates how gender, a core issue in current development discourses is perceived and integrated into rural community development. In doing so, the chapter helps to illustrate how different conceptualizations of gender can impact on the development of a community in the African continent. Thus, the chapter unravels the intricacies imbedded in the concept of gender in this traditional set-up to enable development agents and scholars to be more aware of the possible impact of traditional gender systems in their works. In a nutshell, part one underscores the need to move beyond the perceived and conceptual frameworks to real situations where the intricate internal dynamics function.

Part two of the study has two chapters, comprising chapters five and six. Moving beyond the classical descriptive principles of the phenomenology of religion, the core methodological tool, the second part delves further into the Nankani religio-cultural system to substantiate and illustrate some of the methodological and theoretical issues emerging from the study. In chapter five, some contextual responses are given to some of the nagging problems of field-based studies in the predominantly oral African context. With particular reference to the growing number of 'native researchers' in the African continent, their peculiar position and identity within the politics of scholarship emerges with some contextual innovations for field studies in rural African communities. This is followed up with chapter six. The chapter continues to provide a reflective engagement with some of the recent discourses in theory and method with a focus on the role of the researcher within the discipline of religious studies. It provides a multidimensional perspective on the current debates on identity and the dynamics of the 'insider/outsider' position of the researcher. Intricately interwoven with field data, the process illustrates the peoples' perspectives as well as their encounter with the concepts. Taking development beyond the material domain, the chapter provides opportunities for further theoretical development.

The concluding chapter examines some of the outstanding issues in the study. Without necessarily prescribing formulas for solutions, it provides further explanations to some of the emerging issues with a view to enabling those concerned to ascertain the role of religion (ATR) in sustainable development among the Nankani. Outlined as chapter seven, it challenges and clarifies the community's perspective on the international feminization of gender, underdevelopment and poverty. The chapter draws the investigation to a close with the understanding that presenting an indigenous analytical perspective to modern development is an important contribution to the discourse as it provides an opportunity for 'mending the broken pieces'.

In all, this book seeks to engender understanding on the continuing influence of African beliefs and practices on modern development in Africa. In the past, the approach of development was based on getting development to the grass-roots but with the persistent lack of progress, the emphasis is now aimed at promoting grass-roots development. The study argues that even though the African religio-cultural worldview is a major determinant in sustainable rural development, the inability of the parties involved to consider each other's viewpoints is a major problem. Unravelling this through the dynamics of encounter, power and the politics of negotiation from the perspective of the Nankani, the study has provided some avenues for 'mending the broken pieces' in the area of ATR and rural development. At the same time, this enquiry has provided a platform for the documentation of some aspects of the indigenous Nankani beliefs and knowledge systems as well as their engagement with contemporary debates in this area of study. With the continuous loss of indigenous knowledge, largely due to its oral nature and the death of its indigenous leaders, this study is an opportunity for the preservation of the data and a contribution to knowledge.

'Mending the Broken Pieces' therefore provides the opportunity for stock-taking and dialogue. The study illustrates that rural African communities are not passive recipients of Western modes of development but active partners of the development agenda, even if such an engagement is covertly undertaken or perceived.

Acknowledgements

I wish to first of all express my gratitude to my principal supervisor, Professor James L. Cox. Not only is he the reason for my choice of the University of Edinburgh, I am grateful for his dedication to me and my research and allowing me to critically engage his perspectives on theory and method and the study of African Religion, even though his consent was not sought prior to this. I am grateful to my second supervisor, Dr. Afe Adogame, for support, critical comments and contributions. My appreciation also goes to all the staff and students of the Religious Studies Programme for their comments, contributions and support.

At home (Ghana), I want to sincerely thank my niece Miss Adeline Amenga-Etego for being there and caring for my kids while I have been at study. My debt of gratitude goes to my entire family, natal and filial, for their love and support. I wish also to thank the entire Nankani community for offering me the opportunity and their wisdom to carry out this study. Again, my special thanks to the members of staff, Department for the Study of Religions, University of Ghana, especially Professor Elom Dovlo, for their encouragement and support. The contributions of Professors Kwesi Yankah and John S. Pobee, and Mrs. Christy O. Badu are highly appreciated. I owe special thanks to the University of Ghana for securing the GETFund scholarship for my studies. With much love and admiration I thank the management board of Volta Hall for their bond of sisterhood.

I am grateful to Mercy Amba Oduyoye and Professor Elizabeth Amoah (Ghana) and their friends Shannon Clarkson and Letty Russell (USA), especially to Clarkson whose untiring efforts obtained grant support from the United Methodist Women and Sister Fund, USA, for my studies. Thank you to these women and women's organizations. I am most grateful to Professor Gerrie ter Haar (ISS, The Netherlands) for the diverse ways in which she contributed to my academic development and to this work in particular. To CORDAID, The Netherlands, I am thankful for the contribution towards my 'field study' and their beneficiary organisation, NABOCADO-Ghana, for providing an insightful link on the process of rural development.

I wish also to thank Dr. Anne Pankhurst (Edinburgh), for her timely and meticulous proof-reading of the whole text; and her husband, Dr. Richard Pankhurst, for generous friendship, interest and support. I also thank all those who have been of diverse help to me during this period of study, among whom are David Philpot (Edinburgh), my research assistants, Navrongo DCE and Planning Officer. To the Directors of the Upper East Regional House of Chiefs, Regional Immigration Office, Regional Population Office, Regional Statistical Service and Navrongo District Girl-Child Education Desk (Ghana), I remain grateful. Finally, I am grateful to Professor James Christopher Thomas (Legon) and Mr. Ike Kwofie for the immense help given me as I sought to transform my PhD thesis into this book.

Abbreviations

ADRA	Adventist Development Rural Agency
AEAs	Agricultural Extension Agents
ATR	African Traditional Religion
CENSUDI	Centre Sustainable Development Initiative
CIDA	Canadian International Development Agency
CRS	Catholic Relief Services
DA	District Assembly
DCE	District Chief Executive
FBO	Faith Base Organization
FGDs	Focus Group Discussions
GAD	Gender and Development
GID	Gender Identity Disorder
HIPC	Highly Indebted Poor Country
IDIs	In-depth Interviews
IGAs	Income Generating Activities
IMF	International Monetary Fund
KNDA	Kassena-Nankana District Assembly
MOWAC	Ministry for Women and Children's Affairs
NABOCADO	Navrongo-Bolgatanga Diocesan Development Office
NGO	Non-Governmental Organisation
NHRC	Navrongo Health research Centre

NIH	National Institute of Health
NQ	Negative Questioning
PO	Participant Observation
RULIP	Rural Livelihood Improvement Project Proposal
SAP	Structural Adjustment Programme
SQ	Situational Questioning
UER	Upper East Region
UK	United Kingdom
UNESCO	United Nations Educational, Scientific and Cultural Organization
US/USA	United States of America
UWR	Upper West Region
WAD	Women and Development

INTRODUCTION

Chapter One

THE LIE OF THE LAND

> The study of African religions is one important way of
> understanding African ways of thought.[1]

This statement by Okot p'Bitek observes the pivotal role of religion in the life of the African. This Ugandan poet, ethnographer and song critic, contributed significantly to the analysis of the relationship between 'African Traditional Religion (ATR)' and Western scholarship in 1970. He places religion at the core of understanding Africans and their way of life. This investigation generally focuses on the relationship between ATR and sustainable rural development in sub-Saharan Africa.

Religion in this context refers to the indigenous religions of Africa. Recent studies have traced the conception and development of this broad religious identity of the African continent to a historically constructed Western discourse.[2] This notwithstanding, the resultant product(s), including the term ATR, are now firmly rooted and institutionalized in African discourses, educational institutions and politi-

---

1   Okot p'Bitek, *African Religions in European Scholarship* (New York, Chesa-
    peake: ECA Associates, 1990), 119.
2   Henk J. Van Rinsum, "'Knowing the African': Edwin W. Smith and the Inven-
    tion of African Traditional Religion," in *Uniquely African? African Christian
    Identity from Cultural and Historical Perspectives*, ed. James L Cox and Gerrie
    ter Haar (New Jersey and Eritrea: African World Press, 2003), 39-66 and David
    Chidester, *Savage Systems: Colonialism and Comparative Religion in Southern
    Africa* (Charlottesville and London: University Press of Virginia, 1996).

cal structures.[3] Without neglecting these underlying perspectives, its current usage transcends these boundaries to the ordinary Ghanaian frame of understanding. That is, it reflects an understanding that simply views the diverse designations of the African religious identity as distinct religious categorizations within the religiously pluralistic Ghanaian society.[4] Thus, the descriptions 'African', 'indigenous' or 'traditional' religions are used coterminously with the acronym ATR in this study. Similarly, the term 'African' as used in this study is descriptive of religion, culture, people and refers broadly to the sub-Saharan geographical area, either as noun or adjective.

This appeal to the study of African religions seeks a new perspective, one that is different from its epistemological origins. Its author, p'Bitek, acknowledged that Africa's religion had played a facilitating role in the understanding of the African in the past.[5] However, he argued that these were primarily geared to meet Christian evangelism, colonialism and Western imperial interests rather than a realistic interest in the African or the African religion.[6] This makes the above statement ambiguous, deserving further clarification. So p'Bitek preceded the statement with arguments justifying what he perceived as the underlying interest of early scholarly works on the continent, noted above. In addition, he called for a re-orientation to the study of African religion(s). This quest, he contends, aims at a new understanding, one that studies the indigenous religion from its own perspective and for

---

3   Jacob Olupona, "The Study of Religions in West Africa," in *The Study of Religions in Africa: Past, Present and Prospects*, eds. Jan Platvoet, James Cox and Jacob Olupona (Cambridge, Roots and Branches, 1996), 214-5. See also Hendrik Johannes Van Rinsum, *Slaves of Definition: In Quest of the Unbeliever and the Ignoramus* (The Netherlands: Shaker Publishing, 2001), 112.

4   J. S. Pobee, "Church and State in Ghana, 1949-1966," in *Religion in a Pluralistic Society: Essays presented to Professor C. G. Baëta in celebration of his retirement from the service of the University of Ghana, September 1971*, ed. J. S. Pebee (Leiden: Brill, 1976), 121-44 and Geoffrey Parrinder, *Africa's Three Religions*, 2nd ed. (London: Sheldon Press, 1976).

5   Meyer Fortes, *The Dynamics of Clanship among the Tallensi: Being the First Part of an Analysis of the Social Structure of a Trans-Volta Tribe* (London: Oxford University Press, 1945). Allman and Parker views Fortes' work on the Tallensi religio-cultural system as facilitating British colonial rule. Jean Allman and John Parker, *Tongnaab: The History of a West African God* (Bloomington and Indianapolis: Indiana University Press, 2005), chapter 5.

6   p'Bitek, *African Religions in European Scholarship*, 3.

its own sake. As Van Rinsum puts it, it is a call for a "careful study, in an honest fashion, in their own contexts, and within their own conceptual framework!"[7] This led some scholars to note p'Bitek's work as a "turning point" in the subject area.[8]

Nonetheless, some of p'Bitek's subjective stands and critical analyses raise concerns and questions.[9] There is a sense in which his resolve to de-Hellenize the religions of Africa have equally de-religionized or perhaps predicted the death of the indigenous beliefs and practices.[10] Not only will diviners be abandoned, but to argue one-sidedly that the Akan proverb, 'no one teaches a child God' has no religious import raises concerns.[11] Is p'Bitek saying that everything about the African is religious? If so, what do we do with his analysis of this Akan proverb, or his critique of other African scholars? On the other hand, is he saying the "African ways of thought" can be deciphered through the religious dimension? Is religion used as a prelude or a justifier? The intention is not to critically evaluate the above statement or p'Bitek's work. The use of the statement at this point is to draw attention to the ambiguity surrounding religion and the African way of life or worldview. Although it draws attention to the centrality or influential role of religion as well as the intersection between religion and the African thought pattern, it is not a foregone conclusion. This is where the Nankani (subject group) saying, 'no single hand can embrace the baobab tree', can provide understanding.[12] Although a hand is required for this act, additional hands are needed due to the size of this tree. Even so, this must be within the context of unity of purpose. Of course the question remains as to the aim of embracing the tree. Is it to understand the sacred mysteries of

---

7   Van Rinsum, *Slaves of Definition*, 111.

8   Rosalind Shaw, "'Traditional' African Religions," in *Turning Points in Religious Studies*, ed. Ursula King (Edinburgh: T and T Clark, 1990), 185.

9   Henk J. Van Rinsum, "'They became slaves of their definitions' Okot p'Bitek (1931-1982) and the European Traditions in the Study of African Religions," in *Traditions in the Study of Religion in Africa*, eds. Frieder Ludwig and Afe Adogame (Harrassowitz Verlag: Wiesbaden, 2004), 33-4.

10   p'Bitek, *African Religions in European Scholarship*, 99-100 and Van Rinsum, *Slaves of Definition*, 110-2.

11   p'Bitek, *African Religions in European Scholarship*, 64.

12   Nankani has three different designations. It refers to the language, ethnic group and geographical area, elaborated in chapter two. The proverb is commonly used to advocate unity.

the tree or is it to show that collective efforts and resources are needed to arrive at a single goal?

Irrespective of these ambiguities, p'Bitek's observation deserves attention. This is relevant to the current quest for a greater understanding of the underlying role of Africa's religio-cultural systems to the African lifestyle and livelihood. Even though Afe Adogame has situated this new outlook to the study of Africa's religions "in their own right" within the works of Geoffrey Parrinder, he moves beyond these to project a different perspective.[13] Like Christian Gaba, Adogame argues for case studies with contextual specifics. For these scholars, contextual studies are currently more essential as a contribution to knowledge than the broad works which tend to present sweeping generalizations without adequate details.[14] This enquiry engages these concerns as it specifically investigates the role of religion in development among the Nankani.

Similarly, despite the differing and multipurpose roles of early anthropological studies in Africa,[15] their works revealed forms of interconnectedness within a wide range of endeavours.[16] These include the religion and the socio-cultural as well as the political systems of the traditional society on the one hand, and the daily living of the people on the other hand.[17] It is argued that while some scholars preferred to deal with beliefs separately,[18] others ignored acknowledging such linkages generally.[19] This is irrespective of the fact that even they

13   Afe Adogame, "The Use of European Traditions in the Study of Religion in Africa: West African Perspectives," in *Traditions in the Study of Religion in Africa*, eds. Frieder Ludwig and Afe Adogame (Harrassowitz Verlag: Wiesbaden, 2004), 376.

14   Ibid., 380. See Christian Gaba, "Contemporary Research in African Traditional Religion," *Ghana Bulletin of Theology* 3, no. 4 (June 1968): 1-13.

15   Adam Kuper, *Anthropology and Anthropologists: The Modern British School*, 3rd ed. (London and New York: Routledge, 1996), 107.

16   Jack Goody, *Death, Property and the Ancestors* (London: Tavistock Publications, 1962).

17   Meyer Fortes, *Religion, Morality and the Person: Essays on Tallensi Religion* (Cambridge: Cambridge University Press, 1987).

18   Meyer Fortes, "Some Reflections on Ancestor Worship in Africa," in *African Systems of Thought: Studies Presented and Discussed at the Third International African Seminar in Salisbury, December, 1960*, Preface by M. Fortes and G. Dieterlen (London: Oxford University Press, 1965), 122-42.

19   Allan Wolsey Cardinall, *In Ashanti and Beyond* (London: Seeley Service, 1927).

could not escape the role of religion in their research.[20] Benjamin Ray clearly pointed this out in his study *African Religions*. Ray noted that early British anthropologists concentrated on "the sociological aspects of African culture" to the neglect of its religious dimensions.[21] He observed that even when they did consider religion, it was only to such an extent that it illuminated their study."

The connection between religion, the structure of society and the daily lifestyles of the African is a vital intersection for this exploration. It establishes the grounds on which religion engages the development of the individual and the community. To contextually understand such a role among the Nankani, however, it is necessary to examine the ways in which religion influences the peoples' perceptions, attitudes, and decisions and, subsequently, their activities. This understanding must be sought from the people. A study of this nature must allow the people to speak for themselves. Thus, this is the angle from which this investigation engages the issue of religion and development among the Nankani. The title preface, 'mending the broken pieces', reflects this perspective. Though a symbolic representation of rural African living, it projects as well as illustrates the Nankani approach to sustainable development.[23]

This chapter introduces the subject of study by providing an outline that helps to define and delineate the enquiry. This provides the framework and foundation for understanding. Right from this outset, my field data from the Nankani is integrated into the discourse, a feature that will run through the study. This integrative approach is intended to incorporate structurally the indigenous views.[24] The Nankani are a minority ethnic group with very little written data on them.[25] Most of the indigenous practitioners have no formal Western

---

20   Allman and Parker, *Tongnaab*.
21   Benjamin C. Ray, *African Religions: Symbol, Ritual, and Community* (Engle-
      wood Cliffs, New Jersey: Prentice-Hall, 1976), 7.
22   Ray, *African Religions*, 7-9.
23   See chapter seven, 261-3.
24   Fact Sheet No. III, Population of Ghana: Demographic and Socio-Economic
      Indicators by District, National Population Council, Ghana.
25   The minority ethnic status of the Nankani in this thesis is not derogatory. It is a
      descriptive concept, in the context of establishing identity and privileging. See
      Aidan Campbell, *Western Primitivism: African Ethnicity. A Study in Cultural
      Relations* (London and Washington: Cassell, 1997), 4.

education. This led to an extensive collation of oral field data. The need to integrate this data structurally in such a way that the indigenous views clearly show, allowing the people to speak for themselves, is the basis for this integrative strategy. This however implies that although the views are indigenously conceptualized, they are to some extent dependent on my understanding, interpretation and explanations.[26] In some cases, the vernacular and English versions are provided. Though this multidimensional perspective deserves attention, it is hoped that my multiple identity status within the 'native researcher' context will help to present an indigenous, bottom-up study.[27] The appropriateness of this strategy is in its ability to respond to p'Bitek's quest for an indigenous self-projected study, the current search for a bottom-up approach to sustainable rural development and the phenomenological study of religions.[28]

Two similar, yet opposing, views stand at the crux of this study. Perceived in this context as a 'critique of the other', these standpoints are categorized along the existing polarized lines of Western versus indigenous African perspectives to development. In an era of perceived Western secularization, it may seem astonishing, if not puzzling, that religion, especially ATR, is the focal point of a discourse set against a Western conceptual framework of development. This notwithstanding, there is need for such a study in today's search to alleviate Africa's 'underdevelopment'.

From a conservative Western perspective, ATR is a primitive, backward religion that serves as a stumbling block to the civilization and development of Africa.[29] This perception has its foundation in some early anthropological writings on Africa. The bulk of such conceptions are however found within the myriad of documentations on Africa by

---

26 Peter B. Clarke and Peter Byrne, *Religion Defined and Explained* (London: St. Martin's Press, 1993), 29-32.

27 See chapters five and six.

28 William Brede Kristensen, "The Meaning of Religion," in *Classical Approaches to the Study of Religion: Aims, Methods and Theories of Research, Introduction and Anthology*, ed. Jacques Waardenburg (New York and Berlin: Walter de Gruyter, 1999), 390.

29 Sarah Hesse and Henery Wissink, "Incorporating Indigenous Knowledge Systems into the Field of Development," in *The Quest for Sustainable Development*, eds. William Fox and Enslin van Rooyen (Cape Town: Juta Academic, 2004), 47; John S. Mbiti, *African Religions and Philosophy* (London, Ibadan and Nairobi: Heinemann, 1969), 6-10.

explorers, missionaries and colonial administrators.[30] In spite of the time span, this line of thought continues to flourish, serving as a basis for later scholars who seek to find correlations between indigenous religions and underdevelopment.[31] This line of argument sets out to relate Western development and technological advancement with Western secularization on the one hand, and Africa's dominant religious beliefs and practices with its poverty and underdevelopment on the other. There are however, differing opinions about this correlation within the West. Geoffrey Parrinder's assertion that poverty and underdevelopment are not necessarily a symptomatic reflection of a primitive religion typifies this.[32] In his view, the nature of a religion is not a sufficient index for measuring the development, or otherwise, of a society.

The continuing deterioration of Africa's socio-economic systems, with its apparent signs of hunger, poverty, disease and mass illiteracy, raises concern within an age of global development. The international campaign to end world poverty reached a climax with the 2005 'Make Poverty History' march in Edinburgh. With the theme 'Make Poverty History' and a largely global focus on Africa, the event bears testimony to a worldwide concern over the current poverty and underdevelopment of Africa, especially its rural areas.[33] Even more important is the fact that the campaign was organized around a G8 meeting in which poverty reduction and socio-economic recovery was one of the major issues for discussion on Africa.[34] The presence of the Ghanaian president among four other African presidents was a significant indicator of the African involvement in the current discussions. Yet, the crux of the matter, one that directly connects the issue to the current study, is Ghana's declaration as a Heavily Indebted Poor Country (HIPC) in 2000. Such a self-declaration niches Ghana squarely within Africa's poverty crisis.

---

30   See Chidester, *Savage Systems*.

31   J. Milton Yinger, *The Scientific Study of Religion* (London: The Macmillan Company, 1970), 346-7.

32   Geoffrey Parrinder, *Worship in the World's Religions* (New York: Association Press, 1961), 17-9.

33   2nd July: Make Poverty History Rally in Edinburgh, accessed 18 October 2006; available from http://www.makepovertyhistory.org/2005/index.shtml; Internet.

34   'Africa and Development', Chair's Summary, Gleneagles Summit, 8 July, acceesed 18 October 2006, 2-4; available from http://www.g8.gov.uk/servlet/Front?pagename=OpenMarket/Xcelerate/ShowPage&c=Page&cid=1119518698846; Internet..

Although the impact of the Edinburgh event is debatable, it heightened the international process of civil activism and lobbying within the political sphere. This significantly moved the discourse on Africa's poverty from its hitherto institutional domain to the doorsteps of ordinary citizens of the world. This new dimension further shifted the discourse from its mainstream political and economic focus to specific socio-cultural issues in Africa's communities. Coupled with staggering illustrative graphics and statistics, the civil campaign succeeded in soliciting a wider understanding of the contextual situation of Africa's poverty and underdevelopment.

Creating a paradigm shift, this has broadened the search for solutions to the issues at stake. This also generated a renewed interest in the search for a holistic approach to the crisis in Africa. This has tilted the questions once more to the role of Africa's religio-cultural systems in its development. Could Africa's indigenous religion be a determining factor? If so, what is the role of religion in the development of Africa? With a majority of rural communities engrossed in their indigenous beliefs and practices, the question arises as to what role these practices have in their scheme of development. In response to these concerns, the investigation constructed the question, how will the knowledge of a contextual situation aid in the understanding of religion and its influence on the development of Africa?

Meanwhile, on the other contesting side is the traditional perspective. This opposing view is not just blaming the West and its contact with Africa for most of its problems but is also proposing that Africa should be allowed to find solutions to its own problems. Epitomized in the sayings, 'let Africa be Africa', 'Africa's development is an African problem' and/or 'Africa must evolve its own systems of development'.[35] These perspectives can be traced from early anti-colonialists', pan-Africanists' and nationalists' views to those of the indigenous religious adherents' right down to views expressed by current African scholars.[36]

---

35   Kwame Anthony Appiah, *In My Father's House: Africa in the Philosophy of Culture* (New York and Oxford: Oxford University Press, 1992), 3.

36   Kwesi Yankah, *Globalization and the African Scholar* (Faculty of Arts, University of Ghana Monograph, 2004), 11, 20-4. See also, Martin Minoque and Judith Molloy (eds.), *African Aims and Attitudes: Selected Documents* (London: Cambridge University Press, 1974) and Martin Meredith, *The State of Africa: A History of Fifty Years of Independence* (London, New York, Sydney and Toronto: Free Press, 2005).

In accordance with the opinions expressed on this side of the argument, modern civilisation and development, perceived products of the West, are a bad influence leading to the destruction of Africa's religion and socio-cultural dynamism.[37] The argument observes that the modern approach to development is untenable on the African soil, a perspective that is said to be self-evident in the current crisis. The purported destructive nature of Western civilization and its concept of development are not only detrimental to the African way of life; their erosive element has robbed Africa of its own means of development. During an interview in Naga, Apogpeya, one of the elders of the Cho-o clan observed that, Western civilization and its notion of development is like "setting fire on the dry season grass". Yet, for him, all is not lost. There are always remnant bushes left after every bush burning episode as well as a great expectation of an imminent new growth. The concern of this elder was with the quality of this new blend of 'old shrub' and 'new growth', and its ability to rejuvenate Africa.

Finding an expression in the statement, Africa must rediscover its roots to evolve its own form(s) of development,[38] there is a resurgent call for revival, an African renaissance, and in recent times, the Akan concept *sankofa* ('return and take') is asserted.[39] Yet, despite the varied interpretations given to the term *sankofa*, *sankofa* does not advocate a wholesale return for all that is in the past. Its significance lies in the most essential activity of the symbolic bird. The bird returns to its tail end mainly for the oil or fatty deposit for the purpose of grooming itself. Thus, *sankofa*, more or less, advocates a return to the past basically for those essentials needed in a given context and not a general return to the past. With regard to the untenable nature of Western systems, the above view calls for the retrieval of Africa's valuable resources, resources believed to be embedded in its religio-cultural traditions, as a way out of the present predicament. In this respect, the study is concerned with the indigenous notions and processes of development for possible understanding and negotiation. If the Western notions are untenable, does that imply a complete rejection? If not, what are the

---

37 Douglas E. Thomas, *African Traditional Religion in the Modern World* (Jefferson and London: McFarland and Company, 2005), 43-4.

38 Yankah, *Globalization and the African Scholar*, 15-6.

39 Clyde F. Phillip, *Africa's Role in the Development of major Western Religions* (Miami, Florida: Colonial Press International, Inc., 2002), 15. See also Anon. "Cultural values can't be played down," *Daily Graphic*, Ghana, 26 May 2004, 16.

alternatives or the underlying areas of conflict? And finally, how can they be presented for dialogue?

In the midst of these opposing strands, ATR continues to be the bedrock of life within the current blend of tradition, modernity and religious pluralism.[40] Allison Howell in her study of the Kasena (sic), the other ethnic group that co-shares the Kassena-Nankani District, illustrates this complexity of life among its rural dwellers.[41] This blend of views and life situations has engaged the attention of scholars from various fields of endeavour.[42] Mbiti attests to this in his statement:

> Religion is the strongest element in traditional background, and exerts probably the greatest influence upon the thinking and living of the people concerned...
>
> They [ATR] have been undermined but not overthrown. Modern change is clearly evident almost everywhere and at least on the conscious level. But the subconscious depths of African societies still exert a great influence upon individuals and communities, even if they are no longer the only final source of reference and identity.[43]

Although similar to Howell's observation, Mbiti's expressions are far-reaching. For him, the traditional precepts continue to form the basic foundation for African life and religious practices, irrespective of the current religio-cultural environment.[44]

The role of indigenous beliefs and practices among the Nankani cannot be overemphasized. Despite the prolonged presence of Islam and Christianity in the area, from the fifteenth and early twentieth centuries respectively, the Gurunne language index of the 2000 census religious data recorded an overwhelming percentage of ATR adher-

40   Laurenti Magesa, *African Religion: The Moral Traditions of Abundant Life* (Maryknoll, New York: Orbis Books, 1997), 3-4.
41   Allison M. Howell, *The Religious Itinerary of a Ghanaian People: The Kasena and the Christian Gospel* (Peter Lang, 1997 and Ghana: African Christian Press, 2001).
42   John Beattie, *Other Cultures: Aims, Methods and Achievements in Social Anthropology* (London: Routledge, 1964) and Thierry G. Verhelst, *No Life Without Roots: Culture and Development*, (1987), English translation by Bob Cumming, 1990 (London and New Jersey: Zed Books Ltd, 1990).
43   Mbiti, *African Religions and Philosophy*, 1, 262.
44   Ibid. xi.

ents. According to the 2000 census, Gurunne, which alternates with Nankani as a language variety,[45] revealed the following religious statistics: ATR 90%, Christianity 8% and Islam 2% respectively.[46] This is different from the national data of 69% Christianity, 15.6% Islam, 8.5% ATR and 6.9% Others.[47] This raises questions on ethnic or language compositions, religious affiliations and their impact on national statistics. The contestation of the national figures by the Ghanaian Muslim coalition presented not just a challenge to the credibility of the census, but also, the impact of disaggregated data on people's psyche.[48]

Even more perplexing are the results when the religious data is placed alongside the national poverty index. In this, the Upper East Region (UER) became the poorest region in the country.[49] The report indicated that only one out of every ten inhabitants in the region is above the national poverty line.[50] Although the language index has been significant in situating the Nankani within the framework of the statistics,[51] the data now illustrates a high correlation between the indigenous religion and economic poverty, emerging as a good ground for contextualizing the study. Nevertheless, the arguments advanced by the Nankani, some Non-Governmental Organizations (NGOs) workers in the area and faith-based communities in the country, cast more doubt on the accuracy of some of these census presentations, making the connection questionable. This however re-enforces the debate, calling for a thorough study of the situation.

45   Diedrich Westermann and M. A. Bryan, *Languages of West Africa: Handbook of African Languages,* Part II, (England: International African Institute, 1970), 55, 61, 65 and Peter Barker, *Peoples, Languages, and Religion in Northern Ghana: a preliminary report* (Ghana Evangelism Committee in association with Asempa Publishers, 1986).

46   2000 Ghana Population and Housing Census, Ghana Statistical Service, 'Gurunne', Ghana Languages, accessed 17 September 2006; available from http://www.ghanaweb.com/GhanaHomePage/tribe/languages.php; Internet.

47   Classified, Religions, 2000 Census, accessed 17 septembre 2006 ; available from http://www.ghanaweb.com/GhanaHomePage/general/; Internet..

48   Amos Safo, 'Muslims cry foul over population figures', *News from Africa,* Archive, Ghana, 2002, February, accessed 15 February 2007; available from http://www. newsfromafrica.org/newsfromarica/articles/art_7902.html; Internet.

49   It is one of the ten administrative regions in Ghana. The Nankani are located in this region.

50   This is set against one United States (US) dollar per day ($1.00).

51   'Gurenne', Ghanaian Languages, accessed 23 March 2005 ; available from http://www.ghanaweb.com/GhanaHomePage/tribes/langauges.php; Internet.

Yet, the continuous polarization of the discourse on Africa's development between traditional and Western lines raises questions as to how a study of development in the rural areas can be undertaken. The underlying issues demand an open minded perspective at the point of entry. This is crucial in the context of religious studies, especially as the investigation engages the debate from the indigenous perspective. In other words, what are the hypothetical propositions from which such a study may be carried out?

EMERGING QUESTIONS

How can an understanding of indigenous beliefs and practices, alongside indigenous socio-cultural systems become fundamental to the achievement of any form of sustainable development among the Nankani? This process of understanding should not be one-sided. Both the process of understanding development holistically and from the community's indigenous perspective must entail the active involvement of the people.

The first part of this assertion falls within two broad theoretical frameworks in the study of ATR. The first relates to the oral nature of ATR. This problem has created an astonishing textual void, arousing both scholarly attention and concern, leading scholars to seek research data from the practical lives of its adherents. This has in turn created some theoretical and methodological problems. The second theoretical framework is closely linked to the first. Mbiti contends that the study of ATR should be encompassing, involving a geographical area or community immersed in the daily complexities of life. This perspective responds to the particularities of ATR. It takes into account two of Mbiti's major assertions, both of which are articulated in *African Religions and Philosophy*. For Mbiti, ATR is not universal. It is comprised of 'community' or 'ethnic' groups and therefore geographically based. In this perspective, "[e]ach religion is bound and limited to the people among whom it is has evolved."[52] Consequently, studies need to take these factors on board, bearing in mind that although the issues in each context are uniquely constructed, they are not isolated. They are part of a coherent interconnected system of life in the continent.

---

52   Mbiti, *African Religions and Philosophy*, 4.

Mbiti's second assertion engages the subject of belief and practice. Here, he advocates that adherents of ATR and ATR itself are almost subsumed into one. Mbiti contends that a study of ATR needs to take into consideration the lifecycle of the African. For him, such a study should look at the African perception of life from birth right on till after death.[53] In a statement that reasserts Bolaji Idowu's expression of "In all things...religious",[54] Mbiti states:

> Africans are notoriously religious, and each people has its own religious system with a set of beliefs and practices. Religion permeates into all the departments of life so fully that it is not easy or possible always to isolate it. A study of these religious systems is, therefore, ultimately a study of the peoples themselves in all the complexities of both traditional and modern life.[55]

This clearly illustrates Mbiti's position and emphasis on the study of ATR from an integrated approach.

Despite concerns raised about Mbiti's assertions, the notion of religious pervasiveness has a historical scholarly standing, one that stretches beyond ATR.[56] It is partly based on the ideological perspectives of these longstanding theoretical frameworks that Mbiti's work is criticized.[57] However, even though scholars, including Africans, have been very critical of the conspicuous Judeo-Christian stands of Mbiti and other early African scholarly works, their concerns generally relate to the approach, language and style of presentation and not necessarily the content.[58] Overcoming some of these problems requires contextual studies, a position taken in this investigation. As Dominique Zahan notes, although

---

53   Mbiti, *African Religions and Philosophy*, 3-4.

54   E. Bolaji Idowu, *OLÓDÙMARÈ: God in Yoruba Belief* (London: Longmans, 1962), 1-10.

55   Mbiti, *African Religions and Philosophy*, 1.

56   K. A. Busia, *Purposeful Education for Africa* (London, Hague and Paris: Mouton and Co., 1964), 14; Godfrey E. Phillips, *The Religions of the World* (Wallington Surrey: The Religious Education Press, Ltd., 1948), 24 and George Burman Foster, *The Function of Religion in Man's Struggle for Existence* (Chicago and Illinois: The University of Chicago Press, 1909), 153.

57   p'Bitek, *African Religions in European Scholarship*, 29.

58   Ray, *African Religions*, 14-6 and Byang H. Kato, *Theological Pitfalls in Africa* (Kenya: Evangel Publishing House, 1975), 69-76.

"all African peoples are profoundly religious ... the number and nature of their beliefs are extremely varied."[59] It is these variations that are needed to supplement the emphasis hitherto on similarities.

Focusing on the Nankani facilitates a closer examination of the different perspectives involved. It provides the opportunity for an in-depth study of the Nankani religio-cultural beliefs and socio-political structures. To facilitate this, gender is employed as an analytical tool to cross-examine both the indigenous and modern perspectives of development.[60] The use of gender is strategic. Gender is not only an important factor among the Nankani; it is also a focal issue in current development discourses. This provides a convergence point for further understanding the subject under study.

The objective is to use the activities of NGOs within the Nankani community as an interactive link between religion and sustainable development. NGOs are not just an active developmental link in rural communities; it is they who apply and transform international and national development policies and resources into reality. Working between the above conflicting views, NGOs and their activities in the Nankani area have emerged as a facilitating avenue for understanding the underlying debate. Through this channel, the study examines the community's perceptions of the nature and activities of the NGOs in the Nankani area. With the current proliferation of NGOs in rural African communities, this enquiry focuses mainly on the activities of the Navrongo-Bolgatanga Catholic Diocesan Development Office (NABOCADO). Although a Faith-Based Organization (FBO), it is simply projected as an NGO. The choice of NABOCADO was made after a preliminary field study at the community level, at the start of the study in 2004. The choice was based on three factors. First, it is the oldest NGO in the area, emerging from the first missionary activities in 1906. Secondly, the study area is within its coverage. Finally, like all other local NGOs, it is dependent on international donors for its financial resources. Consequently, its working objectives relate to the

---

59 Dominique Zahan, *The Religion, Spirituality, and Thought of Traditional Africa* (Chicago and London: The University of Chicago Press, 1997), 14.

60 Traditionally, gender is a religio-cultural construct and this forms the core of all analysis. This notwithstanding, gender is a pivotal factor in both instances. Employing gender as an analytical tool brings to light these similarities and difference.

policies of its donor partners, which are largely influenced by international development policies.[61]

The people's choice of NABOCADO was both significant and challenging. The researcher had a past working relationship with NABOCADO and a continuous confessional relationship with its parent body, the Catholic Church. In addition to her community membership, this placed the researcher in a very complex position of the "insider/outsider" debate and the postmodernist discourses on research objectivity and identity status. Yet, as a community based study, the choice was maintained. Growing into a second objective, it examines some of the discussions on theory and method in the context of a 'native researcher' in the study of ATR.

The study focuses on the Nankani speaking communities of the Kassena-Nankana District of the Upper East Region (UER) of Ghana. The Nankani are made up of five traditional communities including two aboriginal (original) ones.[62] The study takes into account the historical experiences of the Nankani. This involves a brief historical account involving the slave raids, caravan trade, British colonial administration and the Roman Catholic missionary activities[63] through independence to the present.[64] This helps to provide the requisite data for understanding the subject group and their development history.

The concept of development from the perspective of the Nankani is also examined. Within the broad spectrum of development activities, the study focuses primarily on the community based work of NGOs, using NABOCADO as the linkage. Seeking a suitable outlet to discuss the internal dynamics of development from the traditional and modern perspectives, gender is employed, bearing in mind its current socio-political nuances. As a result, the contextual understanding of gender will be outlined.[65] The purpose for such an undertaking is also to show how the two parties perceive, construct and engage gender, and the impact of such differing conceptualizations on the development of the area. Thus, the continuous projection of gender and its centrality in this study is based on three main factors. These are: its crucial role

---

61   Paul K. Bekye, *Peasant Development- The Case of Northern Ghana* (Leuven, 1998, 57-9).

62   See chapter two, 99-100.

63   The Catholic Church was the first missionary body among the Nankani.

64   Allman and Parker, *Tongnaab*, chapters 1 and 2.

65   See chapter four.

in the religious and socio-cultural systems of the Nankani; its central placement in modern concepts of development; and lastly, its strategic role as an analytical tool. In other words, gender is the crossroads at which the debate between religion and development, both local and global, meet. Thus allowing gender to manifest prominently in this study is essential for understanding. It helps to provide the platform for 'mending the broken pieces'.

This multidisciplinary character requires a multifaceted methodological approach. In this regard, the historical, psychological, linguistic and other socio-scientific approaches are relevant for their illuminative insights.[66] The importance of these perspectives is not limited to the religious and development analysis. Scholars of gender have also noted that these approaches are significant in any critical discourse in the area; hence, such a broader outlook is relevant.[67] However, at the core of this approach is the phenomenological method, facilitating the focus on the subject community. In identifying phenomenology as the core methodology does not simply amount to concurring with Ezra Chitando's assertion that the approach has gained currency with Africans and their study of ATR. As he himself has pointed out, its usage in the African context is not without due critical evaluations.[68] Its strength is its enabling factor. That is, it enables me to open up and to take a critical look at my own indigenous religion, even as a self-projected 'cultural insider' and 'religious outsider'.[69]

As the search for more efficient and clearer methodologies continues,[70] the need to adjust the available research tools according to each contextual situation is essential. As scholars observed, "[t]he

---

66   Harold W. Turner, "The Way Forward in the Religious Study of African Primal Religions," *Journal of Religions in Africa* 12, no. 1 (1981): 1.

67   Juliana Makuchi Nfah-Abbenyi, "Gender, Feminist Theory, and Post-Colonial (Women's) Writing," in *African Gender Studies: A Reader*, ed. Oyèrónké Oyěwùmí (New York and England: Palgrave Macmillan, 2005), 260.

68   Ezra Chitando, "Phenomenology of Religion and the Study of African Traditional Religions," in *Method and Theory in the Study of Religion* (Leiden: Brill, 17, 2005), 299-316.

69   Two distinct views were encountered during this study. While I viewed myself as a Christian, therefore, a religious outsider to the traditional belief systems, the community saw me as an insider. See chapters five and six.

70   Ursula King, "Historical and phenomenological approaches," in *Theory and Methods in Religious Studies: Contemporary Approaches to the Study of Religions*, ed. Frank Whaling (Berlin and New York: Mouton de Gruyter, 1995), 54.

approaches and subject areas that contribute to the study of religions or religious studies are still developing and this adds vitality to the field".[71] Not only are interdisciplinary studies gaining ground, multi-disciplinary approaches are becoming a part of the academic culture.[72] In these contexts, the phenomenological method does two things. It provides primary data and through this preserves the uniqueness of the religion in question. With such data, a critical engagement can then ensue as demonstrated by this study.

The main aim of this methodological approach is threefold. Firstly, it is multidisciplinary in nature. As indicated, this study is not just a binary research on religion and sustainable rural development; it takes into consideration ethnography as a means of shedding light on the Nankani and their way of life. It also deliberates on gender, which though employed as an analytical tool, is examined in detail to accentuate its importance in the investigation. Secondly, the approach facilitates a critical examination of the different dimensions of the Nankani religio-cultural beliefs and practices. Explicitly elaborated in Ninian Smart's analysis of the *Dimensions of the Sacred*[73] and Mbiti's call to researchers to recognize the encompassing nature of the African religion, these views corroborate well with Harold Turner's call for an inclusive, field-dictated methodological approach.[74] Finally, the phenomenological approach privileges the insider's view. Histori-cally associated with W. B. Kristensen's 'the believers are always right', it has become the core of the phenomenological study of religion.[75] Nonetheless, current scholarship has pointed out that this maxim is not suggestive of an outright endorsement of believers' viewpoints.[76] Inasmuch as it cautions against reductionism, attention is also drawn to issues of reactivity and reflexivity.[77]

---

71   Dominic Corrywright and Peggy Morgan, *Religious Studies: Get set for Religious Studies* (Edinburgh: The University of Edinburgh Press, 2006), 42.

72   Ibid., 43-4.

73   Ninian Smart, *Dimensions of the Sacred: An Anatomy of World's Beliefs* (London: Fontana Press, 1996), 10-1. For his eighth dimension see also Bowie, *The Anthropology of Religion*, 24-5.

74   Turner, "The Way Forward in the Religious Study of African Primal Religions," 1.

75   Corrywright and Morgan, *Religious Studies*, 56-7.

76   Ibid., 57.

77   Ronald Hutton, *Witches, Druids and King Arthur* (London, Hambledon and London, 2003), 259.

In other words, even though the truth or validity of the religion in question is not the ultimate objective of the researcher, the role of the researcher must be critically considered. The dual role of the researcher and its underlying implications for issues of subjectivity and objectivity draws the analysis into a rigorous engagement with the current discourse on *Identity and the Politics of Scholarship in the Study of Religion*.[78] This subject matter and its impact on this investigation is explicated in chapter six. This notwithstanding, the centrality of the phenomenological method is not compromised by the latter discussion. Rather, it enhances it. This is especially useful if such a discussion takes place within the context of James Cox's *naming the phenomena*.[79] From that perspective, the content of that segment simply forms a part of the illuminative processes of the "*eidetic* vision".[80]

In his *Religious Studies: The Making of a Discipline*, Walter Capps reiterates these underlying perspectives in his discourse on the phenomenological method. Capps asserts that the phenomenological approach signifies "an intention to concentrate on phenomena – that is, on the perceptible, manifest, empirical, and sometimes visible features or characteristics of religion".[81] He explains that the phenomenologist is interested in both "the manner and form in which religious phenomena appear in human experience."[82] In other words, the desired "*eidetic* vision" and the processes leading to this vision are all important components of the phenomenological endeavour. Significantly, this also serves as a binding source to the two contested parts of this study. The study embodies both the empirical world of development set within the Nankani community yet pitched against the spiritual world of the Nankani beliefs and practices. Thus, even though the physical world is the primary source of this investigation, the manner and form in which this is perceived, experienced and articulated is of immense

---

78 José Ignacio Cabezón and Sheila Greeve Davaney, "Introduction," in *Identity and the Politics of Scholarship in the Study of Religion*, eds. José Ignacio Cabezón and Sheila Greeve Davaney (New York and Oxon: Routledge, 2004), 1-23.

79 James L. Cox, *Expressing the Sacred: An Introduction to the Phenomenology of Religion* (Harare: University of Zimbabwe Publications, 1996), 33-5.

80 Ibid., 20.

81 Walter H. Capps, *Religious Studies: The Making of a Discipline* (Minneapolis: Fortress Press, 1995), 107.

82 Ibid.

importance to the understanding of Nankani perception, attitude and engagement with modern development.

From the social sciences or development perspective, the phenomenological method presents quite similar characteristics to the qualitative methods. Qualitative methods, it is observed, are becoming an increasing part of recent studies on rural development. Without abandoning their interest in the quantitative results of their projects on beneficiary communities, development agents and institutions are taking a keen interest in qualitative impacts. This is partly in respect of the difficulties in ensuring adequate statistical measurement of rural people's lives and development. These difficulties are evident in statements such as 'the quality of life in target community has improved', 'the standards of living for beneficiaries have improved' or 'enhancing the livelihood of rural communities'.[83]

Qualitative research, like the phenomenological method, encourages a great deal of understanding contextual situations. According to Earl Babbie, the strength of qualitative research lies in its ability to foster an in-depth understanding of its subject of study.[84] Babbie underscores this by noting that qualitative research is of particular relevance for areas which are "relatively new and unstudied."[85] In his conclusion, Babbie contends that qualitative research methods are important in exploratory studies where a researcher is "breaking new ground".[86] He argues that qualitative research methods "can almost always yield new insights into a topic for research."[87] Bogdon and Marshall affirm this assertion by noting the usefulness of qualitative methods in explorative studies. They concur that the qualitative method is essential for investigations into "little understood phenomena, to identify/discover important variables."[88] These are significant declarations because an

---

83   Grace Yennah, "Evaluation Report," Rural Livelihood Improvement Project (RULIP), Navrongo-Bolgatanga Diocesan Development Office, (December 2005), 9.

84   Earl Babbie, *The Practice of Social Research* (Belmont, California: Wadsworth Publication Company, 1987), 285.

85   Ibid., 81.

86   Ibid.

87   Ibid.

88   Robert C. Bogdon, *Qualitative Research for Education: An Introduction to Theory and Method* (Boston and London: Allyn and Bacon In., 1982), 27-30 and Catherine Marshall and Gretchen B. Rossman, *Designing Qualitative Research* (London: Sage Publication, 1989), 78.

in-depth study into ATR and rural African development from indigenous perspectives is quite new, giving the investigation an exploratory character. This collaborative link between the phenomenological and qualitative methods responds to Turner's quest for inclusiveness. Most importantly, it underscores the appropriateness of phenomenology as a useful and efficient methodological approach for the diverse needs of this investigation. Nonetheless, the openness and willingness to engage other perspectives, as noted above, does not change the focus: this is a religious studies investigation from a phenomenological perspective.

Thus, the methodological approach is relevant for unearthing the requisite data within the complex multidisciplinary life of the Nankani. As David Silverman rightly points out, "...often the desire to use multiple methods arises because you want to get at many different aspects of a phenomenon."[89] Even though Silverman expresses reservations on the use of multiple methods, the lack of a suitable methodological model, called for by Turner, for the study of Africa's oral religions and community living makes this multiple approach imperative. As pointed out by Cox's evaluation of studies on Africa's "culture, religions and societies", there have been, and still are, varied and contesting viewpoints in the study of Africa's religio-cultural and social systems.[90] These differences present not just significant insights in themselves, but also, challenges for both African and non-African researchers alike. Terence Ranger's appeal for the use of dialogue and participation to address the present inadequacies in the subject area as well as to provide "understanding [to the] contemporary African realities" is thus laudable.[91]

The multidisciplinary method enables the study to unpack the different yet intertwining layers of ordinary daily living from their religious perspectives. It also helps to identify the relationships or influences involved. As Mbiti points out:

> [T]raditional religion permeates all the departments of
> life, there is no formal distinction between the sacred

---

89   David Silverman, *Doing Qualitative Research: A Practical Handbook* (London, Thousand Oaks, and New Delhi: SAGE Publication, 2000), 50.

90   James L. Cox, "African Identity as the Projection of Western Alterity," in *Uniquely African? African Christian Identity from Cultural and Historical Perspectives*, eds. James L Cox and Gerrie ter Haar, (New Jersey and Eritrea: African World Press, 2003), 25-30.

91   Ibid., 26.

and the secular, between the religious and non-religious, between the spiritual and the material areas of life. Wherever the African is, there is his religion.[92]

During my field study, for example, two points were brought to the fore. The first dealt with the need to understand the historical overview of the Nankani religious and socio-cultural systems. This involves the study of the present with an appreciative grasp of the past and its underlying religio-cultural influences in the daily life-choices and decision making. In an interview, Peter A. Awuni pointed out that, "we follow and do what our ancestors did. But while we strive to keep their ways, we also make some adjustments to some of their good and bad decisions. As you can see, the times are not the same."[93] The second concern stressed the need to give significant attention to culture. Here, the concept of cultural relativity was made evident. At every discussion I was reminded to note that every society has its own culture which shapes its beliefs, thoughts and activities (*tinga woo na ka zoom bune*). The chosen methodological approach addresses these community concerns.

The phenomenological method, with its descriptive and classificatory strands, is able to meet these concerns. Not only does the descriptive element provide a pictorial and narrative enhancement to the understanding of the Nankani by 'outsiders', it also sets the stage for further interpretations and discussions subsequently.[94] This is also advantageous because the believer's point of view allows a phenomenon to be studied within context and brings to the fore Smart's quest for "an empathetic objectivity".[95] This helps to provide a fair understanding of the role of ATR in the modern processes of development.[96]

The notion of attaining a 'fair and empathetic understanding' of a religious tradition through the phenomenological method has been contested by Cox.[97] He did this by spelling out some of the problems

---

92   Mbiti, *African Religions and Philosophy*, 2.
93   It is important to note that although at the time of this study Peter Adocta Awuni was the regent of the Naga chieftaincy, a new chief, Naba Olando A. Awuni III has been enskinned.
94   John B. Taylor, *Primal World Views: Christian Dialogue with Traditional Thought Forms* (Ibadan: Daystar Press, 1976), 68.
95   Smart Ninian, *The Phenomenon of Religion* (New York: Seabury, 1973), 1-6.
96   Parrinder, *Worship in the World's Religions*, 13.
97   Cox, "African Identity as the Projection of Western Alterity," 25 and Parrinder, *Worship in the World's Religions*, 13-4.

involved. For him, even though a critical and methodical perspective is needed, absoluteness is unfounded. In this context, the complex involvement of a researcher and the underlying implication of such an involvement on the concept of objectivity are once more brought to the fore. Although this presents serious constraints on every researcher, it complicates the problems for native researchers. As native researchers, they are classified under the 'insider' category of the 'insider/outsider' debate.[98] As an insider, the individual may possess some basic knowledge of the community, language and some socio-cultural traits. Such an individual may also have access to further information from the subject community. In the African context, the indigenous understanding of belongingness and communal solidarity provides security and trust for respondents to trust the native researcher to do the 'right thing'. Yet, it is this latter point that presents serious challenges to the issue of objectivity and the work of the native researcher. Placed between two differently contesting worlds of intellectual objectivity and filial identity, native researchers may find themselves in a dilemma as to what to do.

Writing on "Phenomenologies and Religious Truth", Merold Westphal acknowledges the problems involved in conducting a scientific and objective study. At the same time, he observes that "we cannot start with nothing".[99] For him the most important thing is to make such challenges clear from the start before addressing them with the appropriate methods. Alluding to Ricoeur, Westphal states that "we cannot see the world from nowhere but only from out of our own history".[100] In other words, the researcher's viewpoint is a crucial factor in any given investigation, irrespective of whether they are Africans researching within their culture or otherwise.[101] In this analytical engagement Cox also acknowledges that, rather than deny our personal involvement in a given study, we should be open and honest.[102] Thus, even though the phenomenological method is not a panacea, it is an appropriate tool for engaging the diverse needs of this discussion. Without neglecting these methodological concerns, its enabling factor

98 Cox, "African Identity as the Projection of Western Alterity," 27.
99 Westphal Merold, "Phenomenologies and Religious Truth," in *Phenomenology of the Truth Proper to Religion*, ed. Daniel Guerrière (U. S. A.: State University of New York Press, 1990), 106.
100 Merold, "Phenomenologies and Religious Truth," 106.
101 Cox, "African Identity as the Projection of Western Alterity," 25-6.
102 Ibid., 25-30.

is crucial, as it allows the study to take its substance from the subject group's perspective.

TERMINOLOGY

Situating key words or terms within the framework of a given study is an integral part of scholarship.[103] This helps to contextually delineate such terms by clarifying their usage for understanding.[104] In this study, these terms are 'Religion', with its specific African variant, 'African Traditional Religion', 'Development', 'Sustainable Rural Development' and 'Gender'. It is important to note that the terms are not readily translatable into Nankani. As a result, they are not specifically delineated, codified or formulated in Nankani as they appear or are understood in English. At the community level, these terms were initially categorized as *sekuul coma yela* (school children's issues). This designation relates to that which is perceived as the 'problems of the educated'. This referential phrase is used by the Nankani to categorize perceived Western or foreign issues that are of interest to the educated in the society. It is a cultural form of alienation and distancing. Given that these terms are technically not indigenous, their construction and formulation are primarily not from the indigenous worldview. The current understanding, interpretations and explanations are however historically and religio-culturally influenced and guided.

Consequently, the delineations were carried out in a comparative manner. Although the format was not the same for each term, the community's perspectives, which are influenced by their religio-cultural tenets, tend to serve as the basis for comparison. For this reason, both the indigenous nuances as well as the comparative perspectives are essential. The analytical processes themselves are equally significant for their contextual understanding. Coupled with a quest to examine the dynamics of the interactive processes, a detailed understanding of each term was discussed during my field study.[105] I have therefore incorporated the terms, just like the rest of the field data, into the work.

---

103 Gerrie ter Haar, "World Religions and Community Religions: Where does Africa fit in?" *Occasional Paper* (Centre for African Studies, University of Copenhagen, August 2000), 1.

104 Graham Harvey, *Animism: Respecting the Living World* (London: Hurst and Company, 2005), xvii.

105 Postgraduate Review Board, School of Divinity, University of Edinburgh, 2005.

Even though the integration of these terminologies is not systematically structured in each chapter, as shown immediately below, I have in some chapters presented them within the framework of 'contextual understanding'. As we encounter each term, therefore, its delineation provides a glimpse into the Nankani pattern of thought, a process that is seen in the interpretation, conceptualization and transformation or indigenization of these foreign concepts into their local variants, providing alternative sources of articulation and information.[106]

RELIGION AND SUSTAINABLE DEVELOPMENT

Among the Nankani, religion (*malma*) is the core of life and livelihood.[107] It characterizes the past, influences the present and determines their future hopes and aspirations.[108] The role of religion in the construction of the Nankani worldview and its subsequent influence on their sense of reality is overwhelming.[109] The most crucial concerns of the Nankani today: family, unity, peace, food security, poverty, disease and mass illiteracy are largely perceived and interpreted within the context of belief and practices. For the Nankani, *Winɛ* (God) is not just a creator; he is the protector and provider of all human needs. Even though this is clearly enshrined in their worldview, as a supreme power source, *Winɛ* does not carry out these activities personally. After creating and sanctioning the individual *paa'la* (showing the way of life or destiny), *Winɛ* relinquishes control and supervision to the ancestors and other spiritual entities. To illustrate this system, the Nankani say, 'when you have a ladle (*biyah*), you do not use your hands to scoop out food from the pot'. Although *Winɛ* still needs to see to the sustenance of his creation, this is done through his ladles (ancestors). It is this understanding of creation, destiny, control, supervision and the

---

106 Timothy Fitzgerald, *The Ideology of Religious Studies* (New York and Oxford: Oxford University Press 2000), 3-32.

107 *Malma* is contextually delineated in chapter two.

108 This was clearly articulated during my fieldwork. Not only is religion perceived as the crux of their well-being, their constant references to the role of religion in the past, present and the need for its centrality in the future depicted this entrenched understanding.

109 This is not peculiar to the Nankani. Omenyo alludes to this in his discussion on the influence of the Akan worldview on the Charismatic Churches in Ghana. Cephas Omenyo, "Charismatic Churches in Ghana and Contextualization," *Exchange* 31, no. 3 (2002): 255-7.

provision of sustenance that the religious base of development (*malgo*) is manifested among the Nankani.

Correspondingly, the structure of the traditional society is believed to have a spiritual significance, having been passed down from the ancestors (*Wine's* managers). This structure, including its gender constructions and systematization, are all imbued with religious connotations.[110] For instance, the view that the traditional Nankani male is responsible for providing leadership and control, including spiritual or religious roles, is perceived as his God given task (destiny). Male family members are not simply secular family heads but spiritual leaders as well. This bestows on them enormous subjective power and authority which does not, sometimes, reflect the current realities. That is, it does not take account of religious pluralism and female rights and freedom. Similarly, it does not take into consideration the current inability of some men to sufficiently meet the needs of the family or changing gender roles. The persistence of these traditional gender divisions, integrated and discussed throughout the study, gives immense superiority to the male gender. Thus, the emerging system is creating a new and complex relationship structure in which the traditional gender roles seem untenable, resulting in conflicts. Besides, the growing complexities of what constitutes the basic needs of the Nankani, as result of today's global influences, continues to pose enormous challenges. This is even more frustrating as they relentlessly grapple with an increasing list of what constitutes their basic needs.

This is irrespective of the fact that the constituents and benefits of *malgo* can be identified and discussed in non-religious terms. For instance, the term development is understood within the context of *tin'malgo/tinga malgo*. *Tinga* refers to the land or earth while *malgo* is a reflection on improvement, betterment, advancement, repair and maintenance. Based on these understandings, *tin'malgo* refers to community improvement or advancement or the processes pertaining to such a state. This presupposes that *malgo* is a composite term with several variations. Within this conceptual understanding, the Nankani say *malgo* is a never-ending process. To this they say: 'no one has ever acknowledged achieving *malgo*'. For them the future is uncertain and each step presents new needs for *malgo*. This is in contrast to Kwame

---

110 Peter McKenzie, *Hail Orisha: A Phenomenology of a West African Religion in the Mid-Nineteenth Century* (Leiden: Brill, 1997), 426.

Gyekye's limitative view of development.[111] Although his perspective will be discussed later, his object based approach in which development must have an elastic end has no room in the Nankani worldview. For the Nankani, development is not viewed or analyzed from the perspective of an object but as a composite system where the religious continuum provides the basis for maintenance and renewal. Thus, although there are different perspectives regarding the term, there is a general notion that at the end of *malgo* lies a better future.

During my field study, various constituents of *malgo* were given. This included *bure* (family), *nuyene* (unity/peace), *diya* (food security), *ko-om* (water), *immasum* (health), and *nungire* (liking/solidarity). In addition to these, the youth spearheaded the inclusion of *sekuul* (schools, as in formal education), *nusi tuuma* (employable or life skills), *tuuma* (work/employment), *soa su-ma* (good roads) and *loa* (transport). Although this second list depicts an emerging trend of difference, change and/or relativity at the community level, the factors listed by the elders were considered fundamental and therefore indispensable.

Remarkably, the process of tabulation concluded with a caution that the above mentioned are meaningless, empty desires, in fact delusions, and may never manifest if the underlying source of *malgo* is not sought or properly tackled. This underlying source is *malma*. In some of the group discussions, it was noted that in the past, things were good, if not, better because people paid attention to *malma* and in return their efforts were blessed. Following that, the elders lamented on the present situation. For them, today's generation is a 'busy for nothing one'. According to these elders, 'the eyes of the current generation are so forward looking that they are unable to see, hence they trip over and destroy that which is lying before them'. This attitude does not only disintegrate the family; it destroys the very source of *nuyene, immasum* and *nungire*, which are essential products, and largely derived from communal ritual gatherings and fellowships. For these elders, the past was good but that has been lost to *nasara* (modernity), the present is madness, and as for the future 'we cannot presume we know'. These sentiments are strongly echoed by Wolfgang Sachs in his critique of the term develop-

---

111   Kwame Gyekye, "Taking Development Seriously," *Journal of Applied Philosophy* 11, no. 1 (1994): 50-5.

ment. For Sachs, "[t]he old ways have been smashed, the new ways are not viable. People are caught in the deadlock of development..."[112]

In view of this state of uncertainty, the elders called for a re-examination of the situation, stocktaking and amendments. The youth (male) related this aspect to the traditional process of fulfilling one's religious, moral or social obligation to parents, elders/leaders, ancestors or gods. According to the youth in Kandiga, despite the individual's personal disposition (destiny or industriousness), he cannot really develop if he neglects his duty to the spirits and his relations.[113] To develop is to be in tune with the spirits, family and community. They observed that, 'a distracted person has no base, no source, hence, is blown helplessly by the wind. How can such a person develop? You need that root to hold on to and to be held. A root to nourish and sustain you and that is why *malma* is important'. In this statement the central theme, 'root', is the spiritual element that supports and binds the people's notion of development to their religion. The phrase 'to hold on to and to be held' connotes a reciprocal form of clinging. This is a process in which the individual's adherence provides the basis to be subsumed into or by the spiritual entity, such that the individual is also protected by the said spiritual force. For them, this is fundamental for development.[114]

Similarly, the conceptualization of 'sustainability' fell within the confines of their traditions and its sources of livelihoods. Linked to maintenance and preservation, the religio-cultural and environmental resources interconnect. One cannot speak of sustainability without due regard for the past and what is currently available. It is only after the past and present are preserved that one is able to incorporate or adapt to new views. In an interview with Juatera, he questioned, 'how can you sustain what you do not have?' Sustainable rural development, therefore, is comprised of *yaaba yela* (ancestral/traditional issues) and *nasara bunu* (modern things). From the perspective of the *tindana* (custodian/land priest) of Kandiga, sustainable community develop-

---

112 Wolfgang Sachs, "Introduction," in *The Development Dictionary: A Guide to Knowledge as Power*, ed. Wolfgang Sachs (London and New Jersey: Zed Books Ltd., 1992), 3.

113 The age range is fifteen to thirty. Below this is the 'child' group. In Kandiga, the youth were interviewed separately. They joined in the community discussions in accordance to their gender. The male group saw this issue as an important factor in their understanding of development.

114 Mbiti, *African Religions and Philosophy*, 2.

ment involves 'holding onto our heritage, and then adding the modern. Can we even do everything? We are supposed to take what we can and leave what we cannot. If a farmer weeds without looking back to see if all is well, is that a farmer?'[115] For him, sustainable development is a process of integration. It is one that takes care of the past, while incorporating the present with the hope of a better future. Enshrined in this perception is an embodiment of choice, a pragmatic selection of the available opportunities.[116] The problem, if any, is perhaps on the choice(s), not tradition *per se*.

Sustainable development, therefore, requires a multi-faceted, participatory, bottom-up approach. It calls for a fuller appreciation and recognition of the diverse rural perspectives and problems. It also involves a careful identification of the needs and opportunities of the specific people. The field discussions suggested development projects must reflect community needs, and also, entail a well coordinated and flexible support system to allow significant changes. The community views are simply absorbed within 'holistic approach to development'. This is however questionable. How can a holistic approach ignore religion, a fundamental driving force in rural African communities? Is this not short of the report of the South Commission where culture and some of its tenets, including religion, were tabulated as important components of development?[117] Nonetheless, it shows theory and practice are not always compatible. In *Beyond Limits*, Donella Meadows *et al* argued that sustainability must involve that which "can persist over generations, one that is far-seeing enough, flexible enough, and wise enough not to undermine either its physical or its social systems of support."[118] Although this definition reflects the Nankani concept of sustainable development, the question remains as to whether this definition can be put into practice.

To contextually understand the phrase 'multi-faceted, participatory, bottom-up approach', there is a need to delve into its Nankani conceptualization. In accordance with their views, participation involves the floating of ideas, ample time for personal and group reflections,

---

115 See Picture 16.

116 Max Assimeng, *Foundations of African Social Thought: A Contribution to the Sociology of Knowledge* (Accra: Ghana Universities Press, 1997), 84-6.

117 The Report of the South Commission, *The Challenge of the South* (New York: Oxford University Press, 1990), 131-3.

118 Donella H. Meadows *et al*, *Beyond the Limits: Global Collapse or a Sustainable Future* (London: Earthscan Publication, 1992), 209.

consultations and a reconvening process where the main discussion takes place. With issues of community importance, consultation may include soothsaying (divination), libation, as well as initiating other appropriate forms of spiritual consultations relevant to the subject matter. For the Nankani, it is only after these processes that conclusions can be considered participatory. It was also noted that participatory decisions may take several attempts, 'not that which is carried out by development workers'. Described as 'sell-offs', the Nankani begrudge the manner in which development meetings are called participatory. Simply put, 'our presence and their pictures of us does not make it participatory, it is time wasting'. Some community members particularly resent the way they are called to meetings. Without prior notification of the core issues (agenda) for discussions, 'we are summoned and asked to represent the respective target groups of their projects'.

The word participation was generally ridiculed by the Nankani when it was put forward for discussion. From the elderly and leadership perspective, *nasara tari yele sune amaa amenga ka borke di* (the modern person/modernity has found a good concept/issue/thing yet, does not understand the very meaning of the word). Interpreted as *nwan* (discuss) or *sö-sɛ* (converse/communicate), it is conceived as the true essence of group or community living. For the elders, life is dependent on participatory discussions and these are the crux of family and community unity.[119] It is the most visible symbol of solidarity, cautioning that discussion in itself does not bestow undue concordance but a shared awareness of divergent opinions. These divergent opinions, they noted, are a good source of knowledge for the participating group. It has the propensity to initiate new ideas and also serve as a genuine source of collaboration and solidarity among people. This notion contradicts Daniel Lerner's view that 'traditional society is non-participant'.[120] Perhaps, what needs to be qualified are the levels and contexts of participation in traditional societies and not participation *per se*. Looked at from this perspective, traditional societies are not an exception; it is a general societal problem. As expressed by the female participants in some of my field discussions, 'when we [community] are called to a

---

119 This might explain why many scheduled in-depth interviews turned into group discussions.

120 Quoted in Rahnema. See Majid Rahnema, "Participation," in *The Development Dictionary: A Guide to Knowledge as Power*, ed. Wolfgang Sachs (USA: Zed Books Ltd, 1992), 116.

meeting and told what is at stake, we respond and contribute to what they [development agents] want to hear. Their minds are already made up. What difference can we make? We are all in it like that.'

Scholars are aware that the application of the term 'participation' is fraught with difficulties. Particularly noted for its ideological tendencies, the multifarious purposes involved in the use of 'participation', in Majid Rahnema's analysis, present uncertainties and anxieties.[121] Is its implementation process strategically planned to coerce indigenous people towards predefined development objectives and goals? Or is it done in an open and enabling environment as a 'real' integrated approach to development?[122] These questions raise concerns for researchers and analysts. It is my contention that if the potential benefit of participation is to be derived, then efforts should be made to extricate biases and coercion. Thus, even though participation is perceived as an inclusive approach to development, the Nankani argued that, the modern view of participation needs to be re-examined. This is because, the desire to share, influence and be structurally involved in the decision-making processes is essential for the Nankani.[123]

It is here that the Nankani encounter most of their problems with development agents. In their attempt to meet the ever growing and complex needs,[124] the Nankani sought partnerships beyond their religious and socio-cultural set-up. Over the years, various relationships have been formed with different development partners. Consequently, the search for partnership has linked indigenous communities with international organizations and their frameworks of development. These relationships produced an unequal power structure, 'the haves' (partners) and 'the have-nots' (community). Despite the attempts, the problems continue to exist. The apparent lack of progress has led to various attitudinal formations at the community level, and speculations by development agents. The need to examine how these partner-

---

121 Ibid., 116-22.
122 Ibid. 116 and Neil Thin, *Social Progress and Sustainable Development* (London: ITDG Publishing, 2002), 96.
123 Pauline E. Peters, "Encountering Participation and Knowledge in Development Sites," *Development Encounters: Sites of Participation and Knowledge*, ed. in Pauline E. Peters (Cambridge: Harvard Institute for International Development, 2000), 6.
124 This process is believed to be rooted in colonialism but exacerbated by globalization.

ship formations have impacted on the development of the people is essential in unravelling the problem.

SEEKING PARTNERSHIP?
INTERNATIONAL DEVELOPMENT AND POLICIES

Seeking partnerships on issues relating to the daily lives of people and community is typical of the Nankani. These alliances are sought in both spiritual and human forms. Although the ancestors are central within the spiritual circle, there are specific deities, spirits, charms and amulets to aid or enhance individual and community interest. A farmer may possess a specific crop or animal deity or charm in addition to his ancestral, territorial or earth spirits.[125] On the human front, life is generally lived in partnership. This is seen in areas of building and construction, farming, hunting, fishing and communal rituals. In all these relationships, the active participation of everyone is essential. Similarly, the aims and objectives of these partnerships are specifically tailored and reciprocally addressed. As the Nankani moved beyond their traditional domain of mutual inclusiveness to the national and international sphere, the arrangement was transformed, destabilizing the traditional system and making it untenable for the external system to function as well. Understanding this requires an explanation.

The advent of colonization and missionary activities among the Nankani introduced dramatic changes.[126] Not only were new systems of governance and religious traditions introduced, the new ways of living like education, Western medicine and health facilities gradually transformed into basic needs in rural African communities. Yet, the fact that these are not part of the traditional system means efforts have to be made, through partnerships, to address such needs. The move to seek human partnership beyond the socio-cultural boundaries of the traditional community led the Nankani to mission houses and colonial officers, a process that is now largely directed at development agents. One of these partners is NABOCADO. Yet, NABOCADO's work in this community depends on financial resources from international

---

125   Rose Mary Akurigu, "A Comparative Study of Sacrifice in Islam and African Traditional Religion: A Case Study of the Islamic Population and the Traditional People of the Upper East Region of Ghana" (B. A. Diss, University of Ghana, 1993), 54-8.

126   See chapter two, 118-24.

funding organizations such as the Cordaid of The Netherlands, Misereor of Germany, Caritas Australia and the Catholic Relief Service of United States of America. All these organizations operate, to some extent, within prevailing international development policies. This has consequently moved the local or culturally specific needs and methods of partnership to the international sphere. At this level, the personalized nature of the Nankani partnership system is depersonalized and counted as a single unit within the global statistics of development partners or beneficiaries. This has not only dissolved the interpersonal relationship structure of the Nankani, it has placed them within the broad frame of development needs, issues or problems. At this level, broad frame policies are formulated to meet the increasing demands of "grassroots" development needs.[127] This process, it may be argued, has set in an uneven or spiral chain of demand and supply of development needs. Subsequently, this led to a myriad of problems and the drive for global solutions has not simply overshadowed diversity, but also, its role as alternative sources of living.[128] This is the situation in which the Nankani find themselves at present.

In a bid to correct the problems arising from the prevailing situation, international development organizations continue to draw-up broad policy frameworks. The aim of some of these policies is to give an inclusive perspective to the different issues arising from former development strategies. Over the years, issues of culture, gender, participation and sustainability have become topical and strategic to the concerns of development. Although these inclusive approaches are essential in today's global world, they continue to present new problems in terms of cultural particularities. Hence, despite the constant search for innovative policies at the international level, there are great difficulties with their implementations in particular contexts. This is not just an issue of religio-cultural differences, very often, what is asked for and what is supplied or the conditions under which such supplies are given are not harmonious.

Unfortunately, the decisions taken are often idealized even when they do not actually reflect the practical realities on the ground. For

---

127 Sylvia Borren, "Development agencies: global or solo players?" in *Debating Development: NGOs and the Future*, eds. Deborah Eade and Ernst Ligteringen (Oxford: Oxfarm GB, 2001), 174-9.

128 Brian K. Murphy, "International NGOs and the challenge of modernity," in *Debating Development: NGOs and the Future*, eds. Deborah Eade and Ernst Ligteringen (Oxford: Oxfarm GB, 2001), 78.

instance, the recent international appeals for the above mentioned strategies, especially, gender, has added new dimensions and compounded the problems of development among the Nankani. This is particularly so with the mainstreaming of gender. Although this is put in place to bridge the existing gender disparities, for a patrilineal African society like the Nankani, this has been stressful and upsetting. Biased to the female gender, the attempt is viewed by some male members as an external imposition, aimed at destroying the traditional religio-cultural system. For these people, opposition is a sign of loyalty to their heritage.

By gender, I am referring to the religio-cultural and social construction of gender which deals with relationships and roles of men and women in a given context. Set within the Nankani traditional religio-cultural context, and serving in this instance as a cultural variant, the international call for gender mainstreaming, which is imbued with a Western conceptual understanding, has left the development programmes among the Nankani at a threshold.[129] This position has resulted in a situation where community development workers are in a deadlock as to how to practically engage and handle the entrenched structural gender issues involved in gender equality, female empowerment, inheritance, access and ownership of property. During my field study, this situation was likened to the proverbial 'stepping into the chameleon's faeces' by Augustine Jude Akanlu.

This is based on a proverb, 'I have stepped into the chameleon's faeces in which washing-up alone cannot help'. It is used by the Nankani to illustrate classical stand-offs. It also refers to cases where important issues are addressed superficially. The chameleon is an important mythical animal. To link something to it implies there are some religious or structural undertones. Thus, although the act of washing may be carried out physically, these do not necessarily resolve the internal dynamics of the problem. The real act of thoroughly cleaning-up and ensuring that the root cause(s) of the situation is properly addressed is left untouched. According to my field study, there are structural issues in the traditional gender construction. To deal properly with these involves serious socio-cultural and religious upheavals. Development workers, who are often drawn up from within the environs, are believed to find such interruptions disturbing. Referred to as, 'they understand

---

129   Judith Butler, *Giving an Account of Oneself* (New York: Fordham University Press, 2005), 11.

the situation themselves'; some community members argued during a group discussion in Kologo that development workers prefer surface dressing. On the other hand, the desire for continuous international support has often led rural community workers to relinquish this duty under the guise of religion and culture while claiming to have made some impact with their superficial dressing. It was thus concluded, 'only time will tell', a view that implies an over-reliance on posterity.

Meanwhile, development workers shelve these difficulties under the broad categories of religion, culture or tradition. Classified as problems, they are presented in development documents as problems resulting from the 'beliefs and practices of target communities'. This classification serves as a 'safe haven' where difficulties are coded with the right rhetoric. A case in point is the issue of *chinchirisi* (*chinchirigo* as singular). These are children classified as evil spirits and eliminated traditionally by a method similar to trial by ordeal. The process is often referred to as, *basiya ti chinchirigo cheya muu-o* (allowing the spirit-child to return to the bush) or *chinchirigo basiga* (seeing off the spirit-child). *Chinchirisi* is the Nankani concept for anomalies.[130] This indicates that such children are not meant to be among people. Their actual home is in the wild space. Their presence in a family might have been a mistake or caused by a hidden spiritual problem, which could lead to revenge. Such children pose potential danger to the well-being of their families and the community at large. Considered in essence as spiritual entities that have strayed their way into the human abode, they are in need of human help to return home. For this purpose, the rite is swiftly carried out without any reservation.

Although significantly reduced, this act is still practice by a few people within the eastern zone of the Nankani community. Although it is known, it is considered a religio-cultural practice of a limited scale, not deserving any serious national attention. Irrespective of the fact that the practice challenges the principles of Human Rights, Rights of the Child and has an impact on child mortality rate, no efforts are made to address it. The Navrongo Health Research Centre (NHRC) has arrived at a tentative understanding with its international donor partner, the

---

130   Amenga-Etego, Rose Mary, "*Chinchirisi*: The Phenomenon of the 'Spirit Children' amongst the Nankani of Northern Ghana," *Legon Journal of the Humanities* XIX, (2008): 183-214. See also, Fiona Bowie, *The Anthropology of Religion: An Introduction* (Oxford: Blackwell Publishers, 2000), 49-51.

Division for Infectious Diseases of the National Institute of Health (NIH), USA, to describe it as a traditional practice. Thus named, 'cultural infanticide' or 'spirit child killing', the practice is left to posterity.

With such opportunities, rural development workers have found an effective outlet to hide comfortably their difficulties, inadequacies or failures. At the same time, the secularisation of international institutions in their approach to development has contributed to these scenarios. Very often, Western donor institutions are either not interested, or are unwilling to probe the reality or otherwise of the allegations brought forward by rural development workers because of their lack of interest in religious issues.[131] Hence, such complex development issues at the community level are often left without proper resolutions. Even where efforts are made, the approach can raise further concerns. For instance, a recent follow-up phone conversation revealed that the above US organization (NIH) was sponsoring a US citizen to undertake a study of the *chincihirisi* phenomenon. Although there is no objection to the research, some people are raising concerns because the approach is from a legal perspective, a view, they suspect, will not fully consider the underlying religio-cultural dimensions. Indigenous communities, therefore, continue to blame modern development programmes for disturbing, disorganizing and/or destroying their religious and socio-cultural systems with the introduction of new issues. They contend some of the modern ideas in development and gender is directly responsible for the erosion of their religio-cultural, economic, and social systems. This makes the NGO sector important for serving as a conduit for international agencies and policies, as well as development players in their own right in the field and this study.

As an introductory chapter, it provides the foundation on which the rest of the study is set upon. Not only has it introduced the subject under consideration, it has also established the view that the study is an integrative, bottom-up approach to the discourse on religion and sustainable rural development among the Nankani. This is enhanced by the chosen multidisciplinary approach, which is underscored by the unique positioning of the phenomenological method.

---

131   Ineke Bakker, "Opening speech by General Secretary of the Council of Churches in the Netherlands," conference report on Religion: a source for human rights and development cooperation, (The Netherlands, September 2005), 43.

PART ONE

Chapter Two

NANKANI IDENTITY AND RELIGIOUS CONSTRUCTION

Our first and most fundamental point is that African religious belief and practice is profoundly historical.[1]

From a historical perspective, Northern Ghana as we know it today is purely the invention of British colonialism, even though nature clearly had a lot to say about its composition.[2]

The raiders descended, the strange protectors took over power and the new spiritual armies pitched their camp; all these to and amongst a people with already a culture quite of their own. ... All three groups caused a cultural confusion among the people they came to. The culture in this area was seemly before these arrivals; the culture became seamy after the arrivals.[3]

"Our tradition says 'history is the torch bearer of life'". This was the first statement of Gerard Akurugo, in my recent interview, as he set out to outline what I generally see as the history of the Nankani and their religion. According to him, the Nankani believe that if you

---

1   Allman and Parker, *Tongnaab*, 6.
2   Yakubu Saaka, "Introduction," in *Regionalism and Public Policy in Northern Ghana*, ed. Yakubu Saaka (New York: Peter Lang, 2001), 1.
3   J. Awia, 'Threefold Encounter in Northern Ghana," in Beverly and Carey's WebPage, accessed 3 December 2004; available from http://mysite.verizon.net/vze827ph/threefold_front.htm; Internet.

do not know your past, you cannot determine your future. The past grants meaning and with it, the understanding that helps to negotiate the future. He remarked that the most common identity question "who is s/he?" traditionally refers to what community, clan and/or family is s/he from? Similarly, a man confidently hits his chest and asks, "Don't you know me? And quickly recounts his ancestry and nothing of himself". Akurugo contended that even though such an account merely situates the person genealogically in a history s/he is not a part of, the aim is to display a sense of pedigree and continuity, and also, to project an underlying logic for the person's future prospects[4]

This underscores the view that 'knowledge is history'. Among the Nankani, knowledge is perceived as a lived experience. This notion is not restricted to the living *per se*. Nonetheless, it does shed light on why the aged, and the ancestors, are crucial in the traditional setup. It is basically for their immense experiential knowledge. The Nankani stress that even the diviner foretells the future on the basis of the past. Be it an interpretation of an act, ascertain an ancestral viewpoint, the search for one's chosen destiny or to predict one's future prospects, the diviner returns to the past to uncover the secrets of the future. In this case, knowledge, religious or otherwise, is intrinsically intertwined with a person or people's history. This stretches from the individual, family, lineage, clan, community to the nation state.[5] As such, religious knowledge is handled with care and transferred with caution. This 'backward – forward outlook to life' has however been identified by Manning Nash as one of the essential traits of ethnicity. From Nash's perspective, tradition represents the past of culture. This past is not stagnant but continuous, producing a present and a possible future. For Nash, it is these features that bestow upon the past its authority. Thus, "the very fact of survival, pastness, and continuity give an aura of authority, legitimacy, and rightness to cultural beliefs and practices".[6] This critically portrays the Nankani conceptualization as a specific formulation of identity. A perspective that may be illustrated by Fredrik Barth as he points out that, "ethnic groupings are categories

---

4   Fortes, "Some Reflections on Ancestor Worship in Africa," 122-3.
5   See Stephen Ellis and Gerrie ter Haar, *Worlds of Power: Religious Thoughts and Political Practice in Africa* (London: Hurst and Company, 2004), 163-5.
6   Manning Nash, "The Core Elements of Ethnicity," in *Ethnicity*, eds. John Hutchinson and Anthony D. Smith (Oxford and New York: Oxford University Press, 1996), 27.

of ascription and identification by the actors themselves".[7] The veracity of this assertion requires further examination.

Consequently, a study of the Nankani invariably includes their socio-political and migratory history.[8] Unfortunately, from the available narrative histories, this will involve individual clan and community histories, a coverage which cannot be pursued in this enquiry. Hence, a brief collective history, within the limits of their present location, will be outlined. For instance, the term 'religion' is inclusively represented as *malma* in Nankani (religion, tradition and culture). Even though *malma* existed as 'practices' prior to the twentieth century, it acquired its current understanding during this period, within the emerging context of religious pluralism. This was a separatist endeavour, with the aim of distinguishing it, as it were, from the intruding religions, with an imbued sense of cultural and ancestral identity. *Malma* as 'religion' is therefore historically embedded.

Nonetheless, the circumstance also makes it a comparative invention. Like Chidester and Fortes, I am tempted to place *malma* within the context of frontier relations of comparative inventions.[9] Yet, unlike these scholars, this invention is from the indigenous perspective. It is an assertion of identity, self-knowledge and representation in the midst of an uncertain invasion.[10] That apart, the comparative generalizations put forward by Fortes do not consider the contextually different frontier situations under which those inventions emerged. The ability to assert oneself is largely dependent on one's level of awareness or knowledge and power relations.[11] The literature shows that, not only were the times of these encounters different, the objectives for which these inventions surfaced were dissimilar. While in the South African frontier, such inventions were carved out from a settler possessive bias,

---

7   Fredrik Barth, "Ethnic groups and Boundaries," in *Ethnicity*, eds. John Hutchinson and Anthony D. Smith (Oxford and New York: Oxford University Press, 1996), 75.

8   See examples, J. Awia, *Navrongo and its Pioneers* (s. l., 1988), 3, 29-31 and Cardinall, Allan Wolsey, *The Natives of the Northern Territories of the Gold Coast: Their Customs, Religion and Folklore* (London: Routledge, 1920), 10-4.

9   Chidester, *Savage Systems*, 20-9 and Fortes, "Some reflections on ancestor Worship in Africa," 122.

10   Joy Hendry, *Reclaiming Culture: Indigenous People and Self-Representation* (England: Palgrave Macmillan, 2005).

11   Allman and Parker, *Tongnaab*, chapter two.

characterized by a brutal, selfish and gross destruction of human lives, the West African frontier, which was environmentally unfriendly, resulted in an extractive approach. This accounts for the area serving as an extractive point of labour for the mineral, cocoa and timber industries in Southern Ghana and as slaves overseas. This underscores the colonial policies in Northern Ghana where efforts were made towards the creation of a labour reserve for the nation's unskilled manpower needs.[12]

In my introductory chapter I affirmed the intertwining relationship between religion and the daily life of Africans through the works of Idowu and Mbiti. Mbiti's call for comprehensive studies, involving territorial groups within their current complex lifestyles was also acknowledged. It is my contention, in this chapter, that such a perspective will foster an in-depth understanding of the Nankani, their religion and their search for sustainable development. Understanding here refers to that which has been aptly carved out by Cox from "the phenomenological term, the eidetic intuition, which implies a seeing into meaning".[13] Similarly, the use of understanding in this investigation goes beyond the traditional descriptive and interpretive stance of phenomenology. It includes an immediate analysis of the data provided to ascertain the possible links between the Nankani religio-cultural system and development.

In this chapter, I attempt, in part, an exploration of this complexity among the present Nankani. To understand the Nankani and that which constitutes their religion, some historical perspective is relevant as indicated by the quotations above, which tentatively presents a summary of this chapter. Thus, the chapter locates the Nankani within the present Ghanaian landscape with its geo-historical nuances. The content is both historical and contemporary. These two factors continue to shape and mould the Nankani and their perspective to life. This consideration is also crucial because the two themes in this study, religion and development, are not just historically imbued with meaning, but dynamic processes as well. While a historical approach is necessary for understanding the people and their religion, a contem-

---

12   Saaka, "Introduction," 3-4 and Jacob Songsore *et al*, "Challenges of Education in Northern Ghana," 224-5.

13   James L. Cox, *Rational Ancestors: Scientific Rationality and African Indigenous Religions* (Cardiff: Cardiff Academic Press, 1998), 83.

porary outlook draws attention to the current realities. This provides a direct engagement with the Nankani with an understanding that is beyond the immediate circumstances, seeing and engaging the issues, as it were, from the community's perspective. This enables the investigation to respond to some of Shaw's observations that until recently, there has been a narrow focus on the understanding, study and presentation of ATR.[14] Although perpetuated by the historical divisions in religion and anthropological studies on Africa, she holds that both apologetic and nationalistic studies from the African perspective have not really been helpful. Although these views have been discussed differently by scholars in the field, including Jan Platvoet,[15] these polarizations of ideas simply sustain the problems, clouding available opportunities for pursuing meaningful and comprehensive studies in the area. There is a need to move ahead, strategise and create new channels and opportunities for the desired results.

The approach of the chapter is 'top-down'. It is also written in the ethnographic present. The structural approach is to adhere to the way the Nankani see themselves. That is, as an identifiable community within a specific location in Ghana. This spatial location is also in cognizance with the acquired sub-nationalistic tendencies of Northerners who view each other as *buri* (Sic. family).[16] Such unified identifications are, however, products of colonialism and postcolonialism. Even so, this notion of identity is different from Hendry's views on the Ainu or First Nations. Although these identity overtones entail some forms of "wrapping", the desire to present a formidable voice, to reject and resist discrimination, or from Saaka's viewpoint, "insulate and isolate the North from the South", and to fight for equal rights and opportunities, sustains this collective cultural and spatial identity.[17] At the same time, the approach affirms the administrative link between the nation's rural communities and central government. This is the process through which the latter is principally responsible for the political and socio-

---

14   Shaw, "'Traditional' African Religions," 183-91. See also, Joel S. Kahn, *Culture, Multiculture, Postculture* (London: SAGE Publications, 1995), x-xi.

15   Jan G. Platvoet, "From object to subject: a history of the study of the religions of Africa," in *The Study of Religions in Africa: Past, Present and Prospects*, eds. Jan Platvoet, James Cox and Jacob Olupona (Cambridge: Roots and Branches, 1996), 105-38.

16   Saaka, "Introduction," 2.

17   Hendry, *Reclaiming Culture*, 1-12 and Saaka, "Introduction," 2.

economic development of the former. That apart, the current under-standing of development in the study area is based on this approach. Finally, the identification of the Nankani as an ethnic group within the national and international sphere is through this approach.

LOCATING THE NANKANI OF NORTHERN GHANA

The designation Northern Ghana or the North refers to the former 'Northern Territories'.[18] According to Hans Debrunner, the area con-stituting the Northern Territories was initially a 'neutral zone' between German Togoland and British Gold Coast until its incorporation in 1901.[19] Debrunner notes that attention was drawn to the area only after the defeat and control of Ashanti.[20] This perhaps explains why earlier anthropologists sought to present the area as a comprehensive unit. In so doing, however, not only did their works lack clarity, some titles were misleading.[21]

Understanding this clustered identity formation can be deci-phered from the geographical and socio-political history of the nation state. Before its establishment as a British colony in 1874, some parts of the South had already come into contact with different Euro-pean groups.[22] This process dates back to 1471 with the Portuguese discovery of *Mina*, "the mine", from which the name Gold Coast emerged.[23] Consequently, the original Gold Coast was the coastal belt. The middle (forest) belt, made up of the Ashanti, was annexed after their defeat in 1900.[24] The Sahel-Savanah (Northern) belt, then referred to as the Northern Territories Protectorate, was incorporated

---

18 H. O. A. McWilliam, *The Development of Education in Ghana* (Longmans, 1959), 34 and F. M. Bourret, *The Gold Coast: A Survey of the Gold Coast and British Togoland 1919-1951*, 2nd ed. (London: Oxford University Press, 1952), 23.

19 Hans W. Debrunner, *A History of Christianity in Ghana* (Accra: Waterville Publishing House, 1967), 202 and Bourret, *The Gold Coast*, 86.

20 Debrunner, *A History of Christianity in Ghana*, 201.

21 Cardinall, *In Ashanti and Beyond* and R. S. Rattray, *The Tribes of the Ashanti Hinterland* (Oxford: Clarendon Press, 1932).

22 J. R. Thackrah, *Twentieth Century History Basic Facts*, Revised, R. F. Stapley (Harper Collins Publishers, 1997), 132.

23 J. D. Fage, *A History of Africa* (London: Hutchinson of London, 1978), 224.

24 Bebrunner, *A History of Christianity in Ghana*, 201.

in 1901.[25] In 1922 the final part, the Mandated Territory of Togoland came under British administration.[26] These initial "four territorial divisions were administered separately until 1946, when the British Government ruled them as a single unit".[27] It is generally observed that, despite the efforts at national integration, these four historical portions have remained pretty much fragmented. Today, although there have been further internal divisions, to create smaller administrative units, comprising regions and districts, this historical outline continues to influence the nation's political, socio-economic and religio-cultural structure. As the title illustrates, it is not a simple case of Ghana but Northern Ghana even though the study is funded with national resources. This is because Northern Ghana is known and accepted as a distinct geographical and political category. Perhaps, this generic term is used because of the inability to obtain a common linguistic identity like the Gas, Akans and/or Ewes. Whatever the case, these linguistic identifications only reinforce the prevailing political situation as they somehow refer to the colonial demarcations.[28]

On the other hand, this articulated Northern identity is also based on its internal dynamics. Before the presence of the British, the North was a fragmented area loosely bound together by similar ecological conditions, slave raids, migrations and the caravan trade. All these had significant impacts on the people and their religions. The significant presence of Islam in the North has its historical root in the last three factors.[29] However, in a sub-heading, 'Islam encouraged', Debrunner ascribed the presence of Islam in the North to British colonial policies.[30] Even though Debrunner's view may be worth noting as a contributory factor to the spread of Islam in the North, the fact that Islam predated British rule in the area and had already established Islamic kingdoms, suggests that Islam was already a force to reckon with at the time of British occupation.

---

25   W. E. Ward, *A short History of The Gold coast* (London, New York and Toronto: Longmans, Green and Co., 1935), 217.

26   Thackrah, *Twentieth Century History Basic Facts*, 132.

27   U. S. Department of State, "Background Note: Ghana," *Bureau of African Affairs*, accessed 9 February 2005, 1-3; available from http://www.state.gov/r/pa/ei/bgn/2860.htm; Internet. See also, The Long Road to Ghana's Independence – September 1997, accessed 9 February 2005, 1-3; available from http://www.greatepicbooks.com/epics/september97.html; Internet.

28   See map 2.

29   Saaka, "Introduction," 2, 7-8.

30   Debrunner, *A History of Christianity in Ghana*, 215.

Besides, when the British moved into the North in 1901, with Gambaga as its first capital, it was already a mixed community of traditional and Muslim adherents. That apart, whereas the pre-colonial Islamic influences in the Bawku area produced a viable Islamic presence, the British attempt to expand the Nayiri chieftaincy to the other parts of the Upper East Region did not produce any Islamic presence. As Allman and Parker have shown, the attempt to impose Nayiri chieftaincy on the area was not successful.[31] Shortly after the establishment of the British administration in the North, Christianity made an appearance, a situation one might argue would not have been possible at the time if the British were not present. In this case, it might be argued, in the light of Debrunner's statement, that British colonial rule rather facilitated the presence and expansion of Christianity in the North.

The Catholic missionary group known as the 'White Fathers', Missionaries of Africa, settled in Navrongo in 1906.[32] These missionaries who had entered into an agreement with the British commander in charge of the North knew that their continuous presence depended on their relationship with the commanders.[33] Together with their own missionary proclamation to first "win local goodwill by providing social services, particularly in health and education", they won not only the admiration of the inhabitants but also of Armitage, the commander in charge.[34] From Navrongo, their mission field expanded to other parts of the North and eventually merged with their counterparts in the South to form the Catholic Church in Ghana. Donald Frazer in his *Future of Africa* has shown how colonial administration served as channels for evangelization in the African continent.[35] Despite the contextual differences, the Navrongo mission station was greatly facilitated by colonial administration.[36]

In a telling article, 'Threefold Encounter in Northern Ghana',[37] Fr. Awia summarized this history and its impact on the area of study. Although the narrative is fused with collaborative texts, the story

31   Allman and Parker, *Tongnaab*, 81-7.
32   Debrunner, *A History of Christianity in Ghana*, 216, 24.
33   McWilliam, *The Development of Education in Ghana*, 37.
34   Ibid., 37, 224.
35   Donald Fraser, *The Future of Africa* (London: Young People's Missionary Movement, 1911), 153-64.
36   Awia, *Navrongo and its Pioneers*, 27.
37   Awia, "Threefold Encounter in Northern Ghana," 1-3.

reflects the common oral narrative pattern on the political and socio-cultural experiences of the Kassena-Nankani people. The phrase 'Threefold Encounter' refers to the Northern sector's encounter with Islam, the British colonial administration and Christianity. Although the encounter with Islam is difficult to trace due to the lack of reliable data, its early presence is acknowledged.[38] Oral traditions have also linked Islam with the Fulani, Mossi and Hausa traders. These traders, whose individual identities proved difficult to establish because of their dress code and religio-cultural practices, are generally identified as the transmitters of early Islam. Fage, however, identifies these people within the fifteenth and sixteenth century "Mande trading activities in the Gold Coast hinterlands".[39]

The encounters brought considerable changes to the people, their religion and culture. The impact of these influences in reshaping the people's philosophical, political, religio-cultural and social systems has been far reaching. These are however relative to each ethnic group. Yet, the need to understand these general influences is still crucial to under-standing the religio-cultural as well as other forms of development in this geo-political area. It is also important for understanding the Nankani, who, in spite of their own unique circumstances, continue to share a sense of belongingness and brotherhood (*buri*) with the rest of the North, perhaps because of their "shared political memories".[40]

The former Northern Territories, commonly known as the North, is now made up of three regions namely Upper East Region (U.E.R), Upper West Region (U.W.R.) and Northern Region (N.R.). Until 1981, the U.E.R. and the U. W. R. formed a single administrative region known as the Upper Region. Although the U. E. R. has two main international border posts linking it to its neighbouring countries of Togo and Burkina Faso, it is overwhelmed by several unauthorised routes, making control of the international boundaries almost impossible. With families, clans and ethnic groups living across borders, it is practically fruitless trying to maintain international boundaries when

---

38   Jacob Songsore, *Regional Development in Ghana: The Theory and the Reality* (Ghana: Woeli Publishers Services, 2003), 23-25 and McWilliam, *The Development of Education in Ghana*, 36.

39   Fage, *A History of Africa*, 90.

40   Max Weber, "The Origins of Ethnic Groups," in *Ethnicity*, eds. John Hutchinson and Anthony D. Smith (Oxford and New York: Oxford University Press, 1996), 36.

the priorities of the indigenous people who live around these borders rest on kinship ties. At present, the region, which was initially made up of three districts, namely: Bwaku, Bolgatanga and Navrongo is now sub-divided into two municipalities and six districts. These are: Bolgatanga and Bawku municipalities, and for the districts, they are: Kassena-Nankana East, Kassena-Nankana West, Bongo, Bulsa, Bwaku West (Zebila), Garu-Timpani and Talensi-Nabdam Districts. While the Garu-Timpani and Talensi-Nabdam Districts were carved out from the Bwaku and Bolgatanga districts in 2004, the Kassena-Nankani West, newest district in the region was carved from the Kassena-Nankani in September 2007. The rest of the old district is renamed Kassena-Nankani East. This notwithstanding, people simply use the old name or refer to it as the Navrongo district. Even though the breakdown of national administrative structures into smaller units are often carried out with the view of accelerating development in the respective areas, the processes are usually surrounded by divergent political negotiations by opinion members of the different communities, ethnic or languages groups among whom the impending split exercise is about to take place.

In such cases, both advocates and lobbyists work towards gaining favour on where to belong or how the new demarcations should be. It was therefore not surprising that at the prime of this study (field study in 2006); such purported political negotiations around the creation of the new Kassena-Nankana West District from the former Kassena-Nankana District stalled my attempt to access the necessary demographic data from the Navrongo Health Research Centre (NHRC). Being a Nankani; that is, belonging to one of the two ethnic or language groups forming the district, and carrying out a study on that select group alone immediately placed my benign study into the prevailing political nuances in the area. The situation was quite upsetting because the research preceded those political negotiations. Besides, the study was funded with national resources and ought to have taken precedence over the local level politics. That apart, as a research institution, I expected the director of the NHRC to rise above the situation, perhaps, because he knows the importance of data to an on going research. Based on such awareness, therefore, I expected some level of possible discussion on the elements of confidentiality, instead of the blatant refusal to provide the demographic data for the study. It is for some of these reasons that the debate on research involvement will continue to linger on in scholarship. This particular case shows the concept of involvement is fluid, as it does not depend on the researcher but can takes different forms.[41]

Two years after the division of the district, there are still quite a number of unresolved problems regarding the specific population or maps of the new (two) districts. Efforts to obtain a clear land mark demarcation of each of the two districts remain an illusion. Part of the difficulty stems from the fact that some communities have some of their members divided between the two districts. A case in point is the Kandiga community. There is also some form of uneasiness, dissatisfaction or a clear lack of understanding as to why Natugnia and Yoa are part of the old district when the rest of the communities surrounding them belong to the new district.[42] Some politically minded people have explained that the creation of the new districts is based on the constituency format because the pattern of the new districts is similar to that of the constituency. This is, however, argued upon with the view that constituencies are created for democratic voting purposes not necessarily for expedient national administration, planning and development. The discussions surrounding these issues clearly show that political expediency and adequate stakeholder national planning can be different scenarios in cases of this nature in Ghana. Yet, irrespective of the above discussion, both districts are still made up of Kasenas and Nankanis. With Paga as the new district capital, the supposedly new district, Kasena-Nankana West District is comprised of the Kasena communities to the West and the Nankani communities of the east, with the exception of Natugnia and Yoa. The rest of the old district (Kasena-Nankana District), now the Kasena-Nankana East District however, maintains the old administrative setup in the Navrongo central, Doba and all the communities to the south of Navrongo, in addition to Natugnia and Yoa.

Coincidentally, therefore, the identity of the Nankani today, as opposed to the prime of this study has not changed dramatically. This is because they interpret the division as a developmental move, arguing that 'it is the only way to get a fair share of the national cake'. The Nankanis still view themselves as one. In a recent discussion with some people, an elder remarked that 'a brother is a brother irrespec-

---

41   See chapter six, 370.
42   See the above named communities in the map of the former Kasena-Nankani District for verification, 137.

tive of where he lives or what outsiders say'. The statement implies that
government and its administrative structures are not only foreign, but
also abstract issues or land marks that do not really affect the internal
dynamics of the family or ethnic group. As indicated above, kinship
ties in Africa do not rest on political or international boundaries. Consequently, I will continue to maintain the identity of the Nankani as
an identifiable ethnic unit in the U.E.R. Besides, all the identifiable
land marks (schools, hospital and prison) discussed in this study have
remained in the old district. That apart, even though it is important to
bring to light the current administrative changes in the study area, this
research was carried out under the previous condition; thus, making it
valid for the context and purpose for which it was undertaken.

Together, the Kassena-Nankana districts formed one of the first
three districts of the U.E.R. It houses one of the main border-posts in the
country; the Paga-Burkina Faso border post. Navrongo was the colonial
administrative and military centre of the region;[43] hence, it houses the
only major prison and the first hospital in the region. It also served as
the Christian mission centre in the North. The first (mission) school
(1907), secondary school, teacher training college and the Navrongo
Campus of the University of Development Studies are all in this district.[44] The district is, therefore, an important component of the region.

Originally created in 1904 as the Navrongo district, the Kassena-
Nankana Districts continue to serve as part of the national administrative set-ups of the country.[45] They are created with two different but
neighbouring ethnic groups: the Kassena and the Nankani.[46] As noted
earlier, Navrongo is the capital of the Kassena-Nankana East, and Paga
is the district capital of the Kassena-Nankana West. English is the official and administrative language in both districts. This is irrespective
of the fact that more than half of the adult population are non-literate,
33.3% male and 21.3% female (literates) respectively.[47] Kassem and
Nankani are therefore used concurrently with English for official and

43 Awia, *Navrongo and its Pioneers*, 3, 29.
44 Awia, *Navrongo and its Pioneers*, 27-31.
45 Nankana, Nankanni, Nankanne and Nankanse are various forms of referring to
    the Nankani. Nankana is used as national administrative district,
46 Awia, *Navrongo and its Pioneers*, 29.
47 Fact Sheet No. III, Population of Ghana: Demographic and Socio-Economic
    Indicators by District, National Population Council, Ghana.

social functions. This multi-linguistic usage is because of the vast differences between the two indigenous languages.

Although parts of the two districts have peri-urban characteristics, the population is basically rural with most of its inhabitants living in dispersed rural communities. These communities are named according to their dialectical variants. The communities are composed of diffused household structures, traditionally made from mud, unbaked bricks and thatch.[48] The districts are largely dependent on a subsistence agricultural economy. Livelihood depends "on agriculture and cattle raising".[49] The Agricultural produce consist of millet, sorghum, corn, rice, groundnuts (peanuts), beans, banbaran (round) bean and a wide variety of vegetables, both wild and cultivated. The livestock comprises cattle, which are the most visible source of wealth, followed by sheep, goats, chickens and guinea fowls. This is supplemented by hunting and river fishing.

In recent times however, both the architectural and agriculture sectors have undergone some changes. The traditional round and oval mud housing structures with the rooftops are built along with other square and rectangular structures.[50] Sometimes, these are built with block, corrugated iron and metal roofing sheets.[51] It is becoming clear that the pictures indicated in the footnotes are used for illustrative purposes, a perspective that was debunked in one of the community discussions as not really being a realistic portrayal of the situation on the ground. Nonetheless, my desire to use pictures, a majority of which are structures is an attempt to project a sense of a true representation of the situation on the field at the time of this study. I am, however, aware of some of the arguments on the use of photography in investigations and the debate as to whether the integration of pictures in findings are meant to indicate "an exact representations of reality" or "not simply the representation of reality, but rather the transfer of a particular view of the world held by the photographer."[52] The latter, having been identified by T. Jack Thompson as a manipulative or propagandist act, in his paper on *Images of Africa*, explained the various uses with which

---

48 Pictures 1, 2, 4 and 5.

49 Bourret, *The Gold Coast*, 85.

50 *Pictures* 2, 3, 4, 5 and 7.

51 Pictures 3 and 8.

52 T. Jack Thompson, *Images of Africa: Missionary Photography in the Nineteenth Century: an Introduction*, Occasional Paper (Centre for African Studies: University of Copenhagaen, February 2004), 3.

pictures where used by missionaries to objectify and portray Africans and their continent. Although this study is not addressing a similar topic, I must state that the incorporation of the pictures in this study is mainly for illustrative purposes.

The agricultural sector has also undergone significant changes with the introduction of soya beans, the rearing of ducks, rabbits and pigs. Even though these new forms of livelihoods are taken up, they are excluded from religio-cultural practices, giving them a purely socio-economic outlook. There is also an increasing use of donkeys for ploughing[53] and the transportation of goods. There is currently a tremendous increase in petty trading in the districts. Even though this is mainly in the area of agricultural produce, processed and unprocessed, there are crafts, traditional wear and other basic commodities. This notwithstanding, these are inadequate for local revenue generation for the districts' development.

Evidence at the community levels show that education, skilled employment and urbanisation continue to influence the movement of people from their local communities to the urban areas of the country. With a significant number of the youth and the productive labour group migrating to the urban South, this has created problems for the subsistence economy. The situation has further produced an unbalanced effect on the socio-cultural and religious structures of the area, since some leadership (religious and secular) positions fall to "Acting" personalities. These factors have contributed to changes in the indigenous patterns of life. In an interview with the then District Chief Executive, Emmanuel Achegwe, in April 2006, he noted out-migration as one of the main challenges of the district.

This broad outline of the political and socio-economic composition of the North seeks to provide an understanding of the general context in which the Nankani, here identified as a rural community, find themselves. The section has outlined the Nankani as a distinct rural ethnic group. It is my opinion that this historical step-down narrative approach is important for the proper identification and understanding of the Nankani within the geographical, political and religio-cultural context of Ghana. Besides that, it has addressed the phrase, 'Northern Ghana'. This is particularly important because the national socio-political development seeps down to rural areas through this channel. Due

---

53   Picture 13.

to this bureaucratic structure; central government, regional, district and community downward administrative process, rural development resources from the national level hardly get to their required destination in good proportions. Nevertheless, the lifestyles, religion and culture of rural communities are continually influenced and affected by the policies and activities within the wider nation. As a historical narrative, therefore, the above provides the background information.

CONSTRUCTING A RELIGIOUS IDENTITY

The term 'religion' has no direct equivalence or translations in Nankani. Fortunately, this problem is now acknowledged. Nancy Ring *et al.* made this clear by stating that "[n]ot all cultures have a term which corresponds exactly to the Latin-derived 'religion'".[54] Writing on the Anufo of Northern Ghana, Jon Kirby made a similar claim, noting that the word 'religion' is "not objectified in their thinking but is rather an aspect of all of life. Religious beliefs and practices form an integral part of life and manifest themselves functionally in modes of action and apparatus for problem solving".[55] This is precisely the case with the Nankani. It is uncertain if an attempt was ever made to identify, translate or define 'religion' in its scholarly context. Although the discussions during my fieldwork revealed an appreciable depth of understanding of 'religion', it was viewed, more or less, as an unnecessary Western concept. Unlike terms such as 'Christians', 'Christ', 'Eucharist' and 'Malam' (Islamic cleric but used for Islam) which have been adopted and localized, 'religion' continues to be isolated and neglected. Persistent efforts to find or identify an indigenous alternative for 'religion' produced two viewpoints.

The first view was a distinction between the three religious traditions among the Nankani. These are the indigenous religion, Islam and Christianity. The second, as I came to understand, represented a form of dissatisfaction over earlier perceptions of the indigenous beliefs and practices.[56] According to the people, this was in opposition to

---

54   Nancy C. Ring *et al, Introduction to the Study of Religion* (Maryknoll, New York: Orbis Books, 1998), 19.

55   Jon P. Kirby, "Cultural Change and Religious Conversion in West Africa," in *Religion in Africa: Experience and Expression*, eds. Thomas D. Blakely, Walter E. A. van Beek and Dennis L. Thomson (London: Heinemann, 1994), 62.

56   This relates to the early notions of ATR as evil superstitions or non-religious.

the manner words were taken from the local language for the Christian liturgy without due regard for their religio-cultural context.[57] Although varied forms of this expression were obtained, the following statement by Abane serves as an illustration.

> So you [plural] now know that ours is also a *pusigo* [religion]. We have never been asked in this way. But what they don't know is that every land has its *zombune*. What can I say, your minds have returned and you now want to find out the truth. If this is real, then it is good. If not, then it's up to you.[58]

This statement presents different layers of thought. At one level, it is an expression of discontent and doubt. As Parrinder observed, although much was written about indigenous religions, the adherents were not asked about their beliefs.[59] On the other hand, there is an emphasis on the differences of cultures and religious practices. Alongside is also an appreciation for the late realization and acknowledgment of the traditional beliefs and practices of the Nankani as 'religion'. Based on these perceptions, further discussions were held to explore the indigenous conception and use of the word *pusigo*.

Pusigo refers to greetings, thanksgiving or prayer. At present, *pusigo* is associated with worship in general. This is because of the Christian use of *pusigo* as worship. Although *pusigo* is linked with 'religion', it is not accepted as an accurate translation. This has to do with its usage. According to the oral histories, the 'Fathers' adopted *pusigo* for their religion.[60] In their attempt to overcome the notions of *pusigo* at the time, they adopted the indigenous name for the Supreme Being, *Winɛ*, transforming both words into the phrase *Winɛ pusigo* (God's

---

57   Examples include: *pusigo, wula* and *kaa'be* (sacrifice). Using *wula* as an example, *wula* is a small calabash. It has multiple uses including those reserved for ritual or libation purposes. It is this ritual *wula* and its religious significance that is adopted as a chalice and used in the Roman Catholic liturgy.

58   *Zombune*, snack made from millet, indicating there are different ways of life and spirituality.

59   Geoffrey Parrinder, *Comparative Religion* (London: George Allen and Unwin Ltd., 1962), 18.

60   The first Christian missionaries among the Nankani were the 'White Fathers' of the Roman Catholic Church. They arrived in 1906 from Burkina Faso.

greeting).[61] This phrase was however translated into 'the worship of God', referring to 'the worship of the Christian God'. The essence of the distinction must be placed within the context of early Christian notions, attitudes and desire to differentiate Christianity as a distinct and the only true religion from ATR. This interpretation however displeased some adherents of the indigenous religion, making *pusigo* an unacceptable translation for 'religion'. Although *Winɛ pusigo* was and still is not generally accepted as the true representation of 'religion', it provided a platform for a common understanding and usage between the Church and the indigenous people. Thus, *Winɛ pusigo* among the Nankani refers to worshiping the Christian God. This presented Christianity as an identifiable religious tradition in the community.

This strategy was then adopted and replicated by the Nankani in their attempt to distinguish Christianity from Islam. The 'Fathers' (*faari duma*) and Christian converts (*faari yire duma*), became synonymous with members of the Christian faith while *Malam duma* was reserved for those of the Islamic faith. According to Akawuni of Kologo, when the missionaries brought in the *lugsingo* (separation or differentiation), "our fathers decided to properly identify them. This is why today we have the *Christa koma*, *malam duma* and *ti ma me malma*". The identifications '*Christa koma*'[62] or '*faari yire duma*'[63], '*Malam duma*'[64] or '*Malam pusiba*'[65] and '*ti ma me malma*',[66] have not only come to designate the three main religions in the area; they significantly introduced a new line of inquiry. This new idea came from the

---

61   *Winɛ* now commonly spelt as *Wine* is the indigenous name for the Supreme Being (God) in Nankani.

62   '*Christa coma*' means 'Christ's children's' but stands for 'God's children', implying these are the followers/children of Christ or those who practice the Christ way.

63   *Faari yiire duma* means 'Fathers' house people'. 'Father' refers to a Roman Catholic priest. 'Fathers house' is used for both the Catholic Church and Christianity. Using 'Father's house' in reference to the Christian church is perhaps symbolic of their pioneering role.

64   Although there are claims of an early presence of Islam in Ashanti, there is no substantive evidence. See, http://www.ghanaweb.com/GhanaHomePage/tribes/langauges.php 23/07/06; Rose Mary Akurigu argued that Islam entered Ghana through the northern sector of the country. See, Akurigu, "A Comparative Study of Sacrifice in Islam and Traditional African Religion," 3.

65   '*malam pusiba*' represents those who pray the Islamic way.

66   This refers to 'our own beliefs, practices, customs, traditions, values and norms'.

word *malma*. Further interviews and discussion on *malma* confirmed that the concept is the closest equivalent and the most acceptable alternative for 'religion'.

In an earlier interview with Abudu Adongo on the meaning and understanding of the term 'religion', he questioned whether I was implying *pusigo* or *malma*. Elaborating further in Nankani, he said, "If it is *pusigo* you are talking of, does a day ever pass without someone saying a prayer? The problem you educated people have is our *malma*." According to Abudu, every society has its own forms of *malma*. Christianity and Islam are examples of the Whiteman and the Arab's *malma*. Probing further to ascertain whether the general understanding of the word *malma* could be used as the acceptable translation of 'religion', he replied:

> My daughter, what kind of question is this? When we say fire has consumed the goat, you ask where the skin is. It is you the educated people who go about differentiating things and giving them all those names – not us.

In other words, the case was closed. His conclusion was drawn from the symbolism of the fire and the consumed goat which leaves no skin. For him, *malma* is religion and there should be no further questions.

In a related interview with Akurugo, he noted that the word *malma* should be taken as a symbolic expression of the Nankani identity and religiosity. After a prolonged discussion with three other elderly relatives on the issue, he concluded that *malma* is "representative of our identity, our uniqueness and our being." Explaining further he said:

> We depend on our traditions, which are our historical experiences. These are situated within our beliefs and practices. So we talk of our heritage. Our heritage is also our culture. This culture embodies these experiences within the context of our environment and our relationship with it. But much of these are passed down to us through the traditions of our ancestors. So, within all these, we find the embodiment of our spirituality which provides meaning and life to our circumstances and our very being. But then, all these are literally understood within the same context of tradition and culture. So, our religion is heavily depen-

dant on these and we have always relied on the ways of our
ancestors to seek *Wine*.[67]

Religion in this case embraces the concepts 'culture' and 'tradition'.
Malma is a compound term, inclusive of that which is seen, heard, felt
and revered as religion within this socio-cultural setting. According
to the Nankani heritage, a great part of *malma* is passed down from
the generations gone. That which is present must be preserved and
passed on to the generations to come. This perspective of religion is
quite similar to Malory Nye's view, "'religion' is not some free-floating
thing that exists outside of the cultural setting".[68] For Nye religion
and culture present reciprocal elements. Like Merrick Posnansky,
Nye contends that, "religion strongly influences the culture, and the
culture is itself the medium through which the religion is experienced
and practiced".[69] Even though the quest to define religion has drawn in
culture and tradition, this does not broaden or complicate the issue of
identification and definition. The basis for this assertion lies in the view
that *malma* is an all embracing term.

The above discussion on 'religion' shows the Nankani description
of ATR is *ti ma me malma* (our own beliefs and practices). This includes
customs, traditions, values and norms, signifying that which is believed
to be indigenous to the people. This provided a link between the indigenous conceptualization and the modern term ATR. Thus deriving its
source from Parrinder's 1954's *African Traditional Religion*, ATR is an
embodiment of the beliefs, practices and customs of the African people.
According to Parrinder, ATR represents the ancient non-Christian,
non-Muslim religious beliefs of Africa.[70] But ATR as an indigenous
African religion today does not seek to exclude Christian or Islamic

---

67   It is important to note that this is a reformulation of the people's views. As a
      retired educationist and elder, Akurugo is often called upon to perform some of
      these intermediary roles.

68   Malory Nye, *Religion: The Basics* (London and New York: Routledge, 2003), 6.

69   Ibid; Merrick Posnansky, "Archaeology, Ritual and Religion," in *The Historical
      Study of African Religion: with special reference to East and Central Africa*, eds.
      T. O. Ranger and I. N. Kimambo (London, Nairobi, and Ibadan: Heinemann,
      1972), 29. For Posnansky, religion is an aspect of culture. Yet this single aspect
      has a far reaching consequence, affecting "all the other facets of social life". See
      also, Capps, *Religious Studies*, 106.

70   Geoffrey Parrinder, *African Traditional Religion* (London: Hutchinson's Uni-
      versity Library, 1954), 10.

influences. Its preoccupation seems to be geared towards the practice and preservation of that which is left, irrespective of the condemnations and influences it has received through history. By implication, it does not only acknowledge the impact of these two religions; it includes slavery, modernity and most importantly, the direct intervention of colonialism which specifically initiated actions for the abolition of some of its ancient practices such as the trial by ordeal. It also accepts the various adaptations as part of its 'new' heritage. In other words, the word 'traditional' does not connote an a-historic, rigid or stagnant religion; a position that has gained the attention of current scholars.[71] This is however not the case. ATR is dynamic and this dynamism is reflected both in ritual performances and symbolic representations. For instance, a gun shot or its equivalent sound from the use of gun powder during funeral performances symbolizes the terror and devastation unleashed on the family, clan and community by death. But this is said to have been originally enacted as a symbolic ritual in memory of the dead and lost of loved ones during the period of the slave raiding in the area. Thus, though the current use of the gun as a religious symbol in funeral rites specifically addresses the issue of loss and death, it is a reminder of the ancestors or people who were either killed or taken away. The gun is also used in other religio-cultural contexts. In some instances captured herbalists or diviners are represented by a gun in their shrines.[72]

While acknowledging that the study of ATR among the Nankani is hampered by the lack of "authentic texts and literature" (written), I concur with Gaba that ATR is a living faith.[73] Unlike Gaba, however, this study is not presenting ATR from the perspective of a lower religion in comparison to the generally acclaimed world religions.[74] In this study, ATR is a robust religion among the Nankani and many Ghanaians.[75] Besides, the independent status of ATR is currently established and

---

71   See David Chidester, *Religions of South Africa* (London and New York: Routledge, 1992), 1; Allman, and Parker, *Tongnaab*, 8-10 and Shaw, "'Traditional' African Religions," 183.

72   See picture 12.

73   Gaba, "Contemporary Research in African Religion," 9.

74   Ibid., 9. See also, Bowie, *The Anthropology of Religion*, 25-8 and ter Haar, "World Religions and Community Religions," 1-12.

75   "Don't Condemn African Traditional Religion," *Daily Graphic* (Ghana, January 12, 2000), 16-7.

argued widely within the context of religious pluralism[76] and inter-religious dialogue. The legitimacy of ATR is also publicly acclaimed in the phrase, 'Africa's three religions'.[77] Nevertheless, I am aware of the latent dynamics of inequalities and subordination involved in these terminologies. Relying simply on these premises would be highly presumptuous. It is within this façade of religious equality that the underlying factor of inequality occurs; therefore, it cannot be ignored.[78]

Notwithstanding the view that Christianity enjoys a superior and dominant role in Ghana, such public acclamations and observances are tainted with that which is now commonly called 'mixing'. Scholars in this category play with words like syncretism or symbiosis, but the bottom-line is, these words make no difference to those involved. Hence, despite its acclaimed public status, Christianity contends with ATR in both the social and private lives of Ghanaians, rendering the national statistics less practical. Manifested in various socio-cultural kinship relations and traditions, 'mixing' is visibly pursued and elaborated in marriage, naming and funeral ceremonies.[79] Ann Marie Bahr notes this scenario as a trend in ATR.[80]

'Mixing' illustrates the continuous influence of ATR in the lives and activities of Ghanaians. Observable practices and scholarly text testify to this practice. For instance, at the national level, most functions are preceded by rituals, including traditional ones. Not only does the state have a national traditional linguist, there are traditional functionaries for national rituals.[81] In the public domain, this is seen in life

---

76   Adairt T. Lummis, "Pluralism, Religious," in *Dictionary of Feminist Theologies*, eds. Letty M. Russell and J. Shannon Clarkson (Louisville, Kentucky: Westminster John Knox Press, 1996), 210-11.

77   Mercy Amba Oduyoye, "The Search for a Two-Winged Theology: Women's Participation in the Development of Theology in Africa, The Inaugural Address," in *Talitha qumi: Proceedings of The Convocation of African Women Theologians 1989*, eds. Mercy Amba Oduyoye and Musimbi Kanyoro (Ghana: Sam-Woode Ltd., 2001), 47.

78   Magesa, *African Religion*, 4.

79   See also, George Ehusani, "Christian Commitment: The African Dilemma," in *African Dilemma: A Cry for Life*, eds. Kofi Appiah –Kubi et al (s. l., Ecumenical Association of Third World Theologians, 1992), 159.

80   Ann Marie B. Bahr, *Religions of the World: Indigenous Religions*, Foreword, Martin E. Marty (Philadelphia: Chelsea House Publishers, 2005), 57-8.

81   Yankah, *Globalization and the African Scholar*, 20-3.

cycle rituals and traditional festivals.[82] Examples include the ongoing ban on drumming and noise making in the national metropolitan city of Accra during the traditional Ga *homowo* festival. Although Accra is a modern democratic city and a national capital, this traditional practice is known and observed by all living within the Ga traditional area, irrespective of their religious inclinations. Attempts by some Pentecostal and Charismatic churches to defy the existing tradition was met with stiff opposition, resulting in a number of violent clashes between some members of the Ga Traditional Council (GTC) and a number of churches from the above mentioned. The four years protracted dispute between the parties in these two religious traditions, Ga traditional and Christian faith, ended with a much more publicized, and perhaps, strengthened traditional position.[83] Although not of the same publicized status, similar practices are found among the Akyim and Ashanti. In these areas, the major festival seasons are preceded by a period of *butu Akyene* (turning the drums up-side-down). On the part of the Nzema and the Ahanta people of the Western Region, the tradition is associated with the Kundum festival. Also known as *esiemu* (hiding), it is the period before the festival where noise making, especially, at night is prohibited. This period of noiselessness is meant for prayers, meditation and other forms of rituals. Some times, according to some traditions, the community spirits and ancestors pay special visits; bearing blessings to their people. Thus, there is no weeping or crying, or drumming and dancing until this ritually prescribed period is over. Consequently, no funerals or merry making are allowed during this period. This traditional prohibition is obeyed and is observed by all inhabitants irrespective of their religious, educational, political or socio-economic status; foreigner or indigenous.[84] These are some of the processes of unconscious dialogues between Christianity and the indigenous religions in Africa.

---

82   Mercy Amba Oduyoye, "Women and Ritual in Africa," in *The Will to Arise: Women, Tradition, and the Church in Africa*, eds. Mercy Amba Oduyoye and Musimbi R. A. Kanyoro (Maryknoll, New York: Orbis Books, 1992), 9.

83   Freda Brobbey, "Understanding the Religious Conflict between the Ethnic Ga Traditionalists and Charismatic Churches in Accra," in *Ethnicity, Conflicts and Consensus in Ghana*, ed. Steve Tonah (Accra: Woeli Publishing Services, 2007), 63-97.

84   "Don't go against traditional laws," *Daily Graphic*, (Ghana, August 17, 2001), 3.

Magesa's book on *African Religion* has also deliberated on some of the intricacies of the general dominance of Christianity in African public sphere *vis-à-vis* its subordination in the private and/or socio-cultural domain.[85] He argues that, while Christianity is often hailed as a dominant religion in public life, ATR underlines every facet of the private life of the African. An examination of Magesa's study however calls for caution. Despite the significance of Africa's moral traditions, there is great need to be mindful not to over romanticize or glorify this heritage wholesale. This is because, some aspects of this same moral code have the potential of precipitating the already precarious position of the vulnerable and marginalized in the African society. As research has shown, some of these moral traditions have been the basis of suppression, domination and dehumanization of the African woman, and children classified as *chinchirisi*.[86]

ATR, however, is not limited to a few adherents or only alive in the area of 'mixing'. It has transcended into the sphere of 'modernity'. This includes health, governance (chiefs), education and identity. The current reference to the indigenous beliefs and practices in Ghana is 'traditional religion'. Being an African nation, the title is shortened. The word 'tradition' is always maintained as core and this preserves its distinct identity from the other religions in the country. The title is also used in the national curriculum. The historic post-independence change of the Department of Divinity at the University of Ghana, to the Department for the Study of Religions in January 1962 was part of creating this national identity, where ATR formed part of the cultural heritage.[87] The process did not just aim at a title change; it created a new direction and phase for the department's curriculum development. The renamed department was required to actively engage ATR as well as other religions in a bid to present a true reflection of the religious reality in the country.[88] In his work on education, K. A. Busia argued that the colonial neglect of the indigenous religious traditions and systems, and the nationalist desire to rediscover and to preserve Africa's religio-cultural

---

85   Magesa, *African Religion*, 5-14.

86   Sheila Minkah-Premo, *Coping with Violence Against Women* (Accra: Asempa Publishers, 2001), 3, 7, 11-12, 26-29 and Nyambura J. Njoroge, *Kiama Kia Ngo: An African Christian Feminist Ethic of Resistance and Transformation* (Ghana: Legon Theological Studies Series, 2000), 81-4.

87   Pobee, "Christian Goncalves Kwami Baëta," 3.

88   Olupona, "The Study of Religions in West Africa," 214-16.

heritage contributed significantly to this renaming and the setting up of the Institute of African Studies in Legon.[89] Undoubtedly, this must have also spearheaded ATR into all areas of academic and national life.

It is important to note the current debates around the term 'Africa' or 'African'.[90] At the moment, any significant engagement with the word 'African' raises questions irrespective of whether or not the researcher is African. This critical position is further compounded if it is paired with the word 'religion(s)'.[91] In either or both cases, two views are often presented. First of all, attention is drawn to the danger of over generalization and its attendant lack of clarity. This critical view guards against undue ignorance as well as the neglect of the implicit vastness and diversity in the continent. These diversities, the recipe of Africa's rich cultural heritage, are inherent in the people, their language and culture as well as their respective histories. Losing this to over-generalization is unacceptable.[92] On the other hand, the second caution draws attention to yet another equally significant factor. Here, it seeks to safeguard the potential neglect or inadequate recognition of what Mugambi calls the "reality of and aspirations for a commonality and homogeneity in the African experience".[93] Fortunately, recent studies have shown a significant awareness of these issues and have sought to guard against them by contextualizing studies to specific subject groups, with indicative attributes and examples to parallel traditions in other African societies.[94] This study is one of such examples.

THE NANKANI

The term Nankani refers to both the people and the language. With the exception of those living in and around the Kassena-Nankana district capital, Navrongo, the Nankanis are mostly found in the rural areas. Traditionally made up of five communities, they occupy the

---

89 Busia, *Purposeful Education for Africa*, 31, 86.

90 Chidester, *Religions of South Africa*, 1.

91 Bahr, *Religions of the World*, 36.

92 Father Richard Nnyombi, "African Traditional Religion (ATR)," accessed 23 August 2006, 1; available from http://afgen.com/atr.html; Internet.

93 J. N. K. Mugambi, *African Christian Theology: An Introduction* (Nairobi: East African Educational Publication, 1989), 5.

94 Tinyiko Sam Maluleke, "Half a Century of African Christian Theologies: Elements of Emerging Agenda for the Twenty-First Century," *Journal of Theology for Southern Africa* 99, (Nov. 1997): 6-7.

eastern, central and southern zones of the original unified district.[95] The communities in the east comprised of Mirigu-Kandiga and Sirigu, which are now part of the Kassena-Nankani West district. The central zone is made up of Nogsenia, now generally called Navrongo, and its environs of Vonania, Nagalkinia, Gongnia, Korania, Gaani, Nayagnia, Pungu and Doba. The third, southern zone has Bui, Kologo and Naga. Out of these communities, Pungu or Pung-yoro and Bui are identified as aboriginal communities. This is contrary to Cardinall's view that there are no aboriginal people in the area.[96] The rest are settler communities with distinct migration histories. Currently, the two aboriginal communities have been subsumed by their neighbours, Navrongo and Kologo. That apart, Nogsenia, Pungu, Nayagenia and Saboro in the central zone have been socialized into the Kassena fold. In an interview with Juatera, he attributed the socialization process to the use of Navrongo as an administrative district. He also noted the area's proximity to Kassena communities and intermarriages as some of the reasons. He however insisted that they are Nankanis and stated that community rituals are still performed in the Nankani language.

The Nankani (people) identified in this study are quite different from those discussed by Cardinall and Rattray. For these scholars, the Nankanni/Nankanse is used loosely for the Frafra, Grunsi and sometimes the Kasena. Rattray's clan classification of the "the Nankanse Tribe", for instance, had none of the above mentioned Nankani groups.[97] Technically, therefore, the Nankani were an eclipsed group. In the process of presenting a general picture of a linguistic and cultural family, he depended largely on the accounts of Aboya to the neglect of specific nuances. Rattray's Nankanse are basically today's Frafra community. For instance, Winkogo, where much of his Nankanse data is taken from, is a Frafra community. Although he has Kologo in his list, he notes that as 'anglice Palago', and this eliminates it from the current demarcation. Thus, despite the use of the identity, there are some problems with its practical application. Yet, his detailed work on the Nankanse is applicable to both Nankani and Frafra communities. On the other hand, Cardinall's work lacks clarity. It is difficult to identify some of the communities in his narratives. One of the few exceptions is his example of

---

95   See the first part of map 3.
96   Cardinall, *The Natives of the Northern Territories of the Gold Coast*, 2.
97   Rattray, *The Tribes of the Ashanti Hinterland*, 235-7.

sacrifice in Sirigu, but he quickly dismissed it with the statement, "There is no need to give further examples. They are all alike in their simplicity and in their straightforwardness".[98] Cardinall generally used Nankana or Navoro (Navrongo) as Rattray used Nankanse. It is quite surprising, though, how these two scholars are locally divided between the Kasena and Nankani. It is my contention that the division may stem from the way they worked on the respective languages. While Cardinall worked on Kasem, Rattray concentrated on Nankanse (Gurunne).

The Nankani community presents a multi-religious background. Although they are predominantly traditionalists, there is quite a large, visible Christian population. This practical manifestation is also a challenge to the statistical data. Thus, it requires further explanations which will be clarified through a discussion on 'mixing' below. Meanwhile, most of the Christians are Catholics and the reason for this is found in the historical narrative given above. A recent incursion of Protestant, Charismatic and Pentecostal churches into some communities is bound to change the situation. Inhabitants are however sceptical of any significant impact in the meantime. This scepticism is based on a perceived notion that this set of Christian orientation is characteristically led by affluence and money. These, they argue, are not part of the Nankani community. They also cited examples of failed attempts by other faiths to buttress their point. The Baha'i faith also made a brief incursion into the eastern corridor, Kandiga, in the 1980s but folded up very quickly. Despite the historical relations between Islam and the North, there are just a few scattered Muslim individuals in some communities. These are usually migrant returnees from Muslim or urban centres. One distinguishing factor, noted by respondents, was the reversion of Muslim converts to ATR. This, they observed, has prevented the growth of Islam in the area.

In an interview with a man in Kandiga, it was revealed that he was baptized into the Catholic faith as a teenager while in school. He remained a Christian even though he was also involved in the traditional beliefs and practices until 1997. On a trip to Kumasi, he converted to Islam, the religion of his employer. Now back in the community, my inquiry as to which religion he belonged to, received the following reply, "We are all in it like that. Who should leave his heritage and ancestors and follow those of others?" In the rest of our

---

98   Cardinall, *In Ashanti and Beyond*, 203.

discussion, the man's claim on heritage and ancestry was well established. On the other hand, his understanding of conversion was interesting and can perhaps be explained with the traditional conception of prayer. According to the Nankani, prayers do not fight each other. It is interesting that those involved refer to this concept instead of the Christian notion of the 'jealous' God, desiring all attention and dedication. Nevertheless, some understanding can be derived from Kirby's studies on the Anufo. Although Kirby questions the concept and content of conversion in Africa, he notes the return to traditional religion is imbued with the "contemporary search for identity and cultural authenticity".[99] In this respect, such temporary conversions may be part of the problem-solving religious tendencies of the Nankani.[100]

Thus, although a good number of the inhabitants verbally profess Christianity, there is a high degree of 'mixing'. 'Mixing' (garngo) here refers to a religious atmosphere in which adherents combine or freely indulge in the different religious traditions and practices in the area. Allison Howell discussed this phenomenon among the Kassena. Undoubtedly, Christianity is perceived as a Sunday religion, a place or building set apart for worship, outside of which much is left to the individual's own choice of spirituality. Thus, for the rest of the week, the individual is left to live within the traditional context in which s/he establishes and confirms his/her true identity. This is typified by Howell's use of the word "real": the real life is outside the church premises. Contrasting their daily lives to the few hours spent in Church on Sundays. Howell elaborates how acknowledged Christians combine traditional rituals and practices with Christian prayer.[101] To meet some of their spiritual needs beyond the designated Sunday worship hours, different forms of Christian fellowships are now being organised in the various communities in the course of the week.

The phenomenon of mixing, illustrated above, is widespread and is practised in various degrees throughout the country. Generally perceived as normal, it has become a socio-cultural characteristic. This raises a number of questions on the census data used in this study. The Gurunne language variant, from which the data showed ATR as a dominant religion (90% ATR, 8% Christians and 2% Muslims), when

---

99   Kirby, "Cultural Change and Religious Conversion in West Africa," 57, 65-6.
100   Ibid, 58, 63-4.
101   Howell, *The Religious Itinerary of a Ghanaian People*, 1.

examined critically, raises the following questions; is the dominance
of ATR in this language group the result of a lack of a clear break by
converts? Is it a full, contented and complete adherence to ATR? Or
is it perceived as an identity status? This is necessary if these statistics
or the issue of mixing are to make sense. While the presence of Islam
is attributed to pre-colonial commercial activities, the missionary
(White Fathers) approach shows there were no stringent attachments
to conversion in the area. This interesting point may therefore provide
some clues to the current state of affairs. As McWilliam explains:

> This Society differed from the others ... not only in the
> direction from which it entered the country, but in its
> whole approach to missionary work. 'Lavigerie's master
> word was adaptation [to local conditions]: the missionar-
> ies must conform to every way except to vice and error.' ...
> win local goodwill by providing social services, particularly
> in health and education; in the second stage, they were to
> give Christian education to individuals who asked for it.[102]

From these backgrounds, no 'tabula rasa' approach was used in this
area. It is plausible, therefore, to argue that the accumulative nature of
ATR enabled adherents to subsume the new religions into the existing
system as alternative outlets, asserting each of these religious identities
only when necessary. This could account for the nature of the statistical
data. Whatever the reason, it does not deny scholarly perspectives on
the accommodative nature of ATR.[103] At the same time, it is crucial to
take into consideration the difficulties of conducting and compiling
census data, especially in Africa, where literacy is a problem and religious variables in questionnaires are sometimes confusing. The analysis
of the South African religious data by Hendriks and Erasmus not only
exemplifies this, but also, the obscure absence of the indigenous religions from their data outline.[104]

---

102 McWilliam, *The Development of Education in Ghana*, 37.
103 Jacob K. Olupona, "Introduction," in *African Spirituality: Forms, Meanings, and Expressions*, ed. Jacob K. Olupona (New York: The Crossroad Publishing Company, 2000), xviii.
104 Jurgens Hendriks and Erasmus Johannes, "Religion in South Africa: The 2000 Population Census Data," *Journal of Theology for Southern Africa*, (March 2001): 88-111, 129.

This notwithstanding, Ghana's census figures also raise questions on the range of people in the area at the time of the last census. As already noted, the Nankani area is rural, with a largely out-migrant population within the productive labour group. As a process set in motion by colonial policies, it has been exacerbated by education, employment and urbanization.[105] Could this have an effect on the religious data? Besides, the census was conducted at the peak of the seasonal out-migrant period, the dry season, when the energetic though largely unskilled labour group travel to seek temporal income earning jobs. Could there have been a difference in the religious data if these groups were present? Even though this cannot be substantiated with the present data, this brief incursion into the multi-religious dimension of the Nankani presents significant insights towards the understanding of the religious data used in the study.

Language is also a vital component of culture. African religion and culture is deeply embedded in its language. Oral traditions (proverbs, myths, rituals and prayers) are all inscribed in language forms.[106] Even though Ghana has adopted English as its national language, local languages are the main medium of communication, especially in the rural areas. Local languages are not just important for information transfer; they are the most vibrant embodiments of the individual or community sense of identity, worldview or general philosophy of life.[107] Kirby has observed that despite the cross-cultural environment of Ghana, peoples' "first language, the 'thinking' language, 'religious' language, is still the most important".[108] This study reflects this perspective. Nankani is not just a language; it is their identity, philosophy and worldview.

Scholars have placed Nankani among the Gur languages of the Niger-Congo.[109] There are also dialectical variations within the villages forming the Nankani. Generally, Nankani is closely related to Frafra.

---

105   Saaka, "Introduction", 3-4.
106   Busia, *Purposeful Education for Africa*, 32.
107   See also, Don Cupitt, *The Meaning of it All in Everyday Speech* (London: SCM Press, 1999), 11-2.
108   Jon P. Kirby, *Ghana Handbook: A Guide for Missionaries to Ghana* (Tamale: Tamale Institute of Cross Cultural Studies, June 1991), 11. Also, Appiah, *In My Father's House*, 3.
109   Bourret, *The Gold Coast*, 85 and Ghana web, "Gurunne," *Ghanaian Languages*, accessed 15 November 2005, 3-4; available from http://www.ghanaweb.com/GhanaHomePage/tribes/languages.php; Internet.

Frafra, known also as Gurunne, is commonly spoken in the Bolgatanga district. Linguists have a hard time placing Nankani. Sometimes it is viewed as an alternate name of Frafra/Gurunne; other times, it is referred to as a dialect alongside Tallensi and Nabdam.[110] This lack of clarity has led to a state where both Frafra/Gurunne and Nankani are held as distinct languages by their speakers.[111] As a distinct language, Nankani is neither standardised nor systematically developed. This is irrespective of Rattray's pioneering work, which is Gurunne and not Nankani.[112] Its spellings are erratic; perpetuated by the dialectical variations, usually patterned according to the community intonation. The original phonetic transcriptions, which employed special phonetic characters, are gradually phased out.

Nankani (language) is both flexible and robust. It articulates the peoples' innermost values. This is particularly enriched by its vibrant and elaborate use of figurative speech. The proverbs, 'the left hand washes the right and the right the left' or 'the elephant says, I will step for my child to drink so that my child would one day step for me to drink', for instance, are not just expressions of reciprocity, dependency and harmonious living. They also convey a sense of responsibility, security and co-operation. On the other hand, when the words *ku dag zanga* (it's not for nothing) are uttered at the sudden death of a young energetic person or on account of a series of misfortunes, such an expression transforms the context beyond the ordinary to the spiritual level. It articulates the peoples' innermost fears and beliefs. In this context, language is not just about morphology, phonetics, syntax and grammar; it is symbolic, and it is this symbolic aspect that immediately assumes the focus of attention in the study of beliefs. This is why the contextual understanding of language is also essential.

Nankani is made up of *malma* (religious, ritual or sacred), *gaasa/bunyul* (profane) and *daarwu* (everyday or secular) ways of *togum* (speaking). This classification is derived from the acceptable language contexts. Primarily, the Nankanis believe words are potent and powerful spiritual entities. This is inherent in both the meaning and usage of some words or sentences. This is especially observed in ritual or

---

110   Baker, *Peoples, Languages, and Religion in Northern Ghana*, 99. See also, Ghana Ethnic Groups: Frafra, accessed on 28 November 2006; available from http://www.ghanaweb.com/GhanaHomePage/tribes/frafra.php; Internet.

111   Cardinall, *The Natives of the Northern Territories of the Gold Coast*, viii.

112   Rattray, *The Tribes of the Ashanti Hinterland*, 130.

taboo language. Here, words or sentences have specific purposes and must be used accordingly. The inability to distinguish and abide by these rules leads to trouble. For instance, it is a taboo to chant, sing or express oneself in some specific language forms outside their ritual settings. In the same vein, certain classes of people like medicine men or soothsayers are expected to be cautious in their use of words. Their status confers on them some form of spirituality. By virtue of this, they could set in motion a chain of unforeseen events. Parents also have a similar language obligation to their children. On the other hand, it is quite common for the mature and elderly to employ profane language in ordinary speech or admonitions. When profane language is not intended for one's peer, then its aim is to teach, buttress or illustrate a point. Sayings such as *a samasia yeiti inga loko ka zue amaa inga wam paale a sira* (the ant says, her item [vagina] is small yet she will readily give it/show it to her husband) or *a ti toa, a ti toa yo-re ka chiri* (quick quick penis does not enter), are used in marriage counselling and also to teach patience, calmness and self-control. The everyday or secular language is that which is associated with ordinary speech.

Unlike the established pattern of language categorizations in Mircea Eliade's *The Sacred and the Profane*[113] and Mary Douglas' *Purity and Danger*,[114] the Nankani are of the view that life is not lived in two extremes. For this reason, the secular category is an important component. Not only does it mediate between the two categories, it provides an avenue for a relaxed atmosphere of living. Situated between the two extremes, it is the domain of normal communication. The emphasis on the secular category forms a departure from the already established pattern which projects a universal binary of 'sacred' and 'profane'. Modern development workers who are not cautious or sensitive in their choice of vocabulary can be perceived as disrespectful.

Nankani is also made up of gendered and non-gendered vocabulary. The gendered meaning of words and sentences depends, to a large extent, on both the sentence structure and the context in which it is used. The majority of gendered language is used figuratively. For instance, the word *Wine*, which is interpreted as the Supreme Deity,

---

113   Mircea Eliade, *The Sacred and the Profane: The Nature of Religion*, trans. Willard R. Trask (San Diego, New York and London: Harcourt, Inc., 1959).

114   Mary Douglas, *Purity and Danger: An Analysis of the Concepts of Pollution and Taboo* (London: Routledge, 1966), 117.

Being or God, is simply perceived as a spiritual entity. (*Winɛ* or God will be used interchangeably for this Supreme Deity.) This notwithstanding, the word *winɛ* also refers to the sky. Similarly, it is associated with the cloud, sun, time and other weather conditions. This is irrespective of the fact that each of these elements has specific names. In each case, *winɛ* is genderless. However, in their active forms, the sun, sky and time are presented as feminine qualities while the cloud, storm, thunder and lightening are masculine. The feminine categorizations relate to the sublime and docile manner in which the elements convey themselves. It also relates to the concept of femininity in the area. On the other hand, the aggressive and violent ways in which clouds, storms, thunder and lightening manifest themselves in this environment have contributed to their association with masculinity. The force and power with which these elements express themselves are related to the masculine demonstration of authority, dominance and control. These classifications are however not strictly compartmentalized. For the Nankani, the calm and collective characteristics of the female can be raised to frenzy and when this happens, its outward expression is 'more than thunder and lightening'. Sometimes, this is referred to as 'burning steadily like the kitchen fire'. This notion is further illustrated in the proverb, 'fear woman and save your life'. Nonetheless, the categorization of the first group of weather conditions as feminine is because they are peaceful, consistent and dutiful like a woman's constant but repetitive daily chores.

The association of *Winɛ* with these natural elements raises some concerns about *Winɛ's* identity and sacredness. As Rattray observes, this association with the sky is ambiguous.[115] It is traditionally argued that the use of *Winɛ* in these contexts is symbolic, indicating the creative source of and the controlling power behind them. Noting that when a case in the chief's court is judged by a *nabia* (prince, also used for all sons of the clan), you do not separate such a judgement from the norm. It stands as the chief's judgement. Nonetheless, these literary connotations should not be totally ignored. The expression *winɛ zuwo* (*winɛ's* head or sky high) could suggest that the sky is really *Winɛ's* head or abode. It could also stand as *Winɛ* is on top of the sky or probably

---

115 Rattray, *The Tribes of the Ashanti Hinterland*, 42-3. See also Eliade's discussion on the Nuer. Mircea Eliade, *From Primitives To Zen: A Thematic Sourcebook of the History of Religions* (New York and Evanston: Harper and Row Publishers, 1967), 607.

somewhere in the sky. The word *zuwo* can be used in different contexts to mean 'head', 'on top of something', 'an item or person with great value or honour' or simply as 'in respect of'. Thus, the use of *Winɛ* in these instances is open to varied interpretations. This ambivalence is however not unique to the Nankani as Parrinder encountered similar cases in his work on *Worship in the World's Religions.*[116]

The gender neutrality expressed in the above implies that *Winɛ*, as a spiritual entity, is genderless. In spite of this genderless impression, however, *Winɛ* is generally identified as male. To explain the novelty and magnificence of *Winɛ*, the Nankani use the expressions, *Naba Awinɛ* or *Nawinɛ* (Chief God). Here, the humanity of *Winɛ* is projected above other manifestations. Perceived and likened to a chief, who by tradition must be male, *Winɛ* quickly acquires a male identity. Such a perception is also possible because of the attributes of creativity, power, authority and control. Among the Nankani, all these are male preserves. Even though women conceive, give birth and nurture children, they are perceived as part of the man's world or property. In the event of a divorce, she loses her children. On the issue of conception, childbearing and nurturing, it is argued that, when someone gives you something to keep, it is not yours, irrespective of the manner or how long you keep it. Thus, the humanity of *Winɛ* in this patrilineal society is masculine, because of the attributes of dominance and control.

It is important to note that despite the presence of these inherent gendered dimensions of the language, Nankani is not normally analyzed in this manner. This exercise is due to the analytical role of gender in this study. Nonetheless, it helps to illustrate how language excludes or undermines women's role or position in some traditional religious contexts. This is another reason why language is an important area of discourse in current investigations.[117]

NANKANI WORLDVIEW

When we think of a people's worldview, we consider their concept of the supernatural, of nature, of man and society,

---

116   Geoffrey Parrinder, *Worship in the World's Religions* (New York: Association Press, 1961), 18.

117   Verena Aebischer, "Knowledge as a Result of Conflicting Intergroup Relations," in *Feminist Thought and the Structure of Knowledge*, ed. Mary McCanney Gergen (New York and London: New York University Press, 1988), 145-6.

and of the way in which these concepts form a system that gives meaning to a people's lives and actions.[118]

The above is one of the classical conceptualizations of the African worldview. Stated by Busia, these types of traditional formulations are currently hotspots of disputation.[119] Questions as to whether these formulations are a result of Christian influence, falling within the concept of inculturation, apologetic or nationalistic frames of discourses, are yet to be resolved. Busia's contention that people "...are influenced in their conduct by traditional beliefs and practices, and by the traditional interpretation of the universe" illustrates this lack of clarity in his own work.[120] Arguably, it stands as a response to the prevailing context of religious pluralism and the place of ATR in the African continent. Such conceptualizations have become the basis for recent queries, bringing about the current drive for localized studies. Nevertheless, these initial frameworks have been fundamental in the imaginative and theoretical processes of ATR, serving as a springboard from which specific details are now examined.

Although localizing African religious studies is not the solution, it has produced specific nuances which are subsequently transforming knowledge. Among the Nankani, for instance, the term 'worldview' is alien, hence, it has no local vocabulary. Yet, when the term came up during my fieldwork, it quickly found currency and was equated to the traditional concepts of *tinga zuwo* (the 'earth's head' or in the world), symbolizing that which relates to the world, and *vam* (life). After a lengthy deliberation *vam* was chosen. This was because the two groups (male and female) each agreed that the essence of the world is the life it contains. It was however observed that *vam* is and must be viewed as a composite term. *Vam* must be seen as a complex web of interdependence sustained in a cyclical motion. This cycle of interdependence is believed to have been created and maintained by a force or power primarily outside, at the same time inside, and somehow, intertwined with its created structure. This controlling force is referred to as *Winɛ panga* (God's power or strength). Although expressed differently, the concept

---

118 K. A. Busia, "The African World View," in *Christianity and African Culture* (Accra: Christian Council of the Gold Coast, 1955), 3.

119 p'Bitek, African Religions in European Scholarship, 102, 107-11; Shaw, "'Traditional' African Religions?" 183-5.

120 Busia, "The African World View," 1.

of 'power' corresponds with some scholarly views on 'force'.[121] Examples include the "*vital force*" among the Bantu[122] and "a force, a power" among the Akans of Ghana.[123] Nonetheless, maintaining the Nankani variant is essential in this discussion. As van Beek and Blakely write, "religion is expressed and experienced in ways and forms offered by [its] culture,"[124] and though cultural expressions can be communicated transculturally, it is "not without loss of meaning and the creation of new meaning".[125] Harvey has observed the multidimensional ways in which words are projected, especially, in the West African religious context.[126]

From the Nankani perspective, this 'power' is not just sacred but also mysterious. No one knows how it came into being and no one needs to know that. The reason being, no one can *pelege Winɛ* (uncover God). Even though the anthropologist Rattray used the word *pelege*, he viewed it from the perspective of colour.[127] *Pelego* is white and *pelege* is used in connection with that which is white, bright and clear. However, when *pelege* is used in relation to the private and personal, it is understood in terms of secrecy. It relates to the mystery and awe surrounding the unknown, that which gives the individual his/her unique identity. To *pelege* someone or thing is to uncover their secrets. In Rattray's case therefore, "*Da pelege ma* ('don't whiten me')", should be understood as 'Don't uncover/expose me'. This is because uncovering or exposing someone renders them vulnerable. Identity protection is vital to the Nankani. For this reason, research data is often given in general forms, detached and rendered as a reported or proverbial speech. The inherent desire to preserve some form of secrecy or anonymity was prevalent in the past. This norm was recorded by Cardinall during the colonial

---

121 E. E. Evans-Pritchard, *Nuer Religion* (New York and Oxford: Oxford University Press, 1956), 317.

122 Placide Tempels, *Bantu Philosophy* (Paris: Presence Africaine, 1959), 30-3.

123 Parrinder, *West African Psychology*, 8, 14; Theo Sundermeier, "Unio Analogica, Understanding African Dynamistic Patterns of Thought," *Africa Theological Journal* 11, no. 1 (1982): 38-9. See also, S. O. Oso, *An Introduction to West African Traditional Religion* (Nigeria, Omolayo Standard Press (NIG.) Ltd, 1978), 20-1.

124 Walter E. A. Van Beek and Thomas D. Blakely, "Introduction," in *Religion in Africa: Experience and Expression*, ed. Thomas D. Blakely, Walter E. A. van Beek and Dennis L. Thomson (London: Heinemann, 1994), 2.

125 Ibid., 3.

126 Harvey, *Animism*, 131.

127 Rattray, *The Tribes of the Ashanti Hinterland*, 238.

labour recruitment exercise in the 1920s. Cardinall noted instances of recruits presenting inaccurate personal identities as:

> Musa Gurunsi, Adamu Kanjaga ... the man's real name thus completely concealed. ... by such concealment it became difficult for an enemy to make evil medicine against one, since the evil spirit conjured to perform the ill deed would be unable to identify their victim.[128]

In this case, using a Muslim name disguises the individual's identity while Gurunsi, which stands as a cultural identity, helps to vaguely locate the ethnic group.

For the Nankani, that which is important is to know *Winɛ panga naam sela wuo* (God's power created everything) and *Winɛ panga n'basi ti ti vua, ge dita, ge gura to* (God's power allows us to live, to eat and guards us). This produces a sense in which this 'power' is disconnected; placed outside the scope of the human realm, enabling it to create yet making itself unknown, continually in control as it administers human destiny, but also, a part of its created self, 'helping lepers drive away flies and wiping the pus from their eyes'. This latter case is because *Winɛ* does not forsake the helpless, confused and dejected in creation (*Winɛ ka baase anintogli bee*).

It is however interesting to state that the Nankanis have no myths of creation. It is as though this is placed within the context of *pelege*. Instead, Nankani myths account for relationships between the spiritual and the natural world, the origin of death, ancestorhood and reincarnation. All efforts to record myths of creation have so far proved futile. The responses to this quest can be summed up with the words of Nsobunu:

> When *Winɛ* created us, he wanted us to know that he was our owner. He showed us how to live; not how we came into being. What is our role in that? [129]

Shutting my investigations in that direction, efforts were made to draw my attention to the issues of life. Explaining the intricacies of life, Nankani mythology notes that, when *Winɛ* created the world, *Winɛ* intended it to be eternal. Humans however got bored and tired of living and appealed to *Winɛ* to intervene in their predicament.

---

128   Cardinall, *The Natives of the Northern Territories of the Gold Coast*, viii.
129   See for example, Fortes, *Oedipus and Job in West African Religion*, 24.

Winε presented a choice. The choice was between the former and the introduction of death. The men convened at the entrance of the house (*zenyore*) to take the decision, but no consensus could be reached. The youth wanted perpetual life, the aged wanted death. A truce was reached when the disputing parties decided to send two animals with their respective answers to *Winε*. With an understanding that the first animal to present the message to *Winε* represents the winning group, a dog was chosen by the youth to carry the news of eternal life while a chameleon was picked by the elderly to carry the message of death. Although the dog led, it stopped when it chanced upon women preparing their meal with meat outdoors; and laid beside the women, waiting and watching to be given a bone. The chameleon with its power of disguise went ahead and delivered the message of death. Similar accounts on the origin of death are reported in Southern Africa.[130]

The aftermath of *Winε's* verdict created a strained relationship between the youth and the aged. To forestall this, *Winε* provided an outlet through ancestorhood. With ancestorhood, deserving individuals who used their first opportunity of life well are not only rewarded, they can return to the world of the living through reincarnation. As ancestors, they are also elevated to a spiritual position where *Winε* delegates some of his power to them to see to the needs and squabbles of their descendants. Having experienced these themselves, they are predisposed to handle them well. Nonetheless, one must show capability for this illustrious task. Thus, *Winε* called on people to live good, harmonious and productive lives. Yet, in order to give the living a part to play in this new order, *Winε* decided that, to be in charge of descendants, one must produce some in his/her life time. This made childbearing a crucial requirement. That apart, to be a judge of character, one must have lived a good life, putting the ancestors' characters out for judgment by the living. Ancestors need descendants to acknowledge, institutionalize and minister to them. For those who want another chance of earthly life, this is also dependent on having descendants and their ability and willingness to procreate. On the other hand, ancestors have a duty to perform. Delegated by *Winε* with a responsibility to their descendants, it is incumbent on them to discharge their duties adequately. This reciprocal perspective is quite visible in ritual performance where the officiate

---

130   See Cox, *Rational Ancestors*, 165-7 and Parrinder, *African Traditional Religion*, 41.

calls on the ancestors to 'let it be' so that they will in turn acknowledge and render thanks. It also explains why ancestors are the central point of reference and the first point of call in Nankani religious practices. Straddling the world of the living and spirit they know what is good and in the process, guide, protect and aid their descendants who look upon them with reverence and anticipation.

For the Nankani, the ancestral spirits are the most important part of their worldview. They have immediate control of the lives and livelihoods of their descendants. They are actively and clearly represented with smaller indoor pots adorned with bangles for female ancestors.[131] Male ancestors are represented with a variety of pots and moulds, adorned with *kure* (hoe blade), *finne* (hoe locker) and *piim* (metal arrow tip). While female spiritual symbols are usually indoors, those of males can be found in and outside the house. Their presence provides a psychological sense of security, blessing and posterity.[132] Adorning a female shrine with bangles relates to the feminine sense of beauty. The use of a pot and its place indoors also relates to the female's role as a cook and her socio-political space in the society. Part of the myth of death also explains that, as a result of the disruption caused on the dog's errand, women no longer occupy the external space. Their space has since been indoors. However, many of their activities, including cooking, are conducted outside during funeral rites. This can be argued as a re-enactment of the origin of death. Meanwhile, the male symbols show their roles as builders, breadwinners as in the case of farmers and hunters as well as sources of security. Their place outside can also be interpreted as a depiction of patriarchal dominance.

Although the basis for this analysis is mythical, it has been "indispensable both to a wider understanding of what 'history' must fundamentally entail in the context of our concern with African religions".[133] Moreover, some prevailing cultural practices can be linked to this narrative. These include respect for the elderly as the repository of patience, diligence and wisdom. Their frailty, like the chameleon, is not despised. Instead, it is revered. Not only is it capable of disguising itself to achieve

---

131   See also Meyer Fortes, *Oedipus and Job in West African Religion* (Cambridge: Cambridge University Press, 1959), 14.

132   Parrinder, *Worship in the World's Religions*, 26. See pictures 11 and 13.

133   Michael Gilsenan, "Myth and the History of African Religion," in *The Historical Study of African Religion: with special reference to East and Central Africa*, eds. T. O. Ranger and I. N. Kimambo (London: Heinemann Educational, 1972), 51-2.

its purpose, those who know how to send or use it are blessed while those it meets are in trouble. In such cases, the latter have to speak to it symbolically for favour and relief. It is said that when one suddenly encounters a chameleon straight ahead with its back to that individual, it is a good omen. To relate to this omen, the individual could enact the process of riding a horse. It is sending a message on your behalf and for your benefit. The enactment process is a sign of acknowledgement. Besides, a horse is not just a symbol of wealth and prestige; it connotes speed. Thus all these form part of the symbolic. On the other hand, if it is facing you, that means bad luck. That individual needs to speak to it, symbolically, to minimise the effect of the bad luck. That apart, the myth also gives meaning to why women's space and domestic chores are secluded, dogs are made to eat last and why they are used for hunting; they must hunt for their bones. Again, children whose behaviour at other people's meal times can be likened to a watchful dog are chastised, driven away, and sometimes denied whatever proceeds they might have had. Sometimes, they are asked if they are dogs.

Cox has examined some of these multidimensional functions as well as the problems surrounding the collection and presentations of African myths in his work on *Rational Ancestors*.[134] However, these myths were not elicited but given by the respondents as part of what I see as the privileges accruing to the insider. Nonetheless, they were also given as lessons to a child. As to whether or not aspects or the whole of this myth is influenced by Christianity is uncertain since the narrator is neither educated nor Christianized. As Kirby has observed among the Anufo, some "traditional belief systems and other traditional structural alignment have remained largely untouched by Christianity".[135]

There is yet another dimension to the interdependence conceptualization of *Winε*, ancestors and the living. In terms of creativity and sustenance, *Winε* is an abstract power source. In terms of relationship and governance, *Winε* is imbued with human qualities, depicted in the name *Naba Awinε*. Although he sees and controls everything, he is very patient and kind, hence he intervenes when it is absolutely necessary.[136] This is also because he is supreme and chiefs hardly engage in manual

---

134   Cox, *Rational Ancestors*, chapter three.
135   Kirby, "Cultural Change and Religious Conversion in West Africa," 58.
136   Geoffrey Parrinder, *World Religions: From Ancient History to the Present* (New York and England: Facts on File Publication, 1971), 62.

work. Thus, rare interventions are made to support the vulnerable, as already illustrated. This limited attention is made possible because *Naba Winɛ* has put in place a mechanism that sees to the constant repetitive, inconsistent and insatiable needs and requests of humans. These are summed up in the word *ninkalinga* (mind dazzling). The expression, "*Naba Winɛ* is right to have handed over the authority of human needs to the ancestors. Who can put up with all these never-ending needs and problems of the human mind and tongue?" explains both the nature of humans and why *Winɛ* created a special spiritual outlet for them.[137] It is unclear if this argument on human inconsistencies among the Nankani corroborates with Olupona's view on the African expression of sympathy or pity for God,[138] or it is simply an aspect in the Nankani concept of person. Nonetheless, the issue of delegation can be linked to the chieftaincy structure. Paramount chiefs have divisional chiefs who rule over limited areas. This viewpoint tallies with the ancestors who are basically responsible for their descendants. If this is so, then this trend of thought might be a later development. This is in view of the fact that this structural formation of chieftaincy among the Nankani is associated with colonialism.[139] It may however derive its source from the traditional concept of the *tindana* (custodian of the land). In the latter case, it predates colonialism to the pre-colonial migrant era.

The Nankani also believe in a dynamic community of spiritual powers. In his book *West African Psychology*, Parrinder clearly elaborates this concept of spirituality in many parts of West Africa.[140] The Nankani do not just believe in a strong spiritual power in nature. The created (humans and nature) must cooperate and collaborate to enable them sustain the power source within them. When this bond is severed, attempts are made through rituals to restore the bond, not necessarily for the sake of the power source, as it is for the life and vitality of creation itself. According to Dominique Zahan, a tree is not felled without

137 Source is unknown. Currently used of people with insatiable needs and complaints.
138 Olupona, "Introduction," in *African Spirituality*, xix.
139 Awia, *Navrongo and its Pioneers*, 3; Der, Benedict G., "Traditional Political Systems of Northern Ghana Reconsidered," in *Regionalism and Public Policy in Northern Ghana*, ed. Saaka (New York: Peter Lang, 2001), 56.
140 G. Parrinder, *West African Psychology: A Comparative Study of Psychological and Religious Thought* (London: Lutterworth Press, 1951), 147-57.

some form of a ritual offering.[141] This is not to say that every tree is a god or spirit. These rituals present opportunities for individuals to take the necessary precautions to avoid any form of friction, accident and to live in harmony with nature. For the Nankani, it is often humans who trespass their boundaries by encroaching on nature for settlement, fuel, food and housing, and it is for this reason that humans must learn to respect and value the inherent power sustaining nature.

Among the spiritual elements of nature, the land spirit is central. Not only does it allow human settlement with its destructive nature and mischief, it has to help sustain the lives on its surface. On the other hand, humans must be reminded, through reprimands, not to take nature for granted. As such, humans and nature must be in contact ritually to sustain a healthy relation. Although it is humans who carry out these rituals, the power in nature sometimes plays a prompting role through spirit possessions, divination and life crisis. The responsibility of sustaining this relationship is on the first settler, the *tindana* and his ancestry. He was the first to encroach on the 'sacred' wild space and so must be responsible.

Similarly, a tree that is close to a house, providing shade and a resting place for its members, may adopt the family in a motherly or fatherly capacity. Each identity goes with its characteristic role and the family would refer to such a tree as mother or father. This is different from ancestor worship. When this relationship is acknowledged and regularized, rituals ensue. Sometimes it is to appease the spirit, that is, if it feels disturbed by the close human proximity. It may also become a reason for relocation if the existing relationship is untenable. These kinds of relationships are extended to other natural bodies and wild animals. In the past, some of these practices led scholars to ascribe animism to ATR, a terminology that was generally rejected,[142] until Graham Harvey's recent re-evaluation of the term. All the same, Parrinder had pointed out, African religion is much more than animism.[143] Harvey's work on 'new animism' offers new and exciting perspectives through which these forms of indigenous worldviews on inter-relationships can

---

141 Dominique Zahan, "Some Reflections on African Spirituality," in *African Spirituality: Forms, Meanings, and Expressions*, ed. Jacob K. Olupona (New York: The Crossroad Publishing Company, 2000), 18.

142 p'Bitek, *African Religions in European Scholarship*, 57; Parrinder, *West African Psychology*, 11-3 and Kato, *Theological Pitfalls in Africa*, 18-20.

143 Geoffrey Parrinder, "The African Spiritual Universe," in *Afro-Caribbean Religions*, ed. Brian Gates (Ward Lock Educational, 1980), 18.

be expressed.[144] The Nankani scenario presents an example of respectful living among a variety of beings. This notwithstanding, there is need for further investigations to substantiate Harvey's new outlook on animism in the Nankani context. At present, this is outside the scope of this study.

These discussions provide reasonable grounds for Kirby's "problem-solving" theoretical perspective on Anufo religion.[145] Unfortunately, it does not respond to the soteriological quest of the Nankani.[146] As Zahan points out, before a study of African religion and its spirituality "we must establish the position occupied by man in African thought and culture, since this is the foundation which will allow us to understand the relationship between God and man".[147] In ATR human beings are neither lords nor servants of their world; they mediate and are in turn, mediated upon by the world around them. Life and all that it encompasses is permeated with both sacred and secular entities, a careful balance of which is required for life and its sustenance. The Nankani believe this and relate to it appropriately. Bahr, for instance, identified this sort of balancing within "the natural, moral and spiritual laws of the universe" in ATR.[148] For Bahr, "African peoples consider their relationships with God, ancestors, and other spirits, other human beings, and animals, plants, and the earth important".[149] An infringement in this cosmic balance leads to serious repercussions. Hence, Bahr sees these intricate dynamics of the African worldview as part of its "worldview *dynamism*".[150]

These cyclical waves of interconnectedness no doubt underscore the perception that life is a complex web of interdependence. Typified by the expression, *la ngalime* (it is complex or mysterious). It is important to note that although this section has been reconstructed as a composite worldview of the Nankani, it is often viewed and discussed as autonomous components according to interest and focus. These

---

144 Harvey, *Animism*.
145 Jon P. Kirby, *God, Shrines, and Problem-solving among the Anufↄ of Northern Ghana* (Berlin: Dietrich Reimer Verlag, 1986), 81-93, 239.
146 Kirby, "Cultural Change and Religious Conversion in West Africa," 64 and Kirby, *Ghana Handbook*, 16.
147 Zahan, *The Religion, Spirituality, and Thought of Traditional Africa*, 6.
148 Bahr, *Religions of the World*, 43.
149 Ibid, 40.
150 Ibid, 45.

individual components include the source of life, the spirits/divinities, witchcraft, ancestors, incarnation or the origin of death.

RELIGIO-CULTURAL DYNAMISM (TRADITION AND CHANGE)

The proverb 'you do not step into the same river twice' is a clear manifestation that the contemporary Nankani is not the same as the historical Nankani.[151] This is reflected in the various stages of Nankani identity development. The identity of the Nankani began to take shape in Rattray's 'tribal' groupings in which he paid attention to the Nankanse. Although his Nankanse is now viewed as an expanded Frafra community in which the Nankanis may be included; the religio-cultural similarities and his close attention to details has placed his work above Cardinall's, making it the only major study ever conducted among the Nankani. Nevertheless, today, a clearer and definite Nankani identity is carved out. Similarly, the encounter between the Nankani and the wider world has not been a static repetitive affair.[152] It has evolved, and is still evolving, renewing itself even as it adapts to the vicissitudes of life.[153]

The need to acknowledge such fluidity as having the ability to effect change is an important step in threading the different strands of experiences and adaptations together. It is also important for negotiating the desired change within the religio-cultural context appropriately. In these instances, memory fills important social and spiritual functions, even as it helps in the transformational and management processes of the communities.[154] It provides a sense of continuity while ushering in a change that is conducive and productive for those involved.

The encounter has been one of constant negotiations, a process that has produced significant religio-cultural dynamism. Notable among this is the self-negotiated term *malma*. In was observed in this context that even where the West did not 'stoop to conquer', as Sanneh puts it, their presence initiated a competitive spirit, leading indigenous communities to philosophize and to articulate their ideas and beliefs

---

151 A Nankani proverb, source is unknown but used to illustrate the fluidity of life's experiences.

152 Appiah, *In My Father's House*, 12.

153 Tempels, *Bantu Philosophy*, 23.

154 Ellis and Ter Haar, *Worlds of Power*, 164-6, 172.

in ways they might not have done.[155] Besides, the different territorial conditions produced different frontier circumstances, enabling the Nankani to self-reflect and respond to the emerging religious identities in their midst. Thus even as the encounter enabled Europe to centre itself with a peripheral surrounding, the peripheral renegotiated its boundaries by carving for itself an identity, believing, 'every land and its way of doing things'.[156] This comparative stance is therefore a significant pointer to the resilience of ATR among the Nankani, accounting for its overwhelming 90% adherents in the 2000 census.

In this section, my intention is to briefly draw on two examples to illustrate some of the significant changes among the people. These are the institution of chieftaincy and education. These are not exhaustive; they are simply deployed as illustrative samples of the contemporary reality among the Nankani. Of these two, the chieftaincy institution is the most difficult to conceptualize. Yet, this shows that change is a dynamic process.

The history of chieftaincy among the Nankani is problematic. This is primarily due to inadequate historical data. This notwithstanding, the available data on the Navrongo chieftaincy provides a glimpse of evidence that there was some form of chieftaincy in the current Nankani area before the British colonial encounter and probably, Islam.[157] There is still a great need of research in the field though, since some written and oral sources perceive the chieftaincy institution in the area as alien.[158] As the Navrongo account shows, it is a migrant community. Nevertheless, the widespread institutionalization of chieftaincy in the North and the introduction of indirect rule led to a paradigm shift in the traditional leadership structure. The sudden change from the predominantly *tindanaship* rule to chieftaincy, with immense colonial empowerment and immediate access to new concepts of wealth, honour and prestige (money, medallions and guards),

---

155   Lamin Sanneh, *Encountering the West: Christianity and the Global Cultural Process: The African Dimension* (London: Marshall Pickering, 1993), 73-6.

156   Chidester, *Savage Systems*, 6.

157   Awia, *Navrongo and its Pioneers*, 27 and Der, "Traditional Political Systems of Northern Ghana Reconsidered," 56-7.

158   John M. Chernoff, "Spiritual Foundations of Dagbamba Religion and Culture," in *African Spirituality: Forms, Meanings, and Expressions*, ed. Jacob K. Olupona (New York: The Crossroad Publishing Company, 2000), 176-97; Collins, *Primitive Religions*, 258-9.

entail unresolved transitional problems, producing frictions over land control and administration with regards to the current concepts of development.[159] While *tindanaship* bestowed power and authority in relation to first settler rights with the land spirit, chieftaincy emerged from later migrations and foreign autocratic impositions. The sudden expansion of chieftaincy, ushered in by the colonial and postcolonial periods, is attributed to modernity and its notion of development.

Unlike the *tindanas*, the status of the chiefs was enhanced by the general application of the native jurisdiction ordinances of 1878 and 1883, which "provided for the recognition of the chiefs" by the colonial government "until 1927".[160] By this generalization, local governance acquired status, just as it acquired a role within the national structure of governance through indirect rule. This also equated some of the newly instituted or imposed chiefs, as Rattray implies, with the well established religio-cultural chieftaincy systems of Mamprugu or Ashanti. As Busia points out, for the Ashanti, the chief and the office of chieftaincy are sacred, constituting an embodiment of both religious and secular roles.[161] The question then arises as to how the sacred/secular dimensions were created by the new chiefs, especially among those for whom chieftaincy did not evolve from the people, aboriginal or settler.

This involved a complex system of adaptations and alliance building with existing chieftaincy institutions resulting in a complex network of alliances. In the process, the colonial medallions were discarded for traditional symbols such as the skin and the *munnga* (red hat).[162] At present, the symbols of chieftaincy in the North and especially the Nankani are the *munnga*, skin and smock, with a ritual installation process called 'enskinment'. This has emerged as a collaborative adaptation of chieftaincy throughout Northern Ghana. In the process, another distinct Northern identity emerged, skin *vis-à-vis* stool in Southern Ghana. The process enabled the system to adapt appropriate religious practices necessary for establishing its sacred identity. This also facilitated co-rulership with the *tindanas*. At present, the

159 Der, "Traditional Political Systems of Northern Ghana Reconsidered," 57-8 and Bourret, *The Gold Coast*, 47.

160 Bourret, *The Gold Coast*, 47.

161 K. A. Busia, *Africa in Search of Democracy* (London: Routledge and Kegan Paul, 1967), 26; K. A. Busia, *The Place of the Chief in the Gold Coast* (Achimota, 1949), 5-9.

162 See picture 15.

two systems are running concurrently, with chiefs commanding both religious and secular roles. This has further relegated the *tindana* to the periphery, sometimes, functioning only as priest to the earth deity.

This complexity is not limited to the Nankani community. Although Ghana is currently a constitutional democracy, its internal administrative structure is made up of the British Canon and the Traditional Customary Law. The latter is administered by the traditional chiefs within their communities.[163] Their authoritative structure is especially visible in the rural areas including the Nankani. Yet, despite having a co-rulership position, the chieftaincy institution is placed within a modern political structure, subjecting it to modernism. For instance, although the ministerial title is constantly changing, it is currently under the Ministry of Local Government and Rural Development. This is further complicated because their consolidated voice has to be channelled through another modern democratic structure known as the Ghana National House of Chiefs. This puzzling yet flexible position of the chieftaincy system within the modern political system presents subtle challenges to the chieftaincy system as a whole and for rural chiefs in particular.

Nevertheless, as a legitimate traditional institution, recognized by law and structurally integrated into the modern democratic system of governance, the role of the chief in traditional religion and sustainable community development is important in this investigation. Not only is the current structure of chieftaincy, especially among the Nankani, a product of colonization, it has transformed the traditional concept of leadership. Chiefs have multiple roles in relation to the spiritual entities, community members and government. At present, chiefs, the local religio-cultural and political leaders, are continually called upon to participate in the development of their communities.[164] The colonial legacy where chiefs worked with colonial officers to "administer justice, enforce ordinances, settle disputes ... supervise such technical work as road building and sanitation" is still identified with the institution.[165] The problem is that because they are expected to function adequately

---

163   Christian Council of The Gold Coast, *Memorandum on The Customary Law Of Inheritance: Addressed to the Chiefs and People of the Gold Coast* (Accra: Christian Council of The Gold Coast), 1934.

164   Daily Graphic, "Chiefs must help promote development," (Ghana, December 1, 2003), Front page.

165   Bourret, *The Gold Coast*, 39.

and effectively in each of these roles, the institution is no longer taken for granted but critically evaluated by all.[166]

On the educational front, the early form of education, a missionary agenda with a Western ideology, produced what McWilliam aptly captured as the "two worlds", separating the literate from the rest of the community".[167] As he observed, "there was no training for tribal citizenship; the best mission schools gave character training of a kind which produced citizens of high quality to serve a different Africa".[168] Consequently, those who acquired this new status also looked down on the others as 'primitive', uncivilized, local, underdeveloped and sometimes, evil. The ultimate desire was often a disassociation from community and its traditional practices. Unfortunately, it was this new category of Africans who took over power and control in postcolonial Africa, serving "a different Africa" that did not really include the needs of rural indigenous communities. The importance of this background is the disparity it created. It also provides significant insights on attitudes and perspectives on rural development, most especially, "endogenous development".[169] Perceiving traditional beliefs and practices as primitive, outmoded and uncivilized, those who participated in them were branded in the same light. As a result, no efforts were made to study, develop or involve traditional systems of development in early postcolonial Africa. Instead, it was a 'forward ever, backward never' march of assimilating Western concepts in a disproportionately different environment.

In an interview with Akawuni on the effect of these early transformations on the traditions and practices among the Nankani, he remarked that, *sela woo la ku daari* (everything has its day). According to him, nature is the school of life and if he learnt well, then, the young bird that has just learnt to make a successful take-off, soars into the sky with delight and freedom, wondering how it ever manages on the ground and wishing never to return. Nonetheless, it soon realizes that it has to return to the ground because *fae ka dunia* (there is no freedom in the world/no permanence). In other words, he believes the children

---

166   Anon., "Interview with Jerry J. Rawlings," in *Ghana: Facts, Pictures and Aspects* (Stuttgart: Association of Churches and Missions in South Western Germany, April 1986), 26.

167   McWilliam, *The Development of Education in Ghana*, 24.

168   Ibid, 25.

169   David Millar, "Endogenous Development: Some Issues of Concern," *Ghana Journal of Development Studies* 2, no. 1 (May 2005): 94-7.

they are losing through education, urbanization and religions pluralism will eventually return. As the interview progressed, Akawuni explained why many traditional people do not send all their children to school. For him, they have always used the issue of resources but that is not the whole truth, it is because "we cannot place all our eggs under one fowl". He pointed out the need to leave some behind to preserve the religio-cultural traditions. As he put it, *naafo bu moo de ti a zoo bona la kuram* (although the cow is in/goes to the bush, its head ends in the fire place or cooking pot). That is to say, irrespective of the individual's adventure, s/he eventually returns home. For this reason, the two groups are made to understand that 'the left hand washes the right and right the left hand', so they should learn to respect and support each other in life. This new line of inculcating reciprocity and interdependence is however now seen as producing a higher dependency load on family relations.

Change among the Nankani as we have seen is twofold. It is one in which the socio-political invariably affected the religio-cultural and vice-versa. But it is also one affected by earlier negative Western attitudes and by this I refer to the indigenous African religions as a whole.

In conclusion, I have identified and delineated the Nankani as an ethnic group in Ghana. From a phenomenological perspective,[170] the discussion depended on history, philosophy along with linguistics and gender as analytical tools. With a special attention to their religio-cultural system as it pertains today, the chapter has acknowledged issues of adoption and adaptation.[171] The extent to which these have been carried out vary according to their religio-cultural and political significance. Nonetheless, these influences have ushered in significant changes that have led scholars to question and to rearticulate their views on the word 'traditional'.[172]

Yet, irrespective of these scholarly perspectives, as Sanneh has observed, no matter how these responses are mediated, it is the indigenous self-reflection, the one which thrives on the remembered past

170 Cox, *Expressing the Sacred*, 32-9.
171 Wim Van Binsbergen and Matthew Schoffeleers, "Introduction: Theoretical explorations in African religion," in *Theoretical explorations in African religion*, ed. Wim Van Binsbergen and Matthew Schoffeleers (London, Boston, Melbourne and Henley: KPI, 1985), 25.
172 Allman and Parker, *Tongnaab*, 6 and Shaw, "'Traditional' African Religions," 183.

that is most important.[173] This underscores Gavin Flood's contention that even though religion is not "outside of history and narrative", it is not the same as history, sociology, anthropology or culture, which as he rightly observes, are heavily loaded with religious phenomena. While lamenting on the shift in the academic study of religion from the transcendent essence, he welcomes the late but steady recognition of the cultural dimension. The importance of Flood's work lies in the relationship he draws between history, culture and religion. He urges the study of religion to move beyond the cultural context to engage its historical perspectives, as this enhances the understanding of the social dimensions. To achieve this, Flood calls for specific cultural studies on religion, a perspective this study addresses.[174]

In this regard, the chapter has brought the investigation into direct contact with current discourses in religion and ethnographic studies. This opens up the study to questions as to how it differs from other religious and/or ethnographic studies. Darlene Juschka, for instance, has called for an active engagement with the post-modern debates. Summed up in the word "posts", she argues that their critical stands on knowledge and its acquisition have been an invaluable contribution.[175] This quest is taken up in chapter six. Even so, Ernest Gellner presents another dimension to this critical stance. His perspective raises different concerns, one that calls for great considerations for authors and their scholarly pursuits. In his concerns, Gellner wonders if postmodernism is not laying too much emphasis on deconstructing the author rather than the text. Expressing his view, Gellner notes that:

> [S]ometimes there seem to be an enormous preoccupation with him, so that a social anthropological study degenerates from having been a study of society into a study of the reaction of the anthropologist to his own reactions to his

---

173 Sanneh, *Encountering the West*, 92.

174 Gavin Flood, *Beyond Phenomenology: Rethinking the Study of Religion* (London and New York: Cassell, 1999), 2.

175 Darlene M. Juschka, "The Writing of Ethnography: Magical Realism and Michael Taussig," *Journal Cultural and Religious Theory* 5, no. 1 (December 2003), 84-105. See also, Jan G Platvoet and Jacob K. Olupona, "Perspectives in the Study of Religions in Sub-Saharan Africa," in *The Study of Religions in Africa: Past, Present and Prospects*, eds. Jan Platvoet, James Cox and Jacob Olupona (Cambridge: Roots and Branches, 1996), 17.

observations of the society, assuming that he had ever got
as far as to have made any.[176]

Notwithstanding these interests and apprehensions, the investigation will engage these concerns in line with current developments in the study of religions and Flood's quest for engagement with wider debates in the social sciences and humanities.[177]

---

176 Ernest Gellner, *Postmodernism, Reason and Religion*, London: Routledge, 1992, p. 23.
177 Flood, *Beyond Phenomenology*, 1-12.

Figure 1: Map of Gold Coast Territories

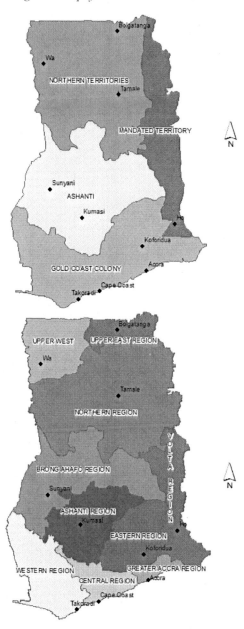

Source: CERSGIS-Legon.

Figure 2: *Map of Modern Ghana Showing the Regions*

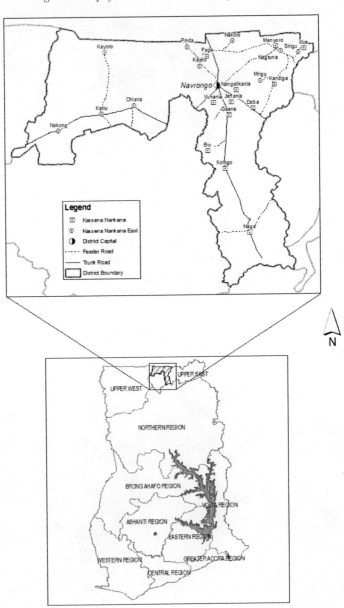

Source: CERSGIS-Legon.

Chapter Three

DEBATING SUSTAINABLE RURAL DEVELOPMENT

In saying 'development', however, most people are now saying the opposite of what they want to convey. Everyone gets confused. By using uncritically such a loaded word, and one doomed to extinction, they are transforming its agony into a chronic condition. From the unburied corpse of development every kind of pest has started to spread. The time has come to unveil the secrets of development and see it in all its conceptual starkness.[1]

Development, as defined in chapter one, presupposes an awareness of some form of underdevelopment. Esteva reflects this effectively into a binary opposition of development and underdevelopment.[2] This conceptualization brings to the fore a two-dimensional view of development, a perspective which scholars have become critically engaged with even as they unpacked their nuances differently.[3] From Esteva's

---

1   Gustavo Esteva, "Development," in *The Development Dictionary: A Guide to Knowledge as Power*, ed. Wolfgang Sachs (London and New Jersey: Zed Books Ltd., 1992), 6.

2   Ibid., 6-7.

3   Bob Sutcliffe, "The Place of Development in Theories of Imperialism and Globalization," in *Critical Development Theory: Contributions to a New Paradigm*, eds. Ronaldo Munck and Denis O'Hearn (London and New York: Zed Books, 1999), 136-45 and Ziauddin Sardar, "Development and the Location of Eurocentrism," in *Critical Development Theory: Contributions to a New Paradigm*, eds. Ronaldo Munck and Denis O'Hearn (London and New York: Zed Books, 1999), 44-9.

viewpoint, the perceived notion of one's state of development cast a downward trend on those thought to be in need of development, setting in place a hierarchical order. Conversely, a desire for development takes into effect one's position of underdevelopment, accepting the impending order and its attendant power of psychological dislocation. Sachs argues that the attendant aspiration to develop is then propelled by an internal illusionist attempt to escape the implicit notion of underdevelopment.[4] Vincent Tucker, however, contends this is a myth, created to set in place a hegemonic structure for those perceived to be developed over the underdeveloped.[5]

Although Sarah Hesse and Henry Wissink do not contest the above, they question the assumed notion and general acceptance of a developed Europe.[6] They note that even the US and UK have not completed their development processes. They also contend that many of the nations in Europe are underdeveloped, viewed as "'countries in transition'" by some scholars.[7] In view of this, they argue that neither the Global North nor Global South can fully claim the status of being 'developed'. By this, they have posited development within the premises of relativity. Hesse and Wissink observe that this erroneous assumption is due to the theorization of development.[8] Identifying the modernization and dependency theories as the core of the problem, they explain how the former drew a correlation between modernity and development, and tradition and underdevelopment. In the ensuing dichotomy, the "traditional ways of life" became defining features of underdevelop-

---

4   Sachs, "Introduction," 1-2. See also Esteva, "Development," 7.

5   Vincent Tucker, "The Myth of Development: A Critique of a Eurocentric Discourse," in *Critical Development Theory: Contributions to a New Paradigm*, eds. Ronaldo Munck and Denis O'Hearn (London and New York: Zed Books, 1999), 1-26.

6   Sarah Hesse and Henery Wissink, "Incorporating Indigenous Knowledge Systems into the Field of Development," in *The Quest for Sustainable Development*, eds. William Fox and Enslin van Rooyen (Cape Town: Juta Academic, 2004), 49. See also Peters, "Encountering Participation and Knowledge in Development Sites," 2-3.

7   Alison Van Rooy, "Good news! You may be out of a job: reflections on the past and future 50 years for Northern NGOs," in *Debating Development: NGOs and the Future*, eds. Deborah Eade and Ernst Ligteringen (Oxford: Oxfarm GB, 2001), 24.

8   Hesse and Wissink, "Incorporating Indigenous Knowledge Systems into the Field of Development," 47-8.

ment; hence, poverty. To forestall this situation, the theory proposed a total makeover. That is, "modernization theorists believe that the only way for development to take place is to rid a society of tradition".[9] The latter, they argue, is preoccupied with forming a centre-periphery relationship structure between the developed and underdeveloped worlds, the articulation of which has strengthened the uneven power base of development. This, the scholars conclude, has led to the denial and exclusion of indigenous knowledge systems from development discourses.

Notwithstanding the depth of theorizations, the world is yet to come to a full and concise grip of what it means to be developed. As scholars have observed, that which constitutes development varies from culture to culture. There are just as many different perceptions and interpretations of development as there are cultures.[10] Underlying this issue is the notion that development is a process. This, the Nankanis have also acknowledged. As to what the itemized constituents of development among the Nankani really mean, one needs to move further to examine what the people perceive as poverty. There is currently a blend in what is generally understood as development, even in this local context, as illustrated by the views of the Nankani youth.[11] Nonetheless, the overriding principles of family, unity and solidarity are emphasized. These values which are based on the traditional notion of family and communal living, articulate both the desires and fears of the emergent society. Family and communal living conceptualize the traditional worldview, bringing it into the immediate realm of the people. In this non-monetary society, these were and still are an important part of security and support or "investments for the future".[12] Not only is it used for organizing communal labour for building, farming or hunting, but also for peace, a vital resource for any form of development. Then again, this simple framing moves beyond the physical to the spiritual realm, encompassing the dead and unborn. It is within this interconnected image of the family that an in-depth understanding of development may be deciphered.

---

9   Ibid, 47.
10 Nolan, *Development Anthropology*, 20-1 and Ambe J. Njoh, *Tradition, Culture and Development in Africa: Historical Lessons for Modern Development Planning* (England and USA: Ashgate, 2006), 1-7.
11 See chapter one, 37-8.
12 Ellis and Ter Haar, *Worlds of Power*, 123.

The family is needed for salvific and ritual purposes. As Fortes explains, a family, most especially a son, is needed for ancestorhood to be effected. Again, the correct performances of earthly rituals have corresponding development implications for the beings in either side of life.[13] That apart, the traditional positioning of males as religious leaders and functionaries places them at the centre of bringing about the spiritual components of development. Meanwhile, in marginalizing females to ritual enactment positions, women have come to depend on men as an integral part of their earthly development.[14]

It is interesting that even though many indigenous rural people do not read these theoretical conceptualizations, they assume and believe that the world outside their scope is better and more developed than theirs. This is worsened by modern means of telecommunication, travel and material goods that are brought into the communities. The internal notion of poverty, not underdevelopment, is entrenched. I refer to poverty because, traditionally, the Nankani language deals with poverty and not underdevelopment. Underdevelopment is derogatory. It is perceived as mal-development in reproductive species. To talk of mal-development or underdevelopment, though currently understood, would be to talk of anomalies or perhaps other spiritual manifestations in nature. On the other hand, poverty is that which is clearly manifest in their lives and to which they have the name *nun-ngo*. In other words, there is an acknowledged sense of poverty but not development. Notwithstanding, the word poverty is beset with varied conceptions.[15] Hence, poverty is not defined but expressed in varied lived experiences.

The discussions of development and sustainable development in chapter one form the foundation upon which this chapter is built. In the earlier discourse, the Nankani perception of development was that of a continuous process of improvement; one that adequately engages their worldview and indigenous resources; one that is focused on 'life' and family. Development is not conceived in terms of 'per capita income' as used in the Ghana 2000 census and demographic data. Development is composite, embracing the sacred and secular in the intertwining realm of daily living.

---

13   Fortes, "Some reflections on ancestor Worship in Africa," 122-5.

14   Agnes Atia Apusigah, "Diagnosing Poverty in Northern Ghana: Institutional versus Community Views," *Ghana Journal of Development Studies* 2, no. 2 (December 2005), 9.

15   Apusigah, "Diagnosing Poverty in Northern Ghana," 6-9.

Yet, viewed as an ideology, religion is said to affect people's thought patterns, from which ideas, perceptions and visions are created and analyzed. The mystification of life, its daily needs and the concepts of poverty and development as shown in chapter one clearly depict this. For Bourdillon, just as ideology presents the social world as an unchangeable natural order, so too religious ideologies mystify life with divine origins and notions. Perceiving mystification as a part of an ideology, he argues, obscures "the human nature of the social order, and therefore its eminently changeable order".[16] Although the underlying principle of the argument is true, the Nankani are not asserting an unchangeable order. They accept *teare* (change) as part of life. Their main concern is the basic tenets of their religion which is linked to their identity. Thus, until this core element is adequately engaged, academic discourses will only be conjectural.

The chapter examines development from within the Nankani perspective. The factors governing this are the traditional worldview and the people's historical experiences. These experiences have contributed significantly to shaping and reshaping the traditional beliefs and practices. Outlined in the second chapter, they have influenced the indigenous perceptions of current developments in their midst. The chapter is in five sections. The first section, contextualizing sustainable development, is a follow-up from chapter one and its aim is to rearticulate the views and to situate them properly in the context of the main discussion on development. In the second, the 'traditional' views on development are examined. This is followed by a historical narrative of the modern experience of development among the subject group. This is further illustrated with an interactive discourse between the traditional and modern approaches through the activities of NABOCADO, the longest standing NGO in the community. The belief in witchcraft and its influence on the people's development is briefly outlined in the context of its contemporary reality and that draws the chapter to a conclusion.

CONTEXTUALIZING SUSTAINABLE DEVELOPMENT

In the community discussions, various constituents of *malgo* (development) were given. As already noted, these included family, unity/peace, food security, water, health, and liking/solidarity. The

---

16   Bourdillon, *Religion and Society*, 8.

youth added formal education, employable skills and sources of employment, and transport and good roads. Although the differences reflect some form of change at the community level, this can also be viewed from a cross-generational perspective or what I already noted as an ever expanding list of basic needs in the modern context.[17] Yet, the view that the first list, led by the elders, is foundational in their notion of development shows the persistence of these traditional models. At the same time, to state that any conceptualization of development is 'meaningless and empty if the underlying source of development (*malma*) is not properly tackled' illustrates the centrality of religion in the psyche of the people; hence, this demonstrates the relevance of p'Bitek's statement at the beginning of chapter one. That is, the link between religio-cultural beliefs and practices, and development, is summed up in the statement made in the male group discussion, 'to develop is to be in tune with the spirits, family and community', provided the basis for their question 'how can such a person develop if s/he has no root to hold onto and be held?'

It is within this context that the concept of 'sustainability' comes into focus. For a person to develop within the confines of their world-view, the traditions and its sources of livelihood should be maintained and preserved to the best of the individual and collective ability. It is in this regard that sustainable development is linked to the past and that which is currently available. The past needs to be adequately articulated, sorted out and preserved within the context of the present. This enables one to clearly interpret, incorporate or adapt meaningfully to the new. Other than this Juatera argued, 'we dislocate ourselves and then soon find ourselves in the middle of nowhere and since the very thing you call sustainable is not there, there will be no development'. This was the premise from which he asked, 'how can you sustain what you do not have?' and followed up with his definition of sustainable rural development as comprising *yaaba yela* (ancestral/traditional issues) and *nasara bunu* (modern things).

The question how can one develop if s/he has no base to stand or spring from raises a very important one from the Nankani. How can one develop without a spiritual source in a traditional setting where religion is encompassing? This question found no immediate answer(s) at the time, when it was reiterated, by the researcher. Similarly, the question found

---

17   See chapter one, 37-9.

no answer from the development workers in the area during the period of the fieldwork. Instead, development workers argued they cannot and do not want to get involved in religious matters. That apart, they have no resources for religious issues. They contended that their presence in rural communities is for development and not for the promotion of the indigenous religions.[18] At this point, we might want to join Robert Chambers to ask whose development are these NGO workers talking about?[19] Are the people in the community right in saying that NGO workers are developing themselves and not the rural poor?[20]

Traditional Concepts of Development

In my field discussions, an understanding was reached with some of the community elders regarding what constitute development in the Nankani setting. The core elements of development emanates from prayers addressed to the ancestors. According to the elders, even though the crux of every ritual is clearly stated at the beginning when the ritual's intentions are declared, the concluding prayer is essential. The concluding prayer affords the people present an opportunity to move from the immediate focus of the ritual to a sphere where communal petitions are made. The petitionary prayer, they concluded, summarises what is traditionally conceived as the essential concepts of development. Illustrating with a general example, they noted the following phrases used in rituals associated with the ancestors:

> *Basiya ti nuyinne ze-le, ti sumasum buna, ti guo gyese, ti dia, gule la ugre kye, ti pogdre basi ti kinkeliga lu, ti bilesi kele.*

> Let there (pl.) be togetherness [unity], that there be health, that there be sleep [peace], that there be food, ruminants and birds at home [wealth], that marriages will be announced and that there be the cries of new born babies.

---

18   These views were repeated several times by a number of the development workers interviewed during my fieldwork. These included officers from the Kassena-Nankani District Assembly, NABOCADO, Widow's Ministry, and CENSUDI. However, due to the appreciative approach to development initiative of CENSUDI they are much more liberal and accommodative in this area.

19   Robert Chambers, *Rural Development: Putting the Last First* (Longman: USA, 1983), 3-10.

20   Peter Batchelor, *People in Rural Development* (Exeter: Paternoster, 1981), 3-9.

The traditional perceptions of each of these terms (unity, health, peace, wealth, marriage and children) form the bedrock of development. They noted that *sumasum* is a state of peace, health and wealth; *guo gyese* is the quest for sound sleep which is ensured when *sumasum* is attained; *guo gyese* embodies security and a peace of mind and body which is free from ill health and disease. It is under these conditions that one can have sound sleep. This is followed by *pogdre* (marriages) which are traditionally announced by the joyous shrill sound called *kinkelinga*. Another necessary condition of development is posterity and this is depicted in the call for the cries of babies (*bilesi kele*).

Yet, even though this prayer was generally agreed upon as the core of the traditional underpinnings of development, differences arose as to what each of the key components of the prayer represented. This was only resolved after a series of lengthy discussions. It was agreed that two distinctions should be made from the interpretations. These were classified as the past and current interpretations. This already shows an acknowledgement of change. In spite of that, before the interpretations were given, the elders quickly introduced a series of proverbs including, *taara nereba di vom buno* (have people rather than wealth) and "a good name is better than wealth". These already subjected the impending interpretations to tradition. The notion of 'a good name' is not dependent on the essence or meaning of the name *per se*, but the desire to live a decent, moral life that brings honour and not shame to the individual and family bearing that name. The former emphasized family and reproduction instead of the youthful desire for material wealth and money.

On the two levels of interpretations, they noted that, traditionally, wealth in the form of food and animals were for consumption, ritual performances or exchange (as in bride wealth), thus "life begets life". In the second interpretation, wealth is conceptualized in the form of cash and other lifeless objects. The question then becomes 'how much is this worth?' in order that it might be sold. They observed that this new development has led to the depletion of local resources. Arguing that as soon as food or animals are sold for money, it is quickly spent on worthless things and this eventually leaves the family with no other means of livelihood except poverty and destitution. Hence, they said "money is but the wind". Citing a 1993 local hit song by Ananyoka, "God made man and everything in it, man made money and money makes man mad", the elders called upon the youth to learn from the song's teaching.

In *Worlds of Power*, Ellis and Ter Haar explain this as a typical phenomenon in agrarian societies. Wealth is reproduced, not created by a multiple effect as pertains to the banking system.[21] Cash gifts are thus used to purchase fowls and ruminants, reinforcing the reproductive system of wealth. Reproduction is thus wealth creation in terms of fertile lands for farming, and fertile animals and humans for birthing.

As the youth emphasized that material wealth and money are an important aspect of development, the elders responded with, "we talk of people and you talk of money, walls [buildings] and rags [clothing]. Don't you know these are but rubbish?" Elaborating on this, the elders noted that they are not against these things but they are worried that the youth are making them indispensable to their lives. Their concern was that these things are *soguro* (rubbish), which humanity has created to make life pleasant; therefore, they should not eclipse the essence of life itself. In an explanatory way an elder asked, "What is the use of walls if there are no people to live in them?" Another elder questioned, "Those children who come from the cities to build, will they call them homes if there were no people to live in them? It is because of us they have homes and they do that because they have families".

The aim was not to devalue money and wealth; it was to instil in the youth the love for family, unity and solidarity as core values in development instead of the current dependency on money. This is especially essential for those living in urban areas. They admitted that most of the families in the rural areas depend on monetary remittances from those in the urban areas for both their sustenance and replenishment of depleted resources. They also admit that most of the urban dwellers support their rural families under difficult conditions, yet they do so because of the relationship. It is therefore imperative for those at home to appreciate and uphold these family values and to make room for those away, not to recklessly rely on money and material wealth and squander the little they have. While agreeing with the priority placed on family, unity and solidarity, the youth called on the elderly to be relatively flexible in their own traditional values of wealth. With reference to ruminants, especially cattle, the youth regretted that so much value is placed on them that it becomes almost impossible to sell them even in difficult circumstances.

---

21   Ellis and Ter Haar, *Worlds of Power*, 119-21.

Contrasting views were made with regard to what is perceived as modern development. This was identified as anti-family. The word anti-family relates to the Nankani understanding of Western individualism and small family size. While the former was linked with family disintegration, the latter was identified with programmes associated with family planning, lower birth rates and population growth concerns. These views were contrasted with the ideal African family life. This included, early and multiple marriages, both of which promoted larger families. These are seen as blessings from the ancestors and a part of renewal in the cycle of life.

Irrespective of the desire for development, there are instances in which one is perceived as not making progress regardless of the efforts made. In this context, a different explanation is brought into focus, *paa-la* (destiny). *Paa-la* is the self-chosen path of life, which originates before birth. Efforts are made during childhood to determine and change bad destinies through rituals. Undetected bad destinies or aspects of it are revealed in the course of life through life crises. Fortes has already observed among the Tallensi that a person's destiny is intrinsically linked to his/her development.[22] Thus we see in this woman's expression, "...my destiny has betrayed me, even if I carry my shea butter under the moon light, it will still melt". The choice of shea butter is very significant, not only in terms of the traditional division of labour but also as to what a woman can clearly claim and own. Shea butter is made from a wild tree. Women do the picking of the fruits and nuts, processing and production of the oil which sets as butter. The process is laborious yet it used to be the only form of oil in the area and it was the ideal woman who had enough butter ready for use at any time. Even though it is preserved as butter, the environmental conditions often make this difficult; hence, women take particular care in its handling. Because of the role the woman plays in its production and usage, it is identified as a woman's property. This raises questions as to what is the value of female property. Is it to do with its function in rituals and family, strenuous method of production or its low monetary value? How can shea butter be compared with cattle, which women are traditionally barred from owning? Nevertheless, for a woman to take the extra precaution of carrying her precious cargo under the moon-

---

22   Fortes, *Oedipus and Job in West African Religion*, 15-37.

light, which is appropriate, yet have it melting, must be beyond her physical control. It must be her destiny betraying her.

In these religio-cultural conceptualizations, other interpretations are derived from the terms family, unity, solidarity and communal living. That is, apart from the traditional factors such as posterity, religious functionaries, security and labour, the formulation continues to serve as an important economic channel in the current system. It is the most visible economic resource base for many rural families. In two of my follow-up field-led interview questions on 'what is development', I asked for people's response to the view that the region is the poorest in the country; and also, how they can show that they are making progress within the modern sphere. Their responses were insightful and significant. Apart from refuting the view that they were the poorest with various religio-cultural resources and tourism indicators, they identified having migrant sons and daughters outside the community. These included the educated, business people and politicians. Other development indicators were their home-based industrious children, children above the basic level of education who are still in school as well as those acquiring employable skills at the moment. These, they pointed out as the most formative sources of the present and future material needs. This is understandable since children are traditionally part of a family's wealth, not only in terms of their presence but also through their material contributions.

MODERN DEVELOPMENT: A HISTORICAL PERSPECTIVE

Development as a concept has eluded any precise definition, consigning it to the use of variables. These variables involve such terms as progress and/or advancement, continually subjecting development to an active process. Drawing parallels from his initial zoological premise, Kwame Gyekye argues that development should "be seen in terms of *adequate responses to the environment in all its complexities*"[23] (his emphasis). By this, Gyekye concurs with the view that to define development simply in economic terms is inadequate. He declares that the economic perspective only looks at "the tip of the iceberg", ignoring

---

23   Gyekye, "Taking Development Seriously," 46-8.

the fundamental part which is a broad based foundation.[24] For him, the phrases "'environment'" and "'adequate responses'" must be seen as encompassing the existential needs of humans and their society. Yet, based on his zoological model, Gyekye argues that development cannot be an act of continuum. By continuum, Gyekye is referring to an endless state of progress. Reflecting on his philosophical background, he contends that even though the notion of a continuum is applied in his native Akan equivalent, *nkoso*, to see development as a continuous process is both epistemologically and logically absurd.[25] Although his contribution to the development debate is logically structured and well thought-out, his views do not really deny the traditional notions of *nkoso*, since the elements of process are still envisaged in his illustration. After all, maintenance and repair are still part of his construction, even if he perceives them as having too little consequence to warrant their inclusion as a continuum. In the case of the Nankani, repair and maintenance are structural components of development. This is because one does not only have to repair or mend broken buildings and objects, but relationships, both physical and spiritual, for the processes of development to ensue. But of course, his paper does not pay attention to the religious component, even though he highlights and discusses at length the moral aspect of culture.[26]

What is unreservedly clear is the objective notion of oppositeness. Development inherently imposes on those who discuss or desire it being drawn into an acute sense of underdevelopment. As Esteva's critical evaluation of the term maintains, from the historic launch of the term on the world stage, 20th January 1949, two-thirds of the world's population was immediately enveloped into a category of underdevelopment.

In a real sense, from that time on, they ceased being what they were, in all their diversity, and were transmogrified into an inverted mirror of other's reality: a mirror that belittles them and sends them off to the end of the queue, a mirror that defines their dignity, which is really that of a heterogeneous and diverse majority, simply in the terms of a homogenizing and narrow minority.[27]

---

24   Ibid, 49.
25   Ibid, 50-2.
26   Gyekye, "Taking Development Seriously," 54-5.
27   Esteva, "Development," 7.

Hence, people desiring development define themselves unsuspectingly by the Other's perspectives, subjecting themselves first to a state of underdevelopment. Invariably they belittle their identity as they seek to escape into the dreams and ideals of the Other.

The practical component of development is usually associated with the elimination of poverty and improvement in the standard of living.[28] By implication, I am departing from seeing poverty as a myth to its real life context described by Apusigah.[29] Similarly, my notion of the standard of living is not limited to Serge Latouche's sense of "material well-being", but the composite system enshrined in the indigenous worldview.[30] This is brought about by education, skills development, employment and high incomes. Other indicators relate to food sufficiency, good housing and health services, including a good provision of social amenities and security. In short, it encompasses a general sense of wellbeing. But development also has a reflective phase. This sets out the steps which should be taken to achieve the desired future state of development. The two components need careful balancing to achieve the desired goal. Any one sided approach is met with criticism. Western approaches are often criticised as dependency driven because of their underlying principles and conditionalities. Within the context of this study, modern concepts of rural development are seen as interventionist measures in which a distributional notion is interjected with the hope of leading a people to some degree of improvement. These different notions raise concerns at the point of destination, including rural African communities like the Nankani.

To examine how some of these issues have manifested themselves among the Nankani, the historical demarcations of pre-colonial, colonial and post-colonial eras need to be considered. As Songsore puts it, we cannot fully grasp the nature or pattern of development in Ghana without "due cognisance of British colonial policy".[31] But this was not

---

28   Peters, "Encountering Participation and Knowledge in Development Sites," 2.
29   Apusigah, "Diagnosing Poverty in Northern Ghana," 6-9. As myth, see, Majid Rahnema, "Poverty," in *The Development Dictionary: A Guide to Knowledge as Power*, ed. Sachs Wolfgang (London and New Jersey: Zed Books Ltd., 1992), 158.
30   Serge Latouche, "Standard of Living," in *The Development Dictionary: A Guide to Knowledge as Power*, ed. Sachs Wolfgang (London and New Jersey: Zed Books Ltd., 1992), 250.
31   Songsore, *Regional Development in Ghana*, 15.

an *ad hoc* endeavour. Therefore there is need for a brief but comprehensive outline of the general system involving the three phases already identified in chapter two.

In his text, *Regional Development in Ghana*, Songsore synthesized what is generally considered the pre-colonial development history of the North. Placed within the trans-Saharan trade between the interior South and the Sudanic states, and punctuated by inter-tribal wars and slave raids, the role of the North as an ancient trade route accrued few benefits.[32] Instead, the era ended with the North depopulated, less developed and set up as a peripheral economy to the South as the ancient trade links gave way to the trans-Atlantic trade. According to Songsore, as trade and commerce gravitated towards the coast and forest sector, the 'stateless' North was without any tangible economic resource, except slave raiding.[33] But this is perhaps because Songsore was focused on the renowned economic resources of development. Even so, the North is endowed with land.

Besides, the trans-Saharan trade had contributed to the development of the market system in the North. The Northern cloth has its root in this period and Der has also situated the development of chieftaincy in this era.[34] These were in addition to the traditional views of development discussed above. As Ellis and Ter Haar have pointed out, pre-colonial wealth or development was vested in people for both their reproductive and labour power, and on animals.[35] That apart, if the perspective that the aboriginal people of the present Nankani area lived underground before the migrant settlers helped them to construct surface housing, then this is yet another form of pre-colonial development.[36] Hence, these examples question our understanding of 'development'.

The colonial period brought a change to rural living and development. As the *tindana* lost out to the chief, the chief also lost part of his power to the colonial administrators. Contrary to the traditional notions of development, the new forms of community development were tied to infrastructure. It introduced the building of new types of residential settlements and homes for the new power brokers, roads,

32   Awia, *Navrongo and its Pioneers*, 31.
33   Songsore, *Regional Development in Ghana*, chapter 2.
34   Der, "Traditional Political Systems of Northern Ghana Reconsidered," 56-9.
35   Ellis and Ter Haar, *Worlds of Power*, 120-1.
36   Awia, *Navrongo and its Pioneers*, 30-2.

toilets, schools and market stores. The initiative, leadership and control of these projects were all taken by the foreign power source, outside the community setting. The chief's role was a social and community resource organizer. In this capacity, the chiefs mobilized the needed human resources as well as other locally available resources such as stones, sand, water and labour. The problem with these new developments was that they were erratic, unfamiliar and uncompromising.[37] The technical knowledge and skill as well as some of the resources were alien to the people and their environment. Such resources included cement, timber, corrugated iron and roofing sheets. Consequently, communities depended on the new political system for the new models of development, creating a dependency syndrome.

This change in the nature and form of development shifted the focus from the available cultural resources to materials which were beyond the reach of the local community. Consequently communities had to depend on foreign resources, knowledge and skills, and an initiator. The resources had to be acquired from outside the communities with money which was unavailable since this was a non-monetary society and they were also not paid for the labour. This dramatic change introduced two new strands to rural development. Thus, it forcefully introduced an adaptation stance, not necessarily based on a local evolutionary method precipitated by improved knowledge, cultural innovations and choice, but by the abrupt interruption.

The poor and underdeveloped status of the area was aggravated when the Gold Coast was restructured to meet the development needs of Britain as a producer of raw materials.[38] With Britain (London) emerging as the decision-making centre, coastal Accra became the transmission or application centre, with the rest of the nation drawn into a vertical centre-peripheral administrative and development oriented structure. The British interest in specific raw manufacturing materials selected gold, diamonds, rubber, timber, cocoa, palm oil and palm kernel. The North was disadvantaged on ecological grounds. Even though some gold deposits were discovered, it was comparatively disadvantageous from a capitalist perspective. Thus, the South emerged as the socio-political and economic centre, requiring infra-

---

37 Basis of 'forced labour', but also, no payments for services rendered. See Allman and Parker, *Tongnaab*, 74.
38 Songsore, *Regional Development in Ghana*, 56

structural development including roads, railways, harbours, administrative setups and other social amenities. Not only were the above developments concentrated in the South, labour was needed to put this new economic system into effect. This resulted in the importation of labour from the peripheral North. The North, then free from being a slave raiding zone, became a labour exporting zone. To facilitate this enterprise, and gradually, policies were put in place. This is generally referred to as the Northern "labor reserve" policies.[39]

Songsore has also argued that earlier socio-economic investment in the South had already produced a competitive class of citizens that "was not to be repeated" in the North.[40] As a result, a strict exclusion of missionary activities, which had the propensity for development especially in the educational sector, was imposed on the North. Debrunner states that an attempt by the Methodist Church to work in Tamale was prevented by the then chief commissioner, Armitage, who said, "'the time has not yet come for the opening up of the north for Christian enterprise'".[41] Consequently, "Northern Ghana fell a century behind the south in terms of educational development" and other forms of development.[42]

The strategic plans provided only minimal education, to standard six, in order that the North could serve as "a cheap, untrained and docile" "labour reserve" for the emerging capital economy. Songsore argues that this was effected with "the policy of induced labour out-migration in Northern Ghana", a policy, he contends, "had far reaching implications for the development of under-development in the region".[43] Described as "deliberate policies of the colonial administration", the labour policy was enhanced by the refusal to develop the North "for fear of halting the migration of labour to the south".[44] Instead, a coercive imposition of a labour recruitment quota system for each of the Northern administrative set-ups was put in place.[45] This was in addition to a "policy of starving the Protectorate of investment funds". This led to the 'free labour' policy. An ambiguous policy devised to secure free labour from the communities to provide the needed

---

39 Saaka, "Introduction," 3.
40 Songsore, *Regional Development in Ghana*, 65.
41 Debrunner, *A History of Christianity in Ghana*, 216.
42 Songsore, *Regional Development in Ghana*, 66-7.
43 Songsore, *Regional Development in Ghana*, 67.
44 Ibid.
45 Der, "Traditional Political Systems of Northern Ghana Reconsidered," 57-8.

local infrastructural development. Together with the imposition of tax (*lampoo*), able people embarked on a self-imposed out-migration process to the South. This was an attempt to be masters of their own destinies but it might as well have fulfilled the colonial policy of induced labour migration. Although this produced a different set of problems, discussed below, it widened the development gap between the North and South.[46] The traditional society was not only intruded, it was stifled and robbed of its main resource, labour. Cardinall, then administrator of Navrongo, glossed over these issues to deal with the belief in secrecy and the protection of personal identity. For him, this was manifested in the use of inaccurate names during the security services recruitment exercise of the district.[47]

Furthermore, as the colony gravitated towards the development needs of Europe, the coastal South became the central colonial administrative enclave. Songsore explains that:

> This tradition not only espouses the view of a dual economy: one traditional and static, and the other modern and dynamic, but also ascribes market forces as playing the key role in the displacement of labour from the 'static' subsistence sector to the emerging 'dynamic' capitalist sector. The labour reserves developing from within the subsistence sector and the wider capitalist economy are considered as separate entities rather than two sides of the same coin: development and under-development, prosperity and impoverishment.[48]

Thus, a formidable centre-peripheral structured economy emerged in the colonial era, with the North bearing the brunt of its negative impact. On all fronts the northern labourer was exploited. Locally, they served as 'free labour' for the construction of roads, administrative and residential buildings. As migrants or through colonial recruitment schemes, they worked either as casual labour or in the mines under unhealthy conditions for poor remuneration, similar to their work on private cocoa farms. Constrained by the emerging capitalist conditions

---

46   Allman and Parker, *Tongnaab*, 86-7 and Songsore, *Regional Development in Ghana*, 6 9-70.

47   Cardinall. *The Natives of the Northern Territories of the Gold Coast*, viii.

48   Songsore, *Regional Development in Ghana*, 66.

in the South, most migrant workers could not remit to their families back home. For those who returned, not much was realized from the endeavour. Consequently, the local economy could neither be stimulated by those left behind nor the out-migrants. The out-migration also had adverse effects on the subsistence agrarian economy, since it was the strong and energetic that migrated. Besides, with the harsh and exploitative experiences of the capitalist South, returnee labourers "contracted drinking habits" and this led to insubordination towards the indigenous leadership structure. Others returned with tuberculosis and venereal diseases.[49] Additionally, others acquired new beliefs or new dimensions to old beliefs and practices, including witchcraft beliefs. Allman and Parker, for instance, have shown how *Tongnaab*, the chief deity of the Tallensi, was renowned for its anti-witchcraft activity in the South even though at home its major concerns were production and reproduction.[50]

Nonetheless, the colonial administration and its out-migrant over-flow did introduce some changes, directly or otherwise. Some of these are still evident in the form of the road network, hierarchical structure of the present indigenous leadership,[51] architectural adaptations and an expanded worldview which has inadvertently impacted on the religio-cultural lifestyle of the North. Some of these religio-cultural influences are in the area of witchcraft. The impact is in the way witchcraft later manifested itself as a powerful negative social phenomenon, inhibiting development, a perspective that is discussed below.

The end of the Second World War (1945) signalled new beginnings for different people in the world. For the West, it was the beginning of a vigorous and progressive form of industrialization and development. The Third World, on the other hand, marked the period with the search for freedom and independence from Western colonial powers.[52] Within the Third World, Africa's liberation struggle came to an end in 1992 with the end of apartheid in South Africa. Nonetheless, the period

---

49   Songsore, *Regional Development in Ghana*, 71-2.

50   Allman and Parker, *Tongnaab*, 107.

51   Der, "Traditional Political Systems of Northern Ghana Reconsidered," 60.

52   Donal Dorr, *Option for the Poor: A Hundred Years of Vatican Social Teaching*, Revised Edition (Dublin: Gill and Macmillan, 1992), 107. See also, Samuel Vinay and Chris Sugden, "Introduction," in *The Church in Response to Human Need*, eds. Samuel Vinay and Chris Sugen (Grand Rapids, Michigan: William B. Eerdmans Publishing Co. and Oxford: Regnum Books, 1987), viii.

marked a controversial stage in the continent's history. Perceived in the West as retrogression, many of the hitherto thriving nations like Ghana moved from being a "Black Star" of Africa in 1957 to a self-proclaimed Heavily Indebted Poor Country (HIPC) in 2001.[53]

The postcolonial era is a rather ambiguous phase, especially if such an era is not simply limited to the early phase of political independence. If such a demarcation is made, then room must be created for that which has been generally described as the neo-colonial era. However, I contend that such boundaries are arbitrary. Thus, the postcolonial era in this context extends beyond the immediate confines of independence. It is the basket in which the diverse political, cultural and socio-economic factors are placed. As indicated above, despite the differences and apprehensions exhibited by the few Northern elite at the time,[54] the independence struggle brought Ghanaians of all walks of life together for a seemingly united front. Epitomized by Kwame Nkrumah's famous 'seek ye first the political kingdom and all others shall be added' proclamation, political freedom became the overwhelming goal, the prelude to all other issues.[55] Unfortunately, political power alone was and still is an inadequate resource for solving the cultural and socio-economic problems that are in existence.[56] Perhaps, Nkrumah was still not fully aware of the magnitude of the problem or of the new colonizing agenda already in motion. Identified by Esteva as "Colonizing Anti-Colonialism", it is not a territorial or implicit political colonization but a technological and material one.[57] Hence, fifty years into independence Ghanaians are still waiting for the fuller manifestation of the phrase, "and all others shall be added". Nevertheless, independence provided new horizons of hope. It gave a sense of identity, dignity and self-esteem to Ghanaians, especially, those who were forced into work by the foreign authority.[58]

53   See Bill Gould, "Structural Adjustment, Decentralization and Educational Planning in Ghana," *Third World Regional Development: A Reappraisal*, ed. David Simon (London: Paul Chapman Publishing Ltd., 1990), 211.
54   Saaka, "Introduction," 3.
55   Meredith, *The State of Africa*, 19 and Pobee, "Church and State in Ghana, 1949-1966," 129.
56   Pobee, "Church and State in Ghana, 1949-1966," 131.
57   Esteva, "Development," in *The Development Dictionary*, 11.
58   Der, "Traditional Political Systems of Northern Ghana Reconsidered," 52-3.

Independence, however, brought no change to the form and manner in which community development was undertaken. The only difference was the change of personnel from British administrators to an elite group of Ghanaians. With the exception of a few infrastructural developments, rural Ghana did not benefit from the major industrial postcolonial developments. Following the precedence laid by the colonial government, the new administrative, commercial and industrial projects of the modernization phase were concentrated in the big urban areas. There was also a territorial downsizing. This led to the division of the North into two regions, the Northern and Upper Regions. The result was further infrastructural development to cater for the administrative wings of government in the respective regions. However, this created new developmental concerns and to some extent, readjusted identities and loyalties in the North. Although political motives have been read into this historical event, such as the break-up of the common Northern front, my concern is to decipher how this new pattern impacted on the development of the Nankani.[59] That is to say, although Northerners still identify themselves as one with the general territorial concern, they owe their allegiances first to their respective communities and regions before the general territorial area of the North.

Other than the administrative infrastructure, projects such as the now defunct meat and tomato factories in the Upper East Region, the Via and Tono dams, and subsequently, the Tono rice mill were established. Much emphasis was laid on administrative structures through which the top-down power structure functioned from the coastal capital city, Accra. The economic and political crises of the mid 1960s to 1980s further led to the concentration of efforts in the urban areas to the detriment of rural communities. Used to waiting for someone to initiate this new form of development, rural communities waited in vain. Community appeals to district and regional offices for assistance yielded only promises. Eventually, some of the early development projects, including the schools, fell into ruins. With no assistance, the people simply retreated to what they know best, their tradition and culture. The life that was introduced "did not see the sunrise", Abudu noted. During the interview, he stated that:

---

59   Songsore, *Regional Development in Ghana*, 93-5.

We were called out to build roads. I mean the ones you
people are now using. I also took part in building this our
village school. These arms that you see were once full of life
and strength. We carried rocks, stones, sand and water for
these things. We even carried grass to Navrongo for some of
the administrators' buildings. But after that, all ended. No
one knew we existed. Oh, except, of course, during voting.
Tell me my daughter, have you seen any zinc [roofing sheet]
or cement product in this compound? If I don't have any,
how do you expect me to get some for the maintenance
of the school or market stalls? Yet we are told we don't
maintain what they have given us. I ask, with what? What
will our soft sand and cow dung do to concrete buildings?
When they came forcing us to put them up, did they ask if
we could maintain them? Child, let's not talk about those
people. We do what we know and to the best of our ability.
All they know is to talk and criticize but do nothing.

This statement puts the rural sentiments on modern development in
perspective. It gives a preview of how development was initiated in this
area, what the people perceive as modern development, one that is different from theirs. Inherent in it is a historical account and summary of
how it started and the state of affairs presently. Most importantly, this
is a personal disillusionment but it fits in well with that which has been
termed the ambiguous 'free labour' policy of the colonial system in the
North.[60] It also shows how development was infrastructurally oriented
without the development of the people.

In chapter two I showed how the colonial administrative system
was simply adopted and maintained at independence with the only
visible change being the subdivisions of the four parts of the Gold
Coast into what is now a ten region administered nation. I have also
shown in this chapter how independence was only a change from the
colonial administrators to an elite Ghanaian group. In other words,
there was little, if any, real attitudinal or structural change to take into
consideration the contextual realities of indigenous socio-cultural
systems. For the cities and urban areas, the process of westernization,
modernization and industrialization was taking effect. This showed

---

60   Allman and Parker, *Tongnaab*, 74, 86-87.

a continuation of the colonial systems and probably the "different Africa" initiated through the new kind of "citizens of high quality".[61]

Subsequently, the Nankani developed a two pronged approach to development. The first approach relied on the communities' own initiative and to a greater extent local resource mobilization, with adaptations. This included new architectural designs, styles and textures, built in addition to the traditional ones. Without abandoning the old, the new has been integrated to form a complex blend of housing structures.[62] For instance, tar is sometimes used in place of cement or the traditional cow dung and together with the black soil used by women to plaster walls, while men add it to sand to mould bricks. The result has been improved, rain resistant, longer lasting buildings. Similarly, the choice of paint is carefully selected, by those who can afford it to warrant its use as an indigenous colour for the traditional colourful designs of wall decorations.[63] The second approach, which is mainly associated with the new order and still follows the Western trend, is left for the 'so-called outsider', particularly the national administrative set-up, to handle. This includes infrastructural and social amenities that do not immediately hinder the way of life.

With the continuous decline of the national economy in the 1980s, Ghana joined the bandwagon of Structural Adjustment Programmes (SAP) with the hope of, at least, stemming the economic decline. In reality, however, the populace felt different. With an acute sense of the failure of SAP nationally, it was nicknamed 'Suffering African People', indicating the fallacy of the programme and an internal scorn of the political leaders for accepting it. Others simply said, 'beggars have no choice', inferring that the political leaders had become public beggars; hence, had to take whatever was put in their plate. SAP as Suffering African People was therefore a slap in their face by the West. This argument presents a two way interpretation of SAP. While one is an assumption on behalf of the donor institutions belittling and teasing Africans, the other is an internal self-reflected scorn inflicted on the ordinary citizens by their leaders. It was significantly engaging to see the rural folks interpret and analyze SAP as experienced realities. Joined by some retrenched labour of SAP, the question was why is it

---

61   McWilliam, *The Development of Education in Ghana*, 25.
62   Picture 3.
63   Pictures 7 and 8.

that 'our leaders never learn to do things for themselves?' The discussion came to a close with a satirical proverb by one of the elders who noted that "if you look for rain, it rains on your rooftop". Although this resulted in laughter, his view was that, it was the Ghanaian leadership which looked for SAP and suffered the consequences of SAP. By implication, rural people, in their own ways, are aware of national policies and can, to some extent, engage in such discussions. They are therefore not ignorant 'by-standers'.

The structural adjustments saw the introduction of various stringent measures.[64] While the masses assessed SAP as a failure, the government, World Bank and International Monetary Fund (IMF) claimed success and Ghana was presented as a model.[65] This success claim was however quickly dismissed in 2001 when a new government assumed power. Ghana was subsequently ushered into the HIPC initiative, proving the masses right. As Jeffrey Sachs puts it, "[b]y the start of the twenty-first century Africa was poorer than during the late 1960s, when the IMF and World Bank had first arrived on the African scene".[66]

One of the legacies of SAP is the decentralization policy of governance. Decentralization is a process through which political power is shared through sub-national units. Among the reasons advanced for decentralization is good governance and development, it is rooted in the current drive for a participatory development. According to F. Saito, this type of participatory approach "signifies that people have the legitimate right to voice their concerns in affairs which affect their lives".[67] He lists the category of people as including the poor, youth, women and minorities. In 1988, the District Assemblies (DAs) concept was introduced in Ghana.[68] Composed of one-third government appointed and two-thirds democratically elected membership, the decentralized

---

64   Paul Streeten, "Structural Adjustment: A Survey of the Issues and Options (1987)," in *Development Studies: A Reader*, ed. Stuart Corbridge (London: Edward Arnold, 1995), 373-9.

65   Augustine M. Ayaga, *Common Values, Contradictory Strategies: A Study of Church, State and NGO Relations in Ghana* (Accra: SonLife Printing Press and Services, 2000), 7.

66   Jeffrey Sachs, *The End of Poverty: How Can We Make It Happen in Our Lifetime*, Forward by Bono (London: Penquin Books, 2005), 189.

67   Fumihito Saito, *Decentralization and Development Partnerships: Lessons from Uganda* (Tokyo: Springer-Verlag, 2003), 38.

68   Ayaga, *Common Values, Contradictory Strategies*, 39.

political structure is headed by a District Chief Executive (DCE), who is appointed by the government. The appointed members are expected to include chiefs and opinion leaders of the district. This is however an area of controversy. The assumption is that the appointed members are picked from the elite and influential members of the ruling party, creating an uneven power structure in the DAs. This purported uneven power structure is based on the view that most of the elected members in the area had hitherto been either illiterate or semi-illiterate.

The role of DAs is to collaborate, spearhead and initiate development with their constituents. Saito has outlined the main areas of DA activities as the forging of relationships between central and local governments (communities), government and the private sector including NGOs, service providers and recipients and lastly, among local authorities.[69] Although there are various problems associated with each of these components, the core problem with the functioning of DAs in Northern Ghana is resource mobilization. As shown by Saito, even though one of the anticipated goals of decentralization was to enhance local revenue mobilization, studies have revealed this as misleading especially in the African context.[70] This has been very disappointing in the case of the Kasena-Nankani District Assembly (KNDA) because of the depth of poverty in the region.

Emerging from the above socio-economic and political condition was a new and vibrant socio-political industry termed Non-Governmental Organizations (NGOs). They clearly distanced themselves from the bureaucracies and failures of governments which were creating unjust societies. They opted to take the side of the poor, exploited, and oppressed as well as the marginalized and excluded, by projecting themselves as the "'civil society'".[71] NGOs proclaimed their roles to include improvements of the living conditions or standards of the above mentioned groups.[72] The steady rise in NGO formations in Ghana got into problems with government when in 1987 government tried to monitor and regulate their activities through an NGO

---

69   Saito, *Decentralization and Development Partnerships*, 2.
70   Saito, *Decentralization and Development Partnerships*, 37-8.
71   Van Rooy, "Good news! You may be out of a job," 27.
72   Jaime A. Joseph, "NGOs: fragmented dreams," in *Debating Development: NGOs and the Future*, eds. Deborah Eade and Ernst Ligteringen (Oxford: Oxfarm GB, 2001), 146.

bill.[73] Even though the bill was abandoned and the impasse resolved, it was not without serious protest from the NGO sector, especially, from religious bodies who were the majority at the time.[74] Despite renewed efforts at collaboration and networking between the state and NGOs, there seems to be no genuine relationship between the two. The KNDA has only sixteen registered NGOs even though it believes the number is about double. Of this number, no religious based NGO is registered. Of the sixteen registered members, only three of them are present in the whole area under study. These are the NHRC, Catholic Relief Services (CRS) and Link. Out of these, only one that is local, the NHRC and it is in the area of health research. The other three are international and are all in education. Even though NABOCADO is similarly present and its presence is acknowledged, it is not registered. The hitherto active role of the Canadian International Development Agency (CIDA) in the provision of water is still acutely remembered and highly recommended by the communities.

NGOs play a vital role through the provision of skills training and capacity building, education, health services and provision of water. Others include job creation and advocacy roles. Although categorized as social welfare roles, they are essential in the rural areas as the government continues to cut down on these services. As rural developers, NGOs are expected to collaborate and work with the DAs and the other national structures in their areas of operations so as to form a concerted front in the overall structure of national development. This presupposes that NGOs are expected to develop their programmes in relation to the national and rural (DAs) development plans. This is however only in theory. NGOs come with their agenda expecting to carve their own niches and to claim their successes. Besides, the 1987 scuffle with government continues to serve as a caution, impeding close collaboration. As Ayaga, himself a development worker in the study area, points out, NGOs do not collaborate well with other stakeholders.[75] This situation is not limited to the state but also among the NGOs themselves. This continues to result in competition, duplication and waste of resources. In spite of these problems, NGOs are an important sector in rural development. From the community's perspective, the

---

73 Ayaga, *Common Values, Contradictory Strategies*, 43-5.
74 Ibid.
75 Ayaga, *Common Values, Contradictory Strategies*, 49.

discussion below highlights the intricate dynamics of NGOs activities among the Nankani. The discussion focuses on NABOCADO, the longest running NGO with international funding.

Navrongo-Bolgatanga Catholic Diocesan Development Office (NABOCADO)

The use of the development sector of the Navrongo-Bolgatanga Diocese as an illustration in this investigation is anchored on two factors. First, it is to treat NGO activities as another attempt at modern rural development. That is, another external interventionist approach with a distinct set of development characteristics. External in this sense does not eliminate national or community participation since the organization is run by indigenous people. It is simply to differentiate it from the traditional form of development. Second, it is based on the community's view of what is modern development and the subsequent link made with the activities of the early missionaries in the area. The church's development office, now known as the Navrongo-Bolgatanga Catholic Diocesan Development Office (NABOCADO), has its history rooted in the Northern missionary activities of 1906. This historical link indicates NABOCADO is itself a sustainable development product, at least institutionally. Growing from an initial missionary welfare programme, it is now a well established organization, with substantial funding support from international donor organizations.

My interest, however, is not on the institution's own development but in its impact on the Nankani community. The aim is to examine how this alternative form of development has contributed or otherwise to rural development. How has the long standing relationship or the development of NABOCADO corresponded with or helped the communities with which it has been associated? What elements of sustainable development can be linked with this hundred-year relationship? Although there were concerns as to how such a link to a Christian organization could be carried out from a traditional perspective, this was resolved under certain considerations. Alison Van Rooy for instance has argued that with "stronger financial footing" and long standing association with their partner communities, these organizations have moved from their "missionary zeal" to "faith-inspired solidarity work", from which they engage even the political.[76] Her view captures NABOCADO approach, a perspective which the community recommends. That apart, the study is community-based and this aims to provide understanding on how NGOs work at the community level. This is irrespective of any counter investigations made at the project level. Another important aspect is that neither the funding sources nor regulations are based on the NBOCADO's religious tenets.[77] Moreover, the communities are the target beneficiaries. If modern development is to be integrated into the rural level, then communities must be given the role to analyze and substantiate the development that is brought to them. This is crucial for community participation.

The importance of this investigation is the manner in which the work of NABOCADO was analyzed at the community level. NABOCADO, as well as all the other development agencies in the area, were identified as exercising a top-down approach to development. This was quickly contrasted with the work of the early missionaries. Similarities were drawn from the colonial administration. By this, I am referring to a situation in which activities are planned at the project level before contacts are made with the community. This included project and community identification, and subsequently, its implementation. Although discussions were held at some point with key collaborators and community leaders, this was reminiscent of the relationship between colonial administrators and chiefs.[78] Some community members felt excluded and some forms of resentments were expressed. Yet these members exercise restraint for fears that any discernible reaction may hinder their communities from being included in future plans.

When I investigated at the project level, NABOCADO prided itself on adopting a bottom-up approach. This is an approach that finds its preliminary processes at the community level. NABOCADO stated that it only responds to communities seeking external help to complement their efforts. Even though efforts made to substantiate this view and others with the general co-ordinator Augustine Ayaga

---

76   Van Rooy, "Good news! You may be out of a job" 20.

77   In a discussion on this issue, references were made to Jesus' response to John the Baptist, the Sermon on the Mount and the call to love one's neighbour as oneself. These were however viewed as additions (some used the word 'excuses') because the mission statement, as articulated in project documents do not include these.

78   Der, "Traditional Political Systems of Northern Ghana Reconsidered," 52-3, 57.

proved futile, my discussions with the Agricultural Coordinator, Joseph Ayembila showed some lapses and inadequacies in the above stated approach. However, this was possible because earlier discussions in Kologo and Naga had already analyzed one of the activities of NABOCADO's Agricultural unit. For these two communities, NABOCADO's notion of a bottom-up approach was rejected with concrete examples. At best, they noted, 'we are asked or informed by the project managers to organize ourselves for meetings. It is often at these meetings that the agenda is made known and decisions taken regarding the project to be implemented'.[79] This contradicts the view that the initiative and project choice originate from the people.

In a discussion with a development agent in Bolgatanga, who prefers to remain anonymous, I was told that the process of community development is quite delicate. He expressed the fear that, if the right thing is to be done, it is most likely that development agents will get into trouble with rural communities. He contended that development agents act upon information and their responses relate to the predetermined project guidelines of donor institutions. In such situations, previous knowledge of their communities are used, sometimes with limited cross-checks, in which no evidence or assurance is given for fear of reprisals from the community. This is because there is often no surety that a project will be funded and sometimes the process of acquiring funding is a long one. Some proposals also undergo significant changes arising from the dictates of the funding institutions. The fear that rural communities might not understand the intricacies involved and think that such agents are using them to collect monies from foreign donors is high. To forestall this, much is done at the project level before communities are contacted for work to ensue.

We may understand this top-down approach, from donor institutions to community development agents, with reference to Chambers' conceptualization of biases. In this case, both donor and local development institutions assume they know and understand what is good for the rural community. This puts the community at the bottom of the chain. Ironically, the call is for the community to participate and sustain projects they have no part in initiating. This recalls the Kandiga

---

79   This assertion is in relation to a 2000-2001 Soya bean cultivation project, implemented with the collaboration from CRS Tamale, Ghana.

discussion on: 'Whose community development is it? And who is participating? Who sustains what?'

NABOCADO: ENGAGING DEVELOPMENT AMONG THE NANKANI

Despite the importance of the above questions, rural-based NGOs continue to impose their views of development on the communities. NABOCADO is no exception. Following its missionary foundation, NABOCADO is engaged in many activities and has a large coverage area, one that covers more than the politically designated region.[80] These activities are in the general area of development, sustainable development and gender. Not only does this pose a problem for effective monitoring, it also demands great resources which NABOCADO lacks. The desire to meet the needs of its ecclesiastical constituency, while at the same time maintaining control of projects and resources, is a major problem. In the process, development activities are spread thinly across these communities, exacerbating the problems of monitoring and management. Consequently, NABOCADO is not able to make any significant impact in the communities. This is especially so in the areas of gender and socio-economic development. NABOCADO might have to consider the view that small is not only beautiful but effective.[81]

This notwithstanding, NABOCADO has made modest contributions towards the goal of enhancing rural livelihood. This however needs a detailed examination and analysis. Women's participation in development activities in the area was found to be higher than men's. Nonetheless, there were male as well as mixed groups. The promotion of soya bean cultivation, small ruminants and poultry production was recommended as having the potential for improving the livelihoods of the people.[82] Although evidence of this was found in some of the Nankani communities, it was not given adequate attention. This is in terms of limited scale, inadequate resource allocation and poor networking with other development agents in the area. Besides, its major

---

80   See also Rural Livelihood Improvement Project (RULIP), Navrongo-Bolga-tanga Diocesan Development Office submitted to Misereor, Germany, March 2002, 5.

81   E. F. Schumacher, *Small is Beautiful: A Study of Economics as if People Mattered* (London: ABACUS, 1974), 52-62.

82   Yennah, "Evaluation Report," 20-1.

donor, Cordaid, has withdrawn from the agricultural sector, creating further financial difficulties in the area.

There has also been some amount of training for beneficiary groups in the community. The level of understanding was good, and subject areas included gender, group dynamics, income generating activities (IGAs) skills and management. Similar training programmes were carried out almost repeatedly by all the NGOs working in the area. They include, Adventist Development Rural Agency (ADRA), Centre Sustainable Development Initiative (CENSUDI), Widows and Orphans Ministry, NHRC, World Neighbours and TechnoServe. Irrespective of the level of understanding, the extent to which the acquired knowledge and skills are applied to real everyday life or integrated into community structures seemed limited. This is however not limited to the field experience; Nolan observes similar characteristics at the donor level.[83]

For example, in the area of development (*malgo*), the inherent traditional notion includes a spiritual element, which the community epitomises as the core element of development. This spiritual element is however lacking in its modern equivalent. Although the modern concept of development is appreciated, it is perceived as lacking substance. In another community discussion in Naga, they elders' argued that modern development does not repair, build upon or improve what they have. The elders called on 'those who say they are bringing us development to sit down and rethink if they have destroyed or built'. They explained that their agricultural heritage has been the used of compost manure; similarly their care of infants, breastfeeding. They noted that modern development introduced fertilizer and baby milk (food supplement). At first, these were given free, later at a price but now you have to *koose nafo la bu bia* (sell a cow and its calf) for fertilizer. This expression reveals two things. Firstly, they are not a monetary economy and therefore have no money to make purchases. The ability to obtain cash for non-traditional products depends on the sale of what they have. Secondly, cows are the highest movable assets and show of wealth among the Nankani. To have a cow with a calf is a prized possession because of its future prospects. For one to sell these two together in order to acquire something else must signify greater loss. Although a hyperbolic expression, it depicts the awareness that they give their

---

83   Nolan, *Development Anthropology*, 233.

prized possessions for things of less value, indicating the impoverishing nature of modern development on the indigenous economy.

For the Nankani, the puzzle with modern development is that, despite all its promises, it does not deliver the goods. Besides, the agents of development "do not know what it means to say sorry. Instead, they return with another idea, pretending it's new and better". Using the two examples in point, they now ask the question, 'what is exclusive breastfeeding and organic farming?' Are these so different from the traditional ways our people had hitherto practised? Yet, they come and say these are new developments. "What is new about them, are they not the same?" they asked. The elders contended that modern development and its agents are thieves. Thieves in the sense that, when people destroy things belonging to others without rendering an apology, they are considered thieves who destroy without taking account. The fact that these practices are presented as new, a process whereby they are called to workshops to be taught is 'an affront to their dignity' (ba de zeesi). They find it most unfortunate that their own children (Africans) whom they sent to learn "with their sweat" (resources) are part of this scheme.

Similarly, they questioned the modern concept of sustainability. It could be argued that NABOCADO's understanding and application of 'sustainability', most especially, 'sustainable rural development', is ambiguous. Is NABOCADO's notion of sustainability institutional or community based?[84] At the project level, the notion was that of maintaining the organization as part of the institutional framework linking the church and communities. References are made to 1981 when the office was formally established and its 1991 restructuring with a more professional focus, distinguishing it from its former phase which was seen as missionary and philanthropic.[85] What is peculiar about Ayaga's study is his inability or refusal to link the modern set-up with its foundation, even though he was part of the re-organization; hence aware of the inherited resources and legacies of the past. At present the desire for a good administrative and financial management system with the potential for attracting a continuous supply of projects is a driving force. These became the indicators of sustainability. When this was analyzed alongside the male discussions on sustainability and development agents at the community level at the Kandiga market, a

---

84   Rural Livelihood Improvement Project, 19-21.
85   Ayaga, *Common Values, Contradictory Strategies*, 47-8.

clear understanding and distinction could be obtained from the two perspectives. From this group's perspective, the concept of sustainability was generally a mockery. The questions 'who or what are they sustaining? Is it their offices, jobs and stomachs or us and our community?' were very informative.

One important area for rural sustainability is a good, viable and active collaborative networking machinery. NABOCADO's collaboration with other development stakeholders at the community level is either inexistent or weak. Getting community people organized around NABOCADO projects to ensure continuity is limited to the beneficiary group and local church leaders. Thus collaboration with locally available structures like the chiefs, *tindanas*, Agricultural Extension Agents (AEAs) and the KNDA and its community Assembly Members appears to be ineffective. In my interview with Emmanuel Achegwe, District Chief Executive, Kassena-Nankana District, he pointed out from his predecessors' handing-over report that even though there were more than sixteen NGOs, only that number had registered. He however pointed out that he was yet to hold a meeting with the NGOs in the area, despite being at post for a year. Tabulating his list of activities and problems in the district, he explained why such a meeting is long overdue. The interview however revealed some structural weaknesses. One of the problems, I will argue, relates to the hierarchical structure of the assemblies. Another factor is either over dependency on the head administrator or the lack of delegation. My earlier interview with the district development planning officer, Richard Ohene, had also revealed the same scenario. NABOCADO, for instance, was not listed in the documents as a partner organization providing services and development to the communities. Thus, NABOCADO's contribution within this political designated structure is not noticed or counted and therefore, not strategically acknowledged in the context of rural or national development. In short, no common front or efforts are made by the development agents in this area to maximize resources.[86]

NABOCADO was variously commended where visible structures were present. That is to say, in Bui for its clinic, Navrongo and its environs for schools, Kandiga for schools and Sirigu for schools, orphanage and clinic. In the eastern zone (Mirigu-Kandiga, Sirigu, Manyoro and

---

86   Ayaga, *Common Values, Contradictory Strategies*, 48-9.

Nabango), NABOCADO is greatly appreciated for its work with the orphanage.[87] This is however a complex issue since these projects, with the exception of the clinics, were not really set up by NABOCADO but the church, its parent organization. The orphanage was formed by the local church when Bishop Akanlu rescued a *chinchirigo*.[88] Again, the schools are not directly managed by NABOCADO but the Catholic Education Unit. Secondly, all of these projects are assisted by the government through the Ministries of Education, Health and Social Welfare Service/SOS School programmes in the country. It is thereby difficult to attribute the success of these programmes solely to NABO-CADO. This notwithstanding it shows the importance of good structural networking and collaboration with existing national machinery. Finally, the identification of infrastructural projects is reminiscent of the colonial era, where this notion of modern development was formed.

In contrast, NABOCADO is summarily dismissed, sometimes rebuked, for its engagements at the socio-economic level. This is the section associated with the Agricultural, and the Gender and Development units. At the project level, it was also the section that encountered great difficulties with senior management. Existing internal communications showed evidence of previous tensions arising between the two projects in this section and the financial and administrative units. The peculiarity of the case is that it involved the whole socio-economic sector. There were internal memos between the general coordinator and unit coordinators as well as general memos.[89] Although these memos showed misunderstandings and tensions between field workers and office administrators, the content of the memos exhibited differences between the two groups of development workers on issues of sustainability. This makes the sector, whose output is often not visible over time, a contentious ground in terms of funding and project implementation.

In terms of gender, project designs generally lack a clear gender vision. This may be attributed to the late incorporation of gender into NABOCADO's scheme of work. The only gender project of the office (1999) was originally designed as a Women and Development (WAD) programme. Although it was expected to be converted and imple-

---

87   In Kandiga, for instance, the orphanage was discussed alongside the issue of spirit-children.

88   See chapter one, 48-50.

89   Gender and Development, and Agricultural Units, 2001- 2002 Office files.

mented as a Gender and Development (GAD) programme by its sponsors, Bilance/Cordaid, management had difficulties in understanding each other in relation to the unarticulated GAD needs of the working document. This is because NGOs activities are usually tailored to meet project objectives and goals. Consequently, no conscious attempts were made to address issues like strategic community gender relations and their impact on the needs and interest of women. My field level discussions revealed that many of the efforts so far have been in the area of gender sensitization and immediate gender needs. Even though women are specifically targeted for trading and skills development these do not address structural issues. The inadequate attention given to strategic gender needs and the inability to fully address gender at its core, has led communities to downplay and ridicule not just NABOCADO's efforts, but all the development workers engaged in the area of gender and socio-economic development. It is my opinion that, unless proper attention is given to the religio-cultural dimensions of gender, some of the misunderstandings, resentment and uncooperativeness of the male members of the community cannot be changed.

Men need not feel jealous and threatened by the fact that more women are given credit support. Similarly, the apprehension that women's economic empowerment is a threat to the patrilineal, male-dominated power structure can be minimized. It was evident in some FGDs that men feel discriminated against by NGOs, especially in credit disbursements, while women are perceived as NGO favourites.[90] According to some men, this is a problem because, "when a woman's hand reaches her mouth, she does not respect". That is, when a woman is capable of caring for herself, she does not respect her husband or the men in charge of her. Paul Willis has discussed some of these dynamics under "Labour and power and patriarchy".[91] Although these dynamics are culturally based, Willis makes a strong argument by stating that these stem "from the ideological division of labour, not simply from the domesticity of the house or patriarchal ideology".[92] When I reiterated the men's remark in the women's group discussion, to solicit their view, the women noted the lack of understanding on the part of their men

90   See also, Rose Mary Amenga-Etego, "Violence against Women in Contemporary Ghanaian Society," *Theology and Sexuality* 13, no. 1 (September 2006), 30-3.
91   Paul E. Willis, *Learning to Labour* (England: Saxon House, 1977), 147-52.
92   Willis, *Learning to Labour*, 149.

and called upon NGOs to re-strategize and to find a way of getting their male counterparts to understand them. For these women, it will be fruitless, even problematic, for them to talk to the men on that. It will simply substantiate the view that they do not respect. Abraham Akrong interprets these as problems accruing from a rigid traditional gender division of labour and its impact on gender boundary crossing.[93]

Without disputing the need for NGO involvement, it is important for Nankani women to self-strategize ways of responding to these challenges from within their religio-cultural resources. Oduyoye has pointed out that religion and tradition are the tools used to underpin African women in subordination and oppression. Hence, it is best to use these same tools as resources of liberation.[94] This may provide the basis for a better acceptance than pure external interventions. An example of this is shown in the study of the Wolof, Serrahuli and Mandinka women of Gambia.[95] "The complex and contradictory ways in which intra-household dynamics are shaped by a new technology reaffirms the need to see work and patriarchal politics as cross-cut by bargaining, negotiating and, on occasion, conflict".[96] Although the Mandinka women's struggle is complex, it shows some problems require multi-dimensional approaches. And this is especially important in Africa where work, property and resource rights are symbolically gendered and religio-culturally stratified and bonded. There are usually alternatives, but where these are not very clear, thus the right of negotiation should be exercised.[97]

Nonetheless, the women argued that their role is not to demean or dis-empower their men because "without our men we won't be women", emphasizing the fact that the female is traditionally accepted as a woman only in the context of marriage. Besides, their position as women in the community is dependent on the men who married them. They noted that their men and the men's power structure are impor-

---

93   Abraham Akrong, "A phenomenology of witchcraft in Ghana," in *Imagining Evil: Witchcraft Beliefs and Accusations in Contemporary Africa*, ed. Gerrie Ter Haar (New York and Eritrea: Africa World Press, 2007), 62.

94   Oduyoye, "The Search for a Two-Winged Theology," 47-53.

95   Judith Carney and Michael Watts, "Manufacturing Dissent: Work, Gender and the Politics of Meaning in a Peasant Society," in *Development Studies: A Reader*, ed. Stuart Corbridge (London, Edward Arnold, 1995), 229-35.

96   Carney and Watts, "Manufacturing Dissent," 233-34.

97   As shown in chapter two. See also Wills, *Learning to Labour*, 171-172.

tant to them as women. This is because the phallocentric power structure defines them as women. Moreover, they do not want to *suke Winɛ
nifo* (prick God's eye i.e. wrong/hurt God). To wittingly demean their
husbands is to hurt *Winɛ* and themselves. With the proverb, "when
the bat tried to urinate on *Winɛ* in its anger, it did so to itself", they
elaborated the complexities of being married women.[98] Interestingly,
the discussion moved into the protracted domestic violence bill which
was then being debated in parliament. Here, the emphasis was not on
the issue of marital rape but what happens to the women and children
as well as their care in the event of a divorce. When it was realized
that no guarantee or adequate provisions were made for women, the
conclusion became *ti yi taare di uusa la bala* (then we will have it like
that and groan in our pain). Is the power to negotiate linked to the
availability of alternatives?

The main discussion was on the view that times are changing (*la
teare me*). This change has affected the traditional socio-economic
lifestyles so that men alone can no longer meet all the needs of the
family. For these women, their role is to help their men, just as in the
past. The only difference is that it is no longer limited to the farm.
They are not competing but rather supporting. This argument must be
considered within the traditional religio-cultural context where marriage is exogamous and initiates females into womanhood. Yet a careful
consideration of the dynamics of the discussion is also important. Are
these religious or are they strategic issues needing specific attention?

On the other hand, although credit support to women has to some
extent empowered them economically and has raised their confidence
level, there are several dimensions to it. In the former case, women
speak of being able to 'supplement household grain requirements',
'provide soup ingredients', 'buy household/kitchen equipments', 'help
to pay school fees', 'send children for health care' and 'provide some
personal needs such as clothes'. These new responsibilities have added
to the workload of rural women, causing untold hardships.[99]

---

98 In the women's focus group discussion in Kandiga, the expressions *darwn Winɛ
surɛ,* (disturb God's heart) and *sa-am Winɛ purɛ* (destroy God's stomach) were
used. It is important to note that similar expressions were used in the discussions
in Naga.

99 Oduyoye, "The Search for a Two-Winged Theology," 50; Niala Kabeer, *Reversed
Realities: Gender hierarchies in Development Thought* (London and New York:
Verso, 1994), 105-7.

Conversely, the amount of credit given to women to undertake IGAs is often so small that the impact is either indiscernible or limited. Thus, the ability to provide the above or some of these depends, to a large extent, on the support from the husband or family, or the ingenuity of the woman. Envious husbands or uncooperative families stifle the women's efforts as these women are left to spend their high interest rate loans on the family. As the women put it, "little by little and everything goes into the kitchen". In such instances, even though the immediate needs are met, the situation returns to its former state. Conditions then become worse for some of these women. Some men use this latter stage of helplessness and loss of self-esteem to ridicule, suppress and bully such women into undue submission. As a man remarked during the discussions at the Kandiga market, "when women are able to lift their hands, they think they can do everything until they realize that it is not easy. At least they can now give men their due respect". This is exacerbated if the women are unable to repay their loans.

In this section, the apparent factor is the politics of power. This is inherent in all levels: gender, community relations and NGO-stakeholder relations. Although the rivalry for stake holding and legitimization claims by individual development agents, government and community leaders may not easily facilitate effective power sharing, some efforts can be made in the area of community gender relations if prioritized.

WITCHCRAFT AND RURAL DEVELOPMENT

Witchcraft is generally perceived as an inimical religio-cultural practice in Africa. Although imbued with good and bad qualities, its public manifestations are usually associated with evil or bad outcomes. It is a common belief that even where witchcraft is associated with good outcome like industriousness, academic success or property acquisition, the achievement is made at the expense of others. Hence, its positive aspects are still tainted with anti-social traits that prevent, put down or use other peoples' resources only to the witch's advantage. This has led to its association with development, casting a shadow on modern development and the general wellbeing of Africans. Meanwhile, although the English vocabulary has gender terminological differentiations, the Nankani word *soa* (witch) is neutral; hence, it is equally applied to males and females.

'Modern development' is used to distinguish it from the traditional modes of development, although there are correlations between the two at the rural level.[100] Nor is there an attempt to deny the link between witchcraft and 'traditional development' since that is the context of its African manifestation.[101] But as Ellis and Ter Haar have pointed out, it was easy to see and perhaps understand within the traditional context, how industrious people developed.[102] The traditional modes of showing empirical evidence of development are however not in consonance with the modern trend. This has brought about misunderstandings, casting doubt and suspicion on some individual achievers. The reverse is equally true as witchcraft can be used as a justification for failure. Thus, it is important to show how modernity has impacted and continually redefined this belief in terms of development. By implication, my objective is not to discuss witchcraft or give a detailed account of the role of witchcraft in rural development.

The importance of this discussion is two-fold. First, it is a follow up on the review of Allman and Parker's discourse on *Tongnaab's* transformation in Southern Ghana into anti-witchcraft deity in chapter five. This discussion helps to explain as well as illustrate the inherent complexities involved in religion and witchcraft belief in this part of the North vis-à-vis the historical development of Ghana. The second purpose is to ascertain the history or development of witchcraft belief and its impact on the development of the Nankani, in relation to the North-South migratory experience. In this respect, I will only highlight that which is relevant to the present discourse. This includes the associated problems of returnees with references to Songsore's recorded cases of poverty, alcoholism, disease and insubordination towards traditional leaders.

It is a fact that the Nankani and their neighbours believe in witchcraft and its potential evil and destructive nature. This is irrespective of the belief in its sacred source. The general view is that its original form has been corrupted. As such, the belief is territorially appropriated. In each local situation, community or clan, deities were traditionally responsible for the control of the anti-social aspects of witchcraft activi-

100   Ter Haar, "Introduction: The evil called witchcraft," 17-8.
101   Elom Dovlo, "Witchcraft in contemporary Ghana," in *Imagining Evil: Witchcraft Beliefs and Accusations in Contemporary Africa*, ed. Gerrie Ter Haar (New York and Eritrea: Africa World Press, 2007), 69.
102   Ellis and Ter Haar, *Worlds of Power*, 120-1.

ties. The territorial deities included some of the *tingana* (earth deities, sing. *tingani*) and the *na-am dongo* (chieftaincy deity).[103] Although these anti-witchcraft deities did and still do not prevent people from becoming witches,[104] their territorial power configurations enable them to control and prevent negative activities within their jurisdiction. As one of the traditional saying goes, 'when situations become critical, you may need fire to fight fire'. The use of other spiritual powers to fight the negative tendencies of witchcraft was thus justified even though it also led to the proliferation of such gods and the belief in witchcraft.

Among the Chaaba clan of Naga, for instance, witchcraft activities are controlled upon contact with the territorial enclave. Any attempt to cause havoc within the clan leads to the death of the witch and not the opponent. On the other hand, a clan member may be attacked and harmed outside the premises of the clan, in which case, the actual manifestation may later take place within the clan. This cannot be prevented since the act occurred outside the deity's sovereign jurisdiction. However, once the perpetuator is identified through divination or confession, the remedy is to commit the person to the clan spirit through oath taking or other forms of ritual activities. In these instances, the alleged witch is made to completely commit him/herself and such evil acts to the deity for life. In serious cases, the suspect may also wear a *dongo* (a little horn filled with the ritual earth of the *tingani* as an amulet) to prevent the person from causing harm in or out of the clan. This type of anti-witchcraft practice is prevalent among the Nankani, Frafra and Tallensi. It is also distinct from that of the Northern Region of Ghana. There is need to consider the differences in practices to avoid the often undue generalization of the 'witch camp' system as a Northern Ghana phenomenon.[105]

For clans which do not have anti-witchcraft spirits, individual clans or household heads may acquire such powers to protect their subjects or families. The much polarized patriarchal gender and the positive/negative dimensions of witchcraft stems from this, inferring that while female witches are often linked to evil, male witches are associated with

---

103 Kirby, "Cultural Change and Religious Conversion in West Africa," 62.

104 Amenga-Etego, "Probing the Religio-cultural Root of Witchcraft among the Nankani," 13.

105 See Ter Haar, "Introduction: The evil called witchcraft," 18; Dovlo, "Witchcraft in contemporary Ghana," 73 and Akrong, "A phenomenology of witchcraft in Ghana," 61.

good intentions.[106] This reference tends to neglect the core point which is based on the view that the original form of witchcraft (sacred and good) can only be transferred genetically through females in childbirth. Thus, its evil trait is acquired differently. Although this questions the stereotypes, diverse practical reasons are advanced to justify the existing claims. Similar to the traditional belief in the origin of witchcraft, the above mentioned male group is generally believed to be good; hence, their environs serve as protective enclaves for the vulnerable from the apparent manifestation of evil witchcraft.[107] Yet, unlike the natural female trait, because this second category is acquired, it is associated with gods, transforming their locations into abodes of anti-witchcraft activities or avenues for subjecting 'stubborn witches' to oath taking.

Although this explanation does not deny the negative expression of witchcraft, it presents it as a sacred (neutral) entity. It also explains and shows the supportive outlets through which its corrupted evil manifestation is controlled within the society. This provides a reasonably stable environment for inhabitants. It is therefore not a lack of a strong belief in or fear of witchcraft as implied by Fortes and, Allman and Parker, in their study of the Tallensi but an inbuilt awareness that, somehow, one is being cared for by the system.[108] Thus, this explains and accounts for the scholarly view that whereas the people in the South were hysterical about witchcraft in the formative years of the nation's development, those in the North were calm and relaxed.

The subsequent account of *Tongnaab* as an anti-witchcraft deity in the South is because of the lack of this in-depth understanding, and the different forms of control mechanisms in this part of the North. *Tongnaab* who has all along played an active, though silent, role in anti-witchcraft activities among the Tallensi is not well understood. As a migrant deity in the South, its presence, power and activities were new and curtailed within its territorial allotment. Yet its ability to meet their specific need led to that focus from which its fame spread. It must however be noted that these are just additional explanations to the Southern situation in which the dominant theories are based

---

106 Dovlo, "Witchcraft in contemporary Ghana," 68, 71; Akrong, "A phenomenology of witchcraft in Ghana," 61-3 and Amenga-Etego, "Probing the Religio-cultural Root of Witchcraft among the Nankani," 3-5.

107 Amenga-Etego, "Probing the Religio-cultural Root of Witchcraft among the Nankani," 6.

108 Allman and Parker, Tongnaab, 223.

on the inherent social tensions arising from it matrilineal system[109] and the socio-economic development of the 1960s.[110] It should also be noted that contrary to Bourdillon's understanding, the Tallensi are not matrilineal and the peripheral status of witchcraft is due to the dynamic religio-cultural understanding of *Tongnaab*.[111]

The above religio-cultural differences played a significant role in the colonial and early postcolonial contacts, causing disruptions to the worldview and development pattern among the Nankani and their neighbours. Having encountered and associated the threat of witchcraft with the internal family structure, wellbeing, progress or success, and in a situation where there was no central spiritual control, many people from the North were affected. Influenced by such an immediate and apparent reality, the fear shook the foundations of their belief. Witchcraft was no longer just linked to death but disease, alcoholism, infertility, laziness and lack of success.[112] With the exception of alcoholism, which was new, all the other factors where hitherto associated with wrong doings like the breaking of taboos, an ancestral reproach or destiny.[113] Disease and death however provided occasions for suspicion but this had to be confirmed by divination. The greatest impact was that the new notions completely overshadowed the local view of *Winɛ sa ka ko, tinga kan di* (if God does not kill, the earth will not eat), which was linked to God and destiny. Consequently, some people would not return home or contribute to the external family for fear of revealing their new status.[114] This fear was compounded if people went home and got sick, experienced problems or died. People who encountered problems blamed their families and local leaders, not only for their inability to protect them but also as being responsible for that individual's predicament.

The recent scenario of interpreting individual development in terms of physical structures or properties has produced a shift in the conceptualization of witchcraft. Buildings have become a crucial

---

109 Fortes, *Religion, Morality and the Person*, 212-5 and M. F. C. Bourdillon, "Witchcraft and Society," in *African Spirituality: Forms, Meanings, and Expressions*, ed. Jacob K. Olupona (New York: The Crossroad Publishing Company, 2000), 186.

110 Akrong, "A phenomenology of witchcraft in Ghana," 57.

111 Bourdillon, "Witchcraft and Society," 186.

112 Dovlo, "Witchcraft in contemporary Ghana," 68.

113 Bourdillon, *Religion and Society*, 212.

114 Dovlo, "Witchcraft in contemporary Ghana," 83.

practical index for measuring, qualitatively and quantitatively, an individual's socio-economic status and development in Ghana. The current surge in modern architecture in rural communities is therefore not solely based on the traditional love of family but also the drive to project one's success and wellbeing. Nonetheless, most of these rural housing projects have multiple interpretations. These include one's communal responsibility and solidarity as well as maintaining a visible structural presence of the family's identity through the preservation of the ancestral home. The Nankani proverb; 'you do not use your left hand to point at your father's house' is often used to depict the pride and privilege given to one's natal home and the undying desire for its preservation. This is one reason why many industrious urban dwellers assist in the construction of houses in their rural communities. It is a desire to be counted and remembered 'at home' even if they are not physically present. It is the desire to belong and an indicative show of intention of a future return, even at death.[115]

The most influential reason for this new phenomenon lies in the current nature of funeral performances. Now referred to as 'funeral celebrations', they offer new and compelling ways of interpreting the surge in rural housing and other family support systems. This is manifested in two forms. On the one hand, urban dwellers returning to rural areas for funeral rites of close relatives, especially mothers or fathers, are eagerly accompanied by staff and/or colleagues, church members, friends, neighbours and the new group classified as 'well wishers'. On the other hand, corpses of deceased urban dwellers are increasingly being sent 'home' for burial. Sometimes, it is the final funeral rites. In these current Ghanaian practices, the occasions have become avenues for various categories of people to travel to the rural areas of the person or family they wish to express their solidarity with. This may be seen as local tourism. Nonetheless, it reawakened the concepts of 'brighten the corner where you are' or 'charity begins at home'. Funerals have become a time not only for mourning but also for exposing one's true identity and concept of family. In such circumstances, the individual's urban status is quickly contrasted and compared with his/her rural and family context. The need to preserve the rural areas for any eventuality has therefore assumed an important part of one's social wellbeing.

---

115   Paul Nchoji Nkwi, "Rethinking the Role of the Elites in Rural Development," 187.

Although these practices have not negated the belief in witchcraft or sorcerers, the current phenomenon has curtailed the overwhelming fear associated with it in the 1960s. Notably within that period was the fear of outstanding progress or success due to witchcraft,[116] this has drastically declined. In the Nankani context, the recent development has reinforced the traditional belief that adherence to traditional norms and values is a formidable protection against evil or anti-social powers. Thus, even though witches are still considered envious and distractive, it is now argued that 'if you do not owe a witch, it has no power over you'. Other explanations are that the activities of witches are not limited by mere absence or distance. Instead, it is believed that the fury of witches is due to discrimination and neglect. The need for inclusiveness is therefore an important factor in adverting witchcraft attacks. This is because an inclusive (extended) family oriented person is protected by the ancestors. Additionally, a person with a strong character brought about by a strong personality spirit or ancestry is immune to witchcraft attacks.[117]

In *Religions of Africa*, Noel King relates a similar belief. He explains how an *nganga* (traditional healer) in Kampala diagnosed ill health and lack of success in urban dwellers as the lack of responsibility to one's "village and its spirits they had left behind perhaps without fulfilling their responsibilities to the living and dead".[118] According to King, the desertion of responsibility by urban dwellers renders them vulnerable to witchcraft and other evil powers. Contributing to the development of family in rural areas is therefore a blessing in which Africans outside their indigenous communities are proactive. This is not to say if a proactive person suddenly encounters misfortunes or dies, there is no suspicion of witchcraft; it may still be assumed that some powerful, revengeful witch somewhere is responsible. Sometimes, his/her own parent may be suspected of using him/her to pay an old debt. It can be argued that everyone is suspect until proved otherwise by a diviner. On the other

---

116   Edwin W. Smith, *The Religio of Lower Races: As Illustrated by the African Bantu* (New York: The Macmillan Company, 1923), 17.

117   H. Debrunner, "The Influence of Witchcraft," in *Christianity and African Culture: the proceedings of a Conference held at Accra, Gold Coast, May 2nd-6th, 1955, under the auspices of the Christian Council*, (Accra: Christian Council of the Gold Coast, 1955), 48.

118   Noel Q. King, *Religions of Africa: A Pilgrimage into Traditional Religions* (New York, Evanston, and London: Harper and Row Publishers, 1970), 57.

hand, this new trend does not prevent people from seeking additional spiritual protection against 'very evil and unscrupulous witches'. But this may still be understood in the terms 'the more protected, the better'.

While writing on *The Influence of Witchcraft* in Ghana, Hans Debrunner touched on one important issue that is significant to this study. In his study, Debrunner rightly identified the psychological conflict brought about by "the old traditional African" culture and Western civilization.[119] According to Debrunner:

> There was a struggle of two systems of economy: the old one which we may call tribal communism with its emphasis on the stewardship of the individual for the clan or the tribe fighting with the western system of private ownership and monetary economy.[120]

In a cynical argument, he stated that the old system suffered as it lost its "good elder" to the modern "successful rascal", "the 'big man'". "The old order, no longer understood and appreciated, was yet acting as a setback. And the new order was yet to be understood".[121] These conflicting values which had hitherto been a challenge under early mission Christianity and Western civilization are gradually being reconciled under the categories, African Christianity, African Renaissance or *sankofa*.[122] Under these new identities, many Africans, including the Nankani of various social strata and gender, engage in diverse practices (building, caring and clothing the families) with nuanced value justifications. In these cases, the old concept of witchcraft, which was hitherto fraught with suspicion, fear, intimidation and terror, is toned down and given a new meaning and understanding.

The belief in witchcraft and its interpretive threat to modern development continues, but its contextual dynamics over time and space, as well as the impact of the changes arising from these, on rural development, should not be overlooked. This incursion, initiated by the literature review of *Tongnaab*, has brought to the fore the importance of such a study in indigenous religions and development.

---

119   Debrunner, "The Influence of Witchcraft," 46.
120   Ibid.
121   Ibid.
122   Nkwi, "Rethinking the Role of the Elites in Rural Development," 181, 191.

In conclusion, this chapter has focused on the Nankani and their understanding and interpretation of development, an understanding that has emerged from their individual and collective self-reflected religio-cultural experiences. With a native researcher, the approach for them has been, 'together, let us tell our story'.[123] From that perspective, the problems of underdevelopment are not completely posited in the past, they are also seen in the continuous unfolding of events. A process that perpetually neglects their religio-cultural heritage and to this, they say, it is time for stocktaking.

As in the preceding chapters, I have employed what Nolan calls "Development Narratives" to posit the different viewpoints.[124] Unlike the Western economic model, the traditional Nankani concept of development is one of reproduction and a communal venture. It acknowledges the need for different resource inputs, but stresses the need for such a composition to instil life, relationships and unity. As the anthropologist Thomas Eriksen argues, in the context of cultural relativism, there is no "intellectual value" in defining development in per capita terms.[125] For Eriksen, local contexts are essential for constructing sociocultural-friendly models of development. The difference in the two conceptualizations is that, in the traditional society, people do not necessarily rationalize to the conclusive ends before embarking on activities. Such rationalizations are often by-products; that is, an after reflection on what people have said and done. In other words, people articulate and act, not write. Taking the funeral example, why would people take time off from their jobs or risk their lives to travel on dangerous roads to show solidarity to non-relations? It is these actions that are articulated through proverbs and sayings. They are not abstract philosophies and theories; they are distilled from practical experience. This is not to say there is no theorizing at all; it is relative to the situation at hand.

What is also significant is that, despite the immense changes, it is quite reasonable to argue that the foundations of Nankani religio-cultural systems and community livelihood are still pre-colonial. The *tindanas*, chiefs and elders are still the recognized community religio-political leaders. Although their authority has declined due to the

---

123 See chapter six.
124 Nolan, *Development Anthropology*, 235-6.
125 Thomas Hylland Eriksen, *Small Places, Large Issues: An Introduction to Social and Cultural Anthropology*, 2nd ed. (London: Pluto Press, 2001), 255.

modern socio-political and national administrative machinery, they are still a major source of power in community development. Technically speaking, no development project can take place in a community without the knowledge and approval of at least one of these leaders. This is particularly important where the allocation of land is concerned.[126] Development initiators in this context need to understand this and to incorporate these people and their views in their notions and discourses on sustainable development.

Nevertheless, the study has continuously shown some ambivalence in the way the different members of the society are perceived and incorporated into the system. This is especially glaring in the area of development. Although this can be viewed from generational, age and gender perspectives, the stance on the gender dimension is exceptional and needs further deliberation. In response to this, the next chapter investigates the Nankani conception of gender and its impact on the development of the area.

---

126 W. T. W. Morgan, "Tropical African colonial experience," in *Tropical African Development: Geographical Perspectives*, ed. M. B. Gleave (Harlow: Longman Scientific and Technical, 1992), 45.

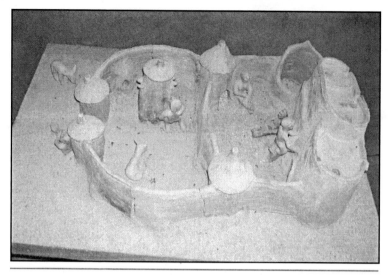

Picture 1: This is a model of the original housing of the Nankani for a single household. Picture is taken from the Catholic Museum in Navrongo.

Picture 2: A traditional compound unit showing a detine (round hut with grass roof) at the extreme end and a de'nyanga on the right. Picture is taken from the rooftop of a higher building in the same household.

Picture 3: Blending tradition with modernity.

Picture 4: Picture taken at the back of a traditional household to show the different structural designs used. The foreground is part of the compound house farm, hence, used for farming during the raining season. See Picture 3:5 for example.

Picture 5: This picture illustrates the scenery of a typical Nankani household during the raining or agricultural season. In the foreground is the early millet crop known as naara. This crop is only sown on the household (compound) farmlands i.e. around residential areas. The picture is taken from a family album.

Picture 6: This is the traditional form of wall decoration. Picture is taken from the Catholic Museum in Navrongo. All the resources for decoration are environmentally friendly, from clay stones and fruit trees. The wood is the ladder for getting onto the rooftop. The others are traditional mats.

141

Picture 7: This is a front view of a de'nyanga. This is an example of the use of tar. Both the wall design and the maintenance work (plastering) involved the use of tar.

Picture 8: This is a part of the Sirigu women's project. This part, which is still under construction, is used as a guest house for tourists. It is a combination of modern building materials and the traditional architectural design.

Picture 9: This is called the kiemaninga in the de'nyanga, with a representation of a woman's pots or store room. It also represents a woman private space. Toolluum is kept in these pots. Picture is taken from the Catholic Museum in Navrongo.

Picture 10: This set of calabashes is the zalinga. It is another spiritual space for a woman. Some of these items are used for funeral rites. Behind the set of calabashes is the traditional grinding mill. This is usually in the second chamber (sadda) of the de'nyanga. Picture is taken from the Catholic Museum in Navrongo.

Picture 11: This is an example of an indoor (compound) sacred site. The bigger mould to the left is founding ancestor of this household. The other two are his descendants and their wives. See the insertion of the pots for the female ancestral shrines.

Picture 12: *This is a shrine of herbalist. The practicing herbalist was taken during the slave trade, with the aid of the gun. The gun is thus a symbolic presence and reminder of this particular ancestor.*

Picture 13: *This is an example of ancestral shrines outside a traditional household. To the left is a constructed hut (ponga) generally used as the male social-political space. These, including the entrance to the household are called the zenyore.*

Picture 14: *Children ploughing the household farm at the beginning of the sowing season with an ox and a donkey. The tradition has been the use of two bulls. Picture is taken in Kandiga.*

Picture 15: *This is the chief of Kandiga and his elder. The chief is wearing a dansika (smock) with the munga (red hat), two of the symbols of chieftaincy in Northern Ghana.*

Picture 16: *The Tindana of Kandiga at the extreme left, wearing a skin. Meeting was originally scheduled as an in-depth interview but he called his elders and it became a group discussion. Picture taken during discussions.*

Picture 17: *Former Meat Marketing Board cattle ranch project housing. Situate on the Kologo-Naga road.*

Picture 18: Inside the Navrongo Cathedral, Catholic Church, Ghana. A mixture of traditional wall designs with Catholic symbols. The triangular designs are the traditional wanzagsi symbol. Perhaps depicting the presence of women or the church as a family.

Chapter Four

THE DYNAMICS OF GENDER IN AN AFRICAN SOCIETY

Poka ka kuuri waafu mwata zuo[1]
(A woman does not behead a snake after killing it.)

The above proverb epitomizes the Nankani conceptual framework of gender. Its importance lies in its role as a boundary marker. According to this proverb, a Nankani woman should not perform or claim leading roles. Additionally, a woman must not claim credit for her achievement(s). In other words, a woman should know the limits of her domain in relation to the traditional gender and gender related structure(s).

In the first place, traditional public leadership roles are often adjoined to religious roles. As a patriarchal society where women are carefully subordinated, Nankani women do not play overt political or leading religious roles.[2] Even where this is visible, they are dependent on male leadership or roles. Their dual identity status, natal and marital, does not favourably expose them to such a mandate since their allegiance at any one moment is held in suspicion. In this regard, although women's specific roles or participation in religion, community and family are crucial, they are regarded as complementary, and therefore, subsidiary.[3] These roles range from their physical presence, preparation of religious meals, observations of rules and taboos as well as the active performance of prescribed rituals. On the other hand, men are traditionally responsible for all manners of leadership roles.

---

1   Nankani proverb.
2   Fortes, *Oedipus and Job in West African Religion*, 12.
3   Betty Friedan, *The Feminine Mystique* (London: Penguin Books, 1963), 13.

These include religious, political, community, family as well as other ritual and social leadership roles. It is a male responsibility to seek religious knowledge and understanding in prevailing situations, through the already all preserved male practice of divination, and to carry out the findings associated with it.[4] With men in the realm of public affairs, heads of families, clan heads, diviners, *tindanas* (land priests) and chiefs, the exhibition of bravery, mastery and control, must also be theirs. It is my contention that this proverb is tailored to secure this end, an all inclusive dominance.

Secondly, the proverb instils the view that a woman's achievement or success story must always find expression in the ambit of a male, no matter how young that male may be. The killing of a snake is perceived as a act of bravery and, therefore, achievement. Traditionally, the only testimony of such bravado is the display of the head of the snake. The Nankani believe that women by nature (fearful and timid) are incapable of the bravery needed for both actions. However, if for any reason, a woman is able to kill a snake, she will still not have the guts to behead it.[5] On the other hand, a male, no matter how young or cowardly, can easily do this. Such a male will then behead the dead snake and claim credit for the brave act. This scenario is translated into virtually every sphere of life, whereby women keep living in the shadow of men. This proverb is a reflection of the gendered way of life among the Nankani. Traditionally, a woman may cultivate a parcel of land but will not lay claim to the farm or the produce as her own. She will have to attribute it to her husband or nearest male kin. A woman may also possess cows, goats, sheep, fowls or she may even construct a hut or compound from her personal resources, but she will not openly or publicly lay claim to them. A male name must be and is always associated with such achievements. It is a male who must always replace her. This indicates that, for the Nankani, a woman can only be glorified through a man.

Women who deviate from this norm are often labelled as strong-headed, or 'men', and sometimes subjected to insinuations and ridicule. This norm was so pervasive in the recent past that it affected the education of girls. In school, girls who showed signs of academic prowess

---

4   Apusigah, "Diagnosing Poverty in Northern Ghana," 61.

5   Janet Sayers, "On the description of psychological sex differences," in *Sex-role Stereotyping,* eds. Oonagh Hartnett, Gill Boden and Mary Fuller (London: Tavistock Publications Ltd., 1979), 48-54.

suffered all sorts of verbal abuse, culminating in some of them dropping out of school. Presently, the situation is different. Even though the proverb is still in use and the norm lingers on, its effect has been weakened considerably by the influence of social change and modernity. This is especially evident in its secondary role. Slow though it has been, the success of the few persistent women who made it through the odds has precipitated an attitudinal change. Social change and modern education have also affected the basic structure of Nankani households and the roles that individuals play therein. Women are becoming *de facto* heads of households as well as sole bread winners. Although different because of the lack of religious duties, the presence of women in modern leadership structures, especially in politics, has not only projected them as capable leaders, but has also broken the monopoly that men held in this area. This is forcing into eventual oblivion the perception that a woman can only be glorified through a man. Indeed, it is now common for Nankani women not only to kill snakes but also to behead them as public testimony of her unlimited capacity and ability.

The reality and interpretations surrounding the status and role of women in many traditional African religions and societies is quite controversial. An article on the role of women in African religion presents such a scenario. Before citing the Akan proverb, "[a] woman is a flower in a garden; her husband, the fence around it", Mbiti acclaims the proverb as "the beautiful comparison and mutual complement between wife and husband". After the citation, however, he concludes with "[s]o the women need all the protection and care men can give them".[6] In this case, one wonders if Mbiti is not simply endorsing the view that African women's status, roles and subsequent edification must be channelled through and by men.

Joseph Akinęle Ọmọyajowo's article in the same volume presents similar viewpoints.[7] According to Ọmọyajowo, the religious sphere "is so fundamentally masculine" that "women are not accorded any visibly prominent status in religious matters".[8] Even though he pro-

---

6   John S. Mbiti, "Flowers in the Garden: The Role of Women in African Religion," in *African Traditional Religions in Contemporary Society*, ed. Jacob, K. Olupona (Minnesota: Paragon House, 1991), 68.

7   Joseph Akinęle Ọmọyajowo, "The Place of Women in African Traditional Religion and among the Yoruba," in *African Traditional Religions In Contemporary Society*, ed. Jacob, K. Olupona (Minnesota: Paragon House, 1991), 79.

8   Ibid., 73.

vides religious resources on the role of women in the Yoruba religion, he continues to articulate what he calls "the male-chauvinist attitude", giving both force and reinforcement.[9] The projection of these views amidst his claims that women cannot remain passive because their contribution to society is essential raises concerns that are similar to those stated above. Like the case of the Syrophoenician woman, is he saying African women should continue to wait for the crumbs that fall from the children's table? (Mark 7:24-30). Ọmọyajowo's view is that:

> Generally and globally, the superiority of men over women has always been taken for granted. Women themselves seem to have internalized this image of female inferiority (a situation in which I have seen the women's liberation or feminist movements as no more than apologetic) and have therefore somehow taken male domination as the natural order of things.[10]

In other words, the current state of discourse on gender in Africa is beset with contradictions and ambiguities. This places emphasis on contextual studies as a means of substantiation. Nevertheless, greater care is needed in the interpretations of the available sources.[11]

This chapter outlines gender from the viewpoint of the Nankani. It examines the influence of contemporary gender perspectives on traditions for an up-to-date consideration on the Nankani and their views on gender. This is discussed in four sub-headings. The first contextually defines gender. This is followed by a discussion on the Nankani religio-cultural conception of gender. The third takes on the interpretations and understanding of modern concepts of gender as a result of current social change. The final part examines the implication of the differing strands and their impact on sustainable development in the community. The latter is discussed as problems and challenges.

---

9   Ọmọyajowo, "The Place of Women in African Traditional Religion and among the Yoruba," 77.
10   Ibid, 73.
11   See Rattray's interpretation of daughters' children. Rattray, *The Tribes of the Ashanti Hinterland*, 161-2.

CONTEXTUALIZING GENDER

Current discourse on gender and its conceptual theory of relationships are generally defined as socio-cultural constructs.[12] Acknowledged as culturally specific, gender is said to embody a set of characteristics that helps to identify the requisite socially acceptable behaviour of the two sexes (male and female) in a given society.[13] Within these broad frameworks, with the exception of the works of feminist theologians, the religious factor is often inadequately expressed.[14] Perhaps, this has to do with the general conceptual understanding of culture as an encompassing phenomenon, embodying beliefs, practices and values.[15] Theoretically, this understanding should be acceptable and accommodating to the Nankani, with reference to their conceptualization of *malma* (religion). This is not so, since for the Nankani, the religious underpinning of gender is not properly articulated.

According to the Nankani, the religious element is 'missing in the cracks'. Consequently, the modern concept of gender is perceived as an abstract, the core of which is *voore* (empty). It lacks the requisite personality which is *vam* (life) to provide the life support needed to make it whole. From this perspective, emptiness cannot hold anything together. In the same vein, it (emptiness) cannot be held. According to this logic, 'emptiness begets emptiness: a complete circle of wasted time and energy'. Simply put, the modern concept of gender is not

---

12   Sally B. Purvis, "Gender Construction," in *Dictionary of Feminist Theologies*, eds. Letty M. Russell and J. Shannon Clarkson (Louisville, Kentucky: Westminster John Knox Press, 1996), 124-5. See also, Lummis, "Gender Institutions," in Russell and Clarkson, 125-6 and Judith Lorber and Susan A. Farrell, "Principles of Gender Construction," in *The Social Construction of Gender*, eds. Judith Lorber and Susan A. Farrell (Newbury Part, London and New Delhi: Sage Publications, 1991), 7.

13   Juliana Makuchi Nfah-Abbenyi, "Gender, Feminist Theory, and Post-Colonial (Women's) Writing," in *African Gender Studies: A Reader*, ed. Oyèrónké Oyěwùmí (New York and England: Palgrave Macmillan, 2005), 259 and Meredith B. McGuire, *Religion: The Social Context*, 2nd ed. (Belmont, California: Wadworth Publishing Company, 1987), 96-7.

14   In most of these cases, religion is simply viewed in terms of social stratification. McGuire, *Religion*, 96.

15   Hannah W. Kinoti, "Culture," in *Dictionary of Feminist Theologies*, eds. Letty M. Russell and J. Shannon Clarkson (Louisville, Kentucky: Westminster John Knox Press, 1996), 63. See also, Verhelst, *No Life Without Roots*, 19.

life-giving. Therefore, it does not possess the requisite tenets to be integrated into the Nankani religio-cultural system.

The argument is that, although modern gender purports to be dealing with the socio-cultural relationships between two sexes, it is in reality amalgamating the existing differences to produce one. It is contended that life is made of differences not unilateral living. Expressing this view in the words, *ba yan eti to za'a la pogsi* (they are now making us all women), some Nankani men explain that what the modern person says and what s/he does are completely different. They noted that the modern view of gender is just one of the passing phases of human existence; a phase they hope might usher in a new sense of understanding and vitality. Something, though they cannot presently articulate clearly, will regenerate the future society by bringing about a new sense of value for life (family life), unity and peace. This is contrasted with what they conceive as a 'decaying world'. As for the current state of emptiness, 'we are all caught in the whirlwind, waiting to see the end'. These pessimistic sentiments fit the post-colonialist Gayatri Spivak's 'vanishing present'.[16] For the Nankani male, there is need to reconsider and properly articulate gender in a more holistic manner. They insist that if gender really entails some cultural significances, then it must be allowed to express itself in the most appropriate way, where and when it is most needed. Thus gender in Africa must also reflect the religio-cultural needs of African societies.[17]

From this philosophical yet reactionary approach to the understanding of the modern concept of gender, the question remains as to what gender is from the traditional viewpoint. There are two main expressions underlying gender which bear the crux of the Nankani conceptual framework of gender. Situated within traditional sayings, they are not only adequately preserved; they serve as quick references in conversations. The saying, *Wine na-am neri sa'la sie'm la bala* (that is how God created the human being) is a core expression that is appropriated by the different sexes as *Wine na-am buda/poka sie'm la bala* (that

16   Chakravorty Gayatri Spivak, *A Critique of Postcolonial Reason: Toward a History of the Vanishing Present.* (Cambridge, MA: Harvard UP, 1999), 337.

17   Brigid M. Sackey, *New Directions in Gender and Religion: The Changing Status of Women in African Independent Churches* (Lanham: Lexington Books, 2006), 60 and Oyèrónké Oyěwùmí, *The invention of women: Making an African sense of Western gender discourse* (Minneapolis: University of Minnesota Press, 1997), 175-6.

is how God created the male/female). These expressions deal basically with the belief that the created sexes are God given. The second saying is expressed in a variety of ways as, *poka de'ne me ba la, poka tuune me ba la/pongne nba la* (that is also the woman's share/own, that is also a woman's work or this is feminine). Again, the feminine attributes are simply swapped with the masculine versions of *huda* and *budaane* to express the view of the male. Its appropriated versions are used to deal particularly with the roles and activities allocated to each sex.

In the first expression, the innate human (male/female) qualities given by the creator are highlighted. They refer to the core biological structure as well as reproductive roles of men and women. These, according to the Nankani, are natural qualities and must be allowed to function as they should. The second, on the other hand, is perceived as partly acquired qualities. These involve the socio-cultural qualities that are specific to each culture. Of particular importance to the Nankani is the belief that those which constitute the socio-cultural are not secular in themselves. First and foremost, they are derived from the creator's gift to that sex and each sex's chosen destiny.[18] Secondly, this implicitness is understood and incorporated into the culture. Finally, this knowledge is derived from the ancestors who have tried and tested these precepts and concepts. Gender is not only traditionally enshrined; the ancestors act as custodians. As a result, any fundamental change should be based on a comparably good and useful insight. Such a change must be one that enhances the well-being of the community and its heritage, 'and not one of emptiness and confusion'.

With this conceptual frame, the traditional definition of gender is "men deciding and women applying".[19] First of all, it is important to note here that the adoption of this definition was not pleasing to some community members.[20] As it is, the definition is loaded with meaning, deserving a critical analysis, since it presents one of the underlying

---

18   See also, Lise Østergaard, "Gender," in *Gender and Development: A Practical Guide*, ed. Lise Østergaard (London: Routledge, 1992), 5-6.

19   This definition was given by Juatera. It was adopted because he was the oldest person among those interviewed. My opinion is that he might still possess the core knowledge and views of tradition.

20   The lack of alternative definitions and the general understanding that the dissatisfaction expressed on the definition was a matter of wording ("too direct") and not in its substance, it was later allowed with due concerns. The protest perhaps shows the dynamics of change.

factors in current gender discourses. This however cannot be under-taken within the confines of this study. Nevertheless, the core of this definition underscores my initial field perspective of 'the critique of the other'.[21] Can the Nankani, who have been so critical about the lack of inclusiveness in modern concepts, be so oblivious of the implications of their own definition?

By implication, gender within the traditional Nankani community is primarily a sex matter. This seems to stand in direct opposition to current gender findings by African scholars, depicting a lack of uniformity in African communities.[22] It therefore calls on African researchers to pay particular attention to contextual issues and to be more open to differences.[23] Nonetheless, the views of Ifi Amadiume and Oyèrónké Oyěwùmí are fundamental and quite applicable to the Nankani. The differences lie in the way the Nankani distinguish between 'formulation' and 'application'. From this traditional perspective, the power to make or formulate laws or rules (decision-making) is a male sex prerogative. However, the application of the laws is largely dependent on women and young men, relative to the power structure. The man's role in terms of application is supervision. In her examination of gender and power, Lynne Segal draws attention to the underlying interconnectedness of "labour, power and desire" and their subsequent unyielding grip on reality. Although contextually different, the facts are the same, presenting some evidence of cross-cultural theoretical frameworks.[24] In other words, the presence of woman-to-woman marriages among the Nankani does not negate the view that this is a provision initiated by men to forestall an imminent male traditional leadership void in a given family. Hence, the differences between this and Amadiume's interpretation of the Nigerian woman-to-woman marriage attest to the different nuances in traditional practices among communities.

21 Despite being critical of the 'Other', there seem to be a lack of foresight in one's own short comings. This understanding is derived from the different analytical overview given by the Nankani vis-à-vis those given by development workers and gender advocates.

22 Ifi Amadiume, *Male Daughters, Female Husbands: Gender and Sex in African Society* (London: Zed, 1987); Oyěwùmí, *The invention of women*, 175.

23 Ifi Amadiume, *Reinventing Africa: Matriarchy, Religion and Culture* (London and New York: Zed Books, 1997).

24 Lynne Segal, *Slow Motion: Changing Masculinities, Changing Men* (London: Virago Press, 1990), 96-103.

Traditionally, therefore, elderly men or leaders do not perceive themselves as part of the framework of gender as in currents discourses. They are outside the scope of gender. With full control of the institutions of power, "authority, control and coercion", these men cannot see themselves subjected to their own constructs.[25] They administer gender and therefore cannot be part of gender.[26] As a result, their physical presence in modern gender discussions is related to their general 'watch dog' roles in the society. They are there to see 'what is new or happening', to know and to understand the new influences, not necessarily to implement or to be transformed. Nonetheless, some aspects of modern discussions on gender are reinterpreted to suit new and challenging situations. For instance, some irresponsible men disguised their act with the slogan, 'what a man can do, a woman can do better'. If this is the case, they argue, their irresponsibility is a test for women to prove themselves. In other instances, the men simply re-phrase the claim by development workers with the expression, 'development workers give their help to women with the conviction that you [women] are better managers, if that is so, why don't you manage all of us'. This type of cynicism in the interpretation and practice of gender is currently a problem.

There are other ways of understanding the current concept of gender among the Nankani. Although influenced by the above, these new interpretations are the most commonly held views in the community. These are however derived from the local understanding of the history of development and gender issues in the area. Here, three interrelated but different definitions of gender can be found. Though basic, these definitions have far reaching implications on the subject matter of this study. In the first place, the general understanding of gender is *p ɔgsi yela* (sic. women's issues). Gender in context pertains to women. Although this definition is closely related to the above discussion, it is particularly situated within women or gender programmes in the community. This relates to earlier projects on Women in Development (WID), Women and Development (WAD) and the current Gender and Development (GAD) from which men generally view themselves as excluded. In addition to male exclusion, the projects addressed issues of women's well-being and empowerment. According to the men, the

---

25 Segal, *Slow Motion*, 97.
26 Warren Steinberg, *Masculinity: Identity, Conflict, and Transformation* (Boston and London: Shambhala, 1993), 133-5.

projects initially dealt with issues of food and nutrition, child care, health and hygiene, petty trading, and agro-processing. These activities fell within the confines of traditional female roles and concept of *pog'mengre* (ideal/good woman). As such, they were accepted and simply classified as *pogsi yela*.

The second understanding is *pogsi na budaasi yela* (men and women issues). Unlike the other, this is principally based on the current GAD approach. It is used by gender advocates and activists. Even though development workers use it, community development animators like John Atuwah reconstructs it as *pogsi na budaasi tin'malgo yela pu'am* (women's and men's development issues) or *pogsi na budaasi lag'gube tire ma-le tinga* (women and men combining efforts for the development of the land). At the community level, however, 'men and women issues' is used for both genders while *a lag'gube nde tin'malgo* (combining efforts to develop the land/combining efforts is the development of the land) is used for GAD. Nankani men view this definition of gender as a new attempt to rope men into women's issues. Consequently, this second definition is overshadowed by the first. With many of the NGOs running GAD or programmes aimed at mainstreaming gender into existing ones, the atmosphere appears saturated with 'women's issues' reinforcing this perceived notion. It is noted that even where NGO activities are said to be inclusive, they do not adequately include men in their entrepreneurial skills development or income-generation schemes.

The third definition is somehow reactionary.[27] This is basically a male perspective and it was presented by men. In this definition, gender is simply perceived as *pognɛ* (feminine). It was at times presented with a dismissive tone. According to the proponents of this view, development workers initially dealt with female issues and with women, but now, *ba yan vaari budasi yan paasa* (they are now adding the men into it). The most resistant men used the words, *ba yan taare di-nra budasi* (they are now pressuring men with it). The basis of this resentment is based on the current drive to involve men in the 'so-called' feminine activities of household chores, child care and agro-processing. Writing on *Religion: Social Context*, Meredith McGuire sees these classifications as a limited form of caste system.[28] This involves the socio-economic, religio-cultural and gender injustices in communities. The strict traditional

---

27   Steinberg, *Masculinity*, 133-4.

28   McGuire, *Religion*, 98.

gender classification is making these men feel *ba base ti budasi lebgra la pogsi* (they are turning men into women), hence a threat to their identity and being. According to Warren Steinberg, male resistance to changing roles is closely tied to both the psychological and sociological environment in which the individuals find themselves. For instance, despite the drive for change, men who exhibit feminine tendencies or are found performing certain female jobs are still called *pog'nindoro* (women-men). Parents are also insistent in maintaining the traditional gender spaces and divisions of labour.

Irrespective of the different representation, gender is used within the context of "men's and women's issues". This was agreed upon at the community level and this makes it culturally specific. Besides, it provides opportunities for the different genders to address their specific development needs as men's issues and women's issues. It is therefore used and promoted by some development workers in the area. Its usage serves as an interacting point between the Western and indigenous views. Although arguable, it is my opinion that this notion of gender was accepted by the various male participants because it continues to provide the framework in which the traditional understanding of gender can be expressed. In addition, it provides avenues for economic opportunities. By this I am referring to the way these new formulations of gender enable traditional women to take on extra responsibilities that yield economic benefits for the entire family. While the latter is encouraged, efforts geared towards female assertiveness, those aimed at her personal and socio-political empowerment are thwarted as shown above.

TRADITIONAL CONCEPTS OF GENDER

It is clear that the Nankani are somehow a gender polarized community. Even though there is no Nankani word for gender, it is perceived as a feminine attribute. Initially understood as *pogsi yela* (women's issues), it has developed into *pogsi na budaasi yela* (men's and women's issues). Conceived as a foreign concept, some Nankani men view 'gender' as a metamorphosis of 'women', the sole aim of which is to lure men into playing feminine roles. There was an insistence, during my fieldwork, that any discussion on the Nankani conception of gender should be rooted in the traditional worldview. That is to say, "that is how God created the human being" or "that is how God created the male/female" and 'to each sex a role was given'.[29]

The discussions on gender in the communities were always re-established within the domains of sex and sexuality. These two provided the foundations through which issues were presented. As shown above, sex and sexuality are perceived religio-cultural constructs. The two categories bestow different status. Sex, although biological, is religiously constructed as male and female and religiously authorized to reproduce through sexual intercourse. Thus, biological sex is divine and static. For this reason, people at either side of the divide must remain as such. Any deviation from this norm, such as a baby born sexless or a hermaphrodite, is open to suspicion and classified as *chinchirisgo*.[30] Perceived as potential evil spirits, these children were, and are to some extent still, ritually eliminated through *nyusigo*. *Nyusigo* is an act of force feeding a child with liquid substances.[31] To help maintain this stereotypical gender framework, efforts are made for children and young adults to conform to the life of heterosexuality, a construct that is currently challenged.[32] Nonetheless, the Nankani adheres to "the two-sex model".[33] Any deviation in adulthood is perceived as *paa-la* (destiny) and for this, spiritual help is sought.

Sexuality on the other hand incorporates the perceived notions of sex and individual sexual preferences. This takes into consideration people's behaviour with regard to the established religio-cultural norms

---

29   These were recurrent themes on all the discussions on gender. This included women even though the nuances were different.

30   Anne Bolin, "Traversing Gender: Cultural context and gender practices," in *Gender Reversals and Gender Cultures: Anthropological and Historical Perspectives*, ed. Sabrina Petra Ramet (London and New York: Routledge, 1996), 25.

31   See chapter one, 48-50.

32   Rosemary Pringle, "Absolute Sex? Unpacking the Sexuality/Gender relationship", in *Rethinking Sex: Social Theory and Sexuality Research*, ed. R. W. Connell and G. W. Dowsett (Carlton, Victoria: Melbourne University Press, 1992), 77 and R. W. Connell and G. W. Dowsett, "Introduction", in *Rethinking Sex: Social Theory and Sexuality Research*, eds. R. W. Connell and G. W. Dowsett (Carlton, Victoria: Melbourne University Press, 1992), 2.

33   Darlene M. Juschka, "Gender," in *The Routledge Companion to the Study of Religion*, ed. John R. Hinnells (London and New York: Routledge, 2005), 230.

of heterosexuality.[34] It includes people's desire for marriage and also, ability for reproduction. Within the sphere of childbearing, one's relationship or care of children is monitored. In the past, women were specially watched for post-natal production of breast milk and general relationship with baby. Wherever problems arose, efforts were made to regularize the 'anomaly'. It was also socio-culturally unacceptable for a woman to engage in post-natal sexual intercourse. It was the belief that such an act polluted the breast milk and hampered the health and growth of the child. Women who engaged in this practice were ridiculed and considered over indulgent.[35] If the women became pregnant, the child was taken from the mother for proper care. Such a child was referred to as a *ngiya*. It must however be noted that these attitudes are currently watered down. This is perhaps due to cross-cultural influences, the introduction of Western health care and family planning services.

At birth the first enquiries and expressions are always associated with finding out the sex of the child. A male child is welcomed as the arrival of the landlord (*yidana*). Its representational name is *Ayidana*. With a female child, the expression is 'another house thing' (*a yema yeri bunu*) and the associated name is *Ayingabunu*. When more females are born, this expression may become *Atignee* (satisfied with cattle) signifying the cows that will be given as bride wealth. A family that begets only females may earn the name *Adogiyeele* (given birth in the wind – as in winnowing). This refers to the view that, like winnowing in the wind, a girl's future destination is not certain until marriage. All these expressions are symbolized and given as names. While the girl-child is defined within the context of an outsider, the boy-child who is perpetually identified as guardian is immediately declared a landlord. These initial declarations become substantive on the third and fourth days when the child is named and incorporated into the society.

Biological sex differentiation is also portrayed by the symbolic ritual presentations at the woman's natal home. For every first born child, a cockerel is sent for a boy and a hen for a girl. This is followed by three days (for boys) and four days (for girls) waiting period before the

---

34   Lloyda Fanusie, "Sexuality and Women in African Culture," in *The Will to Arise: Women, Tradition, and the Church in Africa*, eds. Mercy Amba Oduyoye and Musimbi R. A. Kanyoro (Maryknoll, New York: Orbis Books, 2001), 141.

35   Jane C. Goodale, "Gender, sexuality and marriage: a Kaulong model of nature and culture", in *Nature, Culture and Gender*, eds. Carol MacCormack and Marilyn Strathern (Cambridge: Cambridge University Press, 1980), 134.

naming ceremony is conducted. These numbers are symbolic and are used for demarcating ritual periods relating to the sexes. The numbers have become gender stereotyped for masculinity and femininity. It is significant that the payment of bride wealth and other ritual relationships between in-laws ceases during pregnancy. These relationships can however resume after the baby and mother are reintroduced to the community on their respective symbolic days.

Thus biological sex differentiation is the basic determinant for Nankani gender.[36] It does not only confer on the individual a sense of identity but also, the roles and status of that specific gender. At an early age of between five to seven years, girls are slowly introduced to domestic chores by their siblings and mother. With time, a feminine identity as well as the religio-culturally demarcation of spaces are slowly inculcated in her. At the same age, boys are sent out to the *zenyore* (outside or gate) to be with the male members of the household or society. They are also expected to be engrained in the masculine perspective of life. Recalcitrant girls are driven back by the men or boys outside.[37] This role stereotyping expands as children grow.[38] With time, their spaces, roles and activities are clearly and socially defined. Women remain inside with the domestic and maintenance regime while men are outside with the political, socio-cultural, ritual and economic affairs.[39]

Puberty and courtship mark the threshold of a new identity for both sexes. At this stage, young men are expected to begin to exhibit masculine characteristics of power, possessiveness and control. Young women are expected to show feminine qualities of respect, honour, humility and self-control as well as hard work and good manners.[40] With an exogamous marriage system, daughters serve as a good source of linkage between clans and communities by establishing in-law relationships. Nonetheless, the above qualities are perceived as essential

36   Oyeronke Olajubu, *Women in the Yoruba Religious Sphere*, Forward, Jacob K, Olupona (Albany State: University of New York Press, 2003), 8.

37   Charlie Lewis, "Early sex-role socialization," in *The psychology of Sex Roles*, eds. David J. Hargreaves and Ann M. Colley (London: Harper and Row Ltd., 1986), 98-101.

38   Ruth B. Ekstrom, "Intervention strategies to reduce sex-role stereotyping in education", in *Sex-role Stereotyping*, eds. Oonagh Hartnett, Gill Boden and Mary Fuller (London: Tavistock Publications Ltd., 1979), 217-20.

39   Fortes, *Religion, Morality and the Person*, 206.

40   Sayers, "On the description of psychological sex differences," 50-1.

164

for the maintenance of such relationships. Since it is the woman who must relocate, it is she who needs such sublime character formulation to enable her readjust to her new environment. The boy, on the other hand, needs the power of mastery and domination to enable him subjugate and control the incoming partner. Thus, two different strategies are used to train children and these two lie at the bottom of any current discourse on gender or its power relations.[41]

Marriage marks the stage of maturity.[42] For males, it is the stage where personal ownership and control begins to take shape. With females, ownership and control passes from the woman's natal lineage to the men in her marital lineage. For the Nankani, this transfer of ownership and control does not represent a complete surrender. Patrilineage natal men continue to play supervisory roles over the general welfare of their daughters. Their roles are especially crucial and clearly manifested at death, during the protracted burial and funeral rites of their daughter. Not only is their presence required before burial, they must be informed of the cause of death and the attempts made to save their daughter's life. They are given a full inspection of the body and they provide a burial shroud and mat. In like manner, they must be informed and negotiated with prior to the final funeral rites as they play a crucial part in key areas of the rite. Besides these, a woman's funeral rites are not complete until her 'spirit' is ritually returned to her natal home and reintegrated through other funeral ceremonies with her natal ancestors.[43] Thus, although 'ownership' and control is transferred from the natal family to the marital family, some degree of supervision and 'ownership' is maintained.

In marriage, a woman is expected to be faithful, modest, obedient, appreciative, friendly and serviceable. She is also supposed to be hard working, versatile and creative in the production and management of household staples. These include harvesting and gathering, processing, preservation, storage as well as the judicious use of resources. In addition to these, the ideal woman must be hygienically conscious of herself

41 Kevin Howells, "Sex roles and sexual Behaviour", in *The psychology of Sex Roles*, eds. David J. Hargreaves and Ann M. Colley (London: Harper and Row Ltd., 1986), 269-70.

42 Helen Ware, "Female and Male Life-Cycles," in *Female and Male in West Africa*, ed. Christine Oppong (London: George Allen and Unwin, 1983), 32.

43 Rattray, *The Tribes of the Ashanti Hinterland*, 167 and Fortes, *Religion, Morality and the Person*, 70.

and her environs.[44] For this reason, Nankani women pay a great deal of attention to structural household maintenance, investing time and energy in creative and colourful designs of buildings, pottery, sleeping mats and baskets.[45] On the other hand, men are expected to be possessive, accumulative, domineering and controlling. They must meet the spiritual and material needs of the family, including the provision of food, housing and security. As an agrarian society, men are responsible for the preservation and storage of seed crops and food stored in silos. The silo is a distinct male space and it is a taboo for women to go into a man's silo. Unique male spiritual objects are sometimes kept in silos. Another exclusive sacred space for men is the quiver. This is in contrast to the woman's pots and *zalinga*.[46] The silo is also an economic power source for men. When a woman's household consumption staples are depleted, she relies on the man to provide rations from the silo. This depends on the man's willingness and perception of household needs.

This general conceptualization does not take into consideration the inherent gender differentiations in the system. Although the above is perceived as the standard, in reality this is a male perspective. It does not account for the intricate dynamics of the female gender. For the female, 'the partial outsider', her identity at any given time is dependent on 'the stable insider' (male). Hence, a daughter's identity is dependent on her father or male kin and for a wife, her husband or his male kinsmen. This male dependency does not only characterize the female's identity and status, it also affects the above factors. Without completely relinquishing her previous religio-cultural identity and roles, she takes on her husband's identity, status and all that goes with them. Again, although hard work, good health and physical exuberance are important qualities for marriage, a woman's economic identity is dependent on her husband. These factors are both restrictive and burdensome to the woman.

Nankani women do not own or control land. Access to land depends on their position as wives. Wives 'own' and control backyard gardens where they grow their household vegetables. In the absence of wives, daughters may have access and temporary ownership. Women mainly serve as farm hands on family farmlands as daughters or wives.

---

44 Toyin Falola, *The Power of African Cultures* (Rochester: University of Rochester Press, 2003), 252.

45 See pictures 6 and 9.

46 *Zalinga,* a special kind of a netted rope arranged with calabashes and other ritual valuables and hung in the room. See picture 10.

A woman's access to family farmland depends on having sons or the benevolence of the extended family of her husband.

Animals are a major source of wealth among the Nankani. Ranked third, after family and land, they are the most visible sign of wealth in the communities. These comprise of cattle, sheep, goats, guinea fowls and fowls. Although women can own any or all of these, cattle, sheep and guinea fowls are generally regarded as male preserve while goats and fowls are for both genders.[47] Traditionally, all domestic animals fall under the control, ownership and care of men. These animals were inherited and their uses were restricted to ritual, marriage and gift purposes. As a result, women were traditionally not allowed into this area, since they neither inherit nor care for animals. Angulu Onwuejeowu argues that the exclusion of women from these areas implies men's control over and access to the viable economic opportunities. This limits women's ability to attain economic independence and empowerment, hence re-enforces their dependency status.[48]

In other words, because biological sex categorically renders the Nankani girl-child a relative outsider to her natal identity, she cannot assume any position of authority or leadership. This is because such leadership structures are independent of family and community hence can neither be subsumed by nor transferred to her male affine within the exogamous marriage system. Thus the stable male, who has complete insider status, is entitled to all leadership positions. Similarly, her relatively outsider identity status in marriage disqualifies her from such leadership positions as household head, 'tindana', chief as well as specific spiritual leadership roles. It is for these reasons that Meyer Fortes states that, "[w]omen are never wholly emancipated from male control but marrying out and achieving motherhood frees daughters from parental control".[49]

Yet it is within these sharply divided spaces that personal identity and gender roles can be understood. While men occupy the authoritative, domineering and powerful roles, women are left at the periphery with subservient roles which they now subscribe as God given – a reli-

---

47   These domesticated animals are considered docile in this traditional area; hence, within the range of women.

48   M. Angulu Onwuejeogwu, *The Social Anthropology of Africa: An Introduction* (London: Heinemann, 1975), 23-4.

49   Fortes, *Religion, Morality and the Person*, 198.

gio-cultural heritage. Phoebe Miller notes that among the Afikpo Igo, while "men's world stresses control over land and the laws and religious functions of the community; the women's world is much narrower than the men's and is domestic in nature".[50] The perspective that is often lost in this broader outline of men's control over land, laws and religious functions is their role in the formulation of the norms and values of rural African living. Those who control the religious roles control and command everything and everyone else. This is because every other thing is subject to them and they use religion to legitimize everything. As Songsore puts it, "[t]he most important political and social distinctions were organised along generational and gender lines and power was exercised by council of elders who were often men".[51] It can therefore be concluded that "women are trapped in a male-dominated ideology, which they have internalised and which traps them into gender inequality which impacts on many other areas of their lives".[52]

African gender and feminist scholars are not only contesting what they perceive as an unguarded Western imported gender framework, they are also arguing out a contextual theory of flexibility.[53] Drawing from her matrilineal Akan background, Brigid Sackey argues that any discourse on gender in the African context should be viewed from a three dimensional perspective of "exclusivity, inclusivity and flexibility".[54] Believing that there is no single way to understanding and interpreting the gendered environment in the African continent, she illustrates how these three dimensions can sometimes function synonymously in the person of the queen mother among the Akan.[55] For her, the African scenario defies strict classifications.

Although scholars have variously illustrated this viewpoint, there is still the need to question whether these diverse perspectives are instances of ambiguity or genuine alternative forms of understanding gender in the African context. It is true that some cases defy any strict

50 Phoebe Miller, "Sex Polarity and Among the Afikpo Igo," in *African Religious Groups and Beliefs: Papers in Honor of William R. Bascom*, ed. Simon Ottenberg (India and U. S. A.: Folklore Institute, 1982), 80.
51 Songsore, *Regional Development in Ghana*, 26.
52 Nye, *Religion*, 84-5.
53 Amadiume, *Male Daughters and Female Husbands*, 15 and Sackey, *New Directions in Gender and Religion*, 59-63.
54 Sackey, *New Directions in Gender and Religion*, 50-5.
55 Sackey, *New Directions in Gender and Religion*, 61.

gender categorization but do they not also present ambiguities? Thus we must ask, 'how are those involved interpreting these issues' before such analytical frameworks. In order that an intuitive understanding of the situation may be obtained, African scholars are interrogating not gender *per se*, but the related issues of sex, sexuality and identity in Africa.[56] The variety of issues covered by these scholars in different contexts raises questions as to whether the emerging constructs exhibit a sense of flexibility or ambiguity. To respond to such a critical issue in this study will not be possible. However, a brief examination of some aspects of the Nankani religio-cultural system and its impact on gender can provide some contextual understanding to these issues.

It was not uncommon to find, among the Nankani and their neighbouring Gurusi/Frafras peoples, that a *pog'yuwa* (daughter) was detained to 'stay home' (remain unmarried) in order that she might bear a son(s) to replenish the depleting or ageing male stock of her family.[57] Two options were opened to the daughters in this category. These were to beget the heirs themselves or marry other women to beget such heirs. The choice depended, to a large extent, on the family's preference and the family's predicament. In some cases, both scenarios were practised concurrently, especially, if the expected arrival of the son(s) was delayed. To facilitate an easier grasp of the two categories of women, I will use the term 'daughter' for those playing masculine roles and 'wives' for the women who are married under such contractual agreement. Each of the two options had distinct religio-cultural backing. Irrespective of the fact that both contradicted the standard code of conduct, they were organized within set rules.

In the first scenario, a daughter is officially excluded from the general norm of marriage by a proclamation or vow of her father or her male next of kin. With such promulgation, she must remain a spinster or 'suffer the spiritual consequences of breaking the role' set for her. She becomes a 'taboo' daughter in terms of being available for marriage. All suitors are turned away, noting that she is forbidden to marry. Although qualified persistent suitors may be allowed after such notification, the general interpretation is associated with the man's

---

56 Wairimu Ngaruiya Njambi and William E. O'Brien, "Revisiting 'Woman-Woman Marriage': Notes on Gikuyu Women", in *African Gender Studies: A Reader*, ed. Oyèrónké Oyěwùmí (New York and England: Palgrave Macmillan, 2005), 145-65.

57 See also Rattray, *The Tribes of the Ashanti Hinterland*, 51, 161-2

sexual desires and lust, not marital love. At the same time, his relationship with their daughter has no cultural acknowledgement. His presence may thus be tolerated because of the inherent potential for their
daughter to conceive and beget son(s). She may however be released
from the covenant to marry if the son(s) are delivered. The prohibition serves to declare her as someone 'set apart' and also to secure the
unique masculine role she is called to play. This is because as a patrilineal society, identity is aligned to the male stock. To accept and identify
a daughter's child as belonging to the family, the event must be well
founded and established for the integrity of the future heir and lineage.
Thus such an arrangement must be well known, at least to those who
matter. This is important in distinguishing these children from the
current trend of *yiyen coma* (spinsters' children or children generally
born by daughters outside marriage). The latter case is discussed below.

It is possible, in the first instance, for people to question these
practices in relation to incest taboos. Nonetheless, there are varied perspectives on the subject. As some anthropologists have observed, there
are instances where marriages are allowed after the fourth generation.
Among the Nankani, even though this may be possible through the
female line due to the exogamous system, considering the possibility
that each generation marks a crossing into a new clan. For the male
line, this is still forbidden. In many cases, these people may be living
together, as it were, under a single household. The same applies to
brotherly clans emanating from the same female ancestress. The situation is however different in the case of brotherly clans where the ancestors of the two clans were half brothers. Here, the practice of *yiyen zaba*
('home' or clan lovers) may be possible but not marriage.

The closest example is the Cho-o and the Nyangbisi clans in Naga.
These two are brotherly clans. The two, whose generational history
is beyond the eighth, continue to inherit each other's wives as in the
levirate system. Similarly, divorced women from one clan can remarry
into the other. However, the sons and daughters of the two clans
cannot marry each other. Although it is not allowed, a love relationship between the sons and daughters of these clans can be classified as
yiyen zaba. To allow or accept marriage within these 'brotherly' clans, a
ritual of 'breaking [severing] the calabash' must take place.[58] Although
Rattray described this ritual practice among the Nankannse (Gurunne

---

58   Rattray, *The Tribes of the Ashanti Hinterland*, 177-9.

speakers), his narrative is problematic. This is because even though there is a love relationship, and perhaps children, it is never recognized as a marriage by tradition until the ritual is performed. A calabash, which is a ritual, social and gender oriented symbol, must be severed by the young lovers, in the presence of their elders and ritual leaders to signify an end to the previous 'brotherly' relationship. The calabash with which the 'brothers' drank and ate from is symbolically torn apart (destroyed), bringing that phase to an end. It is only after this that the new relationship, which is an in-law relationship, can ensue. Of course, this act is preceded by various rituals of divination, libation and sometimes sacrifices. This practice, with slight variations, has already taken place in Kandiga within the Bembisi clan.

Children by the 'special' category of daughters were structurally placed. They obtained the same status and roles as sons begotten by other male members of the clan. They took the names of their mother's ancestry. Biological parentage is not demanded, they are religio-culturally begotten. This is religiously explained as an obedient daughter preserving the ancestry. This is different from children begotten by spinsters. Spinsters' children have no religio-cultural or social status or roles in the family or clan. Culturally, this set of children fall below the children of a widow or a divorced woman, whose little children might have followed their mother to her natal home. This notwithstanding, none of these children are structurally integrated into their mother's natal family. They remain outsiders even though they may be taken care of. It is also believed that they are specially looked after by the ancestors because they have no fathers. This is however perceived as a diversion of the spiritual blessings that might have been accrued by the main family members. It is therefore common to see boys from such situations being resettled or relocated in a new home after marriage.

To further illustrate some of the complexities surrounding this practice in our modern era, I refer to a case that was reported in one of the nation's news papers. On Saturday, March 13, 2004, the Ghanaian weekly paper, *The Mirror*, published an article in its front page with the heading: "STAY HOME AND MAKE BABIES: Custom Demands of Seamstress."[59] In that article, the old practice of using daughters to perpetuate a dying patrilineal line became a point of

---

59   "STAY HOME AND MAKE BABIES: Custom Demands of Seamstress", *The Mirror*, Saturday, March 13, 2004, 1.

interaction between tradition and modernity. As published in the paper, the traditional authorities of Zuarungo, a suburb of Bolgatanga in the Upper East Region, were at the centre of the controversy as the Centre for Sustainable Development Initiative (CENSUDI), a gender advocacy NGO based in region was against the practice. The inability of the two sides to solve the case amicably even though the directors of CENSUDI are also from Zuarungo shows the complexity of the situation. In other words, all the parties in this controversy are from the same community, yet they could not resolve the case.

In the second scenario, the 'special daughter' may be allowed or asked to marry another woman to beget the needed son(s). Usually, such marriages are allowed if the daughter is getting past child bearing age. Sometimes, these marriages are arranged if an already married daughter, usually old, returns home to take-up the role of restoring her ancestry. Already past childbearing age, the only possibility of fulfilling such a role is to marry another woman as if she were a child or representative son of her natal family. It must be noted that the latter can only take place during times of misfortunes or crisis resulting in the untimely death of the heir(s). The already married daughter then sees herself as a rescuer. In that context, special arrangements are made between her kinsmen and affine men to reinstate the woman as a daughter, not someone's wife. She must act as a daughter. This is because, if the status of a wife is maintained, the process will find expression in a different context. That is, it will be seen as the woman marrying a younger wife for her husband, another practice engaged by elderly women in the area.[60] Thus, the need to disengage the existing marriage is essential for establishing woman-to-woman marriages. At the same time, daughters cannot role play these marriages in absentia. The saying, *saana ka chire naboa* (a stranger does not go into a ruined or empty house), is often quoted to this effect. A marriage is an invitation to a new home and family not a *daboo* (an empty or ruined house).

This kind of marriage is contracted by the daughter's kinsmen and it is performed using her family name. The wife in such a marriage chooses her sex partners discreetly from the clan or community

---

60   Base on the traditional concept of the ideal woman, some elderly women withdraw from sexual intercourse when their son's wife gives birth. To facilitate this self-withdrawal, they arrange for younger wives for their husbands.

to beget the desired children.[61] The men involved in such a relationship are also aware that they have no claim to the children born through the relationship. Thus, while the living men play surrogate roles, the ancestral name in use begets children posthumously. The woman on the other hand, is not a widow and cannot remarry under the levirate system. The children from this arrangement are accorded full religio-cultural and social status.

Traditionally, the daughters in these roles who had hitherto felt responsible for restoring their ancestry may now have a sense of fulfilment. This is because even though females are culturally socialized to know that they belong to 'another house' through marriage, they are equally told that having a natal home is crucial to attaining identity and dignity in the marriage context. Children are taught the proverb, 'you do not use your left hand to point at your father's house'. Females grow up believing that having a natal home is as much an important part of their life as it is to have a marital home. It is a source of security and pride. This is one of the possible reasons why daughters willingly play such roles. Thus their self-denying role is perceived as a duty and an achievement with spiritual undertones.[62]

The peculiarity of these Nankani narratives lies in the roles and identity status accorded to daughters. Despite the uniqueness of these roles, these daughters are not publicly acknowledged or identified. Neither the children nor 'wives' of the daughters bear their names. Although their surrogate roles are needed, their identity is silenced and hidden in order that the deceased masculine figures identities can be identified and objectified. Moreover, they cannot claim headship of the household or ownership of any form of property therein. Similarly, all these daughters have no overt religious roles, even in their masculine roles. That is, they cannot pour libation, sacrifice or consult a diviner for themselves and the new family members they helped to create. All these roles are controlled by the male next of kin. These kinsmen remain legal custodians until the son(s) are mature enough to take such roles and responsibilities.

---

61 See Parrinder's discussion on sexual morality in African religions. Geoffrey Parrinder, *Sexual Morality in the World's Religions* (London: Oneworld, 1996), 145.

62 Oduyoye, *Introducing African Women's Theology*, 34.

It is my contention that it is not only women's reproductive roles that are exploited but their socio-political roles as well. Women are important and greatly sought after in crisis situations. At the same time, however, the unique roles they play in such situations are obscured by the projection of male identities. Thus denying the identity of women, men are given an undue advantage and an enormous versatility in the society. Although this is not a clear case of inclusiveness or exclusiveness, we cannot simply classify this as a case of flexibility when the identity and freedom of these women are denied. Besides, if the rights of women are an essential part of gender discourses, these must be clearly manifested. The situation also poses questions on the issue of power in the existing gender relations.

These two narratives show that women can and do sometimes play roles outside normal societal gender constructs. Although these examples have added another perspective to the discourse on women's roles in the traditional African society, they have also contributed to the current discussion on woman-to-woman marriage on the African continent. Unlike Amadiume's female husbands and the complex scenario of flexibility among the Gikuyu,[63] the Nankani perspective is quite different. Even though woman-to-woman marriage is not a focal point in this chapter, a brief analytical perspective on some of the issues raised is relevant for understanding the power relations involved. It helps to question the issues of roles, power sharing and women's empowerment.

Woman-to-woman marriage among the Nankani is not an alternative marriage system. It is not empowering to the women involved, and it is not open for personal choice.[64] It is a specific cultural construct for culturally permissible and desperate situations. Even though it is perceived as a final attempt to rescue a family from extinction, such situations were rare. The family is not viewed in the nuclear sense. In the traditional context, the first born son was the heir and cultural legitimate head of all his male siblings. The talk of a family at the verge of extinction refers to a whole masculine generation including its siblings. This is why it was difficult to find a real case for illustration during my fieldwork. It is however difficult to ascertain if the lack of concrete evidence at the time of the fieldwork was due to its

---

63   Njambi and O'Brien, "Revisiting 'Woman-Woman Marriage," 145- 65.

64   Compare with the Gikuyu women. Njambi and O'Brien, "Revisiting 'Woman-Woman Marriage," 147.

infrequent invocation or it is simply dying out. Similarly, it is not clear as to whether the gender-based restrictions surrounding the practice is intended to preserve the dignity of the children or another way of suppressing women's access to power and control. Irrespective of the reasons, the fact that it is still identified as a unique cultural practice worthy of preservation was noted by community leaders.

Caution was however noted when this was contrasted with the current 'sexual revolution'. According to Akurugo, the misapplication of these practices to current sexual behaviour by women and development workers in the region is not only inappropriate but unfortunate. It was particularly noted that due to the freedom and liberty enjoyed by the youth in recent times, some girls 'misbehave' (engage in promiscuous sexual relationships) and when they find themselves in difficult situations they use tradition as a means of escape. What is clear is that the children from these other relationships are not religio-culturally initiated. As a result, they are not recognized, have no legal status and are not seen in the traditional sense as full members of the family. They have no family inheritance and cannot occupy traditional leadership roles in the family, lineage, clan or community. Thus, though they may revert to these traditions to win favour and support from NGOs, their predicament has no cultural grounds. These are some of the problems arising from the current uncritical grasp of Western modernity. This differentiation arose from a discussion in which the current interpretation of *yiyen zaba* and the children born from such relationships presents crisis situation in the area of identity. It must be noted that this new phenomenon is a crisis confronting the Nankani traditional structure. Questions on the rights and roles of children born from these non-traditional religio-cultural structures have to be evaluated and given due consideration in time. Unfortunately, this area has not yet received attention from NGOs or the Social Welfare Service. The most remarkable contribution to this discussion was the linkage between individual freedom, modern social problems and the rising number of street children in the urban areas of Ghana.

This statement is subject to the Nankani worldview where children by unmarried daughters are not family in the first category but relations. In this regard, they are not counted. For the Nankani, family membership or identity is dependent on one's natal home, where natal identity is focused on the male figure. Even though these females are not perceived as 'male' or 'husbands', as in Amadiume's case,[65] the fact that these women's personal identities are not recognized can be questioned. Yet, underlying these Nankani scenarios is the issue raised by feminists on the role of women in maintaining and perpetuating patriarchal structures and systems.[66] Even so the question now remains as to the status of women in these traditional cases. Are these manipulative instruments for an entrenched subordination of women? How do women view these practices? Do they believe that in rescuing and strengthening patriarchy, they are not simply serving their families but themselves? How far is the view that this is a religio-cultural duty accepted? Although these questions present interesting perspectives for reflection on the issues, they are beyond the immediate scope of this investigation.

Despite the differences in gender presentations, some of the issues cut across cultures. Not only is patriarchy a global phenomenon, the use of biological sex differentiation as an important signal for the conceptualization of gender is acknowledged.[67] The names *Ayidana* (The landlord) for a boy and *Ayingabunu* (The outside thing) for a girl serve as illustrations. This premise cannot be overlooked. It underscores all the traits of what it means to be male or female. It puts the individual within identifiable categories where they are then moulded towards their respective future roles.

MODERN CONCEPTS OF GENDER

The current discourse on gender is quite complex.[68] With constant disputations on what is and what is not gender in specific contexts, the debate on generalizations and particularizations seem to be taking centre stage.[69] This is particularly challenging where a number of universal theories are interrogated and contrasted with findings from case

65   Njambi and O'Brien, "Revisiting 'Woman-Woman Marriage,'" 157-60.
66   Mary Daly, *Pure Lust: Elemental Feminist Philosophy* (London: The Women's Press, 1984), 144.
67   Karen Trew, "Identity and the Self," in *Gender and Psychology*, eds. Karen Trew and John Kremer (London, New York, Sydney and Auckland, 1998), 4-7.
68   Bowie, *The Anthropology of Religion*, 111.
69   Lucinda Joy Peach, *Women and World Religions* (New Jersey: Pearson Educational, Inc., 2002), 4-7 and Sackey, *New Directions in Gender and Religion*, 62-72.

studies.[70] The situation is not different in the African context and this raises questions on what it means to speak of gender in the modern context.[71] Are these discourses aimed at developing an integrated approach or producing contextual perspectives? Similarly, are these discourses taking on the religious dimension or are they secular ones?[72] The word modern in this investigation is inclusive. Its purpose is to differentiate it from the Nankani conceptual frame of thought. It acknowledges the various contributions to the debate and helps to prevent the ambiguities surrounding the word Western. As a matter of fact, the discourse on gender has been enriched by the diverse perspectives from around the world.

As in the traditional Nankani perspective, some people are of the view that "biological factors are very influential in shaping the gender roles of men and women in society".[73] For these people, biological sex differentiations other than socio-cultural values determine gender status and role setting.[74] This perspective has been extensively analyzed by feminists and social scientists alike. The extent to which this notion is applied to contemporary gender analysis varies considerably.[75] Unlike Third World feminists, Western feminist studies have generally acknowledged biological differentiations, but at the same time, some of these scholars have moved on to show that there is more to the discourse of gender than biology.[76] Oakley's works have been very useful in providing a cross-cultural perspective to the varied forms of Western debates.[77] According to Archer and Lloyd, the "psychological and behavioural differences between men and women arise from a

70   Deborah L. Best and Jennifer J. Thomas, "Cultural Diversity and Cross-Cultural Perspectives", in *The Psychology of Gender*, 2nd ed. Eds. Alice H. Eagly, Anne E. Beall and Robert J. Sternberg (New York and London: The Guilford Press, 2004), 296-7

71   Oyěwùmí, *The Invention of Women*, 11-27.

72   Judith Evans, *Feminist Theory Today: An Introduction to Second-Wave Feminism* (London: Saga Publications, 1995), 76-105.

73   Stephanie Garrett, *Gender* (London and New York: Tavistock, 1987), 1.

74   Bowie, *The Anthropology of Religion*, 91 and Olajubu, *Women in the Yoruba Religious Sphere*, 8.

75   Sara Salih, *Judith Butler* (London and New York: Routledge, 2002), 49-50.

76   Garrett, *Gender*, 2-37.

77   Ann Oakley, *Sex, Gender, and Society* (London: Maurice Temple Smith Ltd. 1972); *Subject Women*, (London: Fontana, 1982) and *Gender on Planet Earth* (Cambridge: Polity Press and New York: The New Press, 2002).

variety of sources involving both the biological and the cultural".[78] For these scholars, from the threefold linguistic determinant of "masculine, feminine and intermediate", the term 'gender' has assumed the current stereotypical classification of the two sexes.[79] In accordance with the present trend of thought, they argue that its eventual replacement of the differential category of sex alludes to the emerged understanding that gender is more than a biological determinant.

For other feminists and scholars with special interest in gender discourse, the conceptual formulation of biological sex differentiation as the root of gender is the basis of contestation.[80] Anne Bolin has identified five institutionalized forms of gender on the global level,[81] ranging from "[h]ermaphroditic genders, two-spirit traditions" to "rituals in which cross-dressing and/or other cross-gendered behaviours" are accepted. Bolin has shown that the classical two sex heterosexual classification is neither biologically determined nor fixed.[82] Among the diverse forms of explaining diversity in gender in the modern context is the social dimension. According to Lorber and Farrell, gender is:

> [O]ne of the foundations of every existing social order ... women and men are not automatically compared; rather, gender categories (female-male, feminine-masculine, girls-boys, women-men) are analyzed to see how different social groups define them, and how they construct and maintain them in everyday life and major social institutions, such as the family and economy.[83]

They argue for these varied designations of genders, maintaining that there are more than two genders. This is because masculinity and femininity are

---

78   John Archer and Barbara Lloyd, *Sex and Gender*, 2ne ed. (Cambridge: Cambridge University Press, 2002), 17.

79   Archer and Lloyd, *Sex and Gender*, 17-31.

80   Jeanne Marecek, Mary Crawford and Danielle Popp, "On the Construction of Gender, Sex, and Sexualities," in *The Psychology of Gender*, 2nd ed., eds. Alice H. Eagly, Anne E. Beall and Robert J. Sternberg (New York and London: The Guilford Press, 2004), 200-1.

81   Bolin, "Traversing Gender", 22.

82   Bolin, "Traversing Gender," 22-37.

83   Judith Lorber and Susan A. Farrell, "Preface," in *The Social Construction of Gender*, eds. Judith Lorber and Susan A. Farrell (Newbury Part, London and New Delhi: Sage Publications, 1991), 1.

not only socio-culturally specific, they are also generationally influenced.[84] In furtherance of their arguments, they note that there are categories of gender "blenders" among whom are the transsexuals. In this regard, gender has an attitudinal dimension, one that helps to shape life beyond the biological logic. For these scholars, both "construction and reconstruction of differences" in gender categories are integral for the establishment of structures in the area of social domination and subordination.

At present, gender discourses move beyond the superficiality of the traditional argument of biological differentiation and complementarities to issues of discrimination, subordination and domination.[85] Like other post-modern systems of knowledge, the gendered dimensions of life have become text for analysis. The inherent power structures and systems in gender discourses have assumed centre stage in these debates. What is unclear is the understanding of privilege positions, power and authority. The universalization of modern Western power structures and systems, which tend to disregard other forms of power systems in the name of democracy has become another area of concern in such discourses. Contextual investigations have therefore become an important avenue for the evaluation of gender and its inherent dynamics of subordination and domination in societies. For some African feminists and scholars, the debate is centred on whether or not the universal Western oriented principles and assumptions on gender rightly cater for or address the African situation.[86] Although the contributions are fraught with controversies, they have nevertheless introduced new perspectives within the discourse.[87]

As one of the important contributions made to the volume on the *Turning Points in Religious Studies*, Ursula King noted the crucial role of the rise feminism in the area of religion and gender.[88] Bringing a different line of inquiry into the study of religion, women's status and roles in the various religious traditions became an important theme in religious investigations. According to King, until then scholarship on gender had ignored the religious factor and its impact or vice versa on gender. For King, religion is "an important source for the under-

---

84 Ware, "Female and male life-cycle," 15.
85 Ursula King, "Religion and Gender," in *Turning Points in Religious Studies*, ed. Ursula King (Edinburgh: T and T Clark, 1990), 276-7.
86 Amadiume, *Reinventing Africa*, 1.
87 Sackey, *New Directions in Gender and Religion*, 69-70.
88 King, "Religion and Gender," 175.

standing of gender".[89] King argues that the various religious traditions contain precepts, beliefs and practices essential for analyzing gender. Without neglecting the influential role of the secular argument, the present study is focused on the religious dimension and its impact on the conceptual framing of gender among the Nankani. The patriarchal nature of the Nankani society has however promoted the religious views of gender above other perspectives. This has made them view other perspectives, discussed above, as empty and lacking substance. This however needs to be explored and challenged. This is because this perspective continues to project the masculine hegemonic system in place. The desire to maintain this system as the status quo can therefore be viewed as the desire to hold on to patriarchy.

Problems and Challenges

Accordingly, religion is fundamental to gender categorization. Biological sex, which forms the basis for gender identification, differentiation and classification, is a religious determinant. It is not only given by *Winε*, it is also chosen by the individual through the traditional concept of destiny. Thus chosen and sanctioned by *Winε*, the status and roles attached to each sex are consequently determined. The female conceives and bears children. Within this period she is biologically and psychologically burdened and vulnerable. The male, who maintains a stable frame of mind and body, is responsible for providing security and the basic family needs. The manner in which this is carried out depends on the particular context. For the Nankani, this has been illustrated by their forebears (ancestors). Thus the modern perception of gender, which is largely influenced by Western secularism and individualism, ignores this religio-cultural dimension because of its focus on the social dimension.[90] This eliminates the key factors that are essential in the African worldview. This important negation excludes the Nankani from an important engagement, rendering gender as a foreign concept. Although the social aspects of the arguments are not completely rejected, for the Nankani, these are dependent on and/or influenced by the religious element.

---

89   Ursula King, "Religion and Gender," in *Handbook of Living Religions*, ed. John R. Hinnells (London: Penguin Books, 1997), 647.
90   Judith Lorber and Susan A. Farrell (eds.), *The Social Construction of Gender* (Newbury Park, London and New Delhi: SAGE Publications, 1991), 1.

On the other hand, the over simplified assertion that gender is a Western construct, not in consonance with the Nankani or African religio-cultural system, presents a rather limited assessment of gender in this context.[91] Although I concur with the view that a specific socio-culturally constructed view of gender cannot form the yardstick for universal principles, such perspectives can be viewed in relation to the available data to roughly defined plausible universal frameworks. This is because the Nankani religio-cultural milieu presents similar under-pinnings. This calls for a re-examination of the two constructs for proper understanding and dialogue. With the present trend of rapid social change, many Africans are already blending the two systems in their lives. To reject the modern concept and analysis of gender as a Western construct will be meaningless, and as Apusigah asserts, an uncritical romanticization of the African heritage can be dangerous.[92]

In this patrilineal society, mature Nankani men generally con-sider themselves to be outside the scope of gender. Elderly men view themselves as the anchor of power and authority from which com-munity values and norms are directed and ensured. They are the alpha and omega of the physical society. In terms of providing answers to questions of gender, Nankani men do that willingly and most often, with ease. However, this is presented in terms of the 'Other' such as the youth and women. For the elderly, they must maintain the system. In other words, even though gender discussions are held with leaders as the official representatives of the community, these leaders do not see themselves as participants in its implementation. For instance, when some community leaders were asked in my interviews about how their participation in existing gender education programmes had influenced their current roles in the family, they simply laughed and asked if they were the target of 'your' gender programmes. For these community leaders, modern discussions of gender are outside their domain. Gender as a category of reinterpretation is therefore one that is currently articulated with great contradictions and ambiguities. Not only is gender viewed in relation to biological sex, it is still traditionally

---

91   Candace West and Don H. Zimmerman, "Doing Gender," in *The Social Con-struction of Gender*, eds. Judith Lorber and Susan A. Farrell (Newbury Park, London and New Delhi: SAGE Publications, 1991), 13-37.

92   Agnes Atia Apusigah, "Is gender yet another colonial project? A critique of Oyewumi's proposal," A paper presented at the International Political Science Association (IPSA) annual Conference in Durban, South Africa, 2003, 7.

upheld as a God-given system of division of labour, sanctioned by the ancestors and must be maintained.

The drive for African women's rights is therefore a controversial one. According to Oduyoye, "we do not agree on what constitutes women's issues and especially on the method of seeking reconstruction".[93] But this is not a simple issue of method; the religio-cultural diversity of the African continent is making it difficult for Africans to obtain straight forward religio-cultural objectives. As I have shown, gender is not just a scholarly discourse, but one that is prominent at all levels of Nankani society. The need to build "a future in which men are friends [is crucial]. Building that future need not begin by attacking men but by finding methods of bringing change together with them".[94] From Oduyoye's viewpoint, African women "have no past to return to, only a future to build".[95] I discovered during my fieldwork that even though the proper performance of the traditional marriage rites among the Nankani had multiple purposes to which the woman stood as a beneficiary, the added responsibilities are not followed. For instance, the marriage rite served as a bond between the two families. To the affine men, it was a show of respect, capability and responsibility. For the kinsmen, it served as a formal declaration of marriage acceptance and the outward release of their daughter to the in-laws. It is also a responsibility to support and protect their daughter and her children especially when they are very young. Thus, should the marriage fail, the woman's kinsmen are expected to take over responsibility. The main problem is with the woman in her marital home where her lot lies in her own ability to read the 'signs of the times' and to respond properly, perhaps, like a fortune teller. Mary Daly talks of "Canny Women" who understand the difficulties of their situation or as she puts it, "understand the extremity of the conditions under which we struggle to survive and thrive".[96]

93   Mercy Amba Oduyoye, *Daughters of Anowa: African Women and Patriarchy* (Maryknoll, New York: Orbis Books, 1996), 169.

94   Musimbi Kanyoro, "Cultural Hermeneutics: An African Contribution," in *Women's Visions: Theological Reflection, Celebration, Action*, ed. Ofelia Ortega (Geneva: WCC Publication, 1995), 23.

95   Mercy Amba Oduyoye, "Naming the Woman: the Words of the Bible and the Words of the Akan," *Bulletin of African Theology* III, no. 5 (1981): 94.

96   Mary Daly, *QUINTESSENCE... Realizing the Archaic Future: A Radical Elemental Feminist Manifesto* (London: The Women's Press Ltd., 1999), 2.

Writing on 'Faith and Peoples' Struggles For Just, Participatory and Sustainable Life', Samuel A. Kobea identifies two oppositional attitudes on social transformation in society. One of these groups he calls "political realism" and to them he ascribes the desire to maintain the *status quo*. To the first, he considers the "trouble makers who cause disorder and repression" because of their desire for change.[97] The question of how these two perspectives operate in the Nankani context is reflected in the discussion below.

Maintaining the Status Quo

According to the Nankani traditional code of conduct, a woman's place is in the home, well-mannered, respectful, hardworking and serviceable, as well as submissive to the cultural norms and values. She must be nurturing and family conscious. This has already been discussed at length. A woman, it is said, is not supposed to be roaming everywhere, seeking personal and/or political empowerment or making economic achievements her goal. Similar arguments are raised by Hawley and Proudfoot in their contribution to the volume on *Fundamentalism and Gender*. In their study of the American Evangelicals, Hawley and Proudfoot contended that the Evangelical's view of women's crucial role in society is centred on the family.[98] This poses the question as to whether the views expressed among the Nankani can be considered in the same vein. In her paper on "Beyond Belief?", Ellen Armour argued that women are perceived and used as cultural resources. They are used as pawns with culturally imaginary "belief structures" to sustain a male economy.[99] Evaluating Irigaray's work, Armour states retrospectively that, "an inquiry into belief itself is crucial to any inquiry into sexual

---

97   Samuel A. Kobea, "Faith and Peoples' Struggles For Just, Participatory and Sustainable Life," in *Transcending Boundaries: Perspectives on Faith, Social Action and Solidarity, Essays in honour of George Ninan*, eds. Rajendra K. Sail and Ajit Muricken (India: Vikas Adhyan Kendra, and Raipur Churches Development and Relief Committee, 1995), 52.

98   John S. Hawley and Wayne Proudfoot, "Introduction," in *Fundamentalism and Gender*, ed. John Stratton Hawley (New York and Oxford: Oxford University Press, 1994), 4.

99   Ellen T. Armour, "Beyond Belief? Sexual Difference and Religion After Ontotheology," in *The Religious*, ed. John D. Caputo (Blackwell Publishers, 2002), 217.

differences".[100] In her conclusion, Armour argued that the issue is not just religion; it engages various thought patterns. This includes the notion of development. This study calls "attention to the price paid by women and men [development workers and beneficiary communities alike]... for participation in this economy... [it] requires confrontation with pain and loss, not compensation for them".[101]

David Brown has observed that "[r]eligion is one of the activities of life in which people resist change. Religious people do not easily change their ideas or their behaviour".[102] Brown notes that sometimes those who initiate change are labelled deviants and stigmatized. Even so, Brown admits that, like society, religion is dynamic; hence, susceptible to change. As Amadiume explains, "[t]he majority of rural women might not see the demand for equal opportunities as an immediate priority, but it must be argued that they have daughters whose choices they hope will be wider and better than their own".[103] Writing on *West African Traditional Religion*, Awolalu and Dopamu stressed the dynamic nature of society, religion and humanity as a whole.[104] Noting the inevitability of change, they cited examples from some of the changes that have already taken place in the area of taboos and ritual practices. While enumerating the complexities involved in these processes of change, the scholars argued that religion is still on a fertile soil with great potential for rejuvenation and renewal.[105]

The notion of maintaining the status quo within the apparent reality of a religio-cultural dynamism in the subject of gender desires critical examinations. Is it a question of maintaining women in the periphery of the Nankani religio-cultural system? According to Armour's analysis, despite all the "attempts to 'fix' woman in her place; a place that denies her speech, subjectivity, and rights as a woman even as it uses her as a resource to sustain culture...[she] perpetually eludes these attempts to fix her".[106] For a sustained system of development, "women must come

100 Ibid., 215.
101 Ibid., 223.
102 David A. Brown, *A Guide to Religions*, TEF Study Guide 12 (London: SPCK, 1975), 227.
103 Amadiume, *Male Daughters and Female Husbands*, 199.
104 J. Omosade Awolalu and P. Adelumo Dopamu, *West African Traditional Religion* (Ibadan: Onibonoje Press and Book Industries (Nig.) Ltd., 1979).
105 Ibid., 279-85.
106 Armour, "Beyond Belief?" 214.

into their own as women, not as men's others who reflect them back to themselves as they would like them to believe they are".[107]

Christina Larner's contribution to the patriarchal delineation of ideal women is also significant here.[108] She argues that this demarcation does not only provide guidelines for the society's female stereotypes, the women of the society adopt it as the standard code for their own femininity. This "male-delineated ideal" womanhood becomes the archetype through which conformity is sought. Any lack of conformity or deviation by individual women is thus not only confronted by men, but also by those women in support of the status quo. In Ghana, this group of women are referred to as the 'gate keepers'.[109] Larner argues that the failure to recognize patriarchal social structures as divisive among women has been a problem for witchcraft accusations and other concerns of gender in rural Africa.[110] If Larner's assessment is true, the issue of female conformity has a multidimensional purpose. At present, traditional Nankani women depend on their men folk for their spiritual role and its attendant socio-economic and security benefits.[111] Conformity for this set of women, who are still steeped in the religious tradition, is not a choice but a necessity. Nonconformist women are therefore a threat to their welfare and security.

In 'Challenging Patriarchy', Ranjini Rebera[112] asks very pertinent questions on the ambivalent concept of women in society. Why are women perceived to be good and feared as bad? For her, the answer can be been found in patriarchy. She calls for the dismantling of patriarchy. Yet Rebera acknowledges that women have so internalized patriarchy that they have become willing participants and perpetuators of patriarchy.[113] Rebera thus appeals for the use of collective power which has

---

107 Ibid.

108 Christina Larner, *Witchcraft and Religion: The Politics of Popular Belief* (Oxford: Basil Blackwell, 1984), 62.

109 'Gate keepers' refers those who seek to uphold tradition and the traditional roles of women.

110 Larner, *Witchcraft and Religion*, 86.

111 Agnes Atia Apusgah, "Toollum: A Gendered African Concept with Potential for Development," A Paper Presented at the CODESRIA Annual Campus on African Knowledge Systems, Dakar, Senegal, May 2006, 4-5.

112 Ranjini Rebera, "Challenging Patriarchy," in *Feminist Theology from the Third World: A Reader*, ed. Ursula King (London and New York: SPCK/Orbis Press, 1994), 105-12.

113 Ibid., 105-6.

the ability to influence and infiltrate such resistance.[114] This channel of breaking down resistance and establishing new frameworks for women's liberation and empowerment is evident in the rising number of rural women's groups in response to NGO activities. Many women among the Nankani have within the *anaanure* (unity or with one voice) or *asongtaba* (helping each other) group concepts, improved their personal lives as well as rebuilt and restructured their families, securing gradual influences on their community. The issue of maintaining the status quo is thus confronted at various levels.

Consciously or not, Nankani women however continue to teach, endorse and enforce patriarchy in all aspects of their lives. Maintaining, instructing and enforcing traditional gender stereotypes, in their families in the name of tradition and cultural heritage, negate the works of gender and development workers and activists in the area and country. The paradox of belonging and desiring to be free is a thin line. Nonetheless, Nankani women have to discern these boundaries themselves and respond with the appropriate practice. While many Nankani women spend their earnings on the education or training of their daughters, praying, wishing and trying desperately to secure an alternative and better lifestyle for their daughters, they also work hard to transfer the traditional gender stereotypes and their associated roles and concepts of the 'ideal woman' to them. This dilemma continues to enforce and enhance patriarchy and many of its traditional systems.

An example is found in an interview with Aputibunu, a mother of five children, two of whom are girls and the other three, boys. The two girls come after the first boy. These first three are in the community Junior Secondary (JSS) and primary schools. She explained that she works extra hard through a TechnoServe income generation activity (IGA) programme to support her girls in school. She argued that even though she does not want to wait to be proved right or wrong, she cannot imagine that her husband will sell an animal for the educational needs of their girls. This is because of his entrenched notion that they will be marrying out of the family. Although this is a typical traditional viewpoint, Aputibunu noted that 'these days' girls do better in supporting parents than boys'. As such, she was committed in her work to support her girls to acquire education for a better future. Although this can be argued as a case of self-interest, her daughters will at least

---

114 Ibid.,109.

have a chance to improve upon their own welfare. The case however shows that these traditional views are still held by some men even though they would like their sons to marry women who are able to support them. At the same time, it presents a new perspective to rural women's goals and ways of assertiveness. Nevertheless, Aputibunu is caught in the dilemma and social dynamics of rural community living. While I was still interviewing her in her compound, the children arrived from school. After they were given something to eat, all the boys were sent out to the *zenyore* while the girls were asked to carry out some household chores. Asked why she did that, she laughed and said 'you do not understand but my children cannot be different from their peers. Besides, the future is unknown and we have to be prepared for anything'. This is why scholars like Rebera argue that the role of women in traditional society continues to perpetuate patriarchy.[115] Challenging and dismantling patriarchy seem to be two different but competing concepts in practice.

In her article in *Transcending Boundaries*, Shashi Sail looked at how societies use the "socio-economic, religious and cultural fabric" within it as a political mechanism to subject women to a state of vulnerability and powerlessness.[116] Sail does not just discuss the problems arising from this. She shows how women are able to overcome these imposed difficulties and impediments to achieve self determination and empowerment. It is in this endeavour to triumph over prevailing circumstances that some women are seen as breaking the tradition. This is because various initiatives have already taken place. What is more, most of these changes have already received support and are put into practice. The question arises as to what it means to break the tradition. In an article titled 'Rituals and Chastity on Women', Rose Mary Akurigu contemplated in her introductory poem what the women of Naga could do to maintain their valued religio-cultural heritage yet

---

115   Rebera, "Challenging Patriarchy," 106.
116   Shashi Sail, "The Women's Question – Rethinking Gender Politics," in *Transcending Boundaries: Perspectives on Faith, Social Action and Solidarity, Essays in honour of George Ninan*, eds. Rajendra K. Sail and Ajit Muricken (India: Vikas Adhyan Kendra, and Raipur Churches Development and Relief Committee, 1995), 237-8.

minimize the pain and trauma associated with these rituals.[117] Today, most of the rituals associated with adultery and widowhood rites among the Nankani have seen some changes. These can be seen in the areas of clothing during the ritual, the cleansing processes, food habits and attitudes associated with the rituals themselves. Even though the rituals are still occurring, these practices have initiated some form of change. This further raises the question as to what it means to be seen as breaking the tradition.

Breaking Tradition

The endemic patriarchal bias and apparent manipulation of who and what constitutes womanhood are now challenged on various fronts. As noted at the beginning of this chapter, Nankani women are not only killing snakes, they cut off heads and hold them up high for all to see. A majority of Nankani women are searching for new ways of living out their womanhood within their traditional heritage without necessarily compromising their dignity and liberty. These efforts are nevertheless fraught with backlashes. Although traditional arguments of essentialism (innate feminine quality of women) and constructivism (the culturally determined factor of femininity) are used to maintain the status quo, these are no longer satisfactory. Rural Nankani women are breaking from patriarchal norms with a new understanding that these patriarchal systems and characteristics are only maintaining male hegemony. The inability of men to meet the needs of women and family is also precipitating this move. Thus the innate and religio-cultural arguments are now insufficient in maintaining traditional rural women within the status quo.

Morny Joy and Eva Neumaier-Dargyay see 'gender' as a mobile frame of reference. This is because it is constantly reinterpreted to suit specific circumstances.[118] As shown above, gender is not a fixed category. The biological and the religio-cultural constructs are insufficient

---

117   Rose Mary Akurigu, "Chastity and Rituals on Women," in *Where God Reigns: Reflections on Women in God's World*, ed. Elisabeth Amoah (Accra-North, Ghana: Sam-Woode Ltd, 1996), 87.

118   Morny Joy and Eva K. Neumaier-Dargyay, "Introduction," in *Gender, Genre, and Religion: Feminist Reflections*, eds. Norny Joy and Eva K. Neumaier-Dargyay (Canada: Wilfrid Laurier University Press for The Calgary Institute for the Humanities, 1995), 4.

for carving a definite role for today's complex woman. The flexibility of gender, as Amadiume points out,[119] is not a simple issue of classification of "androgynous, bisexual, homosexual, heterosexual, transsexual, as well as those who become eunuchs, celibates, transvestites, and berdache"; it involves and relates to the ever changing roles that women, especially rural women find themselves in,[120] As many rural African women move into masculine roles as a result of necessity, coming from the inability of men to sufficiently play their typical roles of provision and security, traditional gender boundaries are gradually dismantled. As Chinua Achebe in *Things Fall Apart* explains, "[t]hings fall apart; the centre cannot hold"; those traditional stereotypical boundaries cannot hold things together any longer.[121]

Kobea observes that the struggle for recognition, affirmation and participation has brought to the fore the continuous suffering, marginalization and exclusion of women at the various levels of society.[122] Kobea argues that to effectively initiate or effect change, "the best traditions of the people should be respected".[123] For him, no effective and sustainable change can take place "if the culture of the people is not affirmed through it".[124] Kobea however views culture in terms of values, traditions and symbols. This form of clustering every rural problem or activity in the realm of culture clouds the issues at stake and prevents them from receiving the relevant attention to effect the desired positive change.

One of the major religio-cultural changes in the area came through Western education of girls and later through the activities of development agencies which have introduced some changes to a number of the traditional systems. This is irrespective of earlier initiatives when women participated in the colonial 'free' (forced) labour projects. It is also different from the baptism of females by the missionaries. Although for the first time female religiosity was not seen as an appendage to their males but as full, identifiable individuals, the overall structure of the Catholic Church and teachings did not necessitate any change from the community or the people who were converted. It is nonethe-

---

119 Amadiume, *Male Daughters and Female Husbands*, 15.
120 Joy and Neumaier-Dargyay, "Introduction," in *Gender, Genre, and Religion*, 4.
121 Chinua Achebe, *Things Fall Apart* (London: Heinemann, 1958).
122 Kobea, "Faith and Peoples' Struggles For Just, Participatory and Sustainable Life," 56-7
123 Ibid., 65.
124 Ibid., 65-6.

less noted that when the missionaries brought in the Catholic White Sisters, this brought about some change.[125] The main change took place when girls in the area were allowed into the educational system. At this stage, girls were not only taken out of the indoor domestic sphere, they were placed at the same level with the male heirs of the community and subjected to the same system, rules and practices. Educated girls consequently assumed a new status, different from their counterparts who had no education. Although not equal to the educated boys at the community level, they acquired some masculine importance in their families and communities. This enabled them to receive some concessions regarding traditional activities, practices, knowledge systems as well as participating as *de facto* decision-makers of their families. The question of 'what does a woman know' gradually watered down with the education of girls. This had a ripple effect on the entire socio-cultural system of community life.

The education of girls provided avenues for freedom of mobility, speech, delayed marriage life, choice of marriage partners as well as divorce. These initiatives were not only emulated by the non-educated girls, they were pushed beyond the limits set by the educated female. Stories from the Naga chief's house tell of one of the daughters, princess Ayenyela, who, when pushed to marry, took a defiant public oath denouncing marriage altogether and refusing also to stay at home under the protection of her male kinsmen, yet insisted they took full responsibility of her funeral rites. Another princess from the same house confronted the issue of divorce through poisoning.[126] As a result of these incidents, women in this clan gained considerable freedom on marital issues.

Another significant area of change came with the activities of NGOs. This aspect of change greatly benefited non-educated rural women. This sector is very important in its contribution to rural African women's empowerment. Given the general notion of limited economic resources for education and the continuous preference for boys, which has often denied girls the chance for education, NGO activities have become a vital source of empowerment. Through the training of women in various skills of development activities geared

---

125 Rose Mary Amenga-Etego, "Women in the Catholic Church in Ghana" (M. Phil Diss. University of Ghana, Legon Ghana, 1998), 3-4.

126 Stories were repeatedly narrated by members of the Naga Chief house during my field study, between February and June 2006, of how these ladies actions have won considerable freedom for the current generation of daughters.

toward personal and economic empowerment, more rural women increasingly acquired confidence in themselves. This has boosted their self-image and worth, and given some opportunities in family decision-making. Again, through the activities of NGOs, rural women have made great contributions to the rural economy and have helped to develop and sustain their families in difficult times. In her paper on the Afikpo Igbo of Nigeria, Phoebe Millar observed that the contributions of the Afikpo women alleviated famine, improved the relationships, even in polygamous families, and provided "greater wealth and economic security" for the women and their families.[127]

In the Nankani socio-political situation, femaleness as a gender category has its place indoors. In spite of this structural enclosure, Nankani women have transcended the boundary through innovative wall decorations, female-oriented story telling as well as folk songs and dance. These have been and still are important channels where specific views and women's resistance are aired without restraint or fear. Serving as embodiments of religio-cultural continuity on the one hand and as a visible, articulate and a vocal avenue for change on the other, the area deserves more attention than it is currently accorded in research. It is important that whereas the others take place within the ascribed enclosed sphere of women, the latter transcends into the outdoor male sphere. According to Amadiume, traditional folk songs should not simply be seen, to which I must add, and dismissed as the domain of women.[128] For as Amadiume points out, they contain important elements of continuity, change and resistance. This is what makes the Nankani female aesthetics particularly important as a vibrant channel for initiating resistance and seeking change. Although this area of discourse cannot be pursued in detail in this study, it is significant to note that through these channels Nankani women have refused to be

---

127 Miller, "Sex Polarity and Among the Afikpo Igo," 92.
128 Amadiume, *Male Daughters and Female Husbands*, 69.

muted.[129] They may be assigned to the inner sphere of the socio-political spectrum, but their art works have transcended these boundaries.[130]

African scholars are also now beginning to take note of the particular roles these female aesthetics play in traditional culture and religion.[131] Without limiting the varieties to music and dance, scholars are showing how these aesthetic forms are carried beyond the traditional sphere to the Church. The wall decorations of Nankani women have for instance found expressive avenues in the Catholic Church in the area.[132] In the area of music and dance, T. A. Kane has argued that this area continues to be an important feature in the explanation of the diverse issues within the African continent.[133] Pashington Obeng has also noted that dance is "a meaningful avenue to address issues in the open".[134] Arguing on the gendered dimension of African dance, Obeng observes from the Akan that even though women's roles in African dance forms have undergone some considerable changes, women continue to draw inspiration from their music and "dance narratives to address new social and religious circumstances".[135]

It is clear that in rural African communities, socio-cultural patterns of life are rooted in traditional religion and authority. These are further

---

129 See Bowie for 'women as a muted group'. Bowie, *The Anthropology of Religion*, 94-7.

130 In 2002, the UN Secretary General, Kofi Annan, paid a visit to the only organized traditional women's art group in Sirigu to see, encourage and congratulate them. Since then, the group's centre has grown into an important tourist attraction in the region. Accessed 17 April 2007; available from http://www.swopa.org/swopa.htm; Internet.

131 Kofi Yankah, *Speaking for the Chief: Okyeame and the Politics of Akan Royal Oratory* (Bloomington and Indianapolis, Indiana University Press, 1995), 70-81 and Kwame Gyekye, *African Cultural Values: An Introduction* (Accra, Ghana: Sankofa Publishing Company, 1996), 178. See picture 8.

132 See picture 18 for an illustration of Nankani women's wall decorations in a Church.

133 Scholars in African Christianity and culture attest to the importance of African music and dance to the growth of Christianity in Africa. See T. A. Kane *The Dancing Church: Video Impressions of the Church in Africa* (Mahwah, N. J.: Paulist Press, 1991).

134 Pashington Obeng, "Asante Catholicsm: An African Appropriation of the Roman Catholic Religion," in *African Spirituality: Forms, Meanings, and Expressions*, ed. Jacob K. Olupona (New York: The Crossroad Publishing Company, 2000), 381.

135 Ibid., 380-1.

enhanced and protected by traditional values and norms, and encoded by prohibitions and taboos. This enforces a deeper imprint of their religious significance on the people. Modern development projects, however, do not seem to take into serious consideration these underlying factors.[136] In *Religion: The Basics*, Nye underpins religion and culture as the basic factors in the construction of gender in any given society.[137]

As shown by the traditional proverb, the Nankanis have no problem with women's desire for improvement or industriousness. As a matter of fact this is a quality required of women. The problem is in the current woman's desire for self-acknowledgement within the male dominated society. Hence the disapproval relates to the elements of female self-assertiveness and independence. This, however, is the thrust of modern gender initiatives. It is the basis of disparities between the Nankani and the current concept of gender. The question as to how these differences may be bridged is examined further in chapter seven. Hopefully, that will provide additional insights for the individual stakeholders to make informed decisions.

Meanwhile, the search for data as well as the respective engagement with the data in this study involved a number of methodological and theoretical issues worth investigating further. Although theoretical by nature, these issues relate to the general discourse on indigenous peoples and their religio-cultural influences on contemporary notions of development. That is to say, it is an engagement between the indigenous knowledge systems of the Nankani and some of the current discourses on theory and method. This justifies the traditional view that development is not limited to the material but encompasses other spheres of life. The second part therefore presents an elaborate reflective illustration of how the indigenous knowledge systems of the Nankani engage some current debates in research theory and method from the perspective of a 'native researcher'.

---

136   Although development agents use pictures to show the involvement of indigenous socio-cultural systems, some are 'cosmetic', the real issues left untouched.

137   Nye, *Religion*, 73-97.

PART TWO

Chapter Five

THEORY AND METHOD IN INDIGENOUS AFRICAN RESEARCH: RESPONSES FROM THE FIELD

> [T]he nature of the field of study must provide the major control over the methods employed.[1]

By implication, every research is unique. Each requires a distinct mastering and control over methods used in its investigation. Nonetheless, scholarship has shown that nothing starts in a vacuum; it is a built-on process. It is within this context that previous studies become relevant. These either serve as pointers or provide the cracks for others to mend. A historical review of the study of religions provides valuable insights as to how studies in this field have developed. These serve as guidelines for scholars within this sphere of academic endeavour. The need to balance the relative uniqueness of each study within the general framework of the discipline remains a core struggle for the researcher. This challenge is both theoretical and methodological, a reflective engagement of which is a prerequisite for better understanding and appreciation of the new investigation, as well as its contribution to the build-up process. Yet, the enormous presence of diverse theoretical and methodological frameworks, from social scientists and scholars of religion, make such engagements more difficult instead of facilitating them. Attempts at carving out distinct frames for specific studies are therefore becoming complex.

---

1   Turner, "The Way Forward in the Religious Study of African Primal Religions," 1.

The development of the phenomenology of religion as a unique methodological approach for religious studies, as put forward by Cox, is thus significant.[2] Despite the immense contributions from the social sciences and the other subject areas of religion, Cox observes that, "the phenomenology of religion defines the methodology that is uniquely associated with religious studies as a distinct discipline studying 'religion' itself".[3] He asserts, "[o]nly phenomenology provides for the academic study of religions a distinct methodology, justifying its claim to be a field of study in its own right, *sui generis*".[4] This does not only reckon with Turner's caution not to allow the study of religion to be subsumed by other subjects, but as is inherent in Cox's assertion, pursued in "its own right". Beyond this, Cox's text presents specific contextual insights of a West African influence through what he calls the "British School" of phenomenology. Cox who is himself influenced by his African contacts and the British school of phenomenology, which he notes is "sympathetic to the perspectives of adherents", makes this branch of phenomenology intriguing, and perhaps, more suitable for this study.[5] This is because this enquiry is not only situated within the sphere of phenomenology; it is intertwined with all these nuances.

Cox's text is nevertheless subject to interpretation, interrogation and application, especially as it is applied to designated research topics. In this respect, some of the issues in his work will be discussed in details in chapter six.[6] This must not be seen as an issue of inadequacy or disagreement. Rather, it should be viewed within the Nankani saying, 'no single hand can embrace the baobab tree'. The baobab tree, which is personified by the Nankani as a religio-cultural symbol is perceived to possess great mysteries, demanding corporate understanding and applications. The need to 'join hands' or contribute to this understanding is essential. This is not only in terms of the African ethic of 'communal spirit'; it transcends this to contextualization and enculturation. Besides, the need to apply or subject general frameworks to specific socio-cultural contexts is an integral part of the academic enterprise. In *Giving an Account of Oneself* Judith Butler observes the

---

2   James L. Cox, *A Guide to the Phenomenology of Religion: Key Figures, Formative Influences And Subsequent Debates* (London: Continuum, 2006).

3   Ibid., 3.

4   Ibid., 4.

5   Cox, *A Guide to the Phenomenology of Religion*, 5-6.

6   Ibid., 152.

need for universal precepts to be adaptable to particular socio-cultural contexts. Noting that the inability of the universal to respond "to cultural particularity" not only "fails to undergo a reformulation of itself in response to the social and cultural conditions it includes within its scope of applicability" but also violates the "freedom and particularity" of the latter.[7] Therefore, despite the uniqueness of the British school of phenomenology, it is still necessary to subject its broad framework to this specific research since a 'single hand' is insufficient for embracing a baobab tree. Nonetheless, it is still the uniqueness of the British school of phenomenology that renders it suitable for this contextualization.

Even so, the distinctive character of ATR, an oral religion with inadequate expositional written texts in this literary era, presents a peculiar type of difficulty. These distinct characteristics often tilt the load of research to the practical manifestations in which ATR is contextually defined and pursued. These and the phenomenological thrust on scientific objectivity are all problematic areas in recent scholarship. The postmodernist and postcolonial deconstructive stance of understanding a given study questions this arbitrariness on grounds of subjectivity.[8] This has generated much debate on the study of ATR and the key elements of the phenomenological method as well as its pursuit of objectivity.[9] Consequently, the identity and role of the researcher have emerged as crucial determinants in studies of this nature. The emergent dynamics have added more problems to researchers, especially African researches engaging their own religio-cultural traditions.[10] Hence, the search for suitable theories or methodologies for this category of researchers is an increasing challenge.

This puts into operation Ursula King's assertion that "[t]he search for clearer concepts, definitions, and methods is still going on".[11] Scholars are not only informed and encouraged to participate in the search, but also, called to help clarify, substantiate and contextualize them. While this presents another reason to engage Cox's discourse on methodology, it is important to observe briefly the different perspec-

---

7   Butler, *Giving an Account of Oneself*, 6-7.
8   Gellner, *Postmodernism, Reason and Religion*, 23.
9   James L. Cox, *Alterity as Identity: Innovation in the Academic Study of Religions* (Lampeter: BASR, Annual Conference, 1998),1.
10 Cox, "African Identity as the Projection of Western Alterity," 25-6.
11 U. King, "Historical and phenomenological approaches," in *Theory and Methods in Religious Studies*, 54.

tives of Cox and Turner. This is in respect of Turner's statement above. That is to say, while Cox is proposing a guide to the academic study of religions in general, the reference from Turner is dealing specifically with the study of Africa's religions. Thus, irrespective of the time frame, Cox's proposal is a larger framework in which Turner's views may still be located as we address the problems of contextualizing theory and method in Africa's religio-cultural setting.

In his call for a poly-methodic approach, Turner asserts the need to draw upon the rich insights of the human sciences in the examination of Africa's religions. Turner is not the only scholar to advance this line of argument. Benjamin Ray contends that the study of ATR "must be polymethodic and multidimensional".[12] Other social scientists have also shown and expressed in diverse ways the need for an inclusive approach in the study of religion. Posnansky, for instance, has noted the intrinsic relationship between religion and culture, and religion and psychology.[13] In his argument on psychology, Posnansky states:

> [I]t is impossible to escape the psychological dimension in which a religious belief is viewed as part of Man's image of the world and of his own position in relation to the other component parts of that world, the landscape, the climate, the plants and the animals. The psychological boundaries of religion are the most difficult to demarcate.[14]

These inescapable dimensions of interrelationships require measures that will ensure their input without compromising the identity of the field. Unfortunately, there is no guideline to this effect. Though essential, Turner's caution is vague. It is here that the relationship between Cox and Turner, in the right historical order, provides the needed guidelines to the study of ATR. Cox is not only reiterating the uniqueness of religion, he advocates the phenomenology of religion as a responsive methodological tool. Moreover, the phenomenological method sufficiently answers Turner's call for a field-led methodology. Thus the two scholarly perspectives are complementary.

This notwithstanding, Turner's inquest has far reaching consequences. Turner's advocacy for a field-led methodology, even as he calls

---

12   Ray, *African Religions*, 16.
13   Posnansky, "Archaeology, Ritual and Religion," 29.
14   Ibid., 29.

for an appropriate model to meet Africa's religious needs, has contributed significantly to the context of this chapter.[15] While there is a great need for guiding principles, there is equally the need for flexibility and Turner's views encapsulate this. Set within the context of 'Africa's primal religions', his statement also exposes the methodological deficiency in the subject area. Even so, his call is not a grim bewilderment; it is an appeal for an engagement that will rectify the problem. The methodological approach in this study is, to a large extent, a response to Turner's presuppositions. It is field-led, multidimensional, with attempts which aim to respond to some of the inadequacies encountered during my field study. Nonetheless, this is done within the framework of the phenomenology of religion. The general acknowledgement of the limitations of the phenomenological methods and Cox's innovative attempts to move beyond its classical formulations all serve as a convergence point for the methodological innovations employed in this work.

The chapter maintains the general principle of presenting the enquiry from the perspective of the Nankani. Having already identified the methodological approach in chapter one with further substantiation above, the rest of the chapter is organized around one major theme; namely, sources of research data. The breakdown of this has provided two sub-themes: written and oral sources (literature review and field-based methodologies). The peculiar nature of the latter source of data has led to further breakdowns as discussed below.

THE METHODOLOGICAL QUEST

Two groups of sources have been explored for the required data. These are the written text and the oral text, also referred to as oral sources. While the data from the written text is obtained through a selected review of the available literature, the oral sources are gathered through field studies. The written text is simply classified as secondary data. This is irrespective of the sub-classifications of written data into primary, secondary and tertiary data. The essence of this clustering is to give significant attention to the oral sources which are perceived as the main research data. It is my contention that a study aimed at presenting the subject group's perspective, an oral and less documented society, should emphasize the use of the group's own resources or means of representing itself.

---

15   Turner, "The Way Forward in the Religious Study of African Primal Religions," 13.

Oral sources thus constitute the primary source of research data. This data source is based on my field study of the subject group at the individual, group and community levels. The data is gathered from in-depth interviews, focus group discussions and participatory observation. Besides privileging the Nankani point of view, the approach is in consonance with the phenomenological study of religion which is suitable for a field-oriented study in which the findings manifest themselves. Similarly, the approach falls in line with the current desire for a 'bottom-up approach' in rural development. It also answers the qualitative needs of social research which aims for participant or subject group experiences. In view of the crucial role of the primary data, therefore, it has become the key area of discourse in this chapter, giving rise to detailed discussions of the methods used.

The written sources are constituted from various literatures within the confines of this enquiry. This comprises texts on religious studies, ATR, development, gender, cultural and anthropological studies. They also include literature on theoretical and methodological issues. Irrespective of the range, the paucity of literature on the Nankani puts it under restraint. The literature under review, therefore, consists of a few basic texts, relevant for contextualizing the study, bringing out the underlying issues for discussion, filling in gaps and linking it up with "broader contexts".[16] Silverman identifies with Wolcott on this by noting that literature review is not a synthesis of previous works but that which should be used "to connect your narrow research topic to the broader research concerns of the broader research community".[17] Consequently, the rest of the literature will be used to help with the analysis and to situate the study within wider contexts on a "when-and-as-needed basis".[18]

A limited selection of texts is discussed in this section. This choice is based on whether or not the text significantly imparts knowledge on the Nankani. This narrows the selection but is well focused to provide the needed foundation. Within this frame of reference, the work of the British colonial anthropologist R. S. Rattray emerges as the only known text to have directly paid attention to the beliefs and practices of the 'Nankannse'. Contained in his two volume book, *The Tribes of the*

---

16   Harry F. Wolcott, *Writing Up – Qualitative Research* (Thousand Oaks, London and New Delhi: Sage Publication, 2001), 72.

17   Silverman, *Doing Qualitative Research*, 231.

18   Wolcott, *Writing Up*, 72-5.

Ashanti Hinterland, Rattray devoted a large segment of his investigation to a loose group of communities he called the Nankanse.[19] Largely made up of the present Frafra/Gurunne speaking communities, this group had and continues to co-share identities and titles with the Nankani, Tallensi and sometimes the Kasena.[20] Rattray's classification may well depict the struggle to carve out, linguistically, a sense of a larger identity for these communities, hitherto referred to as 'the stateless people', in the nation's transformational history from Gold Coast to Ghana. For instance, while the Kasena and Nankani shared a colonial title of Gurusi/Gurunsi, a title that has a significant bearing on the political clustering of the two ethnic groups in the present political administrative district, a phenomenal change is taking place in which the Nankani are rejecting the title Gurusi as an inappropriate identity description. At the same time, there is a minimal claim by some Frafras to the linguistic designation Gurunne. The current linguistic placement of the Nankani, Frafra and Tallensi under the category Gurunne may be as a result of the ambiguous state of the dialects and languages in the area. This lack of clarity is evident in the manner in which these ethnic groups identify or refer to each other within their communities and language varieties.

My investigation into this referential phenomenon during my field study showed that there are sentimental differences between the titles Nankana, Nankariŋá (Nankarisi) and Guruŋá (Gurusi). These differences are based on the notion of purity or true identity. Although these notions have no significant ethnic or political considerations, it is worth understanding them. Referred to as dialectical negations by Augustine Akanlu, he notes that the Kasenas from the extreme end of the regional boundary refer to the Kasenas and Nankanis to the east as Nankana, designating a less pure Kasena group. The process continues to the point were the Nankanis in the eastern zone refer to the next group, Zokko and the surrounding communities, as Nankarisi. Conversely, the Frafras and Tallensi also refer to those at the West side, Navrongo and surrounding communities, as Gurusi, and beyond this as Yulisi. According to Cardinall, the title Grunshi was use by their neighbours from Burkina Faso to refer to those in Ghana.[21] Despite these ambiguities, the ethnic group identified as Nankani is currently

---

19   Rattray, *The Tribes of the Ashanti Hinterland*, 222-338.
20   Westermann and Bryan, *Languages of West Africa*, 61.
21   Cardinall, *The Natives of the Northern Territories of the Gold Coast*, viii.

well established and this is the significant difference between Rattray's study and the current undertaking.

Although not properly elaborated, substantiated or placed within the framework of gender, Rattray's work contains information that is relevant to current discourses on gender. These relate to issues of female identity, role and status, and their inherent link with inheritance and succession, and of power and authority. Together with Meyer Forte's works on the Tallensi, the two anthropological works provide documented evidence on the intricacies of gender in the north-eastern part of Ghana. Although these issues are referred to in chapter four, they serve as evidence for feminist critique on the lack of gender perspectives in early anthropological works even though their works exhibited the dynamics of gender in the study communities.[22]

Even so, Rattray's work continues to be the only known text on the Nankannse (Guruni/Frafras). Published in 1932, his account remains the landmark documentation on the people. In this text, Rattray documented the structure of the society and aspects of their beliefs and practices. The study enabled him to record some aspects of the language. All these continue to shed light on the Nankani. Nonetheless, his work is circumscribed by its historical setting and colonial administrative oriented objectives.

Great Things Happen by Fr. R. McCoy sheds relevant insights on the contacts between the Nankani and the early Christian mission in the North.[23] Although with a missionary orientation and primarily focused on the Dagaati in the north-western corridor of the country, this text records some of the first signs of modern development through the missionary documentations. These include the earliest missionary provision of formal education, health, agriculture as well as other social services such as sewing and housekeeping for girls. The significance of this text lies in the fact that its contents are rooted in the records of daily missionary life. These historical accounts were recently validated in the narratives of the centenary celebration of the Catholic Church in the Northern Ecclesiastical Province in Navrongo in April 2006. Embedded in the Northern missionary history of 1906, its content

---

22   Christine Obbo, *African Women: Their Struggle for Economic Independence* (London: Zed Press, 1980), 1-3.

23   Remigius F. McCoy, *Great Things Happen: A Personal Memoir* (Montreal: The Society of Missionaries of Africa, 1988), 29-34 and 39-46.

predates Rattray's works. Additionally, its setting in Navrongo and its environs is fundamental to the Nankani communities. Although Navrongo is currently subsumed into the Kassem spoken communities, a product of colonization and urbanization, its position as the starting point of the missionary endeavour among the Nankani is important. Moreover, the role of Navrongo as the missionary development locus gives this study grounds to trace the origin of current development and NGO work, particularly, NABOCADO from the Nankani communities. In my recent field study, it was remarked that while the colonial administration brought division, pain and suffering, 'taking even the little we had away, the missionaries brought relief, comfort and help'.

Among these early texts, the works of Meyer Fortes on the Tallensi stand out as the only extensive and perhaps most comprehensive study on any of the tribes in the north-eastern part of Ghana. Although focused on the Tallensi, Fortes' studies served as the benchmark for colonial governance in the whole area.[24] This had more serious political, religio-cultural and socio-economic implications for the rest of people in the area than is recognized or acknowledged. The fact that the colonial administration in the eastern corridor used Navrongo as their first district illustrates this view. Consequently, the impact of Fortes' studies has a multidimensional relevance to this study as it had, and still has, on the whole region. Its overwhelming documentation of the Tallensi, perhaps as an example of the communities in this part of the country, eventually overshadowed the rest of the ethnic groups, including the Nankani, placing them in a scholarly oblivion. Besides, the theoretical engagement with Fortes' findings by other scholars enables this study to engage with other sources of literature outside this regional scope.[25] This notwithstanding, great caution is taken so as to avoid undue generalization and also to account for the differences or peculiarities between the Tallensi and the Nankani.

Despite the valuable contributions of these earlier texts, their historical location exhibits a limitative factor to understanding the current Nankani realities. The need to transcend this to the contemporary without negating the past is essential. This demands a search into current literature on the Nankani. Unfortunately, it appears there is still no definitive text on the Nankani. As a result, some of the recent general

---

24   Rattray, *The Tribes of the Ashanti Hinterland*, xx-xxii.
25   See for instance, Ray, *African Religions*, 138-40.

works on the region and the country are found valuable for initiating this transition. At the same time, they engage a significant number of issues worth deliberating. With concrete historical underpinnings, the following texts are reviewed to provide this historical link as well as its contribution to the poverty and underdevelopment of the area.

This contemporary set includes *Tongnaab*, by Jean Allman and John Parker, and *Regional Development in Ghana* by Jacob Songsore. The underlying theme of these works is the dislocation of Northern Ghana from the religious, political, socio-economic and historical landscape of the nation state. In their historical study of *Tongnaab* and its complex migratory and transformational dynamism, Allman and Parker succinctly state:

> Those ongoing historical dynamics call into question the shape of much of Ghana's national history. While widely acknowledged as one of the most sophisticated in tropical Africa, the historiography of Ghana remains firmly focused on Asante and the other Akan states of the forest zone. These "stateless" peoples of the northern savanna-including the Talensi, the guardians and mediators of Tongnaab – have long been seen as peripheral to the main narratives of historical change. In the formulation of the early colonial ethnographer R. S. Rattray, these peoples formed the "tribes of the Ashanti hinterland".[26]

The fact remains that Rattray was not the only one to use this term or reference. Fortes referred to the 'hinterland' in his article on "Ritual Festivals and Social Cohesion in the Hinterland of the Gold Coast".[27] Similarly, Cardinall wrote his 1927 book with the title *In Ashanti and Beyond*.[28] From his perspective, the people in the North can simply be categorized in the context of being beyond the centralized Ashanti nation of the emerging Ghanaian state. The import of these designations and their attendant notions of being an insignificant appendage to Ashanti have persisted until the present day, continuing to influence the way the North is perceived in terms of religion, Western civiliza-

---

26   Allman, and Parker, *Tongnaab*, 6.

27   Cited in Allman and Parker, *Tongnaab*, 284.

28   Cardinall, *In Ashanti and Beyond*.

tion, socio-economic development and national politics. Between these two texts, *Tongnaab* stands out for its religio-cultural substance.

Tongnaab, which is partly based on Fortes' studies, focuses on the religious core of the Tallensi. Its historical overview of the Tallensi, analysis of both Rattray and Fortes' works and the strategic roles the two scholars played in facilitating not just the Tallensi but the entire area to colonial governance, is quite explicit.[29] This reiterates the major criticisms of early anthropological studies.[30] That apart, this emphasizes the lack of scholarly literature on the area.[31] Yet, like Fortes, focusing on the Tallensi continues to create an imbalance in our knowledge of the other communities. It is observed that even though some references are drawn from these other communities, they are usually for illustrative and corroborative purposes.[32] Again, despite their attempts to dehistorize the Tallensi and their religion, most of their pictures are picked from the 1920s and 1930s; a representation that still gives the notion of stagnation and historical rigidity. Nonetheless, the study offers a vantage point from which the impact of these colonial and scholarly encounters among the Tallensi impacted on the geographical area. It is from this perspective that *Tongnaab* is most relevant to this study.

Allman and Parker bring to the fore the need to re-examine the idea of 'primitivism' with regard to the Tallensi, therefore, ATR. Rightly observed, if "primitiveness" indicated one's perceived notion of "nakedness" and a "predilection for fetishism" by the other, then there is a great need for a review of such a concept.[33] This is very important for the current context in which indigenous beliefs and practices are acknowledged in their own right as religions. Again, previous notions of 'nakedness' may not only be viewed from the viewpoint of cultural relativism, it also raises questions on today's views on fashion and individual freedom. Even so, the historical notion of nakedness needs to be examined in line with each religio-cultural bodily adornment, and also, within the contextual frame of space and time. This can be considered alongside current discourses on Western and Islamic dress codes. Although the current trend of fashion including bikini, tattoos and

---

29 Allman and Parker, *Tongnaab*, 73.
30 Riall W. Nolan, *Development Anthropology: Encounters in the Real World* (Boulder, Colorado and Oxford: Westview Press, 2002), 65.
31 Allman and Parker, *Tongnaab*, 18.
32 Ibid., 32-7.
33 Allman and Parker, *Tongnaab*, 57, 77-9.

body piercing is another area of comparative interest, it questions the binary concepts of civilized and uncivilized, developed and undeveloped/underdeveloped. This further raises questions on the historical Western constructs of religion, culture and development in the light of the colonial enterprise shown by Chidester's *Savage Systems*.

Closely tied to the question of nakedness is that of the 'origin of clothing' in the area. It is significant that Allman and Parker noted the misrepresentation of the introduction of the cotton cloth to the area. As they observed, the colonial government was not the first to introduce this as 'a first sign of civilization or development'. The mainstay of existing indigenous oral knowledge is that the cotton cloths were introduced to the area by Mossi traders (around the fifteenth century). Their work thus corresponds with this and also illustrates to some extent the problems with colonial administrative reports. Besides, the indigenous cloth or outfit of the area is not identified with the British cotton cloth (Wax Print). The redesigned Islamic-influenced outfit made from the Mossi white and indigo cotton striped cloth commonly called the *mutane* (Mossi piece) is now popularly known by its 'smock' outfits.[34] Not only has it developed in forms different from its original style and colour, it is also used as one of the traditional or national attires in Ghana. Internationally, it is used as part of the indigenous Ghanaian, or African dress code. Made popular by Ghana's first president, Kwame Nkrumah and the recently by ex-president, J. J. Rawlings, the two figures are sometimes seen as the political promoters or heroes of the North and its smock. This sentiment has political ramification in the nation's political system. The important role of this cloth in the construction of a Northern identity and its contribution to the socio-economic development of the people and area has also become significant in recent times.

This discussion is not to simply re-examine and correct misrepresentations, but to illustrate elements of sustainable development in the area. It shows how cultural relevance underlies ingenuity and development. Although this cloth was a trade commodity, it has emerged as the best contextual developed product of the area. It raises a question as to whether the development of the Mossi cloth constitutes a form of resistance to the British colonial enterprise in the area or whether it is based on the relevance and availability of resources and local technology. That is, the integration of the cloth into the religio-cultural

---

34   Picture 15.

practices of the people, the local production of cotton and the ability to produce the cloth locally has engineered its successful transformation into a local product. This is both an example and a challenge to the Western notion of development in the area.

Another significant contribution of Allman and Parker's work is its discussion on the historical migration of *Tongnaab* to Southern Ghana and what is presented as a subsequent metamorphosis into a witch hunting deity. Like Fortes, these two scholars failed to understand the basis on which witchcraft was not a concern for the Tallensi or their neighbouring communities. This shows a continuous lack of grasp of one of the core functions of *Tongnaab* as well as the beliefs and practices in the region. Consequently, this has created a void as to why *Tongnaab* became an active witch-hunting deity in the South, thus creating an impression of a transformation in the activity of *Tongnaab*. The basis on which this gap has been created can be understood in terms of religion and space. It calls our attention to the relationship between religious space and geographical space, and the role of territorial deities. *Tongnaab* is a deity of the Tallensi. Among the Tallensi it controls both space and people. On the other hand, its status in the South as a migrant deity is location-specific. It is believed that the earth deities of those spaces are in control of their territorial spaces. As a guest deity, *Tongnaab* has no geographical or spiritual control over the terrain. Nonetheless, it can act if it is requested to do so within the space allocated to it. This request is interpreted in the form of those people who are brought before it, within its allocated sacred space.

In contrast, as the supreme deity of the Tallensi, no active evil manifestation is allowed within its jurisdiction. Witches are naturally subdued by the power of *Tongnaab* within its territory. On the other hand, invading or recalcitrant witches are ritually presented to *Tongnaab*. Any further activity by this group leads to their mysterious elimination (death) by *Tongnaab*.[35] This belief in the guardianship role of *Tongnaab* relaxes the people, making them less anxious or worried about the dangers of witchcraft. The difference in the activities of Tongnaab in the North and South is not an issue of the transformation but one of territorial sovereignty vis-à-vis subjugation. The situation

---

35   Rose Mary Amenga-Etego, "Probing the Religio-Cultural Roots of Witchcraft among the Nankani," (Institute of Women in Religion and Culture conference paper, Gambaga, Ghana, 2004), 12.

in the South was however aggravated by the socio-cultural differences between the North and South.

Like *Tongnaab*, all migrants from the North to the South acquire new experiences and influences. Some are beneficial while others are perceived as inimical to the local community of the migrants. Thus, the active witch-hunting expeditions in the south and the entire socio-cultural influence of the Southern concept of witchcraft had an adverse effect on most early Northern migrants. Because of the dominance of a matrilineal system in the South, witchcraft is conceived and interpreted differently. According to the Akan, 'the ant that bites you is already in your cloth'. This saying places witchcraft within the family context. In the wake of Western influence, the Akans also held the notion that witches are attracted by one's personal development in the form of education, wealth and affluence. These became destabilizing factors for some Northern migrants whose purpose for travelling was economic. This influence did not only undermine the patrilineal kinship structure of the North and its core values; it greatly affected the pace of development in the area. Some students, business people, wage or salary earners and politicians seldom went back home, supported the extended family or engaged in development work in their home communities for fear of attracting the attention of witches. This attitude contradicted, for instance, the Nankani worldview, which maintains that adherence to family and religion are a security against evil attacks, including witchcraft. Although there is currently a paradigm shift in this perception of witchcraft, the impact of this early phase cannot be underestimated. The beliefs in witchcraft and its influence on development among the Nankani has been discussed in chapter three.

At the end of the second chapter, Allman and Parker came to an important conclusion. For them, the Tallensi refusal to succumb to the colonial authority on its terms was not:

> [B]ecause they were clinging to the refuge of an unchang-
> ing past, but because the terms offered by the British bore
> absolutely no legitimate connection to their real, lived
> history – to their gods and their ancestors – and took no
> account of contemporary change.[36]

---

36 Allman and Parker, *Tongnaab*, 104.

This important observation directly connects this thesis to the core of their study on the persistence and resilience of the religio-cultural dimension. It is the root of that which is often perceived as religious resistance to change or development. Here is one example that shows that change is not resisted *per se*, but because of its lack of religio-cultural inclusiveness. Although this provides further insights to our understanding of the statistical data and discussion in chapter two,[37] can it also be concluded that the resistance of the Tallensi to using their sacred hills for a quarry is an example of anti-development? Definitely not. These are issues of selective choices, pertaining to what constitutes development to those concerned. The choice to put Tong Hills on the National Tourist Board, the continuous negotiations with diverse developmental agencies, and the ongoing consultations to have the hills recognized as a World Heritage site is the community's decision.[38]

How do these processes inform our understanding of rural development? What is evident is that every culture or society has its own priorities and perspectives of what it means to develop. This is an important contribution to the understanding of the current study. In their conclusion, they offer yet another pertinent statement to the effect that development among the Tallensi is not an issue of *per-capita-income*, even though they are a part of the poorest region; but as one the scholars witnessed:

> [T]he complexity and vibrancy of African modernity – a modernity that predates European – and we watched as the boundaries between the local, national, and the global melted before our eyes.[39]

Songsore's text on *Regional Development in Ghana* draws this study into the contextual issues of development in Ghana. His analysis of the dominant theories of regional development brings the ethnic based Nankani into the broader frame of territorial demarcations and the development pattern in Ghana. Although not a religious study, his text addresses the core issues of development in the nation, providing alternative views to the religious undertones of development among the Nankani. His analysis of the Ghanaian situation shows how regional

---

37   See chapter two, 55-7.
38   Allman and Parker, *Tongnaab*, 229-34.
39   Allman and Parker, *Tongnaab*, 236.

development, over space and time, has significantly contributed to the poverty and underdevelopment of the Nankani. In other words, poverty and underdevelopment among the Nankani is not dependent on religion. Thus for Songsore, an examination of the historical, socio-economic and political developments of the nation state is essential in discourses of this nature.

Songsore's own historical analysis places the reconfiguration of trade and power between the eighth/fifteenth and sixteenth/twenty-first centuries at the foundation of the current state of unequal regional development in Ghana. His argument on the shift in trade from "the grasslands of Western Sudan", which relied on the trade routes of the North, to "'the coastlands and forest regions'", with emphasis of centralized political control is significant to the understanding of the Nankani perception of a deteriorating local economy.[40] Northern Ghana, which had served as an indispensable trade route in the pre-colonial era, emerged in the colonial and post-colonial phase as a dislodged periphery in the new socio-economic and political re-configuration. Although my study is a religious endeavour, the main title presupposes that an understanding of the socio-political and economic configuration of the nation cannot be avoided.

That the religio-cultural dimension is not considered in Songsore's text can be viewed as a lack of appreciation for religion as an important resource for development. Nevertheless, Songsore's analysis shows the poverty and underdevelopment of the Nankani is not a religious issue, as contemplated in chapter one. I therefore contend that this view is the product of interpretations and activities of the people involved. Nevertheless, Songsore's identity as a Northerner places him within one of the contesting sides of that preamble (African perspective), thus it contextualizes the debate in this regard.[41]

Despite the relevance of these books in contextualizing the study area, none of them have focused on the Nankani as a subject group of their study. Neither have any among them focused on the religion or the socio-economic development of the Nankani. This lack of prior research on the Nankani makes my investigation unique. Nonetheless, the respective focuses of the above works have been very helpful. However, the integrated nature of this study shows how the two

---

40   Songsore, *Regional Development in Ghana*, 24-5.
41   See chapter one, 8-14.

dimensions can be put together, in a given context, to provide under-standing on religion and its influence on development within the current globalized world.

As indicated at the beginning of this section, oral sources constitute an identifiable source of literature in the study of ATR. 'Oral Sources' is a designated term for the diverse sets of unwritten data sources employed in academic studies. The term oral is used in contrast to written data. Also known as 'Oral Traditions', especially in the Ghanaian context, the two forms of identifications are used interchangeably.[42] Predominantly found in non-literary societies, the term oral is not limited to its practical connotation. It includes a variety of art forms, symbols and dramatic or ritual forms of expressions.[43] The African continent, a major non-literary society, is frequently confronted with its lack of written documentation in the current global literary era. Dependent on a largely unwritten and an inadequate speculative written history, much of Africa's history, religio-cultural, economic and socio-political systems are believed to be contained in this traditional resource.[44] As a result, studies on Africa have had to rely, to a great extent, on these traditional forms of documentation. According to Bahr, even though ATR has no written text, it has "sacred words" and these words are found in the oral traditions.[45]

Despite this acknowledgement, Parrinder's concern about the undocumented nature of Africa's religious data continues to persist.[46] The oral nature of Africa's religions has transcended time and space, and today is acknowledged as an authentic source of data in academic studies. It is therefore misleading to argue that the lack of written documentation means the knowledge of the past has perished.[47] As Mbiti points out:

---

42   Jan Vansina, *Oral Traditions: A Study in Historical Methodology*, trans. H.M. Wright (London: Routledge and Kegan Paul, 1965).

43   Edward G. Newing, "Religions of pre-literary societies," in *The World's Religions*, 4th ed. Ed. Sir Norman Anderson (Inter-Varsity Press, October 1975), 13-7.

44   Emefie Ikenga Metuh, *African Religions in Western Conceptual Schemes: The Problems of Interpretation; (Studies in Igbo Religion)* (Bodija Ibadan: Pastoral Institute, 1985), 1-19; 23-36.

45   Bahr, *Religions of the World*, 40.

46   Parrinder, *Worship in the World's Religions*, 30.

47   Allman and Parker, *Tongnaab*.

> Religion in African societies is written not on paper but
> in people's hearts, minds... Everybody is a religious carrier.
> Therefore we have to study not only the beliefs concerning
> God and the spirits, but also the religious journey of the
> individual from before birth to after physical death...[48]

By this assertion, Mbiti is calling for a different type of study on Africa.
It is one that asks researchers to involve the totality of the lives of the
people, one that can be described as the African lifecycle theory. It
appeals to the researcher to journey with the people through their own
languages, philosophies, customs and practices.

Nonetheless, the search for knowledge in such an encompassing
manner is not only challenging but daunting for some researchers. For
instance, the inability to ascribe knowledge to a specific source or a
limited number of traceable sources but to a whole range of sources
such as myths, proverbs, sayings, names, symbols, music and dance,
rituals and, in fact, a whole way of life seems absurd to these scholars.[49] Today, the presence of written works on Africa, although limited,
provides alternative avenues for accessing or substantiating oral data.
All the same, much of Africa's past, and to some extent present, continues to be veiled in its oral sources. In this regard, an understanding of
Africa's past, the tracking of the changes, and the understanding of the
present, continues to demand of the researcher a complete and objective study of its oral sources. The examination of data in the original
form as well as their present understanding, usage and interpretations
are therefore crucial. In his work on 'The African Spiritual Universe',
Parrinder draws attention to the view that these ancient sources have
assumed modern interpretations.[50]

This brings into context a number of concerns, all raised by Parrinder. This involves his initial lament over the lack of written text on
Africa and the problems this posed to the understanding of the people
and their religion. He writes:

> [C]omplete lack of written documents from within the
> religion. Not only are there no summaries of doctrine
> in ancient African religion, but no written exposition of

---

48 Mbiti, *African Religions and Philosophy*, 4.
49 Parrinder, *Religion in Africa*, 17-38.
50 Parrinder, "The African Spiritual Universe," 16-7.

>spiritual experience, and nothing to tell what it was like to
>be a believer in the old religion.[51]

This expression, though genuine, constitutes one of the misunderstandings or misinterpretations of Africa's religion. The fact that
Africa's religion is not written or doctrinal but practical is not fully
comprehended.[52] Parrinder's desire to bring ATR into conformity with
'world religions', for easy access and understanding was a challenge,
but this was his problem not the religion. Yet like him, other Western
scholars took to writing down aspects of the religion. But Sir Norman
Anderson points out that Africa's written past is inadequate, misrepre-
sented and misinterpreted. The writings of explorers, missionaries and
colonial governors bear the brunt of this criticism.[53] But the criticisms
are not limited to these. They include some of the early and current
scholarly works on Africa.

Subsequently, Parrinder's position of 'lack of written documents'
was transformed to that of no reliable data.[54] Unlike Anderson, he
became critical of modern African scholars who are largely Christians
and not the 'real' practitioners of ATR.[55] This observation is accurate
and it confronts the core of documentation in ATR as well as this
study. Yet, Parrinder is not the only scholar critical of this new trend.[56]
Africans like Okot p'Bitek are not only critical of Western scholarship, including Parrinder's works; he is also concerned with the works
of African scholars. This raises critical questions on this study, for a
professed African Christian conducting this investigation. What do
the Nankani practitioners perceive of this? What role are they playing
to produce a fair representation of their beliefs and practices within
the confines of the study? The answers to these reflections can be deci-
phered below and in chapter six.

The main challenge is about the right (unbiased) understanding,
use and interpretation of oral sources. This area of the subject matter

---

51   Parrinder, *Religion in Africa*, 17.
52   Kwabena Dei Offori-Attah, "African Traditional Religion: Triumphs of Rituals,"
     African Religion, [journal online] accessed 1 September 2006; available from
     http://www2.ncsu.edu/ncsu/aern/afridan.html; Internet.
53   Sir Norman Anderson (ed.), *The World's Religions*, 4th ed. (London: Inter-Varsity
     Press, October 1975), 12-4.
54   Parrinder, "The African Spiritual Universe," 16-7.
55   Ibid., 7.
56   Cox, "African Identity as the Projection of Western Alterity", 25-6.

currently poses various theoretical and methodological challenges to researchers. As researchers grapple with these problems, the issue of providing adequate references to such a contested written past and an oral present becomes a formidable task. Yet, the continuous relevance of these sources, despite growing suspicion and uncertainties from subject communities and intellectual groups, creates problems. Questions as to the best possible ways to present field data in a given study are as crucial as conducting the field study itself. Over the years, various guidelines have been formulated to help researchers in this regard. Unfortunately, these do not adequately address the problems faced by scholars, African or Western, as observed by Turner above. The problems are left to the researchers involved to adapt and/or appropriate the existing methodologies to their given context and study. These are some of the reasons for the methodological innovations employed in this study. In other words, although this investigation subscribed to the use of oral sources, it is conscious of the problems associated with such a methodological choice and takes the necessary steps to meet the needs of this study.

FIELD-BASED METHODOLOGIES

The lack of adequate written data and the resultant reliance on oral sources as primary data on African studies particularly contributed to making fieldwork a priority in this research. Moreover, the current scholarly desire for contextual studies, compounded by a similar desire for a bottom-up approach to rural development, is a crucial underlying factor. Although facilitated by the phenomenological method, obtaining the right and sufficient data to advance this line of argument requires proper identification, structuring and use of appropriate field methods. This has not been easy, especially as the subject group tends to answer questions with queries, riddles, sayings and proverbs. Sometimes, these are interlaced with long genealogical and epistemological narratives. On other occasions, answers are given with a comparative nuance, reflecting what scholars view as 'reactivity' and 'reflexivity' in field studies.

In an attempt to address the prevailing issues, three standard field methods were adapted and used. The extent to which each of these methods was applied in the field varied in response to the culture. Unfortunately, there were some occasions when an in-depth understanding of a phenomenon or subject of discussion could not be obtained due to some prevailing cultural restrictions. As a 'cultural insider', my position provided both clues to these extra insights as well as the limitations imposed on my respondents. The phrase 'cultural insider' refers to my community membership, which has enabled me to belong, to be absorbed by my respondents and has placed me within the scope of a native researcher. At the same time, it indicates an aspect of my own projected sense of outsider status, basically, in the religious and in some contexts, gender and age stratification systems. Although no specific outline is made to discuss the internal dynamics of this relationship between the respondents and native researcher (different levels of perceptions), it is clearly manifested in the study, especially in chapter six. Nevertheless, my insider status enabled me to seek new ways of gathering the requisite knowledge without infringing on the religio-cultural practices and systems. Consequently, three other field strategies were devised to complement the inadequacies encountered in the use of the recognized field methods that were originally strategized for the fieldwork. I refer to these as 'specific field methods' and have subsequently discussed them below. They are so described to reflect their particularity and their contribution to the needs of this study.

In all, twenty-nine in-depth interviews were organized. Thirteen of these turned into informal group discussions with two to nine extra participants in each case, except in three cases where the number kept increasing to the end. Fifteen focus group discussions were organized. Two of these, one male and the other female, were held as community level discussions in Kandiga and were co-organized by the chief. They were the last community discussions and were held simultaneously with three field assistants and a video coverage at the Kandiga market.[57] With the exception of one youth group discussion where two boys of about eight to twelve years sat in and contributed to the gender dynamics in families, participants ranged from the age eighteen to the elderly. My insider status, as well as the repetitive transformation of these discussions into teaching events, facilitated some form of observer participation.[58] Not only were cross-discussions of issues ensuing among participants, I was sometimes asked to participate or contribute to some aspects of the discussion, not as a researcher but as an insider. On these occasions, the roles played by my research assistant(s) became very important, as they wrote down the discussions. This is irrespective

---

57   See picture 8 for details.
58   See chapter six.

of the fact that these discussions were also recorded on audio tapes. In other words, even though my initial preparation for the fieldwork had clear and distinct strategies, these were constantly blurred and transformed at the field level.

Two other assistants were used at the University of Ghana to review the nation's news papers within a guided scope of reference. Their role was to record (extract information) on the types and number of reported cases on traditional religion and its leaders in the context of modern development. This exercise was to help obtain a general overview of what the Ghanaian public expect from its religio-cultural heritage in line with the current trend of life. Two hundred and one cases were identified from three papers between 2000 and 2005. The papers reviewed are *The Daily Graphic*, *The Weekly Mirror* and *The Weekly Spectator*. The captions noted included the need to respect and obey traditions, the important role of ATR in development, the need to support and modify the chieftaincy institution to reflect current trends, different development initiatives of chiefs, and chieftaincy disputes. The varied nature of this data showed that the population was very much interested and is in a constant interactive process of demanding, reprimanding, enforcing as well as paying compliments to its religio-cultural heritage, even in the current context of multi-culturalism, religious pluralism and modernity.

Standard Field-Based Methods

'Standard field-based methods' is used to differentiate acknowledged scholarly methodologies in academic research from those which this study has strategically appropriated to meet its needs. These methods are in-depth interviews (IDIs), focus group discussions (FGDs) and participant observation (OP).

In-depth interviews (IDIs), the direct face-to-face probing technique, were used to gather data from individuals with invaluable knowledge and/or experience on specific aspects of the research. The process involved a formal, semi-structured, time factored programme format for the elite (administrators), and a somewhat 'informal', 'unstructured' format at the community level. The differences enabled me to respond to the specific contexts, especially, of the Nankani tradition. Thus, the latter was formal in that context.[59] There is however no clear cut distinction between the two as they overlap in their applications. As such, IDIs sessions were constantly adjusted to the specific needs of the issues under discussion and the interviewee(s). As observed by Janet Finch, if structured research techniques are used hierarchically in a woman-to-woman interview it is considered perverse and insubordination.[60] This is especially true with elderly women in the Nankani context.

IDIs provided an avenue for a more intensive, interactive and person specific investigative process. This offered data on personal beliefs, motivations, attitudes, activities and experiences. They helped to secure vivid, exclusive accounts of individual personal experiences as well as their impressions about the study. Some of these occasions however unearthed very personal, sensitive and emotional issues. Although these offered significant insights and presented empirical evidence on the psychological role of religion and culture on the individual and his/her development, they are subject to anonymity. Again, even though the majority of these instances related to discussions on gender, the emotional outbursts involved both genders. There were, however, great differences in which each gender category expressed its emotions. For instance, while the males emerged from a position of authority, power and indignation, the female mostly came from a position of pain, sorrow, humiliation and resentment, or from a genuine point of cultural understanding and 'peace-making'. Conversely, there were those who appeared with a sense of what I will call a 'manipulative mastery of the game over power and authority'. These women presented defiant yet controlling attitudes to their lives and experiences. Significantly, most of these were occasions when IDIs were used within the context of situational or negative questioning.

This notwithstanding, IDIs were helpful in clarifying issues raised during FGDs. Likewise, they raised issues that were brought into FGDs for elaboration or substantiation. IDIs were particularly useful for interviewing hard-to-reach individuals, who though valuable, did not turn up for FGDs. It is however worth noting that IDIs are time

---

59 Interview questions were constantly adjusted to suit respective respondents. Besides, some interviews were organized purposely for verifications of previous data.

60 Janet Finch, "'It's great to have someone to talk to': the ethics and politics of interviewing women," in *Social Researching*, eds. C. Bell and H. Roberts (RKP, 1984), 72.

consuming, not only to arrange but also, to conduct. Nevertheless, this may be due to the study area (rural Africa) and subject group (a largely non-literate society).

In *Designing Social Research: The Logic of Anticipation*, Norman Blaikie refers to interview situations as the "*semi-natural* settings".[61] Blaikie asserts that respondents are removed from their natural settings where their lives are lived-out in various activity forms, to a more sedentary place for the needed reflection, recollection and description. Although this is generally true, this study encountered a number of situations that run contrary to his observation. Not only did the female interviewees work during interviews; those who participated in group discussions brought some household chores to the discussion site, thereby juxtaposing the natural with the semi-natural settings. A much more elaborate occasion for fusing the two settings, was during 'situational questioning', where the natural and "*semi-natural*" were almost fused together as they set the context in which the interviews were conducted.

Most rural African women, unlike their counterparts in the developed world, do not have the opportunity to be idle, lonely or bored as put forward by Finch.[62] This is primarily because the so-called 'full-time house-wife' environment and its attendant incidence of isolation is absent in many rural African homes. I do however agree with Finch that a woman-to-woman interview has an added dimension because "both parties share a subordinate structural position by virtue of their gender".[63] This develops bonding and mutual solidarity. In my case, while the elderly women felt happy that their daughter was doing something different and enquired to know my full relations (kinship), the younger ones marvelled and expressed their desire of doing 'something like that'. For others the comment was: 'as for you, you've just rested [you're just free]'. 'Freedom' meant being able to interact and discuss with men in culturally unfamiliar terms but also what they perceived as the drudgery of the life of the domestic rural woman. Yet, as a Nankani woman who sometimes suspends her immediate objective to help with the work of the interviewee, a different understanding or a not-so-different attitude was also adopted. This reduced any form of elite, socio-economic threat and created solidarity within the cultural

---

61   Blaikie, *Designing Social Research*, 28.
62   Finch, "It's great to have someone to talk to," 74.
63   Ibid., 76.

understanding of womanhood.[64] This shares a similar bearing, of a different context, with Finch as she discusses her identity disclosure and as a fellow clergyman's wife, and the relative opening of the channels of communication. For her, interviewees "became warm and eager to talk to me after the simple discovery that I was one of them".[65]

Accordingly, Finch argues that a woman-to-woman interview is 'special'. For her, the shared "status and demeanour as a woman" serves as a converging point.[66] She also states that, the female researcher should be "prepared to expose herself to being 'placed' as a woman and to establish that she is willing to be treated accordingly".[67] This found credence when the women of Kandiga asked me to contribute to one of the male stereotypical assertions about women. Being told 'women do not respect when their hands are able to reach their mouths [can care for themselves]', the female participants felt I was the most appropriate woman to respond since I was within the stereotype. These instances provide additional perspectives from which the classical insider/outsider dichotomy may be further examined.[68] The fluidity with which respondents and researchers navigate these dynamics is significant.[69]

Focus group discussions (FGDs) were sessions in which small groups of homogeneous people were brought together to discuss relevant issues in the investigation. In such groups, the people, especially women and youth, felt more at ease in expressing themselves. It was the most relevant data gathering tool at the community level. The groups were organized according to sex and age. This conformed to tradition hence facilitated the data gathering. Fifteen FGDs were conducted; six in a preliminary study and nine groups in the major field study. They were held in Kandiga, Sirigu, Kologo and Naga communities.

In the preliminary study in 2004, a group composed of men and women encountered problems as the women were less vocal in the mixed group. In order to obtain participants' views on the differences in women's perspectives in mixed group discussions, the question of

---

64   William Foddy, *Constructing Questions for Interviews and Questionnaires: Theory and Practice in Social Research* (Cambridge: Cambridge University Press), 120-4.

65   Finch, "It's great to have someone to talk to". 79.

66   Ibid. 80.

67   Ibid., 79-90.

68   Westerlund, *African Religion in African Scholarship*, 91.

69   See chapter six.

the women's voice was raised. Although, the main reason bordered on the traditional gender structure of this patriarchal society, the women wanted privacy for issues of femininity. Some men also reacted to some of the contributions from women as a lack of respect for men and tradition. In view of this, the main fieldwork excluded mixed groups of women and men but maintained one in which various ages of the same gender were participants. The reason was to examine the differences in attitude and expression, if any, between the youth and mature members in the community, in response to research questions. Whereas there was much excitement and exuberance from the very young ones to participate, and to cite realistic or specific examples, the grown-ups exercised control through eye contact, facial expressions or blank putdowns and counter explanations. What was significant was the level of knowledge and understanding of current issues. Another area of significance was the way in which the young members of the community understood and interpreted the impact of specific modern gender concepts on their families and other community members.

As noted, quite a number of IDIs became FGDs spontaneously at the community level. Some were formed by the individual community leaders or elders who were contacted as key informants for IDIs. At their own discretion, they relayed the content of the agenda to their colleagues and invited their presence and contributions. The IDI session with the *tindana* of Kandiga, for instance, turned into a group discussion composed of him and some members of his council.[70] Others occur when the respondent in an interview situation calls for a collaborator(s) and/or authenticator(s) to some of his views.[71] This related to questions on specific religio-cultural issues with historical significance. On other occasions, such as in Naga, the group started forming as the family head sat at the *zenyore* (main gate) to respond to my interviews. This is however typical of the Nankani where male members join their elder(s) at the *zenyore* for various reasons.[72] The

---

70   Picture 16.

71   Vansina, *Oral Traditions*, 6-7.

72   Reasons given were on the researcher's gender, age and identity. It was also an off-farm season when people were at home and less busy. The absence of crops allowed easy visibility and this led to a much welcomed, though unsolicited, formation of groups. Participants argued that their presence was a demonstration of respect and solidarity for their elders. His acknowledgement and gratitude was shown through tolerance and references made to them.

last type of group formation was one in which participants joined at random. This was just sheer curiosity. These people join as spectators but they eventually participate in the discussion. A similar experience is noted by Allman and Parker in *Tongnaab* about their field work among the Bulsas. Even though all of these groups were formed on the basis of age and gender, the last two disregarded age classifications. One important aspect of these group formations was that they created avenues for teaching and learning, and communal bonding, sometimes without due regard to the researcher's presence.

Although unplanned and unsolicited, causing disruption, consuming time and somehow usurping 'power' and 'control' from the researcher's original plan of action, they provided further avenues for gathering distinct data. Retreating to the background after my questions also provided opportunities for participant observation. Some of the continuing discussions produced significant data on the group or community as a whole. It also provided some understanding of the traditional or institutional frame on which knowledge is imparted to particular age groups or individuals in the society. This process showed some difficulties of applying Western typeset field methodologies within the rural communal setting. The situation continuously called for adjustments, not only to my already prepared Western field-based methodologies but also to time, financial and material resources.

FGDs were therefore used to determine the opinions, attitudes and knowledge held by the target groups. It also gave the participants a good avenue to share information of historical relevance with one another. The relevance of FGDs is that the atmosphere provides greater stimulation than the individual interviews. It was an excellent method for obtaining qualitative data from several respondents at once.

The third method in this category is participant observation (PO). Blaikie describes this as obtaining data from their "natural social settings".[73] PO was useful for obtaining data on beliefs and practices pertaining to rituals, socio-cultural lifestyles and systems, as well as the traditional gender division of labour. My insider status facilitated this easily. As indicated above, PO formed an overlapping tool in the entire field study. I hereby agree with Wolcott that PO is "the core research activity in qualitative inquiry".[74] Although he notes that the

---

73   Blaikie, *Designing Social Research*, 28.
74   Wolcott, *Writing Up*, 66.

perspective underscores his particular interest and reflection on everyday living as the essential empirical element in qualitative research, he is still voicing the opinions of many.[75] Irrespective of his subjective nuance, PO underlies every aspect of fieldwork.

Although the above methods are good tools for gathering field data, they are sometimes inadequate in addressing the specific needs of some studies. This is particularly so in rural Africa with its religio-cultural restrictions. These restrictions are placed in the form of taboos and prohibitions. To overcome some of these problems two practical strategies were applied. These are 'negative questioning' and 'situational questioning'. These additional innovations were used at the community level along with the standard field methods. They were specifically strategized to deal with problems arising from prohibition, secrecy and taboo which in their strictest sense serve to categorise the data in context as 'classified'. On the other hand, the desire to express indigenous perspectives more adequately in academic studies has resulted in the proposed use of 'colloquialism' as a method of presenting the field data. This proposed method enables specified field data from specific socio-cultural contexts to be presented in their 'original' form.[76] These three additional field strategies are discussed below as 'specific field methods'.

Specific Field-Based Methods

'Specific field-based methods' as the phrase implies, refers to three innovative methods devised to circumvent some of the traditional impediments on research data gathering among the Nankani. On the other hand, they also served to compensate the inadequacies in the available field methodologies, in respect to this study. They are so named because they have been developed specifically to meet the field needs of this study.

The codes of taboos, prohibitions and secrecy imposed by oral African communities have, on some occasions, served as impediments limiting the ability of researchers, including natives, from obtaining some required data within the confines of their field data gathering.

---

75   Andy Merrifield, *Henry Lefebvre: A Critical Introduction* (New York and London: Routledge, 2006), 13.

76   Uwe Flick, *An Introduction to Qualitative Research* (London, Thousand Oaks and New Delhi: SAGE Publications, 1998), 148-51.

Serving their roles as 'classified' or 'protected' data categories, similar to classified data in developed or literate societies, some of the data under these protected codes are very important. Yet, set within oral traditions, they may only be obtained by those who matter, at the appropriate periods of ritual enactments, or under a ritual bond. In these circumstances, the inability of researchers to obtain such data may be compromised, and simply shelved as problems.

The strategies in this section are the ways in which some of these excluded sources of data among the Nankani were obtained during my fieldwork. The methods involved an inclusive reporting strategy which takes into consideration some suggestions from the Nankani. These views are essential for a bottom-up approach. The argument from this section is, under some specific contexts, that field data is culturally and linguistically bound. In their work on the *Introduction to the Study of Religion*, Ring *et al.* observed that language is neither neutral nor transparent. According to these scholars "language reveals and shapes our experiences" as much as it conceals them. This has to do with its complex ability to project and/or obscure the "nuances, subtleties, and meanings" of a given experience.[77] What Ring *et al.* failed to observe is our own inhibitions about revealing all of our experiences and beliefs at once and transparently. All the same, I concur with their findings that, "[l]anguage is personal and political: it shapes our private and our public worlds".[78] In the context of Africa, the absence of a literary culture is compensated by a seemingly complex network of language usage, shrouded in figurative forms. The need for such data to be presented within its original context to preserve its socio-cultural relativity and relevance is vital here.

It is within these contested contexts of field and scholarship that these methods are presented. In all, three specific field methods have been included. These are 'negative questioning', 'situational questioning' and 'colloquialism'.

Negative Questioning (NQ)

'Negative questioning' (NQ) is a method in which the researcher strategically rephrases an interviewing question into the negative but

---

77   Ring *et al.*, *Introduction to the Study of Religion*, 140.
78   Ibid., 141.

with relative importance to the respondent or subject community in order to obtain the desired specific data. The rephrased question must be asked with presumed ignorance and innocence, sometimes, as a rejection of the status quo or a protest. The innocent or ignorant perspective must be clearly evident. Although the method may also be used by other field researchers, it would be more useful to native researchers, whose positions as hybrids are deemed inadequate for the knowledge of their traditional beliefs and practices. Although the form and manner in which this method is executed varies, with relative proportion to the relationship s/he maintains with either the respondent or community, the native researcher is in a better position to determine the delicate boundaries on which to tread for the relevant information.[79] Respondents are obliged to disclose or discuss the information needed based on the researcher's filial (membership) identity and the consequential understanding of communal responsibility.[80]

Thus, if used properly, NQ indirectly unlocks the codes of prohibition, taboo and secrecy.[81] The desire to avert any possible communal negative consequence lessens respondents' burdens for divulging secrets and gives authority to the respondents as they seize the opportunity to put things right by explaining and teaching the native researcher (the child of the community) the required lessons. This aspect of intercepting or preventing misfortunes is allowed within the Nankani religio-cultural system. Thus, the respondents are not held liable or accountable for wrong doing and the fear or guilt of violating the norms or sacred law is removed.

A non-native researcher may not receive the same attention because of the lack of filial bond. Since NQ may entail denial or rejection of responsibility, it deals with the intricacies of the clan or community dynamics which a non-native researcher may not be aware of. Likewise, the subject of group responsibility is not applicable to these researchers. Non-native researchers may therefore jeopardize their research with NQ. They may also be charged for wrong doing or be seen as 'foolish', 'mad',

---

79   Foddy, *Constructing Questions for Interviews and Questionnaires*, 129-38.
80   This is based on the belief that any wrong action or decision taken by the native researcher could affect all the members of the group.
81   The drive for specific research data by native researchers in this context must be guided by the indigenous factors surrounding the membership of those secrets. These factors include the type of deity, cult and ritual, or the gender, age and/or status of the researcher within the community.

'rude' or 'arrogant' through the use of NQ. In each of these cases, the aim of obtaining the needed data may be jeopardized.

NQ was used to obtain data on the traditional methods of securing food sustainability; a precondition, according to the Nankani, for development. Traditionally known as 'entering the land or earth', it is the most guarded and solemn ritual performed at night by *tindanas* and their assistant(s) in the rivers/streams, caves or sacred trees/groves of the community. Although this ritual process starts at the physical level by a *tindana* and his team, at his home and the community's earth shrine, the entering into the spiritual depth of the land for the special ritual(s) that dictates and predicts the crops, livestock and fortunes of the following year, is done at night 'beneath the surface of the land'. At the end of the ritual, evidence of the exact successful crop type and the skins of the animals for the coming year are 'brought to the surface' to waiting clansmen. This practice secured and sustained a mutual relationship between the people and the spirit(s) of the land. That apart, this method of forecasting and securing food sufficiency and security enabled the people to channel their resources to where it was most beneficial. Without this religious dimension to the human effort, it is noted, there will be no food security and human efforts are wasted. They argued that the lack of progress by NGOs is because all their efforts towards development are re-channelled into the cooking pot (feeding).

NQ was also used to retrieve data on 'taken-for-granted' traditional or customary practices. In spite of the invaluable lessons in some traditional practices, they have over the years been practiced without due recourse to their history, meaning or the reciprocal values attached to them. Reducing them to mere 'dos' and 'don'ts' of family or community, most of the reasons behind these practices are either getting lost or are absolutely lost. The search to uncover these values for a better understanding of the current difficulties surrounding the practices has become difficult even for native researchers. Even so, the need to ascertain the reasons behind these practices is essential in some studies. In this study for instance, the need to ascertain the reason(s) for the Nankani concept of communal spirit and its essence in the overall understanding of family care, support, and the concept of reciprocity *vis-à-vis* the current antagonistic attitude to individualism was made manifest by my desire to understand the traditional concept of development and sustainability. Although filial relationships and spiritual reasons are known to be the reasons behind the extended family support system, the specific reasons behind this contested reciprocal responsibility are currently not known. Consequently, the rules governing such responsibilities are beginning to wane, resulting in family feuds. Some people have attributed their lack of development to overwhelming extended family demands. This assertion presents serious challenges to the traditional worldview where an individual's progress and well being is tied to his/her generosity and support to the extended family. Yet, the question as to how this system evolved proved difficult to decipher. The concept, 'I am because we are', which was given as one of the answers from respondents, seemed to have been taken as a mystery.

As a developing nation, the minimum daily wage in Ghana (2006) is ¢10,500.00, the equivalent of $1.19.[82] Without minimizing the harsh realities national economies place on their citizens, it is important to note that the economic value of this representational sum varies in their respective countries. Whereas ¢10,500.00 is an averagely sizeable daily income in the African rural areas, the same cannot be said of the countryside of the U.S.A. Therefore, even though these conversions are used, there is need to consider the contextual realities. Besides, the national statistics purport to have 1.7% of the citizens below the national poverty line.[83] Although this is a statistical figure that does not make sense to the living realities of many Ghanaians, worthless to its largely illiterate and subsistence farming population, it may explain why ¢10,500.00 is a daily wage.[84]

At the regional level, however, the national data stated that 76% of the Upper East population was below the poverty line. This high figure placed the region at the bottom, making it the poorest in the country. The disaggregated data further revealed that 9 out of 10 people in the region fall below this poverty line. As members of this region, the Nankani are faced with the same challenges as their counterparts. In other words, an individual Nankani above the poverty line

---

82 OANDA Customized Currency Convert, accessed 4 September 2006, available from http://www.oanda.com/convert/classic; internet.

83 The national poverty indicator is economically valued at an earning below the equivalence of $1 a day.

84 See Ghana Data Profile, A World Bank Group: A World free of Poverty, accessed 4 September 2006; available from http://www.ghanaweb.com/Ghana-HomePage/economy/gdp.php; internet.

is potentially a part carer for 9 other people.[85] This number excludes the individual's nuclear family, if s/he lives outside the region. Thus the pressure from these responsibilities and the current desire for individual economic empowerment and development is resulting in the neglect of filial responsibilities. This has generated problems, some of which have led to accusations and counter accusations, the severing of relations and subsequent allegation of sorcery or witchcraft. In general Ghanaian terms, both the situation of family burden and its degenerated status are now framed into the slogan, 'Pull him[/her] Down' (PHD). This is an ironic depiction of the two poles of this argument. It is the individual's determination to rise against the religio-cultural inhibitive factors projected by the traditional spirit of communal fellowship and sharing that is the core issue.[86]

The initial investigation into the source of this problem, an economic problem with a religio-cultural binding, and its relative impact on both individual and communal development, yielded nothing much. At best, I got the usual: 'this is our culture', 'this is what our fathers taught us' and 'it is part of the African communal way of living'. However, the use of NQ in which my own responsibility to the family was perceived as threatened, unearthed not only the reasons behind this established norm, but also the concepts and internal dynamics underlying the spirit of communalism, development, and sustainability as well as their implications for the overall survival strategy of the Nankani.

Obviously, this is a problem with several dimensions. At one level, it is an economic problem, one that should be dependent on ability, desire and willingness to share within the current system. On the traditional level, however, economic ability and its usage is not entirely dependant on the individual. Much of it is believed to derive its source from the traditional worldview on spirituality and family. The individual's "I am, because we are; and because we are, therefore I am"[87] is not just proverbial but perceived as real and practical.

---

85   In Ghana these are represented by grandparents, parents, uncles and aunties, siblings, nephews and nieces as well as other extended relations.

86   See also Mercy Amba Oduyoye, *Introducing African Women's Theology* (England: Sheffield Academic Press, 2001), 33 and Bourdillon, *Religion and Society*, 140.

87   Mbiti, *African Religions and Philosophy*, 108-9.

Situational Questioning (SQ)

By 'situational questioning' (SQ), I am referring to that uniquely privileged position of the native researcher to use his/her knowledge of the community, language and ritual conventions to acquire specific relevant data.[88] According to the Nankani tradition, words and some grammatical structures are abodes of spiritual power. This is often referred to as 'words are spirits'. The need to use words, especially, ritual words that embody negative tendencies cautiously and within their proper contexts, is a virtue. Recognising the inability of the general public to attain this virtue has led to some form of regulative measures by the ancestors. These are carved out as prohibitions to guide and control their use outside the appropriate context(s). Although some of these words or ritual narratives are a good source of research data, investigations involving or surrounding them are presented in such a way that these prohibitive contexts or words are circumvented or eliminated. Compounded by the largely 'outsider' field researchers in African communities, individual subjective research objectives or tendencies and limited time frames, these issues often escape the attention of field researchers.

In SQ, the native researcher who has privileged knowledge of some of these prohibitions and the conventions surrounding them, can use them, if necessary, to conduct interviews or to verify a point. This method is especially relevant to prohibited ritual data.[89] Comparatively, some restrictive rituals may still be opened for the extended family. This may include the external *i-si* (nephews and nieces) as well as other extended family categories. Such rare opportunities open the door for observations or PO where those unique ritual data can be gathered. This is because, SQ enables respondents to answer, explain or discuss coded rituals practices and vocabulary without fear of breaking taboos. For instance, a male Nankani will not discuss the rituals or aspects of rituals dealing with murder or incestuous sexual purification, restitution and restoration rites, or some specific elements in the final stage of the burial and funeral rites. As such, these aspects of the rituals are eliminated in many narratives. Whereas a non-native researcher may not be sufficiently aware of some of these elements to

---

88   It opens up rare opportunities and helps to explain the intricacies involved. Although the entire data is not used, it helps to inform and enlighten the research.

89   Gaba, "Contemporary Research in African Traditional Religion," 2-3.

probe further, the native researcher might be and avail him/herself to such opportunities for data, if necessary.

The reasons for SQ are connected to the traditional worldview and cosmology. Unwanted rituals or circumstances are not discussed outside their contexts because they have the propensity to regenerate the event. Among the Nankani it is a norm to keep such unwanted situations out of normal everyday conversation and life to keep them at bay. Could this scenario have something to do with the unseen power of the spoken word? Does the 'words are spirits' concept provide any understanding? This is arguable but for the Nankani, an out-of-context discussion, narration or verbal enactment does not only bring bad or painful memories, it is an invitation for the reoccurrence of the actual situation and this should be avoided.

Thus, SQ is suitable for ritual occasions when people re-live, renew and empathise with their colleagues who are undergoing the ritual. The occasion is not created by the researcher; s/he simply taps from it using the right questions. The occasion provides the 'sacred space' – opened to people for teaching, discussions and comparative narrative experiences. SQ is important because it enables people to provide reasons (perceived or otherwise) for their lack of development; some of which are related to either their inaccurate/inadequate performance of a ritual or the neglect/inability to perform a ritual. SQ is however time consuming and calls for adequate preparation and timing as well as the allocation of sufficient time for the ritual event and the interview. While SQ enables the researcher to tap into the respondent(s) emotions and experiences, it also requires the sensitivity (empathy) of the researcher. The advantage of this method is that, it allows the researcher to combine PO with IDIs or FGDs.

At this point, the study raises serious ethical concerns about the native researcher and the use of privileged insider data. Is this a breach of confidentiality? If not, in what context and to what extent are native researchers expected to used data which their privileged positions provides and how can their unique positions as insiders contribute to knowledge? These concerns will be discussed in chapter six.

Colloquialism

Colloquialism addresses some of the problems arising from my field study among the Nankani and the difficulties some reflexive indigenous assertions pose, especially for native researchers, in the academic context. It confronts the two different perspectives already engaged.[90] First, colloquialism seeks to respond to the problematic manner in which indigenous knowledge and information, especially field data, are synthesized and presented in academic studies. And second, it takes into consideration the rising tension created by such systemizations from the indigenous people.[91] The core of this tension from the indigenous perspective lies in their lack of self-expression which sometimes results in discrepancies between written knowledge and indigenous knowledge.[92] Even so, the need to acknowledge the input of some of these translations on indigenous cultures is advocated by some scholars. Sanneh particularly describes the input from the translation of African languages in terms of "indigenous cultural revitalization" and transformation.[93] This is somehow difficult to appreciate in the Nankani context since such an experience is not readily seen.

The Nankani are concerned about how their words are translated into English. With reference to their 'sacred vocabulary', they resented and challenged the manner in which people employ their words out of context and subsequently present incoherent, insignificant interpretations of who they are and what they say. They stressed the view that these spirit-infused words or sentences embody both the individual's and community's spirituality. An illustration of that is when a disturbed or angry mother embraces her chest, breast or stomach and utters the words, 'and this is my own child' or 'is this a child of my womb?' These words move beyond the claim of legitimacy and the pronouncements of parental blessings, to a rebuke or an invocation of a curse to which the child must respond appropriately in placating and seeking forgiveness from the hurting mother. In the absence of the child, the mother might simply convey this message as '*hum* [yes], and you are my own child'. To ignore the first word or the grammatical construction will simply mean to affirm and praise the child. Yet it is partly within this embodiment that the traditional concept of development hinges. Some words of parents, leaders or ritual experts are spiritually potent, impacting significantly on the future of those concerned. It is based on this principle

---

90   See chapter one, 4-8.
91   See also Yankah, *Globalization and the African Scholar*, 20-2.
92   p'Bitek, *African Religions in Western Scholarship*, 65-8.
93   Sanneh, *Encountering the West*, 88.

that the youth of Kandiga alluded to the need to fulfil parental wishes, including the deceased, as a spiritual base for success and development. These expressions also help to distinguish the communal mothering role of the African woman in the extended family system from her biological mothering role. Hence, to overlook the stress in the repetitive possessive nature of the sentence will preclude this aspect.

In his book on African prayers, Mbiti rightly observed that African prayers, for instance, are saturated with poetic elements. He noted the presence of "imagery, rhythm, vividness, use of figures of speech and symbolism, concentration of meaning, and the feeling which touches the innermost parts of one's being." Mbiti however, proceeded to say the poetical rhythms in African prayers "have not been lost even through translation into English". [94] The question we might ask is, even if he assumes the rhythm is not lost, what about the other poetic elements? To what extent were the prayers adjusted to maintain that rhythm? It has become obvious that the translation of one language into another requires compromise.[95] To circumvent some of the challenges involved, some words, phrases or sentences are sometimes written in the local languages before translations, a method that is also used in this study. Unfortunately, sometimes this interpretation has to be done several times and at different levels, a process that does not take into consideration word count or document limitations. Moreover, there are limits to repetitions, in both academic and publishing contexts.[96] For this reason, other avenues must be explored for a wider and more inclusive approach.

Colloquialism is an inclusive method and it caters for relevant socio-cultural specificities and nuances.[97] Its purpose is to help situate and contextualise this research within the oral traditions of the Nankani. For this reason, it gives credence to expressions, communication styles, skills and strategies of the subject group, which may not necessarily conform to the standard academic language norms. For instance, the statement, "when we say fire has consumed the goat, you

---

94   John S. Mbiti, *The Prayers of African Religion* (London: S.P.C.K., 1975), 21.
95   Cox, *A Guide to the Phenomenology of Religion*, 155-7.
96   Yankah, *Globalization and the African Scholar*, 2, 5-9.
97   Kenneth L. Pike, "Etic and Emic Standpoints for the Description of Behavior," in *The Insider/Outsider Problem in the Study of Religion: a Reader*, eds. Russell T. McCutcheon (London and New York: Cassell, 1999, 28-30).

ask where the skin is"[98] presents a number of significant undertones. It projects the importance of animal skin. Historically, it was used for clothing, accessories, rituals and beddings.[99] At present, these skins have acquired global commercial value, especially when used for indigenous artefacts. At the national level, these are classified as non-traditional export commodities, while traditional exports refer to Ghana's mineral resources, cocoa and timber. To be concerned about the skin instead of the animal connotes the importance attached to the skin in relation to the meat. The expression is also to say, 'do I have to spell that out for you? I have already told or given you the core element, the skin.' In other words, if the statement is translated as 'he agreed with the suggestion that *malma* is indeed the local equivalent of religion', the multiple meanings derived from the expression, in terms of the religion, culture and developmental processes would have been lost. The present system of decoding culturally specific language forms and styles, terms and sentence structures, into formal academic standards to avoid "waffle", "padding" or "jargon",[100] stifles, if not alienates, research conducted on African societies.[101] As Yankah observes:

> [O]ur psychological attitudes to language make possible the immediate denunciation as unacademic any discourse not articulated in Euro-American languages. Translate the same discourse into an Euro-American language, and the cross-linguistic rendition almost magically propels it into the realm of academia.[102]

Professor Yankah's accentuation of the situation in this quote shows that the concern of language and its representation or standardization is not just an isolated problem of the rural Nankani, but a sentiment

---

98   See chapter two, 37.
99   Allman and Parker, *Tongnaab*, 60 and picture 16 for the *tindana's* attire. Unfortunately the sitting posture only shows the shoulder strap and a little of the brown animal skin trapped between his back, hand and the tree.
100   Ronnie Cann and Kirsty Woomble, "Thesis Workshop," *Postgraduate Transferable Skills Programme* (College of Humanities and Social Science, University of Edinburgh, February 2005). In this workshop these expressions are used to connote bad or poor academic writing.
101   Pike, "Etic and Emic Standpoints for the Description of Behavior," 29.
102   Yankah, *Globalization and the African Scholar*, 6.

that transcends the boundaries of rural, urban, non-literate and elite in many parts of Africa.[103]

Colloquialism serves as a link, 'mending the broken pieces' between the Nankani religio-cultural nuances and issues of sustainable development with that which is considered standard. It helps to provide evidence on how some religio-cultural views influence the life and activities of the people; hence, their development. Colloquialism in this context should be seen as the community's participatory tool to sustainable development. The underdeveloped and the developed, illiterate and literate, are presented as equal partners in their contribution to knowledge and development. If development is to transcend its economic notions, into a holistic one, inculturalization is essential.

In one of the field discussions on sustainable development, a participant asked if I was serious about finding out the truth of what I was seeking. With a positive reply, I was again asked if I was going to help sustain the answers they were going to give. With another positive reply, noting that my work was in itself part of the process, I was told to do the right thing by writing what they say and not what I want. With the expression, 'when a toad falls into a river, its swims out', I was reminded of the situation I had put myself into as well as the need to get out of it successfully. This has multiple implications but the relevance of these statements is dependent on my identity as a native researcher.[104] Nonetheless, the puzzle began to unravel when Atapugre, an elderly man in the group, noted that 'all we do is to preserve, sustain and develop the White man's culture and things, what has he done for us other than destroy ours'. He contended that 'we have always lost out. This talk about sustainability and development is not for us but them'. In trying to understand the point of his contention, he explained that anytime he had to write a letter to his son in the capital city, the letter did not reflect his views. Instead, the writer 'hovered around like a bee seeking nectar only to produce a honey comb without honey'. He noted that in an effort to get his intentions across the way he wanted them put forward, he changed writers both from within and out of his community, but had the same experience. Subsequently, he challenged the

---

103 Ngũgĩ Wa Thiong'o, "African Languages and Global Culture in the Twenty-first Century," in *African Visions: Literary Images, Political Change, and Social Struggle in Contemporary Africa*, eds. Cheryl B. Mwaria, Silvia Federici, and Joseph McLaren (Connecticut and London: Greenwood Press, 2000), 156.
104 See discussion in chapter six.

view of presenting his words or sentences differently. To his surprise, he was told his choice of words, mannerisms and language structure did not conform to written English. In his frustration he questioned, "whose letter is it? Mine or your English?"[105]

To understand this elderly man one needs to understand the content of the group discussion which started from the concept of development and progressed into the concept of sustainability. As part of the process of development, indigenous people sold food crops and animals for cash to finance their children's education. The process did not just limit their ability to have food reserves; it depleted their livestock and destroyed the traditional process of sustainable development. At the same time, it alienated their children from home, culture and religion. Because of the underdeveloped nature of the community and region, these children have had to move to the urban centres of the country for employment. The problem now arises because the traditional role of the son as a permanent resident, active and supportive member of the traditional household is lost. To maintain whatever is left of this relationship, fathers desire to communicate with their sons. Yet to facilitate this distant communication, they have to rely on an unknown system, the letter, one that is written in English. The difficulty of expressing himself adequately to his son, whom he had helped to develop at the expense of himself, the same one that has caused the separation now becomes the focus of his discontent.

As a methodological approach, colloquialism may facilitate the freedom of expression in which indigenous knowledge, in its original form and construction, can be used in academic writing. According to Smart, "sometimes they [indigenous people] offer illumining terms which we can incorporate into our own".[106] Unlike Smart, however, the emphasis here is not just on terms or in enriching the other, but in acknowledging, accepting, preserving as well as enhancing the indigenous language and knowledge forms. This helps to underpin the concept of sustainability in the indigenous context, as discussed in chapter one. Unfortunately, this is an aspect that is inadequately addressed in academic studies, perhaps due to the conventions of academia.

---

105   This is reminiscent of Okot p'Bitek's *Song of Lawino* in which the husband found the Acholi language primitive and limitative for expressing his answers to his wife. See Van Rinsum, *Slaves of Definition*, 119.

106   Smart, *Dimensions of the Sacred*, 3.

Colloquialism combines well with both negative and situational questioning, as relevant field strategies for the native researcher. Together, they can enrich ethnographical and phenomenological studies of ATR and the African culture. Besides, if the due processes of phenomenology are maintained, then considerations should be given to these propositions since they serve as channels for the *eidetic intuition*,[107] that is, provided *epochē* and *empathetic interpolation* are given due cognisance.[108] They can effectively facilitate the processes of naming of the phenomenon and the description of relationships and processes.[109] In line with Smart's 'evocative expression', which relates to emotions, feelings and values, the presentation of field data within their colloquial context, with all their proverbial analogies, helps to document the identity and knowledge of this specific African community.

Colloquialism is therefore another way of documenting and preserving data on African communities and making it available for further studies. Besides these, it contributes to the sustainability of local resources in the rural development process. In the midst of these complexities, Sanneh cautions that:

> In any case, let not a subtle, avuncular protectiveness push us to the point of claiming that Africans are inherently incapable of coping with Western contact and criticism and should, therefore, be made the exception to the rule of maturity through historical struggle. We would be in danger of promoting such a view were we to disallow any possibility for complexity in indigenous categories and values and Africans' ability to draw comparisons and contrasts from their own resources.[110]

But is this the case? The discussions in this study illustrates that African people do not just cope but are constructively engaged in a process of negotiations. The problem encountered in this study is the desire for responsibly sustainable development.[111]

---

107 Cox, *Expressing the Sacred*, 17-20, 35-8.
108 Ibid.,17-9, 24-30.
109 Ibid., 33-6.
110 Sanneh, *Encountering the West*, 96.
111 See chapter one, 19-20 and Wa Thiong'o, "African Languages and Global Culture in the Twenty-first Century," 156-61.

The search for an appropriate methodology is field-led. The approach has enabled the investigation to respond to the inclusive needs of the Nankani. This has in-turn facilitated a bottom-up approach from which the subject group's perspectives have been brought to the fore. With the phenomenological method, the subjective and objective aspects of the research are interwoven through a descriptive discourse, allowing the field data to manifest itself. This has been enhanced with a content analysis approach, in which the data is revealed through the integrative 'when-and as-needed basis' approach.

'Life is like the disjointed but interconnected search of the *bakolo-dana* (diviner) for his *bakolo-yaala* (divinatory items). It requires body and soul but when all is accomplished, quality is measured by his determination and endurance'.[112] This saying which was constantly applied to me during the field study, referred to my struggles to unpack and repack the content of my bag at each meeting. The content of the bag which included pencils, pens, notepads, a camera, a tape recorder, batteries and cassettes and the entire process of my research endeavour found its contextual understanding in the initiation process of the diviner. Typified in the above Nankani saying, it continues to provide new insights and meanings as the study unfolds itself in writing. As illustrated in this chapter, the most appropriate conclusion for this methodological segment can be likened to the Nankani diviner in search of his divinatory items. Not only is the chapter made up of the search for, and the piecing together of different concepts or viewpoints, like the diviner, after gathering his tools, he makes them the bedrock of his profession. It is my contention that as the saying implies it will facilitate the understanding of this chapter and subsequently, the research as whole.

---

112 The initiation process of the soothsayer entails the discovering and gathering of his artefacts at specific locations known only to the initiators. These items become the items of divination (the eyes of the diviner or objects of decision-making). The test of one's spiritual insight and effectiveness depends on these discoveries. Hence, this initial search is crucial to the diviner's profession.

Chapter Six

THE POLITICS OF INVOLVEMENT

> I believe, that religious studies scholarship now commonly acknowledges the inherent limitations within the phenomenological method. Nevertheless, I contend that we can still use phenomenology to deepen our awareness of the problems entailed in achieving an understanding of religious traditions of which we are not a part without at the same time necessarily accepting all its conclusions. My proposals ... regarding theory and method in the study of African indigenous religions represent my effort at taking the next steps beyond classical phenomenology.[1]

The above statement from the preface of *Rational Ancestors* underpins the key methodological issues engaged in this study. These are the acknowledged limitations and challenges of the phenomenological method, the importance of the method in the study of ATR and the need to move beyond its classical understanding. Subtle though it may be, the outstanding issue in this statement relates to the quest for 'understanding' of the religion of the 'Other' (ATR), a perspective that is being questioned in recent times.[2] Forming the crux of a new line of inquiry, concerns are raised as to whether this is not a ploy by Western scholars for access in the study of ATR. Converging around the "insider/outsider" debate, the question of difference between the 'outsider's understanding' and the 'insider's understanding' in the study of ATR is becoming a ground for contestation. But just as the

---

1   Cox, *Rational Ancestors*, iv.
2   Chitando, "Phenomenology of Religion and the Study of African Traditional Religions," 310-1.

credibility of the Western scholar is questioned, Cox, a member of this group, also thinks the insider perspective of the African may simply be the scholar's own rendition.[3] This raises concern over the quality of research on ATR. The postmodernist deconstructionist attitude to researchers is therefore a welcome contribution to the understanding of scholarship in this context.

It is not surprising that in the concluding chapter of his latest book, *A Guide to the Phenomenology of Religion*, Cox takes the statement 'Phenomenology at the Crossroads' as his title.[4] With this marked statement, Cox recalls the issues at stake, by taking his readers through a series of discourses, with the exception of the "insider/outsider" debate. Yet, even though this issue is not tackled, it is an important area deserving attention. Through his engagement, however, Cox has not only highlighted the current debates, placing them in a single collection makes them more accessible. Besides, his response to the discussion on engaged scholarship is thought provoking.

Without itemizing how some of these issues have been engaged in this study, I have in various contexts shown that even though the concept of the 'sacred' is a core feature of ATR, it is not perceived as a 'Wholly other', that which is 'set apart'. The 'sacred' is part of and is involved in daily life. Not only in the historical context was the supreme entity persistently hit with a pestle and its benevolence wasted by women,[5] this entity as noted in chapter two is still providing directions for the confused and dejected as well as caring for the vulnerable. It is in this context that the application of the phenomenological method to ATR by Africans engages the issues at the 'crossroads'. African scholars, including non-practitioners, do not engage ATR as religious 'outsiders' in the same sense as Westerners. As 'cultural insiders', they form a different category within the "insider/outsider" debate. What then does it mean for Africans to apply the theoretical and methodological principles of phenomenology to ATR?[6]

Cox sees self-disclosure as an important endeavour. It is a dual reflection addressed to the subject group and the academic commu-

---

3   Cox, "African Identity as the Projection of Western Alterity," 25-7.
4   Cox, *A Guide to the Phenomenology of Religion*, 209-47.
5   Parrinder, *African Traditional Religion*, 40-1.
6   Chitando, "Phenomenology of Religion and the Study of African Traditional Religions," 311-2.

nity, yet it must not be seen simply as an issue of objectivity and subjectivity.[7] He agrees that this involves "a world of multiple confessions comprised of competing truth claims".[8] In his concluding reflections, Cox considers the possible concerns emanating from 'diatopical hermeneutics' and 'methodological conversion'. Although he admits they are both tailored to the understanding of indigenous religions within the academic discourse of the scientific study of religion, Cox objects to any view of coercion. For him 'diatopical hermeneutics':

> [W]ill still speak within its own frame of reference, within its own myth. The other confession will do the same. The aim is not to destroy the faith of the either party but to achieve a humane understanding based on the principles that truth is possessed exclusively by none and that understanding is gained best by human interaction based on respect and nonviolence.[9]

His view of non-violence and the non-exclusivity of truth are appealing and also, render his methodological tools applicable to this study.[10] Classifying myself within Adogame's insider-outsider category, discussed below, the question of multiple identities and competing truth claims requires that a researcher should nonetheless adopt a stand from which the investigation can be viewed.[11] At the same time, a nonviolent position ensures the integrity of the subject group, encourages participation, thereby enhancing the search for mutual respect and understanding.

THEORY OR METHOD? A RETURN TO THE FIELD

Two interrelated yet currently distinct issues in academic studies have emerged as major methodological concerns. These are the questions of identity and the place of the native African researcher. Closely

---

7   Cox, *Rational Ancestors*, 138.
8   Ibid.
9   Cox, *Rational Ancestors*, 138.
10   See also Butler, *Giving An Account of Oneself*, 6-7.
11   Adogame, Afe, "To be or not to be? Politics of Belonging and the African Christian communities in Germany," in Religion in the context of African Migration, eds. Afe Adogame and Cordula Weisskoeppel (Bayreuth: Bayreuth African Studies Series, 2005), 99-100.

tied to these is the 'Insider/Outsider' debate. How does an African researcher perceive him/herself in the context of an African study, especially, among his/her community and people? How is s/he perceived and evaluated by the subject group and to what extent can the academic concerns of subjectivity and objectivity be negotiated? To what extent is his/her 'Otherness' validated or repealed by these two identity groups. In what ways or to what extent will s/he engage and negotiate the boundaries of African identity in both the African community and academic objectivity?[12] In other words, how do these contested identities impact on the research methodology or the academic study of religions?

NATIVE RESEARCHER

The postmodernist desire to know the subjective positions of researchers in a given study has undoubtedly necessitated the disclosure of the relational self in this study.[13] From the preceding discussions, the concept of a native researcher and its attendant privileges were noted. This notwithstanding, the question as to who is a native researcher and his/her position in a given academic research, such as this is still inadequately addressed. Again, to what extent is the native researcher an insider or outsider in a given study? And finally, how do these concepts affect the study in question?

Pablo Wright's article on 'Postmodern Ontology, Anthropology, and Religion' presents an interesting entry to this discussion. In this article Wright addresses two issues of great relevance. First, Wright addresses the shift in anthropological studies. Wright asserts that current anthropological studies depict a shift from the rigid "autonomous individual of Malinowskian ethnography, to an open, reflexive subject" of study.[14] He contends that in this new state, the ethnographer does not have to be the "exotic" traveller who "*displaces* his/her being-in-the-world to a different place" to meet the "Other", but could be a native ethnographer who replaces him/herself in "a known place

---

12   Yankah, *Globalization and the African Scholar*, 15-6.
13   Gellner, *Postmodernism, Reason and Religion*, 23 and Juschka, "The Writing of Ethnography," 85.
14   Pablo G. Wright, "Postmodern Ontology, Anthropology, and Religion," *Culture and Religion: An international, interdisciplinary journal* 1, no. 1 (May 2000): 86.

but with a different (epistemological) agenda".[15] Simply put, the native researcher is one who returns to his/her own society for the specific purpose of research.

Secondly, Wright brings to the fore some of the differences between non-native and native researchers. Here, Wright explains his surprise encounter and experience of what he states as the "non-arbitrary relationship" between the spoken language and action. By clearly admitting his lack of prior knowledge on the subject matter and the inability of Western methodologies to adequately address the issue beforehand, Wright revealed the differences between the two groups of field researchers.[16] In furtherance of this point, his claim of unpreparedness alludes to the view that native researchers, working as insiders, might have some knowledge on the problem of language and its varied forms of articulation. For instance, the correlation between language and its mystical power relations might not produce such significant surprises to native researchers since this might have been a part of their cultural heritage and upbringing.[17]

Wright's article also reiterates the challenge to current Western oriented field methodologies. How adequate or universal are these methodologies for researchers and their individual fields of research? Originally formulated for the study of the 'Other', how is the current surge in native researchers affecting these methodologies?[18] If their inadequacy is felt by Wright, then we can continue to ask, how adequate they are for the native researcher who displaces him/herself within his/her own environment as a result of a new agenda? Still within this context, how do native researchers adequately present themselves and their new agenda to their 'subject group' for the required data, and the findings to the scholarly world? In what ways and to what extent can the open minded and reflective native researcher present objective findings within the scientific study of religions? So far, two perspectives to these problems have emerged. These have largely been argued within the context of the 'insider/outsider' debate and the discourse on identity. To what extent then have these discussions contributed to knowledge and to this investigation in particular?

---

15   Ibid., 87.
16   Wright, "Postmodern Ontology, Anthropology, and Religion," 88.
17   See also Westerlund, *African Religion in African Scholarship*, 91.
18   Linda Tuhiwai Smith, *Decolonizing Methodologies: Research and Indigenous People* (London and New York: Zed Books Ltd, 1999), 1-17.

Lamin Sanneh underscores this inherent difficulty for native researchers in his critical analysis of the work of Magema Fuze, a nineteenth century Christian convert. Fuze according to Sanneh, having been converted and educated by John Colenso, produced a unique ethnographic account of his people, the Zulu. *The Black People*; the translation of Fuze's book was published in 1979. Although Fuze's book is used by Sanneh as a reflective piece on the Christian encounter with Africa, it indicates that boundaries are never completely crossed. Not only does the old continue to give a sense of identity and meaning to the new; the new, which provides a wider horizon for the old, also creates a feeling of alienation from within its own boundaries.[19] Thus, the analysis of Fuze's work opens the door to the complexities of the native African researcher. For even as Sanneh acknowledges the importance of Fuze's work, he does not hesitate to note that Fuze "himself 'stood at the frontier of the clash of cultures, values and interests'".[20] From Sanneh's analysis, we encounter the contrasting worlds of the native researcher through such words and phrases as: "influence", "strands", "straddles", "linkages", "lives in several worlds at once" and "[t]he care and accuracy with which he describes the details of Zulu rural life...".[21] While this exhibits the difficulties with which the native researcher struggles to negotiate within the boundaries, "between old and new worldviews, tradition and modernity",[22] Sanneh also brings to the fore, issues of Western imperialism and cultural subversion.[23] This places the native researcher within a different frame of research dynamics where he/she must be aware of the complexities of his/her role.[24] Thus, Sanneh's analysis of Fuze's book offers illuminating insights to this subject matter.

ENGAGING THE INSIDER/OUTSIDER DEBATE

> Whether they are insiders or outsiders, scholars are concerned both to obtain accurate descriptions of the insiders'

---

19   Sanneh, *Encountering the West*, 93-5.

20   Ibid., 93.

21   Ibid., 94.

22   Afe Adogame and Ezra Chitando, "Moving among Those Moved by the Spirit: Conducting Fieldwork within the New African Religious Diaspora," *Fieldwork in Religion* 1, no. 3 (2005): 257.

23   Sanneh, *Encountering the West*, 89-92.

24   See also Van Rinsum, *Slaves of Definition*, 120-61.

> experiences of religion and to assess the ways that religion
> functions in the lives of individuals and community.[25]

This is the crux of all academic pursuits. Yet, the inherent dynamics of such an endeavour has led to the current concern and quest for understanding the place of the researcher in a given research. The need to locate this discourse in the context of the Nankani as part of the insider account is relevant to the general understanding of the debate, chapter and study as a whole.

Among the Nankani, the concepts "Insider/Outsider" are perceived and analyzed at three interrelated levels of 'in', 'inside' and 'insider', and 'out', 'outside' and 'outsider'. To be 'in' means to be safe, protected, covered or enclosed, calm and quiet. It offers security, stability and warmth but more importantly, it presents the notion of seclusion, hidden from exposure thus embodying the element of secrecy and mystery. According to the Nankani, the problem of the latter group of characteristics is that this perception of 'in' is at the risk of being strangled to death. To overcome this problem, 'in', which is viewed as a possessive element, must be reinterpreted and understood in the context of 'inside', since to be 'in' is conceived in relation to being inside something else. Thus, having been encased, it becomes the responsibility of the encasing element to protect that which is 'in' from dying on the one hand and being hidden from other predatory elements on the other. It is at this point that 'in' is interpreted and preserved in the form of and through myth and ritual.

Acknowledging this transformation is to render 'in' into exposure and danger, hence the responsibility of the encasing element is expanded upon. To explain the imposition of responsibility on the encasing element, the Nankani have sought to do this from the basis of necessity and relevance, noting that to encase something involves some form of imposed value, negative or positive. Whatever the case, the desire to hide it from others must be strong; hence, the question of responsibility. It is at this point that the encasing element, in the human context of person, family, clan or community, is perceived in terms of the insider. The level to which the insider circle widens depends on the importance and the generational cycle of that which is encased. To the Nankani, therefore, the insider dimension is perceived in terms

---

25   Ring *et al*, *Introduction to the Study of Religion*, 59-60.

of secrecy and its attendant notion of security for those to whom it matters. From this dimension, 'inside' knowledge and its transmission are mainly for the purview of those 'insiders'. To buttress this view, the saying 'walls cover issues' is used as an illustration. Metaphorically phrased,[26] these walls are the insiders whose duty is to serve as the protective wall covering those important issues.

The opposite is true of 'out', 'outside' and 'outsider'. 'Out' has the elements of wildness, recklessness, a mark of being pursued or possessed at any time and by anybody, insiders and outsiders alike. 'Out' is predisposed to any and everybody, including strangers or foreigners. This characteristic mark of exposure is its main source of danger. Hence, that which is 'out' takes new forms, a process that is likened to the chameleon. As a result of this flexibility and adaptability, its life is ensured; nonetheless, its true identity, like the authentic colour of the chameleon, may be lost. This explanation has a significant bearing on this study. For instance, the general or common knowledge among ordinary Nankani on the composition of the current Nankani communities has the tendency to exclude three important communities because of their overriding language differences. Bui and Pungu tend to be perceived as migrant communities of Bulsa and Kasem, while what is now loosely called Navrongo is said to be over-influenced by the Kasem community. Other scholars have referred to Bui as "a subchiefdom of Kologo", representing another interpretation of the situation of the outsider.[27] The latter perception is also a reflection of the chieftaincy configuration of the Nankani communities in which Kologo holds a paramount title while Bui has a divisional status. These perspectives were initially adopted in this study. However, when these preliminary findings were discussed during my major field study, I was reminded by the elders to be attentive to the levels of information available and to adhere to the traditional community formation and leadership structure. With directives to the appropriate or knowledgeable persons in these communities, this aspect had to be reinvestigated, followed by the necessary adjustments.

---

26   Based on the reality of the enclosed style of home-building. See pictures 1 and 2.
27   J. M. Hunter, "Elephantiasis: A Disease Development in North East Ghana," *Bulletin of the Ghana Geographical Association* 36, no. 5 (1992): 635, quoted in Songsore, *Regional Development in Ghana*, 290.

This case brings into focus two scholarly perspectives on the insider debate. From Smart's perspective, the insider "can be terribly wrong about her tradition, ignorant about or insensitive to the variety of her religious heritage".[28] On the other hand, Afe Adogame reclassifies the insider perspective into *insider-insider* and *insider-outsider*.[29] He observes that there are ways in which insiders may still be outsiders. Although these two perspectives shed further light on this discussion, the circumstances are still different. Considering the context and content of this discussion, the latter is more akin to my case than the former.

In his article 'To be or not to be?' Adogame enumerates four levels at which the insider/outsider debate can shed more light on existing realities. These four levels are the *"Insider-Insider, Insider-Outsider, Outsider-Insider, and Outsider-Outsider"*.[30] Relating each of these categories to the varied identifiable contexts in which my position, though placed within the insider category, can be excluded because of gender, age or the degree of insider position as discussed above, I find myself belonging relatively to the first three classifications. The shifts between the 'insider' and 'outsider' status is further influenced by education, marriage, urban dwelling and employment which is different from the rural subsistence living. At the general level however, the elders, leaders and ritual experts maintain my identity within the insider category by virtue of being a daughter and wife of the wider Nankani community. Nonetheless, this insider is not comparable to their own insider-insider position. On the other hand, anthropologists like Rattray and Fortes as well as migrant settlers and wives can be considered within the outsider-insider while tourists or strangers remain in the outsider-outsider categories. Even here, there is still a sense in which the latter can be included in the outsider-insider category. Traditionally, unidentified strangers and lost persons are taken to the chief or *tindana*. As leaders and custodians of the community, these strangers belong to them until such time that things are sorted out. Within this period, they acquire a temporal identity as people belonging to the land, hence its leaders. This is because of a notion that no one enters and stays in a land if the spirits of the land do not welcome them. Besides, supposed strangers can be spirits (malevolent or benevolent). Receiving such people

---

28   Smart, *Dimensions of the Sacred*, 4.
29   Adogame, "To be or not to be?" 99-100.
30   Adogame, "To be or not to be?" 100.

in a relative degree of insider status can therefore become a blessing or turn misfortunes around. This traditional conceptualization of the "Insider/Outsider" debate further problematizes the discourse to such an extent that this binary issue becomes one of relativity.

Based on these Nankani epistemological explanations, the two concepts were then discussed with the notion that there are different levels of knowledge and modes of its acquisition among the Nankani. Using the above analysis as a background, the "insider" dimension was understood within the context of *pu-oam* or *pu'rum* (inside). *Pu'rum* also refers to internal, personal, or secret knowledge and behaviour individuals engage in. *Pu'rum* according to the Nankani is very personal and it is also interpreted as that which is in the stomach. In this respect, the words *deo* (room) or *yi'rum* (home) are used to shed more light on the subject matter. Unlike *pu'rum*, *deo* deals with such knowledge or secrets that are related to a relatively nuclear family or to the extended family who trace their family to a single *yaaba* (ancestor). Having descended from one ancestry, the people in this category perceive themselves as members of the same room. By extension, this categorization is applied to *yi'rum*, *bure* (paternal line) and *so-o* (maternal line) as the circle of classification widens.[31] This concept is also applied to members of cults and secret societies. In other words, to talk of the "Insider" within the Nankani conceptual framework is relative.

Likewise, the concept "Outsider" is framed within *yenga* (outside). Here, anything that does not pertain to the 'inside' is a subject of the 'outside'. Unlike the inside, outside knowledge is not secretive or particularly sensitive. It embodies the general culture or public knowledge and behaviour. This notwithstanding, *yenga yela* (outside issues) or *yenga bunu* (outside things) may sometimes refer to some *pu'rum*, *deo* or *yi'rum* issues that have become public knowledge over the course of time. An individual may also move from the category of the *deo* to the *yenga* depending on the circle from which knowledge is sought. Marriage, Western education or urbanization also transfers insiders to the insider-outsider categories. Just like the insider position, therefore, the outsider category is relative. In other words, insider/outsider categories are tied to the concept of family and identity. The more precise the claim of identity or belongingness, the more the individual is an insider

---

31   Rattray views this concept of secrecy as security measure. Rattray, *Tribes of the Ashanti Hinterland*, 238-9.

and the more its secretive elements are enforced and protected. Thus, the insider/outsider dimensions among the Nankani are tied first and foremost to identity and subsequently, to the concept of relativity.

As a patrilineal society, a child of a male Nankani is an insider; a position that is fixed and unchallenged. In this position, all public (outside) knowledge is at the disposal of both the insider and outsider. However, the insider status may enable him/her to acquire other categories of knowledge through the established networks of relationships. That is, knowledge that is not intended for general community display but restricted to a clan, household or family. To the outsider, this is subject to other types of status such as the extended family system, cult or secret society membership or marriage. Unlike the last category, the exogamous marriage system among the Nankani produces that which may be classified alongside the 'insider-outsider category', a category that is basically sex and/or gender oriented. Because of the centrality of marriage in traditional societies, women acquire insider information related to their age. Perceived as a 'wandering hermit', she is traditionally not a good candidate to divulge insider secrets, especially in marriage, until old age when commitment is certain. At this age, her desire for or chances of divorce and remarriage are limited. This differentiates the Nankani perspective on putting women in leadership or ritual positions from some African communities where menstrual blood seems to be the dominant point of reference. Thus, even though old age is a common denominator, the underlying reasons differ. The equation of menopause to maleness hence a sign of purity and a qualifying factor for leadership is not a norm among the Nankani. Menstrual blood has no general taboo or dangerous inferences.[32] For the Nankani, the core issue is to protect family secrets from a woman who is capable of remarrying and divulging her previous secrets.

With respect to the relativity of knowledge and its acquisition processes, the following analogy was given. According to tradition, a child is simply told that it is a taboo to talk while eating. As s/he grows, the idea of choking is introduced; however, at puberty s/he is also told to pay attention and listen so as to respond to any emergency call. In this respect, knowledge is itself classified into levels and to justify this, they say knowledge and wisdom are not put in a race, neither are they bought; they are acquired. The process and degree of acquisition is

---

32   Douglas, *Purity and Danger*, 119.

intrinsically linked to one's identity status and the relevant indices of age, sex, and status.

It is in this area of knowledge dissemination and acquisition that differences between insider and outsider status are manifested. The general notion is that an insider has the privilege to participate in knowledge acquisition while an outsider imagines it. For instance, an outsider (for example, one who has never been a widow or gone through widowhood rites) can never be an insider, experience or re-experience this process simply by knowledge acquisition, it remains an imaginative process. Moreover, the content of knowledge imparted at any given time is relative to the contexts discussed above. In this regard, *pu-rum yela* are the most relative. In a related example, the people from the Cho-o clan of Naga noted with respect to a man who had been taken by a river, a crocodile god known as Asabalika, in his youth for three days. Though he is still alive, he does not talk about it. Accordingly, though there is common (outsider) knowledge of the incident and the related rituals, the insider perspective is unknown. These are *pu-rum yela*. Thus, the saying 'walls cover secrets' applies to such personal cases. Despite the privileges of the insider position, the Nankani contend there are always degrees of limitation, a relatively limited position where every insider shares with an outsider. This provides contextual evidence to Cabezón's argument that the insider position does not necessarily privilege the researcher.[33]

Nevertheless, the insider maintains his/her privileged position because of the concepts of identity and relationships.[34] This was evident during the field work, when my respective insider positions of child, wife and *is'nga* (niece), were relevant identity disclosure strategies for accessing information. Of course, my subject of study and gender did expose me to some of the traditional barriers that directly exclude females from specific insider data. However, as the respondents noted on several occasions in the Naga discussions:

---

33   José Ignacio Cabezón, "Identity and the Work of the Scholar of Religion," in *Identity and the Politics of Scholarship in the Study of Religion*, eds. José Ignacio Cabezón and Sheila Greeve Davaney (New York and Oxon: Routledge, 2004), 43-59.

34   See by extension, Fortes' discussion on levels of congregational worshipers of the ancestor cult. Those levels indicate the individual's insider status to that ancestor. Fortes, "Some Reflections on Ancestor Worship in Africa," in *African Systems of Thought*, 122-3.

> You and what you are doing are the very subject we are
> talking about – *teare* [modernity]. Anyway, as we say, the
> world is changing, and if we refuse the truth to our own
> child and wife, would we rather give it to the stranger? Oh
> no, the ancestors will scream. So, if this is of benefit to you,
> then it is of benefit to all of us. After all, it all comes back
> to us: is she not our daughter and our wife? That is it.

In this context, I was not only given the permission to carry on with my studies; the statements presented some of the underlying advantages of the insider. From a gender analytical point, my achievement is to their credit because I belong to them.

The above analysis has produced two contextual explanations to the current discourse on the "Insider-Outsider" debate. It questions the assumed knowledgeable position of the scholar and draws the discourse into the community's context. The analysis has shown that a researcher's insider or outsider status alone does not determine his/her access to field based data but that the community's internal dynamics on what and who falls within these categories matters. This introduces two levels with which the current debate may be structured to cater for the emerging complexities, a methodological level and community descriptive and analytical level. With these two, the methodological level will continue to pursue the researcher's position while the other examines the community's views and its contribution to the study.

CONTESTING IDENTITIES

Central to the contemporary debate on the insider/outsider dimensions is the question of identity, the socio-cultural location(s) of scholars and their research. Although this has a historical footing in the Enlightenment era, there has been a paradigm shift. The perceived notions of the detached, neutral and objective scholar have generally given way to an acknowledged impact of identity and location on research.[35] As José Ignacio Cabezón and Sheila Greeve Davaney point out:

---

35   José Ignacio Cabezón and Sheila Greeve Davaney, "Introduction", in *Identity and the Politics of Scholarship in the Study of Religion*, eds. José Ignacio Cabezón and Sheila Greeve Davaney (New York and Oxon: Routledge, 2004), 3-4.

> The identity and subjectivity of the scholar and their rela-
> tion to the knowledge and scholarship he or she produces
> are now firmly established as central theoretical concerns.
> Many contemporary scholars see variables such as race, eth-
> nicity, nationality, gender, class, and sexual orientation, on
> the other, as an important aspect of their self-understanding
> as scholars and as inextricably related to the questions they
> ask and the claims they make within and for the academy.[36]

Cabezón challenges the stereotypical scenarios implicit in identity politics.[37] Quite important also is the reverse way in which he handles the
complexities involved in this type of identity politics.[38] The embedded
renegotiations and boundary crossings which I have had to constantly
address in terms of my identity, and with which my subject group and
culture have had to engage, in order to come to terms with this relatively new scenario, present constant challenges and contradictions. The
benign manner in which one is imbued with stereotypical feminine,
ethnic, cultural or religious identities does not often meet the scholastic
scrutiny desired. For me, these are not just contemporary theoretical
issues but real concerns as issues of ethnicity, gender and cultural identity are in constant renegotiation for community solidarity as well as the
daily economic quest for survival. Having an indigenous woman enquir-
ing about information to which she is not entitled can be daunting, yet
being aware that it is part of *teare* enables respondents to negotiate with
the current situation in order to respond appropriately.

Thus, while some of the works in *Identity and the Politics of Scholarship in the Study of Religion* are motivating, they do not adequately
address my case. As the scholars: José Ignacio Cabezón, Francis X.
Clooney, Rita M. Gross, Tazim R. Kassam and Kwesi Wiredu, relate
and discuss the stories underlying their multiple identities and scholarship, the seemingly unique position of my own identity and the identity
of my subject group continue to emerge as different. Whereas I reason
with Cabezón's assertion that the insider position does not unduly
privilege the researcher in his/her study, Gross calls for "a scholar-
practitioner". Though not a new idea, this raises questions. Who is a
scholar-practitioner? Is Gross by implication presenting the Western

---

36   Cabezón and Davaney, "Introduction," 4.
37   Cabezón, "Identity and the Work of the Scholar of Religion," 43-59.
38   Ibid., 55-6.

stereotypical individualist stand of one's profession of faith? If so, what role will the African play, who by virtue of the religio-cultural setting, lives within the confines of the religio-cultural traditions, despite a personal profession of a different religion. In other words, what identities are ascribed to a person who preferentially opts out of a religion, yet professing membership with its religiously enshrined cultural heritage returns to both the culture and religion for scholarly pursuits? It is, perhaps, in this lack of clarity in terms of cultural specificity that these forms of ambiguous categorizations differ.

Yet in a rather complicated manner, neither culture nor religion perceives the individual, described above, as an outsider, especially if that individual stays within the religio-cultural boundaries of gender and age. Actually, the religio-cultural system persistently maintains that individual's identity as an insider through its practices. As disclosed during my field study: *fu ka tiea, fu me ka boa. Fu yesi ta perime dita* (you have not changed and you are not lost to us. You went out searching and eating).[39] While pondering on the implication of this saying within the context of existing theories on the receptiveness and accommodative nature of ATR, another member of the group remarks: *fu ti'siri la be-em? fu menga sa pu ka lemwa, fu kure kan kuliwa?* (What are you thinking of? even if you do not return in person, won't your funeral come home?).[40] Could this claim of an eventual return, irrespective of the state in which one returns, present a key to a new understanding or a perspective on the concept of receptiveness in ATR? Although worthy of investigation, this cannot be pursued within the limits of this study.

Nevertheless, we must probe further. What does the Nankani proverb 'the guinea chick follows the hen, but it knows its parent is a guinea fowl' mean? Does it further suggest that the individualistic con-

---

39 This is symbolically drawn from the traditional free range style of poultry keeping. In this system, fowls are left to range after the morning feed and return in the evening. Thus, the current religious affiliations of individuals are tactically accommodated within this notion.

40 Apart from participating in family and traditional activities, the return of pensioners or the aged, these statements also deal with personal practices including marriage, naming and funeral rites. The sending of corpse to their natal communities for burial and/or the performance of final funeral rites are perceived as the final return (of the free range fowl) and the reconfirmation of the traditional identity.

fessions of other religions are viewed as temporary, or perhaps, necessary processes for the time being because those individuals will eventually return? Or, is it perceived as an expansion of the individual's religious horizon? Can it be argued that these adherents are not particularly worried about these 'conversions' because the family, community and cultural systems are maintained? According to Mbiti, to be religious is to belong to a family, clan and community, and to participate in these.[41] Pushing this further, can it be argued that these processes should not simply be perceived as tolerance and accommodation but as part of the individual's religious development? Not one in which the individual abandons the old to acquire the new one but takes on the new as an additional spiritual dimension. If this view is to be investigated, then research must approach it from the indigenous perspective and re-examine the theoretical basis of conceiving ATR as accommodative, transparent and adaptable. It also calls on scholars in African religions to reconsider these dynamics. ATR is not confessional or individualistic, although communal and participatory, its core ritual responsibilities are vested in designated leaders. These leaders are expected to act for the communal good, with or without the individual's consent. This is different from the confessional, individualistic religions which call on the individual to take an active role whether they are leaders or not.

Does this liberal representation by the Nankani support Kwesi Wiredu's claim that questions on identities are intellectual problems?[42] Even so, we must ask the question: what is identity among the Nankani? How is identity perceived and formulated? And finally, what is its impact on this study? In the first place, no discussion of identity within this geographical region can be complete without due consideration of the works of the anthropologist Meyer Fortes on the Tallensi. Even though his work documented the core issues of identity among Tallensi, it provides the landmark documentation of identity for the entire region.[43] Writing on the Tallensi, Fortes succinctly observes that

41   Mbiti, *African Religions and Philosophy*, 2. See also Gyekye, *African Cultural Values*, 3-4.
42   Kwesi Wiredu, "Identity as an Intellectual Problem," in *Identity and the Politics of Scholarship in the Study of Religion*, eds. José Ignacio Cabezón and Sheila Greeve Davaney (New York and Oxon: Routledge, 2004), 212-3.
43   Fortes, *Religion, Morality and the Person*, 194 and 197.

identity "is rooted in ancestry".[44] Fortes' observation is based on this core factor:

> A person's social and juridical identity is irrevocably fixed by his membership by birth of his father's lineage and his connection with other lineages through his mother. This determines where he lives and gets his living, and what his life chances are.[45]

For the Nankani, like the Tallensi, the answer to the question 'who is your father?' is the threshold for establishing ethnic identity. The question of space and location as in place or country of birth is irrelevant. Likewise, it does not recognize other systems like the matrilineal system which dominates the Southern sector of the country. These rigid categorizations of identity into matrilineal and patrilineal descent present great problems in cross-cultural marriages.[46] This conceptual frame of identity also encounters difficulties when a foreign (male) national enters into a marriage relationship with a Nankani female and brings forth children, even if they are in Ghana. Technically, these children, though Ghanaians, do not derive their ethnic or cultural identity as Nankani. The Nankani becomes an extended identity, described by Fortes in terms of the "connection with other lineages through his mother".

Again, despite the apparent simplicity underlying Fortes' description of identity, the system contains complex gender dimensions. For, while a man's cultural and ethnic identity is permanently determined at birth through his father, a woman's identity is understood in multiple and transitional terms. As a daughter, her identity is fixed to her father's lineage. At marriage, she assumes her husband's identity, by affinity, especially as she moves into his lineage. Despite this cultural identity transfer, her natal identity is not completely relinquished. In other words, by Nankani tradition, a married woman maintains, although to a limited degree, her natal identity in addition to her marital one. Her husband is required by tradition to recognize this dual identity as

---

44   Ibid., 193. This should be understood against the background that the ancestors are the most important and immediate spiritual component of the Tallensi religion and worldview

45   Ibid., 194.

46   In the past, these marriages were likely to encounter some antagonistic rejection or struggle for children.

an in-law, and to fulfil all obligations arising from them.[47] This duality, however, underscores the social injustices underlying the place and role of women in the traditional society. It casts doubt on the true identity of married women. Which is a woman's true identity and how does this affect the interpretation of her allegiance to any one identity in the context of marriage?[48]

The above can be viewed as a cultural collateral, designed to protect daughters who as a result of the exogamous system marry outside the community, and therefore, may be susceptible to abuse. In this case, the changes in a woman's identity are compensated by the seminal retention of her natal identity; an assured identity to which she can always return, even after death.[49] This also acts as a surveillance system as the woman's family and natal community are entitled to supervise her welfare, though to a limited extent, in her marital home and community. Although the implications for this tradition on the well-being and development of women have been observed above, it is still important to reiterate that it is the underlying cause of her absence from the dominant structures of authority and power among the Nankani.

On the other hand, this feminine dual identity, which was originally created for the special nature of the daughters, has assumed a new dimension. The traditionally fixed identity and role of sons as permanent residential heirs and landlords has undergone some changes in modern times. The lack of the continuous residential status of sons due to education, urbanization, migration or employment, has tentatively placed these categories of sons under the dual feminine construct of identity. In other words, irrespective of where they are or whatever citizenship they adopt, as a result of modernity, their identity in their natal home is still assured. Like the local free-range fowls, these sons are only considered to be out looking for food with the hope of returning.

---

47 Fortes, "Some Reflections on Ancestor Worship in Africa," 126-7.

48 These factors underpin the many underlying issues of gender and development among the Nankani. The rigid determination of identity stated by Fortes, and its role in understanding allegiance, underscores the issues of inheritance and leadership.

49 By implication, the dual identity status of females, created during marriage, are re-united in the final funeral rite at her natal home. This is a major difference between the genders in terms of funeral rites. Nonetheless, it may serve as an important cue to understanding the 'free range fowl' concept. See also Fortes, "Some Reflections on Ancestor Worship in Africa," 126-7.

Distinctively different from the identity status of daughters, sons who are traditionally enshrined within the leadership structure have no difficulties in assuming leadership positions at any time.

It is with respect to these scenarios that Francis X. Clooney's title, "Neither Here nor There" seems appropriate.[50] Seeing a bit of myself in most of the discussions as they grapple with the concept of identity and, at the same time, disagreeing, rejecting and still feeling left out, impressed on me a true understanding of the concepts of "plurality, fluidity, and complexity" of identity in today's world.[51] How can one effectively explain that, although s/he does not profess a religion, s/he lives and practices the religion in the context of community and belonging? Well, this is the case. As Africa's cultural identity continues to be intertwined with her religious identity, many Africans will continue to cross boundaries.[52] The desire for African names, the African family's sanctification of marriage and death rites, the African rites of passage, all allude to this scenario of interconnectedness.[53]

Judith Butler's response to the question of identity in 'Collected and Fractured' serves as an interesting analytical piece from which to interrogate the concept of identity. Butler requests our understanding of the varied conceptual readings arising from the word identity. Apart from her stimulating discourse on the intellectual shift from the singular notion of identity to the complicated network(s) of identities, Butler observes the inherent "burdens" of culture, "historical formation and contextualization; the possibility of agency, social transformation, representability, and recognizability in both linguistic

---

50 Francis X. Clooney, (S. J.), "Neither Here nor There: Crossing Boundaries, Becoming Insiders, Remaining Catholics," in *Identity and the Politics of Scholarship in the Study of Religion*, eds. José Ignacio Cabezón and Sheila Greeve Davaney (New York and Oxon: Routledge, 2004), 99-111.

51 Tazim R. Kassam, "Balancing Acts: Negotiating the Ethics of Scholarship and Identity," in *Identity and the Politics of Scholarship in the Study of Religion*, eds. José Ignacio Cabezón and Sheila Greeve Davaney (New York and Oxon: Routledge, 2004), 138.

52 See the complexities in Appiah and his father's identity negotiation and boundary crossing between family and religion. Kwame Anthony Appiah, "In My Father's House: Epilogue," in *African Gender Studies: A Reader*, ed. Oyèrónkè Oyěwùmí (England, Palgrave Macmillan, 2005), 341-54.

53 Fulfilling both the cultural and traditional marriage practices to confirm and affirm one's marriage status, the only stage that the individual African has reasonable control over attests to the challenging circumstances.

and political terms" to the current conception of identity.[54] She argues that the intrinsic desire of this current shift is, perhaps, to counter-act the "false and exclusionary generalizations of 'man'" for "cultural specificity".[55] Yet, in Butler's own understanding, the very notion of cultural specificity produces ambiguities, an understanding of which we may infer from the above. Does the notion of specificity in identity discourse connote similarities in a sense in which the two words, speci-ficity and identity, may be used interchangeably or dissimilarities with the potential danger of solipsism? The contribution of this insight to the current study, the question of globalization through development and the Nankani insistence on *tinga woo naka zoom buni* (every land with its way of doing things), presents grounds for further examination even though it cannot be pursued in this research.

Meanwhile, it is important not to lose sight of Butler's subject of positioning. In positioning she conceptualizes identity within the context of both speaker and listener, and the inbuilt power relations such positions present.[56] During my field study, I was constantly drawn to the 'they-us' dichotomy in which the Nankani projected their speaker position in relation to the world outside. The inclusive 'us' by which I was incorporated into the subject group's position manifested clearly when my identity as a Nankani was used to deny me access to the statistical data from the NHRC.[57] With reference to the general frame of my field discussions, however, the subject of positioning was used to reflect on the Nankani analytical perspective of the concept of participation. The questions 'who is a participant and what is the person called to participate in? Whose agenda and terms of reference are participants made to participate in? And finally, to what length or extent are participants allowed to participate?' evolved as necessary questions. The question of identity became very important in relations to development and the call for participation. Identity is tied to self-

---

54   Judith Butler, "Collected and Fractured: Response to *Identities*," in *Identities*, eds. Kwame Anthony Appiah and Henry Louis Gates Jr. (Chicago and London: The University of Chicago Press, 1995), 439-40.

55   Ibid., 441.

56   Judith, "Collected and Fractured," 440.

57   As stated in chapter two, although the NHRC is a public institution, my identity as a Nankani became a reason for the denial of the 2006 Nankani demographic data. The alleged political lobbying fort autonomy among the two groups in the joint Kasena-Nankana district became the underlying factor for the decision.

esteem and dignity. Similarly, positioning is linked to identity. Positioning is also used as a power symbol, full of authoritative nuances. The frequent positioning of African communities at the listening, participating and receiving ends is therefore a serious challenge to their dignity and identity. This is especially so when the traditional concept of positioning, which is based on age, sex, generational dynamics and leadership structures is subverted by the emerging constituents of economic power, modern knowledge and technology. In these encounters, the rural communities are critically examining their identities in relation to their subject positions *vis-à-vis* the international discourse on participatory and sustainable development.

Although the postmodernist recognition of flexibility, fluidity and multiplicity of identities has helped to provide multiple standpoints from which one can view and articulate a given study, it continues to raise questions about the moral obligations of the insider.[58] Hence, finding oneself in a similar predicament to Jacobs, the recurrent combinations of religious and cultural narratives within the context of identity preservation and authentication is a serious challenge.[59] While this engages and, perhaps, addresses the cultural insider position, it elicits questions in relation to one's gender based outsider positions. This is a significant issue when, in the study context, religion and culture are preserved as one and inseparable.

THE DISENGAGED SCHOLAR?

According to Francine Fournier, Sub-Director General for Social and Human Sciences, UNESCO, Paris, this is the era where organizations and researchers should pay close attention to their relationship.[60] Although collaborations have long been established by anthropologists and colonial administrations, Fournier's statement appeals to a continuous engagement. She observes that social sciences have already "acquired

---

58   Janet L. Jacobs, "Transitional Identities: Self, Other, and the Ethnographic Process," in *Personal Knowledge and Beyond: Reshaping the Ethnography of Religion*, eds. James V. Spickard, J. Shawn Landres and Meredith B. McGuire (New York and London: New York University Press, 2002), 93.
59   Ibid., 97.
60   Francine Fournier, "UNESCO and Participatory Research," *People's Participation: Challenges Ahead*, Complied and Analyzed by Orlando Fals Borda (New York: Apex Press, 1998), 23.

the status and capacity to forecast and to intervene in everyday life". Thus she states that they are "currently expected to contribute" not only to the policy making processes but also, "explicating the ideas and paradigms implicit in social movements, in the economic decision and in political change". For her, this is essential for "preventing social disarrays".[61] In this regard, Fournier sees researchers as part of the "problem-solving" mechanism of society.[62] Similarly, Yankah contends that:

> The construction of knowledge, access to knowledge, the transfer of knowledge, and the application of knowledge have been said to be currently determining levels of development. The central issue is that of relevance; for if the purpose of education is the actual improvement of human life on the planet, in the global context, scholarship should be concerned with the application of knowledge to address the pressing needs of society.[63]

The issue of involvement is not only political but relative, if not, a scholarly rhetoric. The issue is not streamlined. Without proper delineation of what it means to be an engaged scholar it will be equally difficult to demarcate disengagement clearly. As shown in the various works of Westerlund, Juschka and Cox,[64] in what sense and to what extent is the line between the personal or nationalistic interest *vis-à-vis* pure scholarship drawn? In some rural African societies, entire communities are still counting in single digits the number of scholars emanating from the area as part of their cumulative sense of development. For instance, in a historical overview of the educational system in Northern Ghana, the scholars, all of whom are Northerners, noted that there was only one graduate at the time of Ghana's independence (1957) and the second was in 1960.[65] In such contexts and where the idiom, 'I am because we are' is still prevalent, the question of involvement or disengagement is questionable. Is this another piece of individualistic

61 Ibid., 23.
62 Ibid., 24.
63 Yankah, *Globalization and the African Scholar*, 1.
64 David Westerlund, *African Religion in African Scholarship: A Preliminary Study of the Religious and Political Background* (Stockholm: Almqvist and Wiksell International, 1985), 44-63; Juschka, "Writing of Ethnography), 88 and Cox, *A Guide to the Phenomenology of Religion*, 225-33 and 239-42.
65 Songsore, *et al*, "Challenges of Education in Northern Ghana," 226.

Western conceptual baggage in the academia? As the Nankani say, 'you cannot step into water and expect to remain dry'. As shown in the insider-outsider discussion above, the scholarly endeavour is an engaged enterprise, one in which the subjects and objects as well as the contexts are engaged in relative degrees. Recent studies (deconstructionist and feminist studies) have illustrated diverse reflective nuances of this.[66] Hence, the issue of engagement will continue to be argued in relative terms. The issue is, in what context, for what purpose, and to what extent such engagements will feature.

That which needs consideration and careful articulation is the place of indigenous scholars, as in the case of African scholars investigating African religions. While straddling different worlds of religions and cultures as well as socio-political consciousness, in which the colonial and postcolonial are embodied, critiques of their works cannot and should not be placed, simply, in binary positions. These are not just apologetic or nationalistic reflections; they display complex forms of encounters and engagements.[67]

THE NATIVE RESEARCHER AND ISSUES OF SENSITIVITY

The question of how sensitive or ethical native researchers are in the presentation of their insider or privileged information to outsiders is yet another crucial area of contemporary discourse. To understand this situation, I will again draw from my field work and the concept of *teare*. *Teare* (change) is the key for responding to this concern. The Nankani are aware of the subtleness of change and this is evident implicitly in this very study. Under normal circumstances, a son should be undertaking this study but that is not the case. Rather, a daughter (myself) is doing it. In my interview of Juatera, he lamented that 'our children have become children of the market. They have no time for themselves, how then can they learn from their fathers. The *wee* [marijuana] and *apatheshi* [traditional Ghanaian gin] is destroying our land'. With an implied absence of interested sons, a daughter's interest is welcomed. The roles played by daughters in the restoration of the family in times of need is essential for understanding why people gave me access and their knowledge even though they knew I was going to 'write and teach others'. It is an honour that a daughter, who is also

66   See Westerlund, *African Religion in African Scholarship*, 44-63.
67   Shaw, "'Traditional' African Religions," 182-5 and Chidester, *Savage Systems*.

a wife in some instances, is not only academically ambitious but also interested in the traditions. The need to give her access and 'teach her properly' is equated to equipping her with the right information so that 'her listeners and readers' will know and understand that *tinga woo la ka zoom bune* (every land has its way of doing things).

The issue of teaching the traditions was particularly welcomed. The understanding that the educational system in Ghana has little or no information on the traditional practices of the Nankani or North was not appreciated. From the contributions of some students who were in the group discussions, much of that which is taught in the Ghanaian educational system on ATR is based on Akan, Ga, Ewe and to a lesser extent, Dagomba traditions. The expression *ti ma nuu lagidena la Ghana dunma* (are we also Ghanaians) was quickly uttered and the desire to be included in the list was expressed. An elder in the group asked if they had not heard of the proverb, 'if your mother is in the kitchen, you are sure to eat'. It was observed that this problem was either due to the lack of material from the area or because the sons and daughters of the area had not taken that area of study in the educational system seriously.

The sayings, 'is she not our daughter? Her *malgo* (development) is also ours' and 'you do not use your left hand to point to the direction of your house', already discussed, show that a Nankani woman's wellbeing and development is a projection of the family name (the masculine identity). In other words, this can be interpreted as helping a daughter of the community is in fact developing the self, as in community. In my earlier discussions on development, I made known that having a child in higher education, travelling out of the community and being in a gainful employment, were all considered as signs of development. Thus, this process is part of development.

This is not to deny that the research is a sensitive one. I have already indicated the NHRC's denial of the 2006 demographic data on the Nankani community, based on my insider status. I have also observed that some community members refrain from confrontation with community development agents for fear that their communities will be excluded from future development initiatives. Thus my critical analysis of community and/or NABOCADO, the traditions or perhaps the choice of the focal community, discussion groups and elders are all potentially sensitive domains. As Raymond Lee and Claire Renzetti have pointed out "*a sensitive topic is one that potentially poses for those involved a substantial threat, the emergence of which renders problematic for the researcher and/or the researched the collection, holding and/ or dissemination of the researched data*". (Emphasis in original)[68] I have throughout the study presented my findings in collective terms, from the community perspective, unless where necessary and this I hope helps to preserve anonymity. Nonetheless, I have already alluded to the saying 'there is no shame in the day of delivery'. This statement which depicts exposure, pain, uncertainty, expectant joy, a new beginning as well as a renewal of humanity through the new birth, primarily calls for truth telling. There is always some form of anxiety for letting out insider information but this fear is already minimized by our awareness of *teare*. Besides, the subject of secrecy and confidentiality are contained in the analysis given on the insider-outsider discussion. As George Watson rightly points out, "a subject may converse without revealing all that he knows".[69] And finally, the notion that access to insider knowledge is relative to one's insider status, serves as a self-regulatory mechanism in this study.

The chapter has responded to some of the emerging issues. I have substantially related my fieldwork on the Nankani to how the diverse issues of this study have been understood, perceived, interpreted and engaged from within their religio-cultural lens. This is not only insightful; it enhances our understanding on the acquisition and presentation of the field data. The stretches of interconnected relationships have in different ways revealed an engendered position in which the socio-cultural dynamics of power have contributed to both the topic and the emerging trends in the study of religions.

Chitando's view on the acceptance of the phenomenological method by African scholars and students is not to be taken literally. For this is not without reflections, concerns and criticisms as he himself has shown and as illustrated in this study.[70] It is the method's ability to

---

68 Raymond M. Lee and Claire M. Renzetti, "Problems of Researching Sensitive Topics: An Overview and Introduction," in *Researching Sensitive Topics*, eds. Claire M. Renzetti and Raymond M. Lee (London and New Delhi: SAGE Publications, 1993), 4.

69 George Watson, *Writing a Thesis: a guide to long essays and dissertations* (London and New York: Longman, 1987), 54.

70 Chitando, "Phenomenology of Religion and the Study of African Traditional Religions," 308-13.

present a multifaceted descriptive perspective of a phenomenon, one that enables African researchers to undertake a critical study of their own religio-cultural traditions that has facilitated its acceptance. Thus, while the search for appropriate methodologies continues, the phenomenological method remains a viable tool through which African researchers and students, in the current era of religious fanaticism and fundamentalism, open up to the multi-religious perspectives of their communities and the world at large. Such an opening also draws attention to the limitations surrounding current methodologies. This challenges them to respond and contribute to the search for appropriate tools for the study of ATR as found in chapter five.

In case we not only become slaves of definitions,[71] but also of theories and methodologies, there is need for a judicious engagement with the religio-cultural resources,[72] in order to mend the broken pieces for *malgo* to ensue. As the saying goes, *ba taari la yam basira nwanya/ngwanga nyoro* (it is with wisdom that you dispose of the intestines of a monkey).[73] Thus, despite the limitations and the debates arising from the phenomenological method, I have gone beyond the narrative descriptions to provide analysis where necessary. As in the study title, life and development is about mending broken pieces. It is about participatory discussion (*sosika*), one in which we may not agree or have a smooth discussion (*zoka*), nonetheless, we may still learn from one another. For the Nankani, religion is not an individual enterprise, and so it is with development. Similarly, development, individual or collective, is not a distinct category, it is inclusive. Education as a modern component of development is expected to reflect this perspective (consciously or unconsciously), as I have illustrated in this study. Even though the extent to which one is engaged varies, all participants of religion and development discourses are engaged parties.

---

71   Van Rinsum, *Slaves of Definition*.
72   Olupona, "Introduction," in *African Spirituality*, xviii.
73   Diviners are not trained but called. This is usually by the spirit of an animal. One of these is the monkey. Although it is not forbidden to eat it, its intestines are associated with some mythical beliefs, that of company and a moving nature. Thus, to dispose of it one has to deploy a scheme in which a temporal excuse is given to put the intestines down in order to move away and consequently disappear. If this is not properly done the spirit will follow and posses that individual as a diviner.

Consequently, sustainable development among Nankani is neither focused on environment nor economics; it is all embracing, with religion as an integral part in respect to providing meaning and moral value to life giving situations. They consider the available resources as prime factors, serving as a base for expansion and a guide in the search for the new. Within the framework of 'mending the broken pieces', all these form 'tradition' influencing both culture and religion, and contextualizing the concept of religio-cultural dynamism as discussed in chapter two.[74] My engagement with theory and method in this study therefore is yet another response to the call for a 'holistic' search for sustainable development from an African woman's perspective within the current discourses in religious studies. It is a response where traditional concepts engage the modern to illuminate and develop further our understanding on the subject matter. For the Nankani, the continuous engagement with the different components of life situations is a way of life and livelihood. To live, develop and sustain life is about 'mending the broken pieces'. It is for this reason that 'mending the broken pieces' is not an abstract phrase, but a search aimed at soliciting understanding from the visible and the invisible world as we encounter in the concluding chapter below.

---

74   See also Pictures 8 and 12.

CONCLUSION

Chapter Seven

MENDING THE BROKEN PIECES

The European too easily tends to ridicule the notion that upsetting the rhythm of human life, by administrative or missionary methods, is generally regarded by the people as liable to bring down a series of natural disasters. 'The crops will not grow, hens will not lay, women will not bear children ... So often has this cry been heard, simply on account of the construction of a road in some part of the forest[1]

The traditional way of life is closely bound up with religion and religious beliefs in such a way that there is a mutual interdependence of religion and culture ... African Religion provides a holistic view of life. It enables persons to understand and accept their status and identity and passes on beliefs that explain prevailing conditions. African Religion teaches its adherents how to survive and thrive in the world in which they have been placed. This religion undergirds the shaping of the moral, social and the political, and even, at times, the economic. Hence, the moral obligations that weigh so heavily on African women are firmly hooked on to beliefs.[2]

Although differently presented, these statements are complementary. In a preliminary study of *African Religion in African Scholarship*, Westerlund pointed out that there are great differences between Western and African perspectives and presentations of ATR.[3] Much of this, he believes, is based on the individuals or their collective 'religious

---

1   Parrinder, *West African Psychology*, 15.
2   Oduyoye, *Introducing African Women's Theology*, 25.
3   Westerlund, *African Religion in African Scholarship*, 87-91.

and political background'. Even so, the differences are essential as they each and collectively contribute to the understanding of the subject matter. Throughout this study, the disputes between development and African communities occur around the nature of African spirituality, its connection to the African worldview and its inherent notion of interdependence.[4] Parrinder captured the depth of the problem by adding that "[p]erhaps such a world-view may have paralysed the mind, or prevented its free development; so it appears to us".[5] Yet, as gladly as Parrinder seems to wish for the disappearance of such 'ill-founded superstitions' he is also worried that "Africa's spiritual and living world-view" would be replaced by a "superficial and purely materialistic outlook".[6] Although it is impossible to decipher the depth of his concerns, Oduyoye provides some insight to the inter-connectedness and the respective moulding of the African mind and attitude to life. For her, "[w]hatever is adopted, adapted, assimilated or ignored comes from a gradual interaction and not from imposition".[7] The need to note this so as to carefully negotiate on some crucial elements of this worldview would be essential for sustainable development among the Nankani. As Olupona elaborates, "Africa's religious heritage bestows upon its people a worldview and a value system; it bestows a personal and social orientation to life. As Africa enters the twenty-first century, it faces new spiritual, social, and economic challenges, which it must surmount with resources from its own religious and cultural heritage".[8] Mobilizing this resource will be a significant contribution to the development of rural Africa.

At the same time, we are drawn to the dynamics of gender and the view that religion and culture is differently experienced and presented according to one's gender. Oduyoye's remarks above enjoin us first to think of this as part of the structural network of interconnectedness and then, its effect on the African woman. As an African woman, she observes that the African woman is brought up with a sense of community, one in which "African women are programmed to live for

---

4   Oduyoye, *Introducing African Women's Theology*, 34-5.
5   Parrinder, *West African Psychology*, 16.
6   Ibid.
7   Oduyoye, *Introducing African Women's Theology*, 34.
8   Olupona, "Introduction," in *African Spirituality*, xviii.

others", others as in family and community.[9] While this illuminates our understanding of the various roles of Nankani women, discussed in this study, it also illustrates the important role of gender as a tool for 'mending the broken pieces'. But while the importance of gender in development initiatives has been generally acknowledged, women's specific (contextual) views have not really been taken into consideration. As illustrated in the field discussions under NABOCADO, the Nankani female identifies herself as a woman only within the context of marriage, the context within which she assumes full and active responsibility in family and community life. Understanding the perspectives in this context as well as the wider context of relatedness and inter-dependence are essential in mapping out development strategies for the area. These structural views call on development initiators to listen and consider the voices on the ground when drawing up development programmes. While the Nankani want development, the men do not want to be perceived as 'irresponsible and ineffective' and the women do not want strained family relationships or to unduly take on all the burdens of the family and process of development. Even though Olupona reports that "[w]omen have a significant place in African religious heritage", he does so with a sense of balance as he explains, "[i]ndeed, the complementarity of male and female principles and values ... is portrayed as essential for the survival of any African community".[10] These internal dynamics, which have been engraved on Africans by their specific religio-cultural contexts, needs serious attention from those working with and within them.

In chapter six the main issues arising from the study, in relation to contemporary discourses on research objectivity were examined. Within that discussion evolved my view that the issue of objectivity and research involvement are contextually relative. That is, each research context, in relation to the researcher, affects both the approach and content which invariably has an impact on the output. Clearly manifested in its respective presentation of the problem (Western and African) in chapter one, some of the inputs of chapter five, the view is further strengthened by the underlying tone of the two state-

---

9   Oduyoye, *Introducing African Women's Theology*, 31. See also, Mercy Amba Oduyoye, *Hearing and Knowing: Theological Reflections on Christianity in Africa* (Maryknoll, New York: Orbis Books, 1986), 122.

10   Olupona, "Introduction," in *African Spirituality*, xviii.

ments heralding this chapter. But whereas this study acknowledges the importance and influence of these contemporary debates on research, as a significant move in the history and development of scholarship,[11] its focus continues be on p'Bitek's quest for "understanding African ways of thought".[12] 'Mending the broken pieces' provides this glimmer of light from the Nankani for the various stakeholders in the subject matter to work with.

It is clear that both indigenous communities and development agents have often not given due consideration to each others' viewpoints in their respective schemes of work. This has caused misunderstandings between the parties irrespective of the fact that they both aspire to what is perceived to be the same goal. This chapter discusses how some of these misunderstandings and misrepresentations may be avoided, if not minimised, by shedding more light on some of the issues that have emerged from the study. The chapter is in three parts: discussing the problems and challenges; gender, development and the feminization of poverty; and lastly, development in partnership. This provides additional resources for understanding the concept of 'mending the broken pieces' as the study concludes.

PROBLEMS AND CHALLENGES

The most important challenge to modern development stems from the ambiguities arising from the term 'development'. As shown, scholars have deliberated extensively as to the real meaning of the word and what its constituents are. The fact that this is not only culturally relative but historically influenced cannot be denied. Over the years, efforts are made to understand both the term and to respond to the changes in its trail. William Watts identifies some of these challenges as poverty in the midst of plenty, environmental degradation, depletion of non-renewable resources, rejection of traditional values, uncontrolled urban spread and uncontrolled economic systems.[13] For him, this has culminated in drawing an opposition to the entire concept of development. Arguing that it has already run its course and should

---

11   Cox, "African Identity as the Projection of Western Alterity," 34-6.

12   See chapter one, 1-3.

13   William Watts, "Foreword", in *The Limits to Growth: A Report for the Club of Rome's Project on the Predicament of Mankind*, eds. Dennis L. Meadows *et al* (London: A Potomac Associates Book, 1972), 10.

be laid to rest, Sachs concludes that development is an illusion and a disappointment. For him, "it did not work"; besides that, it "has grown obsolete".[14] What Sachs is yet to comprehend is why "[t]hough doubts are mounting and uneasiness is widely felt, development talk still pervades not only official declarations but even the language of grassroots movements".[15]

Sachs' analogy of the cycle of life, birth and death fails to understand that words and ideas are not as mortal as humans. Perhaps Sachs needs assistance from the Nankani worldview where some words are believed to possess some form of potency. According to this view, certain words are delicate and must be handled with care; otherwise, they can easily transform into new forms, taking on life forms that can be engaging and enduring. This then requires a much more strenuous effort to bring them under control.[16] The spontaneous proclamations of the development agenda after independence in Africa, Asia and South America, for instance, have rather profusely given more life to 'development', not death as Sachs wishes.[17] Its continuous transformational processes have enabled it to reproduce or take on new characteristics like participatory development, sustainable development or sustainable rural development.

These amendments are not by themselves miraculous. Problems continue to arise with regard to the different socio-cultural contexts. Also, questions as to whether rural African communities share the same goals, visions and aspirations as those of the West are becoming crucial. To what extent and in what context are objectives shared? Do rural African communities have a say in what is introduced to them or is it forced on them because they are perceived as poor and underdeveloped? How many of their concerns and aspirations are taken into consideration when development programmes and projects are planned and implemented? How are rural African communities responding to these forms of development? Some of these questions have already been explored. So far, it is evident that to achieve sustainable development among the Nankani, the religio-cultural systems and the underlying structures governing gender needs to be unearthed, analysed, discussed

---

14   Sachs, "Introduction," in *The Development Dictionary*, 1.
15   Ibid.
16   See chapter five, 156-8.
17   Ellis and Ter Haar, *Worlds of Power*, 172.

and streamlined. This can be done in a constructive and participatory manner with all the stakeholders, noting the weaknesses and strengths from both parties, taking along the respective people's heritage with a careful reflection of the contemporary situation.[18] This can then be used as a reference for consensus building and negotiations.

Although there is a growing awareness that indigenous knowledge and resources alone cannot cope with today's growing needs, the reverse is also considered as being incapable of redeeming the African continent and its rural problems. This is because indigenous needs, desires and aspirations have assumed complex dimensions. Aware of these, the incorporation of relevant modern knowledge and resources is important for the enhancement of indigenous systems. Nonetheless, the search for and process of integration can be done in a friendly manner to forestall indignation. Success in such programmes however depends on the manner and extent to which indigenous cultural values are balanced with those of modern science and technology.[19] Thus, development as a process can be cumulative to both parties.

There is still no correct understanding or interpretation of the indigenous socio-economic system. Traditional communalism is often interpreted in terms of communism or socialism. Yet these systems are not in consonance with the traditional one. As Martin Minoque and Judith Molloy write, "[t]raditional social organisation often did not possess the character attributed to it; the viewpoint is a romantic one".[20] These new concepts are based on ideological backgrounds that are strategically and constructively different. Nevertheless, the Nankani saying, 'it is for the sake of beans that stones are oiled' provides understanding for these misrepresentations. It implies that under normal circumstances, stones will not be cooked with oil as food, yet their presence in food sources may well provide that opportunity. In other words, the misunderstandings are because of the similarities in the systems. This notwithstanding, the traditional economy acknowledges class, status, individualism, gender and age. The recognition of individual initiatives

---

18   A. K. Awedoba, *Culture and Development in Africa: with special references to Ghana, Some Basis Issues,* Vol. 1, (Legon: Institute of African Studies, University of Ghana, 2002), 18-9.

19   John C. Afele and Kofi V. Anani, "Indigenous Knowledge Systems," in *Global University Systems,* accessed 4 November 2004; available from http://www.mapzones.com/world/africa/ghana/cultureindex.php; Internet.

20   Minoque and Molloy, *African Aims and Attitudes,* 4.

and achievements is clearly evident in Igbo culture.[21] Even so, through its extended family or communal solidarity system, the poor and vulnerable obtain support. The lack of proper understanding and balancing of these factors has led to the varied applications of development strategies by different African governments, with little success.

Tanzania's socialist approach to the traditional concept Ujamma is one such example. Ujamaa was part of the search to involve "the people as a whole" in the nation's efforts towards development. It was a good attempt at dealing with participatory rural development in the modern sense.[22] But Nyerere's adaptation of the concept, though laudable, failed to take into account the traditional factors of individual achievements and ownership of property. The communal concepts 'we' and 'ours' take into consideration some perspective of the individual as in 'I'. Nankani traditional communities, for instance, have recognizable individuals who excel in specific fields.[23] The difference is that these individual achievers are perceived as unique blessings to the family or community. Hence, their services are sought. To completely eliminate that for the communal 'our land', 'our crop' and 'our shop' did not only nullify the presence of these exceptional individuals within the communities but also eliminated the spirit of individual hard work and talent development as well as the spiritual component binding these factors.[24] Secondly, rural development is not about forming new rural communities, but aiding existing ones to improve even within their existing cultural heritage. Rural living has no single theme; in like manner, rural development cannot be singularly focused as Ujamma type of development. Nor can it be achieved by the simple provision of new settlements, roads, educational and health facilities.[25] Most importantly, to have ignored the traditional elements of spirits and

---

21   See Victor C. Uchendu, 'Concubinage among Ngwa Ibo of Southern Nigeria', *Africa: Journal of the International Institute* 35. No. 2 (April 1965): 188; accessed 18 December 2008; available from http://www.jstor.org/ stable/1158231?seq=2; Internet.

22   Sigvard von Sicard, "African Socialism: Communism or Communalism, A Case Study," *Africa Theological Journal* 11, no. 1 (1982): 27.

23   Rattray, *The Tribes of the Ashanti Hinterland*, 266-8.

24   Meredith, *The State of Africa*, 253-4.

25   Meredith, *The State of Africa*, 255. See also, Minoque and Molloy (eds.), *African Aims and Attitudes*, 86-92.

ancestors, by dislocating people, sometimes forcefully from their old settlements, was a major disruption to their spirituality and worldview.

Similar initiatives in Ghana by Kwame Nkrumah did not yield the needed results. In his desire to develop the Anaafo coastal community in Cape Coast as a modern seaside estate, Nkrumah built the Ola estate to relocate the people. The traditional community refused to relocate to the inland modern estate, citing among their reasons their unwillingness to leave their ancestral and spiritual 'home'. Likewise, the programme which resulted in the development of 'state farms' in various parts of the country, including the Oil Palm plantation in Pretsea in the Western Region, did not materialize because the people saw the projects as *aban dea* (for government) and *aban edwuma* (government work), not theirs. The same can be said of the cattle ranch located on the Kologo-Naga road in the Nankani community. Meant to supply the meat factory that was located in Zuarungo in the regional capital, the project failed and now its infrastructure is in ruins.[26] The personal, family and community ownership forms of conceptualization and commitment were not cultivated. Perhaps, because there were no religio-cultural links with these projects, people had no moral or religious obligations towards them. It is worth noting that the modern system of governance is still perceived as foreign in comparison to the traditional one (chieftaincy). Development activities initiated by perceived 'foreign bodies' do not carry the same religio-cultural significance and responsibilities. It is unclear as to who the project initiators at the community level were. Similarly, I am unsure of the nature and extent of the educational campaigns that were attached to these initiatives. What is certain is these factors have diverse effects on rural development projects; hence, the need to learn from these experiences by paying closer attention to the complexities of community resistance.

While agreeing with Chitando's view that the phenomenological method is quite loose, I disagree that it is unable to "embrace approaches that emphasise religion and gender, the environment, sexual orientation and others".[27] The apparent lack of research in these areas need not be construed as an inability of the method. This is a hasty conclusion. As shown in this study, the method does not limit the study of gender, espe-

---

26   See picture 17.
27   Chitando, "Phenomenology of Religion and the Study of African Traditional Religions," 311.

cially if scholars accept that phenomenology relates *To the Things Themselves*.[28] The indigenous African religion, as in the Nankani religion, is not wholly other, that which is set apart. It is relational and reciprocal. It is this uniqueness that has led to its superimposition on all areas of community and people's life.[29] Therefore, if the method, despite its "conviction that religion is unique, irreducible and a discipline in its own right" can be applied to ATR, then it is my contention that it is equally capable of responding to these other concerns, which hinge on religion. It is important to note that the Department for the Study of Religions, University of Ghana, has for the past eight years applied phenomenology to the study of religion and gender in a course 'Gender Issues in Religion and Culture'. The course, structured to reflect the religio-cultural dynamics of the nation, is taught by a team embracing Islam, Christianity and ATR. Besides, this study illustrates that such endeavours are possible.

What is more, the study also calls on development agents not to focus their drive for gender equality narrowly on women's economic or political empowerment. In line with the current realities, the question 'who is a woman' or 'where does the Nankani woman belong' need examination, thus requiring a place in gender discussions in the area. At present, women are traditionally perceived as appendices to men in their roles as fathers, brothers, husbands or even as sons. Even so, it is still common to hear a married woman's parents tell their daughter 'go home', meaning her matrimonial home. The same statement can also be issued at the matrimonial home, especially when trouble arises. The question then becomes, where does she belong? The issue arising from this is that women have no permanent identity or status of their own. Although the traditional provision of a dual identity can be interpreted as a flexible form of empowerment, one which women can use to escape or manipulate male dominance, it is also a source of disempowerment as it is used to toss women about.[30] Judith Butler advances a similar argument in relation to the gender identity disorder (GID) diagnostic requirement for sex transformation.[31] These forms of sub-

---

28   A. Sharma, *To the Things Themselves: Essays on the Discourse and Practice of the Phenomenology of Religion* (New York, Gruyter, 2001), quoted in Chitando, "Phenomenology of Religion and the Study of African Traditional Religions," 299.

29   Chitando, "Phenomenology of Religion and the Study of African Traditional Religions," 311-2 and Gyekye, *African Cultural Values*, 3-4.

30   See chapter four.

31   Judith Butler, *Undoing Gender* (New York and London: Routledge, 2004), 75-101.

version find expression in Susan Faludi's *Backlash*.[32] For just as the lack of a static identity deprives women of inheritance, power and authority, so also does it impinge on their commitment to development.[33] For instance, the name Ayingabunu not only conveys a sense of alienation, it presents the female as an 'Other'. She belongs to outsiders, and in that capacity, she contributes to the property of that 'Other'. As shown in this study, the male understanding and diagnosis of my gender and insider status, in relation to my field data requirement was couched in terms of "if this is of benefit to you, then it is of benefit to all of us. After all, it all comes back to us: is she not our daughter and wife? That is it".[34] This may be reinterpreted as a repossession of that which is given, including the prospective achievement and the outlet through which that achievement is made. This form of conceptualization can be a disincentive for females to adopt a strong desire for development that goes beyond the immediate and/or personal needs.

This aligns with the perception that women are poor. She belongs to others; hence, her resources and possessions belong to these 'others'. Consequently, she is without property, inheritance, power or authority because she must submit to those to whom she belongs. In other words, if the African religio-cultural heritage provides survival strategies for its people,[35] a strategy which Oduyoye contends programmes women to live for others,[36] then the scholarly projection of gender complementarity needs to be re-examined.[37] These contradictions do not order well for understanding or policy making and they contribute to misinterpretations. Otherwise, the concentration of development resources on women will either continue to feed the existing system or breed conflict and division.[38]

---

32 Susan Faludi, *Backlash: The Undeclared War against Women* (London: Vintage, 1992).

33 Rose Mary Amenga-Etego, "Traditional/cultural practices which impinge on women's development in the Upper East Region," unpublished paper on Tradition and Women's Underdevelopment (Upper East Regional Population Service seminar, Bolgatanga, 5th July, 2002), 3.

34 See chapter six, 370.

35 Olupona, "Introduction," in *African Spirituality*, xviii.

36 Oduyoye, *Introducing African Women's Theology*, 31.

37 Olupona, "Introduction," in *African Spirituality*, xviii and Mbiti, "Flowers in the Garden," in *African Traditional Religions in Contemporary Society*, 68.

38 See chapter three, 185-9.

Culturally, women are perceived as a part of the man's world and property. This complex situation extends even to the modern educated, working or industrious woman. Not only are their properties socially perceived as their husband's properties, it is a common practice to see the properties of women in this category taken over by their spouses during divorce or by their in-laws at his death. This practice is not limited to the Nankani; it is widespread in Ghana. Among the Akans, rooms are sometimes locked and keys taken to prevent the widow(s) access to the man's 'supposed' property until the *abusua* (family) have presided over the inheritance, one in which the man's maternal nephew has custody. The Akan proverb, 'if a woman buys a gun, it is placed in a man's room' subtly nuances this subversive tendency among the matrilineal Akan, whose women pride themselves on their overt political authority and economic rights.[39] The need to consider these subversive elements underlying the current economic and socio-political empowerment programmes is crucial for sustainable development in rural African communities.

GENDER, UNDERDEVELOPMENT AND THE FEMINIZATION OF POVERTY

The feminization of underdevelopment and poverty is widely acknowledged by scholars and development agents alike. According to Brian K. Murphy, "[i]t is no secret that where there are poor people, the majority and the poorest among them will be women and children".[40] Although this observation is quite true, the placement of women and children together in these discussions raises concerns. Not only does it place women at the level of children as vulnerable, incapable of self-care, childlike, needing security and control, it perpetuates the subservience of women. It gives credence to the traditional notions that women are children. Such generalizations, therefore, strengthen the historic gender-based bias and oppression. Although 'boy children' have better religio-cultural rights than women among the Nankani, the generational and age stratifications impinge on this, giving women leverage in daily living. The above categorization thus exposes women further to domination and control. It is not surprising that the initial

---

39   See also Oduyoye, *Hearing and Knowing*, 123.
40   Murphy, "International NGOs and the challenge of modernity," 70.

debate surrounding the creation of the Ministry for Women and Children's Affairs (MOWAC) in Ghana included these concerns.

As Murphy himself noted, women are not passive members of their societies or families. They often bear the brunt of their families' and communities' survival. Among the Nankani, for instance, it is the woman who is blamed for a wayward child. Again, whereas women and children may be presented as poor, a child's poverty is dependant on the mother, if not, an already impoverished family or society. A woman's poverty also exists because she gives all she has.[41] A child's poverty is because s/he depends on the mother for his/her immediate needs. This may be contrasted with the traditionally (assumed) prosperity of men which thrives on preservation and accumulation.

One of the important discoveries in this study was through my discussions with the elderly men and women. According to this group, women are not perceived as poor in the traditional context. They explained that although women could generally be viewed as poor due to their overt lack of control over property like cattle, sheep, crop produce stored in granaries or households, these items were traditionally considered as family property with ancestral ownership.[42] Technically therefore men had no property of their own. Male ownership was seen in the family context and the ultimate concern was to preserve what they possessed for posterity. By this, men acted as custodians. It was explained that, with collective property, consultations, sometimes rituals had to be performed before the use of specific items.

On the other hand, female property which depended on their industriousness was fully regarded as women's private or personal properties. Ayogwine Awuni[43] explained that women had control over

---

41   See chapter three, 86. The alleged gains of women are numerated in terms of their contribution to household expenditure.

42   This situation has changed. These inherited properties are either no longer in existence or have greatly diminished. The breaking down of the extended family system has also led to the distribution of family properties to individual control and ownership.

43   Ayogwine Awuni is a widow of the late chief and second mother of the Naga chief's house. The current landlord and his wife (father and mother) are both younger. They have acquired their positions because the man belongs to a senior generation. Although Ayogwine is older and has acquired her knowledge and skills as result age and experience, she is second to the younger woman who is accredited as the mother of the house.

their property, regardless of its nature or quantity. Properties which consisted of small portions of diverse foodstuffs and other items were properly preserved and kept for emergencies in women's storage pots in their *detinma* (round huts), traditionally known as *toolluum* (warmth or heat). Men were barred by taboo to search or take anything from these. In the eastern zone, these pots were placed in the *kiema'niga* (in front of the ancestors) in the *de'nyanga* (feminine or ritual room).[44] Although the current discussion contributes to our understanding of Apusigah's arguments on *toolluum* as a gendered concept and a potential for sustainable development, the issue here is on women's personal property and ownership. Women's *toolluum* items, although often used for the family's welfare, were privately owned.

The manifestation of women's poverty, it was argued, is associated with the transformation of subsistence economies to cash economies without the requisite resources or avenues for the generation of the needed cash. It was observed that not only have modern women stopped using and preserving indigenous foodstuffs and items, the concept of *toolluum* is disappearing. The conversion of things into cash and the storage of feminine property in modern gadgets such as bags and trunks have also broken down the traditional gender barriers to individual ownership. Without such boundaries, unscrupulous men and sons now have unauthorized access to women's property simply by means of destruction. This refers to the destruction of the locks or gadgets used in households. Similarly, the venture into male oriented property is projected as not being helpful to Nankani women. This is because women often revert to the culturally accepted means of seeking male permission before the use of such property, including animals. In other words, women have lost their position of strength in the traditional sector without any real gain in the modern setup. The lack of sustainability in the area of traditional skills and resources is viewed as a loss of diversity and an alternative source of living. This is seen as a problem of modern development which is interpreted as one that focuses on acquisition and not preservation.

On the other hand, the women who attended the focus group discussions analyzed their gains or development within the modern sphere in terms of the freedom to choose between the old and new forms of living. Others included formal education, training in new skills, and

---

44   See pictures 9 and 10.

other modern alternative sources of living. The latter was elaborated in terms of trading or engaging in a variety of paid jobs. The different perspectives presented by these women should not be seen as conflicting, but as a discussion on alternative forms of rural living. Nonetheless, the problem remains as to how women can secure, control or have unlimited access to their property within the 'modern' rural context. Rural development planners and researchers need to carefully investigate as well as consider these lines of discourse in their programmes. As Griswold remarks, the drive towards globalization is indirectly fostering "a renewed sense of cultural particularism – new boundaries, rooted in ethnicity, religion, and geography" are constantly being raised.[45]

This is not to imply that there is no poverty or underdevelopment among Nankani women. Like the pastoralist societies of East Africa, the self-proclaimed statement "the poor are not us", though contextually defined, does not eliminate the view that, they are getting poorer in comparative terms.[46] These scenarios call on development agents to look beyond superficial expressions to the underlying factors in their target communities. Observed by Oduyoye above, the African religion enables people to accept their identities and status. There is no doubt that the perception of the female as a partial 'outsider' has in many ways affected her attitude to development. Besides, this traditional notion of a partial 'outsider' continues to influence the upbringing of females in terms of care, education and skills training. Proper care at childhood is said to have an impact in one's adult life. The gender based disparities in child care arising from overwork, poor nutrition, few or inadequate educational opportunities or training have placed women in a disproportionate position. This needs proper attention, not scholarly justification which may otherwise perpetuate it.

Development in Partnership

In *Rural Development*, Chambers argued for the removal of all forms of biases, negative stereotypes and prejudices as well as self-interest and egos of development planners, initiators, donors and

---

45   Griswold, *Cultures and Societies in a Changing World*, xviii.

46   David M. Anderson and Vigdis Broch-Due, "Poverty and Pastoralism: Deconstructing Myths, Reconstructing Realities," in *The Poor Are Not Us: Poverty and Pastoralism in Eastern Africa*, eds. David M. Anderson and Vigdis Broch-Due (Oxford: James Curry Ltd., 1999), 4.

workers from development programmes and activities. He argues that poverty and underdevelopment do not constitute lack of knowledge or wisdom. Environmental and cultural knowledge in given situations are crucial components to a successful and sustainable development initiative. Indigenous knowledge and resources are vital components in every human adventure and so it must be with sustainable development. His call to "putting the last first" within the development hierarchy is thus a welcome move and contribution to this study. Yet we might still question his view on 'the last'.[47]

Writing on the sub-heading; "Whose Priority?" both Chambers and Batchelor address the core issue of rural development, although from different perspectives.[48] Understanding the needs and priorities, and at the same time, the fears and anxieties of the rural people is crucial for rural development. Batchelor argues that development initiatives should be self-driven by the beneficiaries. Beneficiaries need to desire the particular development initiative, for them to participate in or lead the process. They should, however, be well equipped with the different possibilities, insights, and improved skills to effect the change. This includes the necessary logistics and financial support. But even in these contexts, anticipated outcomes should be reasonable because the impact could be just a little step or improvement at a time, even though a giant leap is possible.[49] Whatever the situation, Batchelor insists, "we must start from what really matters to people".[50] We see this in the way Aputibunu handles her children.[51] Batchelor's work is very revealing and relevant in the way he recounts the diverse self-realisation points of expatriate development workers in rural Africa. As of now, some indigenous development workers have adopted this old trend. Although, many reasons can be given for this, including what Chambers calls the "Elite bias",[52] much of it weighs on the desire of development workers

---

47   See Carolyn Long, *Participation of the Poor in Development Initiatives: Taking their Rightful Place* (London and Sterling: Earthscan Publication Ltd., 2001), 64-5.

48   Chambers, *Rural Development*, 141-8. See also Batchelor, *People in Rural Development*, 3-10.

49   Batchelor, *People in Rural Development*, 3-10.

50   Ibid., p. 4.

51   See chapter four, 162-3.

52   Chambers, *Rural Development*, 18.

to meet the goals and objectives of their donors in the West.[53] These goals that are often set within prescribed times and periods have in many occasions thrown reality out of the way.

The need to identify and understand the different coping strategies adopted by rural African communities in terms of gender, poverty and development is another dimension to a possible successful and sustainable venture.[54] In many cases, people employ a variety of ways to cope with given situations. While music composition and dance or dance drama can be adopted by both sexes as channels of free speech and resistance, women also use the opportunity of wall decorations as an added avenue for voicing and projecting themselves.[55] Another strategy for addressing the emergent gender base roles and responsibilities amidst poverty has been to travel to urban centres in search of jobs. However, sometimes these women are unable to secure what they expect and subsequently find themselves entangled in the difficulties of urban life.

Among the major concerns raised in *The Limits to Growth* are the rising levels of poverty in the midst of plenty, environmental degradation, the depletion of non-renewable resources, the rejection of traditional values, uncontrolled urban spread as well as uncontrolled economic systems.[56] The report argues that these factors do not just occur in varying proportions in the different societies but that they interrelate with each other and their impact is often extensive although not immediate. Humanity's failure to recognize these factors as a composite unit, and to foresee a future impact at the initial stages, is therefore a problem.[57] The professionals in this discourse argue that, "[a] person's time and space perspectives depend on his culture, his past experience, and the immediacy of the problems confronting him on each level".[58] These factors must therefore be critically considered when embarking on projects at the rural level. Although the report forecasts a limit to growth, it calls for alternative options aimed at establishing "a condition of ecological and economic stability that is sustainable far into the future".[59] In its sequel, *Beyond the Limits*, Donella Meadow

---

53   Campbell, *Western Primitivism: African Ethnicity*, 58-9.
54   See chapter three.
55   See picture 6.
56   Watts, "Foreword," 10.
57   Watts, "Foreword," 11.
58   Meadows *et al*, *The Limits to Growth*, 18.
59   Ibid., 24.

et al declare, "[s]ustainability does not mean no growth", rather, its stress is on quality, not sheer physical expansion.[60] Acknowledging the peculiarities of rural livelihoods and environment, and the adoption of measures tailored to each specific need and situation, is one feasible step towards this qualitative growth. Sustainable rural development should therefore take a multi-faceted, participatory, bottom-up approach. It must aspire to a full analytical appreciation and recognition of the diversity of rural problems. This should entail the identification of the needs and opportunities of rural people. It must also have a good coordinated and flexible support framework to allow significant changes and adjustment to ongoing programmes. The scholars referred to this as a holistic approach to development.

According to Olivier de Sardan, this is part of the development rhetoric.[61] How can rural development be holistic if the African religion, the driving force in rural African communities, is not considered? Apusigah's analysis of community views of poverty in Northern Ghana was based on the religio-cultural dynamics of spirituality and its corresponding influence on wealth, development and general wellbeing. Her study shows that an adaptation of the institutional perspective alone is inadequate.[62] As Guy Hunter aptly puts it, Africans want *The Best of Both Worlds* and indeed, this is a challenge to development initiatives in Africa.[63]

When Mbiti says "Africans are notoriously religious"[64] and Idowu "in all things religious"[65], we might wonder what these expressions mean in the context of development. Yet set in a wider context or earlier scholarly perspectives we may glean some more understanding from George Foster. Foster had earlier argued that the idea that "man is incurably religious and will find his way back to religion again after he has lost it" is based on the fact that humans have "vested interests".[66] Even though current debate on religion and secularization in the West provides

60   Ibid., 210.
61   Jean-Pierre Olivier de Sardan, *Anthropology and Development: Understanding Contemporary Social Change*, trans. by Antoinette Tidjani Alou (London and New York: Zed Books, 2005), 4-5.
62   Apusigah, "Diagnosing Poverty in Northern Ghana," 6-9.
63   Guy, Hunter, *The Best of Both Worlds? A Challenge on Development Polices in Africa* (London, New York and Toronto: Oxford University Press, 1967).
64   Mbiti, *African Religions and Philosophy*, 1.
65   Idowu, *OLÓDÙMARÈ*, 1-10.
66   Foster, *The Function of Religion in Man's Struggle for Existence*, 153.

avenues for questioning this line of thought, the ambiguity surrounding the nature and context of religion, justifies the resurgence of this claim.[67]

Nevertheless, we might need to join the women of 'The Circle' in "Treading Softly but Firmly" in our attempt to unlock the potentials of the African worldview. Like the Nankani women, 'The Circle' women are aware of the "ineffectiveness of confrontation as a means to an end".[68] In their search for gender-justice, 'The Circle' is engaged in local studies as a means to understanding the relevant religio-cultural tools needed for effective negotiation. As Ola Rotimi has illustrated in his classic African play *The Gods Are Not To Blame*, it is the lack of tolerance and respect for each other's views and lifestyles that drives his plot and sustains underdevelopment. According to Rotimi, "when trees fall on trees, first the topmost must be removed",[69] and this process requires action. The need to move beyond the perceived to the reality, from lip-service and political rhetoric to practice, is essential. It is time therefore to start unpacking from the topmost part of the rubble, perhaps, starting with the biases associated with rural African development. As shown in this study, it is not religion *per se*; it is the uncooperative nature of the different stakeholders. Yet, as the popular saying clarifies, 'you can't have your cake and eat it'. As Helder Camara holds, "[t]here can be no real development without the humility to be sensitive to local culture, however rudimentary it may be, without attention given to community development, and without that creative and animating participation which is rightly called the corner-stone of development".[70] The need for all parties to reconsider their respective stands is essential for 'mending the broken pieces'.

'Mending the Broken Pieces'

'Mending the broken pieces' is a significant phrase in this study. It encapsulates both the traditional Nankani way of life as well as the

---

67   Fitzgerald, *Ideology of Religion*, 98-118 and Nye, *Religion*, 177-206.

68   Isabel Apawo Phiri and Sarojini Nadar, "Introduction: 'Treading Softly but Firmly'," in *African Women, Religion, and Health: Essays in Honor of Mercy Amba Ewudziwa Oduyoye*, eds. Isabel Apawo Phiri and Sarojini Nadar (Maryknoll, New York: Orbis, 2006), 2.

69   Ola Rotimi, *The Gods Are Not To Blame* (London: Oxford University Press, 1971), 22.

70   Helder Camara, *Church and Colonialism* "London and Sydney: Sheed and Ward, 1969), 32-3.

nature of rural development work in Africa. It reflects the day-to-day life situation of rural African living, taking into consideration the Nankani religio-cultural traditions, which, although centred on the ancestors, reflects a life of interdependence, receptiveness, incorporation and renewal. It is a life that is constantly making efforts to mend disruptions and broken relationships. This projects a sense in which development within this local context also needs a mending of the two worldviews, balancing each other effectively through an appreciative and participatory approach.[71] Besides these, it is symbolic, reflecting the way this investigation is composed and structured, the diverse issues discussed and its presentation as a collective unit. Finally, it re-emphasizes the view that even though gender is noted as a crucial component of development, its contextual understanding is essential for negotiating rural development.

On the other hand, the phrase metaphorically projects an image of a society that is fragmented religiously, culturally, socially, politically and economically as a result of historical and current global changes.[72] This situation has placed the Nankani in a complex position in which the people are finding it difficult to move forward in their bid for development. Even so, they are also aware that a withdrawal to the past is equally impossible.[73] In spite of such awareness, the present situation has created nostalgia for a vaguely defined past as the best form and source of development, without a full consideration of its implications.[74] This shows that the present state of development in the Nankani area is largely understood as a product of contradictions in previous political and development interventions. These contradictions, although based on the failures in previous development interventions, also reflect the failure of community development workers to consider an input from the religio-cultural heritage of the Nankani. As a symbolic prefix to the

71   Franciska Issaka and Charlie Ewine, "Introduction to Appreciative Inquiry: Questions of Difference," (UK and Napoka Development Associates, Ghana, Unpublished document, 2005), 1-5.

72   *Tongnaab* presents some examples of the struggles and changes that are taking place. Allman, and Parker, *Tongnaab*.

73   See, Ama Atta Aidoo, *The Dilemma of a Ghost* (London: Longman, 1965), 50. Also depicted in the Nankani proverb, 'The farmer farms forward, not backwards'.

74   Max Assimeng, *Foundations of African Social Thought: A Contribution to the Sociology of Knowledge* (Accra: Ghana Universities Press, 1997), 84-9.

title, 'mending the broken pieces' introduces the notion of possibilities for the Nankani and development agents in the area to move beyond the present impasse, in a spirit of cooperation and participation. This will enable them to forge ahead in their efforts to overcome the problems of underdevelopment. 'Mending the broken pieces' does not seek to provide a formula of restoration but to provide an avenue for a possible 'understanding' of the religio-cultural heritage of the Nankani and their aspirations in modern development.[75] Thus, the study charts a new path for religion and sustainable development in the area.

In this investigation therefore, development is not simply configured in terms of economic achievement, scholarly or technical knowledge acquisition. Neither is sustainable development focused on the environment and nature's resources.[76] These two concepts involve a whole range of variables in which the religio-cultural with its imbued sense of communal solidarity is intrinsically intertwined. Central to this network is the role of gender, perceived as an inseparable part of the system. Yet, this is another core area of difference between the 'traditional' and 'modern' concepts of development. Hence, it is the area that calls for attention in the current pursuit for Africa's development. Closely associated with this is the question of power. It is in this context that the dynamics of community based power is subtly employed to the disadvantage of Western oriented forms of development. Having been subjected to discrimination and abuse, their attitude to current notions of development is one of caution and criticism.

For the Nankani, development is composite. Scholars refer to it as 'holistic'. Unlike the scholarly perspective, where the non-verifiable religious dimension is often excluded, the Nankani hold onto the religious variable as a key resource. In that respect they question, 'how can community development be holistic when religion, the most influential factor in the rural African community is left out?' For them, it is in the interweaving of the visible and the invisible resources of life that provides the basis for development. This has therefore unveiled the scene in which the politics of negotiation in the actual field of the development enterprise has evolved as the agenda for discussion.

---

75   Cox, "African Identity as the Projection of Western Alterity," 28.
76   Mostafa Kamal Tolba, *Sustainable Development: Constraints and Opportunities* (London: Butterworths, 1987), 205-8 and J. Sachs, *The End of Poverty*, 192.

While criticisms from indigenous people rage on, alternative and coping strategies are explored and developed alongside. This attests to the view that the success or otherwise of development projects in communities depends, to a large extent, on the participants' evaluative perception. Yet, by viewing and making such decisions in the context of their religio-cultural traditions, the Nankani have substantiated current scholarly notions that the term 'tradition' is a dynamic construct.[77] It also attests to the perspective that ATR underlies every facet of the African's way of life. In this regard, the study enriches the debate on rural African development with new insights and possible grounds for dialogue and negotiations. It has also contributed to knowledge through its epistemological analysis of key terms and its engagement with current discourses in theory and method in the study of religions. Moreover, its examination of the dynamics of gender has unearthed insightful contextual information, serving as primary data on the understanding of womanhood, gender, woman-to-woman marriage and the feminization of poverty and underdevelopment.

The study has also opened up areas for further investigation. These include a thorough religio-cultural study of the *chinchirisi* phenomenon, the socio-political and migratory history of the Nankani and its impact on their religion, religious pluralism and the concept of 'mixing' and its possible impact on religious data in census statistics in Africa, the need for an in-depth study of chieftaincy and governance, and witchcraft among the Nankani as well as their impact on the people's development. The issue of gender and identity, with special reference 'single mothers' (daughters), is also an important area for future research.

In conclusion, we may still ask the questions 'what is development?' and 'whose development is this statement dealing with?' The Nankani sayings, 'every land with its way of doing things' and *gobga nu peri zuo to pera gobga* (the left washes the right and the right the left), illustrate that differences emanating from a variety of nations and traditions are part of life. Like the hands, however, the essence is in complementing each other, not obliterating the other. I have shown in this investigation that for the Nankani, life without the mystical is not just impossible; it is perceived as empty and fruitless. Well-being depends on the good will and benevolence of the spiritual world and this is mediated

---

77   Chidester, *Religions of South Africa*, 1.

through rituals and good human relations, reciprocity. On the other hand, development organizations and workers, partly as a result of the enlightenment ideology, exclude religion and the mystical from their schemes of development. In this context, the mystical is superstition, and superstition is something that must be rid of for development to ensue. From this study, that distinction is problematic, representing the very basis of the divergent approaches to development. The need to relate to the above proverbs and the question 'whose development?' is crucial in 'mending the broken pieces' for sustainable development among the Nankani. Moreover, sustainable development among the Nankani is inclusive, engaging the new with understanding from the indigenous religio-cultural resources. Yet, the call for an understanding of the indigenous perspective is not to say that indigenous people are incapable of responding to modernity and its thought forms.[78] The resolution to the problems will result from acknowledging and understanding differences as well as allowing these differences to make their contributions to life as expressed in the above proverbs.

---

78   Sanneh, *Encountering the West*, 96.

Bibliography

"Religion and Development at the Crossroads: Convergence or Divergence." BIC Document no. 02-0826; accessed 23 November 2004. Available from http://www.bicun.hahai.org/02-0826.html.

"The Long Road to Ghana's Independence." (September 1997). Accessed 9 February 2005. Available from http://www.greatepicbooks.com/epics/september97.html.

"Where Are We Now? Ghana's Realization of the MGD'S and the GPRS: The Voices of Ghanaians. An alternative report by an independent consultancy team. August 2005.

208th General Assembly Presbyterian Church (U.S.A.). *Hope for a Global Future: Toward Just and Sustainable Human Development.* Louisville, Kentucky: The Office of the General Assembly, 1996.

Adogame, Afe, and Ezra Chitando. "Moving among Those Moved by the Spirit: Conducting Fieldwork within the New African Religious Diaspora." *Fieldwork in Religion* 1, no. 3 (2005): 253-270.

_____. "To be or not to be? Politics of Belonging and the African Christian communities in Germany." In *Religion in the Context of African Migration*, edited by Afe Adogame and Cordula Weisskoeppel, 97-114. Bayreuth: Bayreuth African Studies Series, 2005.

_____. "The Use of European Traditions in the Study of Religion in Africa: West African Perspectives." In *Traditions in the Study of Religion in Africa*, edited by Frieder Ludwig and Afe Adogame, 375-81. Harrassowitz Verlag: Wiesbaden, 2004.

Aebischer, Verena. "Knowledge as a Result of Conflicting Intergroup Relations." In *Feminist Thought and the Structure of Knowledge*, edited by Mary, McCanney Gergen Mary, 142-51. New York and London: New York University Press, 1988.

Afele, John C. and Anani, Kofi V. 'Indigenous Knowledge Systems', in Global University Systems, accessed 4 November 2004. Available from http://www.mapzones.com/world/africa/ghana/cultureindex.php.

Aidoo, Ama Atta. *The Dilemma of a Ghost*. London: Longman, 1965.

Akintan, Oluwatosin. "Cultural Values: A Factor in the Realization of Women Empowerment in Ijebu-Land." In *African Culture and the Quest for Women's Rights*, edited by Dorcas Olu Akintunde, 125-33. Ibadan: Sefer, 2001.

Akrong, Abraham. "A phenomenology of witchcraft in Ghana." In *Imagining Evil: Witchcraft Beliefs and Accusations in Contemporary Africa*, edited by Gerrie Ter Haar, 53-66. New York and Eritrea: Africa World Press, 2007.

Akurigu, Rose Mary. "Chastity and Rituals on Women," In *Where God Reigns: Reflections on Women in God's World*, edited by Elisabeth Amoah, 87-96. Accra-North, Ghana: Sam-Woode Ltd, 1996.

_____. "A Comparative Study of Sacrifice in Islam and African Traditional Religion: A Case Study of the Islamic Population and the Traditional People of the Upper East Region of Ghana." B. A. Diss. University of Ghana, 1993.

Alasuutari, Pertti. *Researching Culture: Qualitative Method and Cultural Studies*. London, Thousand Oaths and New Delhi: Sage Publicans, 1995.

Allman, Jean and John Parker. *Tongnaab: The History of a West African God*. Bloomington and Indianapolis: Indiana University Press, 2005.

Amadiume, Ifi. *Male Daughters and Female Husbands: Gender and Sex in an African Society*. London: Zed Press, 1987.

_____. *Reinventing Africa: Matriarchy, Religion and Culture*. London and New York: Zed Books, 1997.

Amenga-Etego, Rose Mary. "Chinchirisi: The Phenomenon of the 'Spirit Children' among the Nankani of Northern Ghana." *Legon Journal of the Humanities* XIX (2008): 183-214.

_____. "Probing the Religio-Cultural Roots of Witchcraft among the Nankani." Institute of Women in Religion and Culture. Unpublished conference paper, Gambaga, Ghana, 2004.

_____. "Traditional/cultural practices which impinge on women's development in the Upper East Region." Upper East Regional Population Service Seminar, Unpublished paper. Bolgatanga, 5th July, 2002.

_____. "Violence against Women in Contemporary Ghanaian Society". *Theology and Sexuality* 13, no.1 (September 2006): 23-46.

_____. "Women in the Catholic Church in Ghana." M. Phil Diss. University of Ghana, 1998.

Amoah, Elizabeth. "Women as portrayed in some African proverbs." In *Embracing the Baobab Tree: The African Proverb in the 21st Century*. Vol. 5 of African Proverbs Series, edited by Willem Saayman, 203-213. Pretoria: University of South Africa, 1997.

An Agenda for Growth and Prosperity: Ghana's Poverty Reduction Strategy 2002-2004, Executive Summary, March, 2002.

Anderson, David M. and Vigdis Broch-Due, "Poverty and Pastoralism: Deconstructing Myths, Reconstructing Realities." In *The Poor Are Not Us: Poverty and Pastoralism in Eastern Africa*, edited by David M. Anderson and Vigdis Broch-Due, 3-20. Oxford: James Curry Ltd., 1999.

Anderson, Sir Norman, ed. *The World's Religions*. 4th ed. London: Inter-Varsity Press, October 1975.

Anon. "Interview with Jerry J. Rawlings." In *Ghana: Facts, Pictures and Aspects*. 26-27. Stuttgart: Association of Churches and Missions in South Western Germany. April 1986.

Appiah, Kwame Anthony. "In My Father's House: Epilogue." In *African Gender Studies: A Reader*, edited by Oyèrónkè Oyěwùmí, 341-54. England: Palgrave Macmillan, 2005.

_____. *In My Father's House: Africa in the Philosophy of Culture*. New York and Oxford: Oxford University Press, 1992.

Apusgah, Agnes Atia. "Is gender yet another colonial project? A critique of Oyeronke Oyewumi's proposal." A paper presented at the International Political Science Association (IPSA) annual Conference in Durban, South Africa, 2003.

_____. "Toolluum: A Gendered African Concept with Potential for Development" A Paper Presented at the CODESRIA Annual Campus on African Knowledge Systems. Dakar, Senegal, May 2006.

_____. "Diagnosing Poverty in Northern Ghana: Institutional versus Community Views." *Ghana Journal of Development Studies* 2, no. 2 (December 2005): 1-14.

Archer, John and Barbara Lloyd. *Sex and Gender*. 2nd ed. Cambridge: Cambridge University Press, 2002.

Armour, Ellen T. "Beyond Belief?: Sexual Difference and Religion After Ontotheology." In *The Religious*, edited by John D. Caputo, 212-26. Oxford:Blackwell Publishers, 2002.

Assimeng, Max. *Foundations of African Social Thought: A Contribution to the Sociology of Knowledge*. Accra: Ghana Universities Press, 1997.

Awedoba, A. K. *Culture and Development in Africa: with special references to Ghana, Some Basis Issues*. Vol.1. Legon: Institute of African Studies, University of Ghana, 2002.

———. *Studies in Kasem Phenetics and Phonology*. Revised and Enlarged Edition. Language Monographs No. 5. Legon: University of Ghana, 2002.

Awia, J. "Threefold Encounter in Northern Ghana." Accessed 3 December 2004. Available from http://mysite.verizon.net/vze827ph/threefold_front.htm.

———. *Navrongo and its Pioneers*. S. I., 1988.

Awolalu, J. Omosade and P. Adelumo Dopamu. *West African Traditional Religion*. Ibadan: Onibonoje Press and Book Industries (Nig.) Ltd., 1979.

Ayaga, Augustine M. *Common Values, Contradictory Strategies: A Study of Church, State, and NGO Relations in Ghana*. Ghana: SonLife Printing Press and Services, 2000.

Babbie, Earl. *The Practice of Social Research*. 5th ed. Belmont, California: Wadsworth Publication Company, 1989.

Bahr, Ann Marie B. *Religions of the World: Indigenous Religions*. Foreword by Martin E. Marty. Philadelphia: Chelsea House Publishers, 2005.

Bakker, Ineke. "Opening speech by General Secretary of the Council of Churches in the Netherlands." In *Religion: a source for human rights and development cooperation*. The Netherlands, September 2005.

Barker, Peter. *Peoples, Languages, and Religion in Northern Ghana: a preliminary report*. Ghana Evangelism Committee in association with Asempa Publishers, 1986.

Barth, Fredrik. "Ethnic groups and Boundaries." In *Ethnicity*, edited by John Hutchinson and Anthony D. Smith, 75-82. Oxford and New York: Oxford University Press, 1996.

Bascom, William R. and Meiville J. Herskovits, eds. *Continuity and Change in African Cultures*. Chicago: University of Chicago Press, 1959.

Batchelor, Peter. *People in Rural Development*. RURCON, 1981.

Beattie, John. *Other Cultures: Aims, Methods and Achievements in Social Anthropology*. London: Routledge, First Pub., 1964, Reprint, 1992.

Bekye, Paul K. *Peasant Development- The Case of Northern Ghana*. Leuven, 1998.

Bell, Catherine. *Ritual Theory, Ritual Practice*. New York and Oxford: Oxford University Press, 1992.

_____. *Ritual: Perspectives and Dimensions*. New York and Oxford: Oxford University Press, 1997.

Bening, Raymond B. "Administrative Boundaries of Northern Ghana, 1898-1951." In *Regionalism and Public Policy in Northern Ghana*, edited by Yakubu Saaka, 13-33. New York: Peter Lang, 2001.

Best, Deborah L. and Jennifer J. Thomas. "Cultural Diversity and Cross-Cultural Perspectives." In *The Psychology of Gender*, 2nd ed. Edited by Alice H. Eagly, Anne E. Beall and Robert J. Sternberg, 296-327. New York and London: The Guilford Press, 2004.

Blaikie, Norman. *Designing Social Research: The Logic of Anticipation*. Cambridge: Polity Pres, 2000.

Bogdewic, Steven P. "Participant Observation." In *Doing Qualitative Research*, 2nd ed. Edited by Benjamin F. Crabtree and William L. Miller, 47-69. Thousand Oaks, London and New Delhi: Sage Publications, 1999.

Bogdon, Robert C. *Qualitative Research for Education: An Introduction, to Theory and Method*. Boston and London: Allyn and Bacon In., 1982.

Bolin, Anne. "Traversing Gender: Cultural context and gender practices." In *Gender Reversals and Gender Cultures: Anthropological and Historical Perspectives*, edited by Sabrina Petra Ramet, 22-51. London and New York: Routledge, 1996.

Booth, Wayne C., Gregory G. Colomb and Joseph M. Williams. *The Craft of Research*, 2nd ed. Chicago and London: The University of Chicago Press, 2003.

Borren, Sylvia. "Development agencies: global or solo players?." In *Debating Development: NGOs and the Future*, edited by Deborah Eade and Ernst Ligteringen, 171-88. Oxford: Oxfarm GB, 2001.

Bourdillon, M. F. C. "Witchcraft and Society." In *African Spirituality: Forms, Meanings, and Expressions*, edited by Jacob K. Olupona, 176-97. New York: The Crossroad Publishing Company, 2000.

_____. *Religion and Society: A Text for Africa*. Zimbabwe: Mambo Press, 1990.

Bourret, F. M. *The Gold Coast: A Survey of the Gold Coast and Briish Togoland 1919-1951*. 2nd ed. London: Oxford University Press, 1952.

Bowie, Fiona. *The Anthropology of Religion: An Introduction*. Oxford: Blackwell Publishers, 2000.

Bradley, David G. *A Guide to the World's Religions*. Englewood Cliffs, N. J.: Prentice-Hall, 1963.

Brokensha, David. *Social Change in Larteh, Ghana*. Oxford: Clarendon Press, 1966.

Brown, David A. *A Guide to Religions*. TEF Study Guide 12. London: SPCK, 1975.

Brown, Karen McCarthy. "Writing about "the Other," Revisited." In *Personal Knowledge and Beyond: Reshaping the Ethnography of Religion*, edited by James V. Spickard, J. Shawn Landres and Meredith B. McGuire, 127-33. New York and London: New York University Press, 2002.

Busia, K. A. "The African World View." In *Christianity and African Culture*, 1-6. Accra: Christian Council of the Gold Coast, 1955.

_____. *Africa in Search of Democracy*. London: Routledge and Kegan Paul, 1967.

_____. *Purposeful Education for Africa*. London, the Hague and Paris: Mouton and Co., 1964.

_____. *The Challenge of Africa*. New York: Frederick A. Praeger, 1962.

_____. *The Place of the Chief in the Gold Coast*. Achimota, 1949

Butler, Judith. "Collected and Fractured: Response to *Identities*." In *Identities*, edited by Kwame Anthony Appiah and Henry Louis Gates, Jr. 439-47. Chicago and London: The University of Chicago Press, 1995.

_____. *Giving an Account of Oneself*. New York: Fordham University Press, 2005.

_____. *Undoing Gender*. New York and London: Routledge, 2004.

Cabezón , José Ignacio and Sheila Greeve Davaney. "Introduction." In *Identity and the Politics of Scholarship in the Study of Religion*, edited by José Ignacio Cabezón and Sheila Greeve Davaney, 1-23. New York and Oxon: Routledge, 2004.

_____. "Identity and the Work of the Scholar of Religion." In *Identity and the Politics of Scholarship in the Study of Religion*, edited by José Ignacio Cabezón and Sheila Greeve Davaney, 43-59. New York and Oxon, Routledge, 2004.

Camara, Helder. *Church and Colonialism*. Translated by William McSweeney. London and Sydney: Sheed and Ward, 1969.

Campbell, Aidan. *Western Primitivism: African Ethnicity. A Study in Cultural Relations*. London and Washington: Cassell, 1997.

Capps, Walter H. *Religious Studies: The Making of a Discipline*. Minneapolis: Fortress Press, 1995.

Cardinall, Allan Wolsey. *In Ashanti and Beyond*. London: Seeley Service, 1927.

_____. *The Natives of the Northern Territories of the Gold Coast: Their Customs, Religion and Folklore*. London: Routledge, 1920.

Carney, Judith and Michael Watts. "Manufacturing Dissent: Work, Gender and the Politics of Meaning in a Peasant Society (1990)." In *Development Studies: A Reader*, edited by Stuart Corbridge, 224-39. London: Edward Arnold, 1995.

Chambers, Robert. "Beyond "Whose Reality Counts?" New Methods We Now Need." In *People's Participation: Challenges Ahead*, Complied and Analyzed by Orlando Fals Borda, 105-30. New York: The Apex Press, 1998.

_____. *Rural Development: Putting the Last First*. Longman: USA, 1983.

Chernoff, John M. "Spiritual Foundations of Dagbamba Religion and Culture." In *African Spirituality: Forms, Meanings, and Expressions*, edited by Jacob K. Olupona, 257-74. New York, The Crossroad Publishing Company, 2000 176-197; Collins, 1978.

Chidester, David. *Religions of South Africa*. London and New York: Routledge, 1992.

_____. *Savage Systems: Colonialism and Comparative Religion in Southern Africa*. Charlottesville and London: University Press of Virginia, 1996.

Chitando, Ezra. "Phenomenology of Religion and the Study of African Traditional Religions." *Method and Theory in the Study of Religion*, (2005): 299-316.

Christian Council of The Gold Coast. *Memorandum on The Customary Law Of Inheritance: Addressed to the Chiefs and People of the Gold Coast*. Accra: Christian Council of The Gold Coast, 1934.

Clarke, Peter B. and Peter Byrne. *Religion Defined and Explained*. London: St. Martin's Press, 1993.

Clooney, Francis X, S. J. "Neither Here nor There: Crossing Boundaries, Becoming Insiders, Remaining Catholics." In *Identity and the Politics of*

Scholarship in the Study of Religion, edited by José Ignacio Cabezón and Sheila Greeve Davaney, 99-111. New York and Oxon: Routledge, 2004.

Coleman, John A, S. J. "Religious Social Capital: Its Nature, Social Location, and Limits." In *Religion as Social Capital: Producing the Common Good*, edited by Corwin Smidt, 33-47. Texas: Baylor University Press, 2003.

Collins, John J. *Primitive Religion*. New Jersey, Littlefield: Adams and Co., 1978.

Connell, R. W. And G. W. Dowsett. "Introduction." In *Rethinking Sex: Social Theory and Sexuality Research*, edited by R. W. Connell and G. W. Dowsett, 1-4. Carlton, Victoria: Melbourne University Press, 1992.

Corrywright, Dominic and Peggy Morgan. *Religious Studies: Get set for Religious Studies*. Edinburgh: The University of Edinburgh Press, 2006.

Cox, James L. *Alterity as Identity: Innovation in the Academic Study of Religions*. Lampeter: BASR Annual Conference, 1998.

_____. *A Guide to the Phenomenology of Religion: Key Figures, Formative Influences and Subsequent Debates*. London: Continuum, 2006.

_____. *Expressing the Sacred: An Introduction to the Phenomenology of Religion*. Harare: University of Zimbabwe Publications, 1996.

_____. *Rational Ancestors: Scientific Rationality and African Indigenous Religions*. Cardiff: Cardiff Academic Press, 1998.

_____. "African Identity as the Projection of Western Alterity." In *Uniquely African? African Christian Identity from Cultural and Historical Perspectives*, edited by James L Cox and Gerrie ter Haar, 25-37. New Jersey and Eritrea: African World Press, 2003.

_____. "From Africa to Africa: The Significance of Approaches to the Study of African Religions at Aberdeen and Edinburgh Universities from 1970 to 1998." In *European Traditions in the Study of Religion in Africa*, edited by Frieder Ludwig and Afe Adogame, 255-64. Harrassowitz Verlag: Wiesbaden, 2004.

_____. "Intuiting Religion: A Case for Preliminary Definition." In *The Pragmatics of Defining Religion: Contexts, Concepts and Contents*, Jan G. Platvoet and Arie L. Molendijk, edited by Jan G. Platvoet and Arie L. Molendijk, 267-84. Leiden, Boston and Koln: Brill, 1999.

_____. "Methodological Considerations Relevant to Understanding African Indigenous Religions." In *The Study of Religions in Africa: Past, Present and Prospects*, edited by Jan Platvoet, James Cox and Jacob Olupona, 155-71. Cambridge: Roots and Branches, 1996.

Cronin, Ann. "Focus groups." In *Researching Social Life*, 2nd ed. Edited by Nigel Gilbert, 164-77. London, Thousand Oaks and New Delhi: Sage Publications, 2001.

Cupitt, Don. *The Meaning of it All in Everyday Speech*. London: SCM Press, 1999.

d'Azevedo, Warren L. "Gola Womanhood and the Limits of Masculine Omnipotence." In *Religion in Africa: Experience and Expression*, edited by Thomas D. Blakely, Walter E. A. van Beek and Dennis L. Thomson, 343-62. London: Heinemann, 1994.

Daly, Mary. *QUINTESSENCE... Realizing the Archaic Future: A Radical Elemental Feminist Manifesto*. London: The Women's Press Ltd., 1999.

Davidman, Lynn. "Truth, Subjectivity, and Ethnographic Research." In *Personal Knowledge and Beyond: Reshaping the Ethnography of Religion*, edited by James V. Spickard, J. Shawn Landres and Meredith B. McGuire, 17-26. New York and London: New York University Press, 2002.

Debrunner, H. "The Influence of Witchcraft." In *Christianity and African Culture: the proceedings of a Conference held at Accra, Gold Coast, May 2nd-6th, 1955, under the auspices of the Christian Council*, 46-50. Accra: Christian Council of the Gold Coast, 1955.

_____. *A History of Christianity in Ghana*. Accra: Waterville Publishing House, 1967.

Delmos, Jones. "Towards a Native Anthropology." *Human Organisation* 29, no. 4 (Winter 1970): 251-59.

Der, Benedict G. "Traditional Political Systems of Northern Ghana Reconsidered." In *Regionalism and Public Policy in Northern Ghana*, edited by Yakubu Saaka, 35-65. New York: Peter Lang, 2001.

Donal Dorr. *Option for the Poor: A Hundred Years of Vatican Social Teaching*. Revised Edition. Dublin: Gill and Macmillan,1992.

Douglas, Mary. *Purity and Danger: An Analysis of the Concepts of Pollution and Taboo*. London: Routledge, 1966.

Dovlo, Elom. "Witchcraft in contemporary Ghana." In *Imagining Evil: Witchcraft Beliefs and Accusations in Contemporary Africa*, edited by Gerrie Ter Haar, 67-92. New York and Eritrea: Africa World Press, 2007.

Ehret, Christopher. "Language Evidence and Religious History." In *The Historical Study of African: with special reference to East and Central Africa*, edited by T. O. Ranger and I. N. Kimambo, 45-49. London: Heinemann Educational, 1972.

Ehusani, George Rev. Fr. "Christian Commitment: The African Dilemma." In *African Dilemma: A Cry for Life*, Papers from the EATWOT West Central African Sub-regional Conference, 1991, edited by Kofi Appiah –Kubi et al, 159-65. s.l.: Ecumenical Association of Third World Theologians,1992.

Ekeya, Bette. "Woman, For How Long Not?" In *New Eyes for Reading: Biblical and theological reflections by women from third world*, John S. Pobee and Bärbel von Wartenberg-Potter, 59-67. Geneva: World Council of Churches, 1986.

Ekstrom, Ruth B. "Intervention strategies to reduce sex-role stereotyping in education." In *Sex-role Stereotyping*, edited by Oonagh Hartnett, Gill Boden and Mary Fuller, 217-28. London: Tavistock Publications Ltd., 1979.

Eliade, Mircea. *From Primitives to Zen: A Thematic Sourcebook of the History of Religions*. New York and Evanston: Harper and Row Publishers, 1967.

_____. *The Sacred and the Profane: The Nature of Religion*. Translated by Willard R. Trask. San Diego, New York and London: Harcourt Inc., 1959.

Ellis, Stephen and Gerrie Ter Haar. *Worlds of Power: Religious Thoughts and Political Practice in Africa*. London: Hurst and Company, 2004.

Esteva, Gustavo. "Development." In *The Development Dictionary: A Guide to Knowledge as Power*, edited by Wolfgang Sachs, 6-25. London and New Jersey: Zed Books Ltd., 1992.

Evans-Pritchard, E. E. "For Example, Witchcraft." In *Rules and Meanings*, edited by Mary Douglas, 24-25. London: Penguin Education, 1973, 24-25.

_____. "Where the Women are, the Cattle are not." In *Rules and Meanings*, edited by Mary Douglas, 38-44. London: Penguin Education, 1973.

Fact Sheet No. III. Population of Ghana: Demographic and Socio-Economic Indicators by District. National Population Council. Ghana.

Falola, Toyin. *The Power of African Cultures*. Rochester: University of Rochester Press, 2003.

Faludi, Susan. *Backlash: The Undeclared War Against Women*. London: Vintage, 1992.

Fanusie, Lloyda. "Ethnography." In *Researching Social Life*, edited by Nigel Gilbert, 145-64. London, Thousand Oaks and New Delhi: Sage Publications, 2001.

_____. "Sexuality and Women in African Culture." In *The Will to Arise: Women, Tradition, and the Church in Africa*, edited Mercy Amba Oduyoye and Musimbi R. A. Kanyoro, 135-45. Maryknoll, New York: Orbis Books, 2001.

Fielding, Nigel. "Ethnography." In *Researching Social Life*, 2ⁿᵈ ed. Edited by Nigel Gilbert, 154-71. London, Thousand Oaks and New Delhi: Sage Publications, 1993.

Figures, Rev. R. J. "A Summary of the Conference Discussions." In *Christianity and African Culture*, edited by Nigel Gilbert, 62-72. Accra: Christian Council of the Gold Coast, 1955.

Finch, Janet. "'It's great to have someone to talk to': the ethics and politics of interviewing women." In *Social Researching: Politics, Problems and Practice*, edited by C. Bell and H. Roberts, 72-90. RKP, 1984.

Fitzgerald, Timothy. *The Ideology of Religious Studies*. New York and Oxford: Oxford University Press, 2000.

Flick, Uwe. An *Introduction to Qualitative Research*. London: Thousand Oaks, and New Delhi: SAGE Publication, 1998.

Fortes, Meyer. "Ancestor Worship." In *African Systems of Thought: Studies Presented and Discussed at the Third International African Seminar in Salisbury, December, 1960*, 16-20. London, New York and Toronto: Oxford University Press, 1965.

_____. "Kinship and Marriage among the Ashanti." In *African Systems of Kinship and Marriage*, edited by A. R. Radcliffe-Brown and Daryll Forde, 252-84. London, New York and Toronto: Oxford University Press, 1950.

_____. "Some Reflections on Ancestor Worship in Africa." In *African Systems of Thought: Studies Presented and Discussed at the Third International African Seminar in Salisbury, December, 1960*. Preface by M. Fortes and G. Dieterlen, 122-42. London: Oxford University Press, 1965.

_____. *Oedipus and Job in West African Religion*. Cambridge: Cambridge University Press, 1959.

_____. *Religion, Morality and the Person: Essays on Tellensi Religion*, Cambridge: Cambridge University Press, 1987.

_____. *The Dynamics of Clanship among the Tallensi*. London: Oxford University Press, 1945.

Foster, George Burman. *The Function of Religion in Man's Struggle for Existence*. Chicago, Illinois: The University of Chicago Press, 1909.

Fournier, Francine. "UNESCO and Participatory Research." In *People's Participation: Challenges Ahead*, Complied and Analyzed by Orlando Fals Borda, 23-25. New York: Apex Press, 1998.

Frazer, Donald: *The Future of Africa*. London: Young People's Missionary Movement, 1911.

Freeman, Christopher. "Malthus with a computer." In *THINKING ABOUT THE FUTURE: A Critique of THE LIMITS TO GROWTH*, edited by H. S. D. Cole *et al*, 5-13. London: Chatto and Windus, 1973.

Friedan, Betty. *The Feminine Mystique*. London: Penguin Books, 1963.

G8 Gleneagles Summit, 2005. "Africa and Development', Chair's Summary, 8 July; accessed 18 October 2006. Available from http://www.g8.gov.uk/servlet/Front?pagename=OpenMarket/Xcelerate/ShowPage&c=Page&cid=1119518698846.

Gaba, Christian. "Contemporary Research in African Traditional Religion." *The Ghana Bulletin of Theology* 3, no. 4 (June 1968): 1-13.

Ganusah, Rebecca Yawa. "Rites of Birth and Initiation into womanhood among the Ewe-dome of Ghana: A Theological and Ethical Perspective." PhD Diss., University of Edinburgh, 1999.

Garrett, Stephanie. *Gender*. London and New York: Tavistock, 1987.

Gayatri, Chakravorty. *A Critique of Postcolonial Reason: Toward a History of the Vanishing Present*. Cambridge, MA: Harvard UP, 1999.

Gellner, Ernest. *Postmodernism, Reason and Religion*. London and New York: Routledge, 1992.

Ghana Home Page. "General Information about Ghana." accessed 17 September 2006. Available from http://www.ghanaweb.com/GhanaHomePage/general.

Ghana Poverty Reduction Strategy 2002-2004: An Agenda for Growth and Prosperity, Analysis and Policy Statement, February 20, 2002.

Gilchrist, Valerie J. and Robert L. Williams. "Key Informant Interview." In *Doing Qualitative Research*, 2nd ed. Edited by Benjamin F. Crabtree and William L. Miller, 71-88. Thousand Oaks, London and New Delhi: Sage Publications, 1999.

Gilsenan, Michael. "Myth and the History of African Religion." In *The Historical Study of African Religion: with special reference to East and Central Africa*, edited by T. O. Ranger and I. N. Kimambo, 50-70. London: Heinemann Educational, 1972.

Goodale, Jane C. "Gender, sexuality and marriage: a Kaulong model of nature and culture." In *Nature, Culture and Gender*, edited by Carol MacCormack and Marilyn Strathern, 119-42. Cambridge: Cambridge University Press, 1980.

Goode, William J. *Religion among the Primitives*. Introduction by Kingsley Davis. Illinois: Free Press, 1951.

Goody, Jack. *Death, Property and The Ancestors*. London: Tavistock Publications, 1962.

Gould, Bill. "Structural Adjustment, Decentralization and Educational Planning in Ghana." In *Third World Regional Development: A Reappraisal*, edited by David Simon, 210-27. London: Paul Chapman Publishing Ltd., 1990.

Griswold, Wendy. *Cultures and Societies in a Changing World*. 2nd ed. Thousand Oaks, London and New Delhi. Pine Forge Press, 2004.

Gross, Rita M. "Religious Identity, Scholarship and Teaching Religion." In *Identity and the Politics of Scholarship in the Study of Religion*, edited by José Ignacio Cabezón and Sheila Greeve Davaney, 113-32. New York and Oxon: Routledge, 2004.

Gyekye, Kwame. "Taking Development Seriously." *Journal of Applied Philosophy* 11, no. 1 (1994): 45-56.

_____. *Tradition and Modernity: Philosophical Reflections on the African Experience*. New York and Oxford: Oxford University Press, 1997.

Hart, Chris. *Doing a Literature Review: Releasing the Social Science Research Imagination*. London, Thousand Oaks and New Delhi: Sage Publications, 1998.

Harvey, Graham. *Animism: Respecting the Living World*. London: Hurst and Company, 2005.

Hawley, John S. and Wayne Proudfoot. "Introduction." In *Fundamentalism and Gender*, edited by John Stratton Hawley, 3-44. New York and Oxford: Oxford University Press, 1994.

Hendriks, Jurgens and Erasmus Johannes. "Religion in South Africa: The 2000 Population Census Data." *Journal of Theology for Southern Africa*, (March 2001): 88-111.

Hendry, Joy. *Reclaiming Culture: Indigenous People and Self-Representation*. England: Palgrave Macmillan, 2005.

Hesse, Sarah and Wissink, Henery. "Incorporating Indigenous Knowledge Systems into the Field of Development." In *The Quest for Sustainable*

Development, edited by William Fox and Enslin van Rooyen, 47-61. Cape Town: Juta Academic, 2004.

Hill, P. "Cocoa-Farming and the Migratory Process in Ghana, 1894-1930." In *Underdevelopment and Development: The Third World Today*, edited by Henry Bernstein, 97-114. England: Penguin Books, 1973.

Howell, Allison M. *The Religious Itinerary of a Ghanaian People: The Kasena and the Christian Gospel.* Lang, 1997. Ghana: African Christian Press, 2001.

Howells, Kevin. "Sex roles and sexual Behaviour." In *The psychology of Sex Roles*, edited by David J. Hargreaves and Ann M. Colley, 268-86. London: Harper and Row Ltd., 1986.

Hunter, Guy. *The Best of Both Worlds? A Challenge on Development Polices in Africa.* London, New York and Toronto: Oxford University Press, 1967.

Hutchinson, John and Anthony D. Smith. "Introduction." In *Ethnicity*, edited by John Hutchinson and Anthony D. Smith, 3-14. Oxford and New York: Oxford University Press, 1996.

Idowu, E. Bolaji. *African Traditional Religion: A Definition.* London: SCM Press, 1973.

_____. *OLÓDÙMARÈ: God in Yoruba Belief.* London: Longmans, 1962.

Issaka, Franciska and Charlie Ewine. "Introduction to Appreciative Inquiry: Questions of Difference." UK and Napoka Development Associates, Ghana, Unpublished document, 2005.

Jacobs, Janet L. "Transitional Identities: Self, Other, and the Ethnographic Process." In *Personal Knowledge and Beyond: Reshaping the Ethnography of Religion*, edited by James V. Spickard, J. Shawn Landres and Meredith B. McGuire, 88-99. New York and London: New York University Press, 2002.

Jeffries, Richard D. "The Sekondi – Tatoradi General Strike, 1961." In *Third World Lives of Struggle*, edited by Hazel Johnson and Henry Bernstein, 131-41. London: Heinemann for Open University, 1982.

Joseph, Jaime A. "NGOs: fragmented dreams." In *Debating Development: NGOs and the Future*, edited by Deborah Eade and Ernst Ligteringen, 145-62. Oxford: Oxfarm GB, 2001.

Joy, Morny and Eva K. Neumaier-Dargyay. "Introduction." In *Gender, Genre, and Religion: Feminist Reflections*, edited by Norny Joy and Eva K. Neumaier-Dargyay, 3-9. Canada: Wilfrid Laurier University Press for The Calgary Institute for the Humanities, 1995.

_____. "Postcolonial and Gendered Reflections: Challenges for Religious Studies." In *Gender, Religion and Diversity: Cross-Cultural Perspectives*, edited by Ursular King and Tina Beattie, 28-39. London and New York: Continuum, 2004.

Juschka, Darlene M. "Gender." In *The Routledge Companion to the Study of Religion*, edited by John R. Hinnells, 229-42. London and New York: Routledge, 2005.

_____. "The Writing of Ethnography: Magical Realism and Michael Taussig." *Journal for Cultural and Religious Theory* 5, no. 1 (December 2003): 84-105.

Kabeer, Niala. *Reversed Realities: Gender hierarchies in Development Thought.* London and New York: Verso, 1994.

Kahn, Joel S. *Culture, Multiculture, Postculture.* London: SAGE Publications, 1995.

Kandiyoti, Deniz. "Identity and its Discontents: Women and the Nation." *WLUML DOSSIER 26*, (October 2004): 47-60.

Kanyoro, Musimbi. "Cultural Hermeneutics: An African Contribution." In *Women's Visions: Theological Reflection, Celebration, Action*, edited by Ofelia Ortega, 18-28. Geneva: WCC Publication, 1995.

Kassam, Tazim R. "Balancing Acts: Negotiating the Ethics of Scholarship and Identity." In *Identity and the Politics of Scholarship in the Study of Religion*, edited by José Ignacio Cabezón and Sheila Greeve Davaney, 133-61. New York and Oxon: Routledge, 2004.

Kato, Byang H. *Theological Pitfalls in Africa.* Kenya: Evangel Publishing House, 1975.

Keesing, Roger M. *Cultural Anthropology: A Contemporary Perspective.* 2nd ed. Harcourt: Brace Jovanovich College Pub., 1935.

King, Noel Q. *Religions of Africa: A Pilgrimage into Traditional Religions.* New York, Evanston and London: Harper and Row Publishers, 1970.

King, Ursular. "Historical and phenomenological approaches." In *Theory and Methods in Religious Studies: Contemporary Approaches to the Study of Religions*, edited by Frank Whaling, 41-176. Berlin and New York: Mouton de Gruyter, 1995.

_____. "Religion and Gender." In *Handbook of Living Religions*, edited by John R. Hinnells, 647-66. London: Penguin Books, 1997.

_____. "Religion and Gender." In *Turning Points in Religious Studies*, edited by Ursula King, 275-86. Edinburgh, T and T Clark, 1990.

Kinoti, Hannah W. "Culture." In *Dictionary of Feminist Theologies*, edited by Letty M. Russell and J. Shannon Clarkson, 63. Louisville, Kentucky: Westminster John Knox Press, 1996.

Kirby, Jon P. "Cultural Change and Religious Conversion in West Africa." In *Religion in Africa: Experience and Expression*, edited by Thomas D. Blakely, Walter E. A. van Beek and Dennis L. Thomson, 57-71. London: Heinemann, 1994.

_____. *Ghana Handbook: A Guide for Missionaries to Ghana*. Tamale: Tamale Institute of Cross Cultural Studies, June 1991.

_____. *God, Shrines, and Problem-solving among the Anufɔ of Northern Ghana*. Berlin: Dietrich Reimer Verlag, 1986.

Kobea, Samuel, A. "Faith and Peoples' struggles For Just, Participatory and Sustainable Life." In *Transcending Boundaries: Perspectives on Faith, Social Action and Solidarity, Essays in Honour of George Ninan*, edited by Rajendra K. Sail and Ajit Muricken, 52-69. India, Vikas Adhyan Kendra, and Raipur Churches Development and Relief Committee, 1995.

Kristensen, William Brede. "The Meaning of Religion." In *Classical Approaches to the Study of Religion: Aims, Methods and Theories of Research, Introduction and Anthology*, edited by Jacques Waardenburg, 390-97. New York and Berlin: Walter de Gruyter, 1999.

Kuper, Adam. *Anthropology and Anthropologists: The Modern British School*. 3rd ed. London and New York: Routledge, 1996.

Larner, Christina. *Witchcraft and Religion: The Politics of Popular Belief*. Oxford: Basil Blackwell, 1984.

Latouche, Serge. "Standard of Living." In *The Development Dictionary: A Guide to Knowledge as Power*, edited by Wolfgang Sachs, 250-63. London and New Jersey: Zed Books Ltd., 1992.

Lee, Raymond M. and Claire M. Renzetti. "Problems of Researching Sensitive Topics: An Overview and Introduction." In *Researching Sensitive Topics*, edited by Claire M. Renzetti and Raymond M. Lee, 3-13. London and New Delhi: SAGE Publications, 1993.

Lerner, Gerda. "Men's Power to Define and the Formation of Women's Consciousness." In *Issues in Feminism: An Introduction to Women's Studies*, 4th ed. Edited by Sheila Ruth, 442-7. London and Toronto, Mayfield Publishing Company, 1997.

Lewis, Charlie. "Early sex-role socialization." In *The psychology of Sex Roles*, edited by David J. Hargreaves and Ann M. Colley, 95-117. London: Harper and Row Ltd., 1986.

Long, Carolyn. *Participation of the Poor in Development Initiatives: Taking their Rightful Place*. London and Sterling: Earthscan Publication Ltd., 2001.

Lorber, Judith and Susan A. Farrell. "Preface." In *The Social Construction of Gender*, edited by Judith Lorber and Susan A. Farrell, 1-5. Newbury Part, London and New Delhi: Sage Publications, 1991.

_____. "Principles of Gender Construction." In *The Social Construction of Gender*, edited by Judith Lorber and Susan A. Farrell, 7-11. Newbury Part, London and New Delhi: Sage Publications, 1991.

Lorde, Audre. "The Transformation of Silence into Language and Action." In *Issues in Feminism: An Introduction to Women's Studies*, 4th ed. Edited by Sheila Ruth, 173-5. London and Toronto: Mayfield Publishing Company, 1997.

Lummis, Adairt T. "Gender Institutions." In *Dictionary of Feminist Theologies*, edited by Letty M. Russell and J. Shannon Clarkson, 125-6. Louisville, Kentucky: Westminster John Knox Press, 1996.

_____. "Pluralism, Religious." In *Dictionary of Feminist Theologies*, edited by Letty M. Russell and J. Shannon Clarkson, 210-1. Westminster John Knox Press: Louisville, Kentucky, 1996.

MacDonald, Susan Peck. *Professional Academic Writing in the Humanities and Social Sciences*. Cardbondale and Edwardsville: Southern Illinois University Press, 1994.

Macrae, Clare. "Divinities and Ancestors in Encounter with Christianity: In the experience and Religious History of the Early Irish and the Akan People of Ghana." PhD Diss., University of Edinburgh, 1995.

Magesa, Laurenti. *African Religion: The Moral Traditions of Abundant Life*. Maryknoll, New York: Orbis Books, 1997.

Make Poverty History. "Edinburgh 2005." accessed 18 October 2006. Available from http://www.makepovertyhistory.org.

Maluleke, Tinyiko Sam. "Half a Century of African Christian Theologies: Elements of Emerging Agenda for the Twenty-First Century." *Journal of Theology for Southern Africa* 99, (Nov. 1997): 4-23.

Mama, Amina. *National Machinery For Women in Africa: Towards an analysis*. No.1 of *National Machinery Series*. No. 1, Ghana, Third World Network, 2000."

Marecek, Jeanne; Mary Crawford and Danielle Popp. "On the Construction of Gender, Sex, and Sexualities." In *The Psychology of Gender*, 2nd ed. Edited by Alice H. Eagly, Anne E. Beall and Robert J. Sternberg, 192-216. New York and London: The Guilford Press, 2004.

Maret, Pierre de. "Archaeological and Other Prehistoric Evidence of Traditional African Religious Expression." In *Religion in Africa: Experience and Expression*, edited by Thomas D. Blakely, Walter E. A. van Beek and Dennis L. Thomson, 183-95. London: Heinemann, 1994.

Marshall, Catherine and Gretchen B. Rossman. *Designing Qualitative Research*. London: Sage Publication, 1989.

Maxwell, John, ed. *The Gold Coast Handbook*. The Crown Agents for the Colonies, 1928.

Mbiti, John S. "Flowers in the Garden: The Role of Women in African Religion." In *African Traditional Religions in Contemporary Society*, edited by Jacob K. Olupona, 59-72. Minnesota: Paragon House, 1991.

_____. *African Religions and Philosophy*. 2nd ed. London: Heinemann, 1990.

_____. *Introduction to African Religion*. London, Ibadan, Nairobi and Lusaka: Heinemann, 1975.

_____. *The Prayers of African Religions*. London: S.P.C.K., 1975.

McCoy, Remigius F. *Great Things Happen: A Personal Memoir*. Montreal: The Society of Missionaries of Africa, 1988.

McGuire, Meredith B. "New-Old Directions in the Social Scientific Study of Religion: Ethnography, Phenomenology, and the Human Body." In *Personal Knowledge and Beyond: Reshaping the Ethnography of Religion*, edited by James V. Spickard, J. Shawn Landres and Meredith B. McGuire, 195-211. New York and London: New York University Press, 2002.

_____. *Religion: The Social Context*. 2nd ed. Belmont, California: Wadworth Publishing Company, 1987.

McKenzie, Peter. *Hail Orisha: A Phenomenology of a West African Religion in the Mid-Nineteenth Century*. Leiden: Brill, 1997.

McVeigh, Malcolm J. *God in Africa: Concepts of God in African Traditional Religion and Christianity*. Massachusetts: Claude Stark, Cape Cod, 1974.

McWilliam, H. O. A. "Ferguson, Samori, and Babatu." *Ghana Teachers' Journal*. London and Edinburgh: Published for The Ministry of Education, Ghana by Thomas Nelson and Sons Ltd. No. 27 (July 1960): 34-43.

_____. *The Development of Education in Ghana*. London: Longmans, 1959.

Meadows, H. Donella *et al*, *The Limits to Growth: A Report for the Club of Rome's Project on the Predicament of Mankind*. London: A Potomac Associates Book, 1972.

Meadows, H. Donella, Dennis L. Meadows and Jøegen Randers, *Beyond the Limits: Global Collapse or a Sustainable Future*. London: Earthscan Publication Ltd, 1992.

Meredith, Martin. *The State of Africa: A History of Fifty Years of Independence*. London, New York, Sydney and Toronto: Free Press, 2005.

Metuh, Emefie Ikenga. *African Religions in Western Conceptual Schemes: The Problems of Interpretation; (Studies in Igbo Religion)*. Bodija Ibadan: Ibadan Pastoral Institute, 1985.

Millar, David. "Endogenous Development: Some Issues of Concern." *Ghana Journal of Development Studies* 2, no. 1 (May 2005): 92-185.

Miller, Phoebe. "Sex Polarity and Among the Afikpo Igo." In *African Religious Groups and Beliefs: Papers in Honor of William R. Bascom*, edited by Simon Ottenberg, 79-94. India and U. S. A.: Folklore Institute, 1982.

Ministry of Women and Children's Affairs, Ghana's Second Progress Report on the Implementation of the African and Beijing Platform of Action and Review Report for Beijing +10, Final Draft Document, June 2004.

Minkah-Premo, Sheila. *Coping with Violence Against Women*. Accra: Asempa Publishers, 2001.

Minnich, Elizabeth Kamarck. "Transforming Knowledge." In *Issues in Feminism: An Introduction to Women's Studies*, 4th ed. Edited by Sheila Ruth (ed.), 448-63. London and Toronto: Mayfield Publishing Company, 1997.

Minoque, Martin and Judith Molloy, eds. *African Aims and Attitudes: Selected Documents*. London: Cambridge University Press, 1974.

Moore, Brooke Noel and Richard Parker. *Critical Thinking*, 6th ed. Mountain View, California, London and Toronto: Mayfield Publishing Company, 2000.

Morad, Stephen D. "The Founding Principles of the African Inland Mission and Their Interaction with the African Context in Kenya from 1895-1939: the Study of a Faith Mission." PhD Diss., University of Edinburgh, 1997.

Morgan, W. T. W. "Tropical African colonial experience." In *Tropical African Development: Geographical Perspectives*, edited by M. B. Gleave, 25-49. Harlow: Longman Scientific and Technical, 1992.

Mugambi, J. N. K. *African Christian Theology: An Introduction*. Nairobi: East African Educational Publication, 1989.

Murphy, Brian K. "International NGOs and the challenge of modernity." In *Debating Development: NGOs and the Future*, edited by Deborah Eade and Ernst Ligteringen, 60-85. Oxford: Oxfarm GB, 2001.

Narayan, Uma. "Undoing the 'package picture' of cultures." *WLUML DOSSIER* 26, (October 2004): 1-4.

Nash, Manning. "The Core Elements of Ethnicity." In *Ethnicity*, edited by John Hutchinson and Anthony D. Smith, 24-8. Oxford and New York: Oxford University Press, 1996.

Nasimiyu-Wasike, Anne. "Christianity and the African Rituals of Birth and Naming." In *The Will to Arise: Women, Tradition, and the Church in Africa*, edited by Mercy Amba Oduyoye and Musimbi R. A. Kanyoro, 40-53. Maryknoll, New York: Orbis Books, 1992.

Navrongo-Bolgatanga Catholic Diocesan Development Office. "Rural Livelihood Improvement Project (RULIP)." Misereor, Germany, Revised. March 2002.

Nida, Eugene A. *Customs and Cultures: Anthropology for Christian Missions*. USA: Harper and Brothers, 1954.

Njambi, Wairimu Ngaruiya and William E. O'Brien. "Revisiting 'Woman-Woman Marriage': Notes on Gikuyu Women." In *African Gender Studies: A Reader*, edited by Oyèrónké Oyěwùmí, 145-65. New York and England: Palgrave Macmillan, 2005.

Njoroge, Nyambura J. *Kiama Kia Ngo: An African Christian Feminist Ethic of Resistance and Transformation*. Ghana: Legon Theological Studies Series, 2000.

Nkwi, Paul Nchoji. "Rethinking the Role of the Elites in Rural Development: A Case Study from Cameroon." In *Development Encounters: Sites of Participation and Knowledge*, edited by Pauline E. Peters, 175-96. Cambridge: Harvard Institute for International Development, 2000.

Nnyombi, Father Richard. "African Traditional Religion (ATR)." accessed 23 August 2006. Available from http://afgen.com/atr.html.

Nolan, Riall W. *Development Anthropology: Encounters in the Real World*. Boulder, Colorado and Oxford: Westview Press, 2002.

Nwachuku, Daisy N. "The Christian Widow in African Culture." In *The Will to Arise: Women, Tradition, and the Church in Africa*, edited by Mercy Amba Oduyoye and Musimbi R. A. Kanyoro, 54-73. Maryknoll, New York: Orbis Books, 1992.

Nye, Malory. "Editorial: Culture and Religion." *Culture and Religion: An international, interdisciplinary journal* 1, no. 1 (May 2000): 5-12.

_____. *Religion: The Basics*. London and New York: Routledge, 2003.

Oakley, Ann. *Gender on Planet Earth*. Cambridge: Polity Press and New York: The New Press, 2002.

_____. *Sex, Gender, and Society*. London: Maurice Temple Smith Ltd. 1972.

_____. *Subject Women*. London: Fontana, 1982.

Obbo, Christine. *African Women: Their Struggle for Economic Independence*. London: Zed Press, 1980.

Obeng, Pashington. "Asante Catholicsm: An African Appropriation of the Roman Catholic Religion." In *African Spirituality: Forms, Meanings, and Expressions*, edited by Jacob K. Olupona, 372-400. New York: The Crossroad Publishing Company, 2000.

Oduyoye, Mercy Amba. "Naming the Woman: the Words of the Bible and the Words of the Akan." *Bulletin of African Theology* III, no. 5 (1981).

_____. "The Search for a Two-Winged Theology: Women's Participation in the Development of Theology in Africa, The Inaugural Address." In *Talitha qumi: Proceedings of The Convocation of African Women Theologians 1989*, edited by Mercy Amba Oduyoye and Musimbi Kanyoro, 31-56. Dayter Press, 1990 and Ghana: Sam-Woode Ltd., 2001.

_____. "Women and Ritual in Africa." In *The Will to Arise: Women, Tradition, and the Church in Africa*, edited by Mercy Amba Oduyoye and Musimbi R. A. Kanyoro, 9-24. Maryknoll, New York: Orbis Books, 1992.

_____. *Beads and Strands: Reflections of an African Woman on Christianity in Africa*. Yaoundé, Regnum and Clé: Regnum and Clé in Association with Paternoster Press, 2002.

_____. *Daughters of Anowa: African Women and Patriarchy*. Maryknoll, New York: Orbis Books, 1996.

_____. *Hearing and Knowing: Theological Reflections on Christianity in Africa*. Maryknoll, New York: Orbis Books, 1986.

_____. *Introducing African Women's Theology*. England: Sheffield Academic Press, 2001.

Offori-Attah, Kwabena Dei. "African Traditional Religion: Triumphs of Rituals." *African Religion*; accessed 1 September 2006. Available from http://www2.ncsu.edu/ncsu/aern/afridan.html.

Ofie-Aboagye, Ester. *The Role of National Machinery in Implementing the Beijing Platform for Action*. No. 2 of *National Machinery Series*. Ghana, Third World Network, 2000.

Ogwang, Ernest Okello and Beverly J. Stoeltje. "Gender Presentations in African Folklore." In *African Folklore: An Encyclopedia*, edited by Philip M. Peek and Kwesi Yankah, 143-6. New York and London: Routledge, 2004.

Olajubu, Oyeronke. *Women in the Yoruba Religious Sphere*. Forward by Jacob K. Olupona. Albany State: University of New York Press, 2003.

Olupona, Jacob K. "Introduction." In *African Spirituality: Forms, Meanings, and Expressions*, edited by Jacob K. Olupona, xv-xxxvi. New York: The Crossroad Publishing Company, 2000.

_____. "The Study of Religions in West Africa." In *The Study of Religions in Africa: Past, Present and Prospects*, edited by Jan Platvoet, James Cox and Jacob Olupona, 211-9. Cambridge: Roots and Branches, 1996.

Omenyo, Cephas. "Charismatic Churches in Ghana and Contextualization. *Exchange* 31, no. 3 (2002): 252-77.

Ọmọyajowo, Joseph Akinẹle. "The Place of Women in African Traditional Religion and among the Yoruba." In *African Traditional Religions in Contemporary Society*, edited by Jacob K. Olupona, 73-80. Minnesota: Paragon House, 1991.

Onwuejeogwu, M. Angulu. *The Social Anthropology of Africa: An Introduction*. London: Heinemann, 1975.

Oso, S.O. *An Introduction to West African Traditional Religion*. Nigeria: Omolayo Standard Press and Bookshops Co. (NIG.) Ltd, 1978.

Østergaard, Lise. "Gender." In *Gender and Development: A Practical Guide*, edited by Lise Østergaard, 1-10. London: Routledge,1992.

Oyěwùmí, Oyèrónké. "Preface." In *African Gender Studies: A Reader*, edited by Oyèrónké Oyěwùmí, xiii-xiv. New York and England: Palgrave Macmillan, 2005.

_____. *The Invention of Women: Making an African Sense of Western Gender Discourse*. Minneapolis: University of Minnesota Press, 1997.

p'Bitek, Okot. *African Religions in European Scholarship*. New York: Chesapeake, ECA Associates, 1990.

Parkin, Robert. *Kinship: An Introduction to the Basic Concepts*. Oxford: Blackwell Publishers, 1997.

Parrinder, Geoffrey. "The African Spiritual Universe." In *Afro-Caribbean Religions*, edited by Brian Gates, 16-25. Parris Scott V: Ward Lock Educational, 1980.

_____. *African Traditional Religion*. London: Hutchinson's University Library, 1954.

_____. *Comparative Religion*. London: George Allen and Unwin Ltd, 1962.

_____. *Religion in Africa*. London: Pall Mall Press, 1969.

_____. *Sexual Morality in the World's Religions*. London: Oneworld, 1996.

_____. *West African Psychology: A Comparative Study of Psychological and Religious Thought*. London: Lutterworth Press, 1951.

_____. *World Religions: From Ancient History to the Present*. New York and England: Facts on File Publication, 1971.

_____. *Worship in the World's Religions*. New York: Association Press, 1961.

Patel, Pragna. "Difficult Alliances: Treading the minefield of identity and solidarity politics." *WLUML DOSSIER* 26, (October 2004): 37-46.

Peach, Lucinda Joy. *Women and World Religions*. New Jersey: Pearson Educational Inc., 2002.

Peters, Pauline E. "Encountering Participation and Knowledge in Development Sites." In *Development Encounters: Sites of Participation and Knowledge*, edited by Pauline E. Peters, 1-14. Cambridge: Harvard Institute for International Development, 2000.

Denis, Philippe. "The Use of Oral Sources in African Church History." accessed 12 December 2004. Available from http://www.hs.unp.ac.za/theology/denis2.htm.

Phillip, Clyde F. *Africa's Role in the Development of major Western Religions*. Miami, Florida: Colonial Press International, 2002.

Phillips, Godfrey E. *The Religions of the World*. Wallington Surrey: The Religious Education Press, Ltd., 1948.

Phiri, Isabel Apawo and Sarojini Nadar. "Introduction: 'Treading Softly but Firmly.'" In *African Women, Religion, and Health: Essays in Honor of Mercy Amba Ewudziwa Oduyoye*, edited by Isabel Apawo Phiri and Sarojini Nadar, 1-16. Maryknoll, New York: Orbis, 2006.

Pike, Kenneth L. "Etic and Emic Standpoints for the Description of Behavior." In *The Insider/Outsider Problem in the Study of Religion: a Reader*, edited by Russell T. McCutcheon, 28-36. London and New York: Cassell, 1999.

Platvoet, Jan G. "From object to subject: a history of the study of the religions of Africa." In *The Study of Religions in Africa: Past, Present and Prospects*, edited by Jan Platvoet, James Cox and Jacob Olupona (eds.), 105-38. Cambridge: Roots and Branches, 1996.

_____. "To Define or Not to Define: The Problem of the Definition of Religion." In *The Pragmatics of Defining Religion: Contexts, Concepts and Contents*, edited by Jan G. Platvoet and Arie L. Molendijk, 245-65. Leiden, Boston and Koln: Brill, 1999.

_____. and Jacob K. Olupona. "Perspectives in the Study of Religions in Africa." In *The Study of Religions in Africa: Past, Present and Prospects*, edited by Jan Platvoet, James Cox and Jacob Olupona, 7-36. Cambridge: Roots and Branches, 1996.

Pobee, J. S. "Christian Gonclaves Kwami Baëta – A Personal Appreciation." In *Religion in a Pluralistic Society: Essays presented to Professor C. G. Baëta in celebration of his retirement from the service of the University of Ghana, September 1971*, edited by J. S. Pebee, 1-4. Leiden: Brill, 1976.

_____. "Church and State in Ghana, 1949-1966." In *Religion in a Pluralistic Society: Essays presented to Professor C. G. Baëta in celebration of his retirement from the service of the University of Ghana, September 1971*, edited by J. S. Pebee, 121-44. Leiden: Brill, 1976.

Posnansky, Merrick. "Archaeology, Ritual and Religion." In *The Historical Study of African Religion: with special reference to East and Central Africa*, edited by T. O. Ranger and I. N. Kimambo, 29-44. London: Heinemann Educational, 1972.

Pringle, Rosemary. "Absolute Sex? Unpacking the Sexuality/Gender relationship." In *Rethinking Sex: Social Theory and Sexuality Research*, edited by R. W. Connell and G. W. Dowsett, 76-101. Carlton, Victoria: Melbourne University Press, 1992.

Purvis, Sally B. "Gender Construction." In *Dictionary of Feminist Theologies*, edited by Letty M. Russell and J. Shannon Clarkson, 124-5. Louisville, Kentucky: Westminster John Knox Press, 1996.

Quarles van Ufford, P. & Schoffeleers M. eds. *Religion and Development: towards an integrated approach*. Amsterdam: Free University Press, 1988.

Radcliffe-Brown, A. R. and Daryll Forde, eds. *African Systems of Kinship and Marriage*. London, New York and Toronto: Oxford University Press, 1950.

Rahnema, Majid. "Participation." In *The Development Dictionary: A Guide to Knowledge as Power*, edited by Wolfgang Sachs, 116-31. London and New Jersey: Zed Books Ltd., 1992.

_____. "Poverty." In *The Development Dictionary: A Guide to Knowledge as Power*, edited by Wolfgang Sachs, 158-76. London and New Jersey: Zed Books Ltd., 1992.

Rattray, R. S. *The Tribes of the Ashanti Hinterland*. Oxford: Clarendon Press, Vol. I and II, 1932.

Ray, Benjamin C. *African Religions: Symbol, Ritual, and Community*. Englewood Cliffs, New Jersey: Prentice-Hall, 1976.

Rebera, Ranjini. "Challenging Patriarchy." In *Feminist Theology from the Third World: A Reader*, edited by Ursula King, 105-12. London and New York: SPCK/Orbis Press, 1994.

Report on Environmental Concerns and the Commonwealth. *Sustainable Development: An Imperative for Environmental Protection*. London: Commonwealth Secretariat, August 1991.

Ricoeur, Paul. *Figuring the Sacred: Religion, Narrative, and Imagination*. Minneapolis: Fortress Press, 1995.

Ring, Nancy C., Kathleen S. Nash, Mary N. MacDonald, Glennon Fred and Jennifer A. Glancy. *Introduction to the Study of Religion*. Maryknoll, New York: Orbis Books, 1998.

Roberts, Mary Nooter. "Secrecy in African Orature." In *African Folklore: An Encyclopedia*, edited by Philip M. Peek and Kwesi Yankah, 407-9. New York and London: Routledge, 2004.

Ruth, Sheila. "Women's Spirit and Men's Religion." In *Issues in Feminism: An Introduction to Women's Studies*, 4th ed. Edited by Sheila Ruth, 473-80. London and Toronto: Mayfield Publishing Company, 1997.

Ryan, Patrick J., S. J. "African Muslim Spirituality: The Symbiotic Tradition in West Africa." In *African Spirituality: Forms, Meanings, and Expressions*, edited by Jacob K. Olupona, 176-97. New York: The Crossroad Publishing Company, 2000.

Saaka, Yakubu. "Introduction." In *Regionalism and Public Policy in Northern Ghana*, edited by Yakubu Saaka, 1-11. New York: Peter Lang, 2001.

Sachs, Jeffrey. *The End of Poverty: How Can We Make It Happen in Our Lifetime*. Forward by Bono. London: Penquin Books, 2005.

Sachs, Wolfgang. "Introduction." In *The Development Dictionary: A Guide to Knowledge as Power*, edited by Wolfgang Sachs, 1-5. London and New Jersey: Zed Books Ltd., 1992.

Sackey, Brigid M. *New Directions in Gender and Religion: The Changing Status of Women in African Independent Churches*. Lanham: Lexington Books, 2006.

Safo, Amos. "Muslims cry foul over population figures." *News from Africa*. Archive, Ghana, 2002, February, accessed 15 February 2007. Available from http://www.newsfromafrica.org/newsfromarica/articles/art_7902.html.

Sail, Shashi. "The Women's Question – Rethinking Gender Politics." In *Transcending Boundaries: Perspectives on Faith, Social Action and Solidarity*, *Essays in honour of George Ninan*, edited by Rajendra K. Sail and Ajit Muricken, 237-49. India: Vikas Adhyan Kendra, and Raipur Churches Development and Relief Committee, 1995.

Saito, Fumihito. *Decentralization and Development Partnerships: Lessons from Uganda*. Tokyo: Springer-Verlag, 2003.

Salih, Sara. *Judith Butler*. London and New York: Routledge, 2002.

Samuel, Vinay and Chris Sugden. "Introduction." In *The Church in Response to Human Need*, edited by Vinay Samuel and Chris Sugen, iii-xii. Grand Rapids, Michigan: Regnum Books, Oxford: William B. Eerdmans Publishing Co. 1987.

Sanneh, Lamin. *Encountering the West: Christianity and the Global Cultural Process: The African Dimension*. London: Marshall Pickering, 1993.

Sardar, Ziauddin. "Development and the Location of Eurocentrism." In *Critical Development Theory: Contributions to a New Paradigm*, edited by Ronaldo Munck and Denis O'Hearn, edited by Ronaldo Munck and Denis O'Hearn, 44-62. London and New York" Zed Books, 1999.

Sawyerr, H. "Traditions in Transit." In *Religion in a Pluralistic Society*, edited by J. S. Pebee, 85-96. Leiden: E. J. Brill, 1976.

Sayers, Janet. "On the description of psychological sex differences." In *Sex-role Stereotyping*, edited by Oonagh Hartnett, Gill Boden and Mary Fuller, 46-56. London: Tavistock Publications Ltd., 1979.

Schumacher, E. F. *Small is Beautiful: A Study of Economics as if People Mattered*. London: ABACUS, 1974.

Segal, Lynne. *Slow Motion: Changing Masculinities, Changing Men*. London: Virago Press, 1990.

Shaw, Rosalind. "'Traditional' African Religions." In *Turning Points in Religious Studies*, edited by Ursula King, 183-91. Edinburgh: T and T Clark, 1990.

Sicard, Sigvard von. "African Socialism: Communism or Communalism, A Case Study." *Africa Theological Journal* 11, no. 1 (1982): 26-35.

Silverman, David. *Doing Qualitative Research: A Practical Handbook*. London, Thousand Oaks, New Delhi: SAGE Publications, 2000.

Smart, Carol and Barry Smart. "Women and social control: An introduction." In *Women, Sexuality and Social Control*, edited by Carol Smart and Barry Smart, 1-7. London, Boston and Henley: Routledge and Kgan Paul, 1978.

Smart, Ninian. *Dimensions of the Sacred: An Anatomy of the World's Beliefs*. London: Fontana Press, 1996.

_____. *The Phenomenon of Religion*. New York: Seabury, 1973.

_____. *The World's Religions: Old Traditions and Modern Transformations*. Cambridge: Cambridge University Press, 1989.

Smith, Donald Eugene. ed. *Religion, Politics, and Social Change in the Third World: A Sourcebook*. New York: The Free Press and London: Collier-Macmillan Ltd, 1971.

Smith, Edwin W. *The Religio of Lower Races: As Illustrated by the African Bantu*. New York: The Macmillan Company, 1923.

Smith, Linda Tuhiwai. *Decolonizing Methodologies: Research and Indigenous People*. London and New York: Zed Books Ltd, 1999.

Songsore, Jacob. *Regional Development in Ghana: The Theory and the Reality*. Ghana: Woeli Publishers Services, 2003.

_____, Aloysius Denkabe, Charles D. Jebuni and Steven Ayidiya. "Challenges of Education in Northern Ghana: A Case for Northern Ghana Education Trust Fund (NETFUND)." In *Regionalism and Public Policy in Northern Ghana*, edited by Yakubu Saaka, 223-39. New York: Peter Lang, 2001.

Southall, Aidan. *Social Change in Modern Africa*. Forward by Daryll Forde. London, New York and Toronto: Oxford University Press, 1961.

Spickard, James V. and J. Shawn Landres. "Introduction: Whither Ethnography? Transforming the Social-Scientific Study of Religion." In *Personal Knowledge and Beyond: Reshaping the Ethnography of Religion*, edited by James V. Spickard, J. Shawn Landres and Meredith B. McGuire, 1-14. New York and London: New York University Press, 2002.

Spradley, James P. *Participant Observation*. USA and London: Harcourt Brace Jovanvich College Pub. 1980.

Steinberg, Warren. *Masculinity: Identity, Conflict, and Transformation*. Boston and London: Shambhala, 1993.

Streeten, Paul. "Structural Adjustment: A Survey of the Issues and Options (1987)." In *Development Studies: A Reader*, edited by Stuart Corbridge, 368-82. London: Edward Arnold, 1995.

Sundermeier, Theo. "Unio Analogica, Understanding African Dynamistic Patterns of Thought." *Africa Theological Journal* 11, no. 1 (1982): 36-62.

Sutcliffe, Bob. "The Place of Development in Theories of Imperialism and Globalization." In *Critical Development Theory: Contributions to a New Paradigm*, edited by Ronaldo Munck and Denis O'Hearn, 135-54. London and New York: Zed Books, 1999.

Swetnam, Derek. *Writing Your Dissertation: How to plan, prepare and present your work successfully*. 2nd ed. Oxford: How to Books, 1997.

Talamantez, Ines. "Images of the Feminine in Apache Religious Tradition." In *After Patriarchy: Feminist Transformations of the World Religions*, edited by Paula M. Cooey, Willaim R. Eakin and Jay B. McDaniel, 131-45. Maryknoll, New York: Orbis Books, 1991.

Taylor, John B. *Primal World Views: Christian Dialogue with Traditional Thought Forms*. Ibadan: Daystar Press, 1976.

Tempels, Placide. *Bantu Philosophy*. Paris: Présence Africaine, 1959.

Temu, Peter E. *The Unspoken Truth About Globalization: Eight Essays*. New York, Lincoln and Shanghai: iUniverse Inc., 2007.

Ter Haar, Gerrie. "Introduction: The evil called witchcraft." In *Imagining Evil: Witchcraft Beliefs and Accusations in Contemporary Africa*, edited by Gerrie Ter Haar, 1-30. New York and Eritrea: Africa World Press, 2007.

_____. *World Religions and Community Religions: Where does Africa fit in?*. Occasional Paper, Centre for African Studies, University of Copenhagen, August 2000.

The Report of the South Commission. *The Challenge of the South*. New York: Oxford University Press, 1990.

Thin, Neil. *Social Progress and Sustainable Development*. London: ITDG Publishing, 2002.

Thomas, Douglas E. *African Traditional Religion in the Modern World*. Jefferson and London: McFarland and Company, 2005.

Thompson, T. Jack. *Images of Africa: Missionary Photography in the Nineteenth Century: an Introduction*. Occasional Paper: Centre for African Studies, University of Copenhagaen, February 2004.

Thorpe, S. A. *African Traditional Religions: An Introduction*. Pretoria: University of South Africa, 1991.

Tolba, Mostafa Kamal. *Sustainable Development: Constraints and Opportunities*. London: Butterworths, 1987.

Trew, Karen. "Identity and the Self." In *Gender and Psychology*, edited by Karen Trew and John Kremer, 3-14. London, New York, Sydney and Auckland: Arnold, 1998.

Tsikata, Dzodzi. *Lip-Service and Peanuts: The State and National Machinery for Women in Africa*. No. 11 of *National Machinery Series*. Ghana: Third World Network, 2000.

Tucker, Vincent. "The Myth of Development: A Critique of a Eurocentric Discourse." In *Critical Development Theory: Contributions to a New Paradigm*, edited by Ronaldo Munck and Denis O'Hearn, 1-26. London and New York: Zed Books, 1999.

Turabian, Kate L. *A Manual for Writers of term Papers, Theses, and Dissertations*, 6th ed. Revised by John Grossman and Alice Bennett, Chicago and London: The University of Chicago Press, 1996.

Turner, Harold W. "The Way Forward in the Religious Study of African Primal Religions." *Journal of Religions in Africa* 12, no. 1 (1981): 1-15.

_____. *Living Tribal Religions: An Introductory Survey of the Religious lives of Tribal Societies in a Thematic Basis*. S. I., 1970.

_____. *Living Tribal Religions*. London: Ward Lock Educational, 1971.

U.S. Department of State. "Background Note: Ghana." *Bureau of African Affairs*. February 2005, accessed 9 February 2005. Available from http://www.state.gov/r/pa/ei/bgn/2860.htm.

United Nations Development Programme. *Human Development Report 1993*. New York: Oxford University Press, 1993.

Van Beek, Walter E. A. and Thomas D. Blakely. "Introduction." In *Religion in Africa: Experience and Expression*, edited by Thomas D. Blakely, Walter E. A. van Beek and Dennis L. Thomson, 1-20. London: Heinemann, 1994.

Van Binsbergen, Wim and Matthew Schoffeleers. "Introduction: Theoretical explorations in African religion." In *Theoretical explorations in African religion*, edited by Wim Van Binsbergen and Matthew Schoffeleers, 1-49. London, Boston, Melbourne and Henley: KPI, 1985.

Van Rinsum, Hendrik Johannes. *Slaves of Definition: In Quest of the Unbeliever and the Ignoramus*. The Netherlands: Shaker Publishing, 2001.

_____. "'Knowing the African': Edwin W. Smith and the Invention of African Traditional Religion." In *Uniquely African? African Christian Identity from Cultural and Historical Perspectives*, edited by James L Cox and Gerrie ter Haar, 39-66. New Jersey and Eritrea: African World Press, 2003.

_____. "'They became slaves of their definitions.' Okot p'Bitek (1931-1982) and the European Traditions in the Study of African Religions." In *Traditions in the Study of Religion in Africa*, edited by Frieder Ludwig and Afe Adogame, 23-38. Harrassowitz Verlag: Wiesbaden, 2004, 23-38.

Van Rooy, Alison. "Good news! You may be out of a job: reflections on the past and future 50 years for Northern NGOs." In *Debating Development: NGOs and the Future*, edited by Deborah Eade and Ernst Ligteringen, 19-43. Oxford: Oxfarm GB, 2001.

Vansina, Jan. *Oral Traditions: A Study in Historical Methodology*. Translated by H. M. Wright. London: Routledge and Kegan Paul, 1965.

Verhelst, Thierry G. *No Life Without Roots: Culture and Development*. 1987, Translated by Bob Cumming., London and New Jersey: Zed Books Ltd, 1990.

Vickers, Jeanne. *Women and the World Economic Crisis*. Women and World Development Series. London and New Jersey: Zed Books Ltd., 1991.

Wa Thiong'o, Ngũgĩ. "African Languages and Global Culture in the Twenty-first Century." In *African Visions: Literary Images, Political Change, and Social Struggle in Contemporary Africa*, edited by Cheryl B. Mwaria, Silvia Federici and Joseph McLaren, 155-61. Connecticut and London: Greenwood Press, 2000.

Ward, Barbara. *Progress for a Small Planet*. England: Penguin Books, 1979.

Ward, W. E. *A short History of The Gold Coast*. London, New York and Toronto: Longmans, Green and Co., 1935.

Ware, Helen. "Female and Male Life-Cycles." In *Female and Male in West Africa*, edited by Christine Oppong, 6-31. London: George Allen and Unwin, 1983.

Warren, Michael. *Communications and Cultural Analysis: A Religious View*. Westport, Connecticut, London: Bergin and Garvey, 1992.

Watson, George. *Writing a Thesis: a guide to long essays and dissertations.* London and New York: Longman, 1987.

Weber, Max. "The Origins of Ethnic Groups." In *Ethnicity,* edited by John Hutchinson and Anthony D. Smith, 35-40. Oxford and New York: Oxford University Press, 1996.

West, Candace, and Don H. Zimmerman. "Doing Gender." In *The Social Construction of Gender,* edited by Judith Lorber and Susan A. Farrell, 13-37. Newbury Park, London and New Delhi: SAGE Publications, 1991.

Westerlund, David. *African Religion in African Scholarship: A Preliminary Study of the Religious and Political Background.* Stockholm: Almqvist and Wiksell International, 1985.

Westermann, Diedrich and M. A. Bryan. *Languages of West Africa: Handbook of African Languages.* Part II. England: International African Institute, 1970.

Willis, Paul E. *Learning to Labour.* England: Saxon House, 1977.

Wiredu, Kwasi. "Identity as an Intellectual Problem." In *Identity and the Politics of Scholarship in the Study of Religion,* edited by José Ignacio Cabezón and Sheila Greeve Davaney, 209-28. New York and Oxon: Routledge, 2004.

Wisdom, Mark. "'What Is Trokosi System?'" In *Where Silence is no Longer and Option, Where Silence is no Longer an Option,* edited by Elizabeth Amoah and Mercy Amba Oduyoye, 31-9. Accra-North, Ghana: Sam-Woode Ltd, 2000.

Wolcott, Harry F. *Writing Up – Qualitative Research.* Thousand Oaks, London and New Delhi: Sage Publication, 2001.

Wright, Pablo G. "Postmodern Ontology, Anthropology, and Religion." *Culture and Religion: An International, Interdisciplinary Journal* 1, no. 1 (May 2000): 85-94.

Yankah, Kwesi. *Globalization and the African Scholar.* Faculty of Arts, University of Ghana Monograph, 2004.

————. *Speaking for the Chief: Okyeame and the Politics of Akan Royal Oratory.* Bloomington and Indianapolis: Indiana University Press, 1995.

Yennah, Grace. "Evaluation Report." Rural Livelihood Improvement Project (RULIP). Navrongo-Bolgatanga Diocesan Development Office. December 2005.

Yinger, J. Milton. *The Scientific Study of Religion.* London: The Macmillan Company, 1970.

Zahan, Dominique. "Some Reflections on African Spirituality." In *African Spirituality: Forms, Meanings, and Expressions,* edited by Jacob K. Olupona, 3-25. New York: The Crossroad Publishing Company, 2000.

_____. *The Religion, Spirituality, and Thought of Traditional Africa.* Chicago and London: The University of Chicago Press, 1997

FIELD RESPONDENTS

Name	Place	Date
Abane	Doba	28/05/06
Abudu Adongo	Naga	11/09/04
Adagwine	Kologo	11/09/04
Agnes, Atia Apusigah	Navrongo	
Albert K. Awedoba	Legon	14/07/06
Alex Amenga-Etego	Kandiga	17/06/06
Helen Amenga-Etego	Kandiga	13/04/06
Apogpeay	Naga	13/03/06
Aputibunu	Naga	21/02/06
Asobayire	Kologo	11/09/04
Atarah	Kandiga	09/03/06
Augustine Jude Akanlu	Navrongo	13/04/06, 06/05/06, 18/05/06
Ayogwine Aweni	Naga	21/04/06
Daniel Tabazuuing	Bolgatanga	07/03/06
Daniel	Wa	29/03/06
Danoye Oguntola-Laguda	Wa	29/03/06
David Millar	Bolgatanga	
Emmanuel Achegwe	Navrongo	27/04/06
Gemma Kazaresam	Navrongo	17/05/06
Gerard Akurugo	Naga	11/09/04, 12/03/06, 09/04/06, 23/06/06

Henry Amenga-Etego	Kandiga	10/05/06
John Atuwah	Bolgatanga	08/03/06
Joseph Ayembila	Bolgatanga	06/03/06
Juatera	Navrongo	14/04/06
Margaret Mary Issakka	Bolgatanga	29/05/06
Mary-Emil Amenga-Etego		
Melanie Kasise	Bolgatanga	29/05/06
Ncho Akawuni	Kologo	10/09/04, 14/03/06, 09/05/06
Nchobunu	Kologo	21/04/06
Peter Adocta	Naga	12/03/06
R. K. K. Maaldu and Richard Kazaresam	Navrongo	14/04/06
Richard Ohene	Navrongo	12/04/06
Silvester Aganmikire	Bolgatanga	07/03/06
Sophia	Kandiga	13/04/06
Tindana	Kandiga	10/05/06
Yusif Akudugu	Bolgatanga	08/03/06

Index

Women and Development (WAD)
125, 159, 175
Women in Development (WID)
159
Wright, Pablo G. 213, 242, 243

Yankah, Kwesi 10, 11, 61, 192,
232-234, 242, 260
Yennah, Grace 21, 121
Yinger, J. Milton 9

Zahan, Dominique 15, 16, 80-82
Zimmerman, Don H. 181
Zulu 244